Genocide:

Approaches, Case Studies, and Responses

Genocide:
Approaches, Case Studies, and Responses

Graham C. Kinloch, *Florida State University*
Erik Allardt, *Professor Emeritus, University of Helsinki*
Mihran Dabag, *University of Bochum (Germany)*
Brij Mohan, *Louisiana State University*
Franco Ferrarotti, *University of Rome*
Arthur S. Wilke, *Professor Emeritus, Auburn University*
Medardus Brehl, *University of Bochum (Germany)*
Tarique Niazi, *University of Wisconsin, Eau Claire*
Lydia Aran, *Hebrew University*
Raj P. Mohan, *Auburn University*
Max Koch, *University of Ulster*
Kristin Platt, *University of Bochum (Germany)*
Kurt H. Wolff, *Brandeis University*
James Jenkins, *Auburn University Libraries*

Foreword by
Erik Allardt

Edited by
Graham C. Kinloch & Raj P. Mohan

Algora Publishing
New York

Library of Congress Cataloging-in-Publication Data —

Genocide : approaches, case studies, and responses / Graham C. Kinloch and
Raj P. Mohan, editors.

p. cm.

Summary: "Fourteen authors analyze factors behind genocidal situations
worldwide, with detailed case studies, and an evaluation of attempts to prevent
genocide and of the implications for human rights policies, with a particular concern to develop new and practical insights"

Includes bibliographical references and index.

ISBN 0-87586-379-5 (soft cover: alk. paper) — ISBN 0-87586-380-9 (hard cover:
alk. paper) — ISBN 0-87586-381-7 (ebook)

1. Genocide. 2. Genocide—Case studies. I. Kinloch, Graham Charles. II. Mohan,
Raj P.

HV6322.7.G448 2005

304.6'63—dc22

2005001188

Printed in the United States

To all victims of genocide, past and present

TABLE OF CONTENTS

FOREWORD 1
Erik Allardt, Professor Emeritus, University of Helsinki

PREFACE 5

INTRODUCTION 7
Graham C. Kinloch & Raj P. Mohan

PART I. THEORETICAL APPROACHES TO GENOCIDE 13

CHAPTER 1. THE POSSIBLE CAUSES AND REDUCTION OF GENOCIDE:
AN EXPLORATION 15
Graham C. Kinloch, Florida State University
 Defining the Term 16
 Sociological Background 17
 Theories of Genocide 18
 Comparative Case Studies 21
 Possible Prevention 28
 Towards a General Theory of Genocide 29
 Policy Implications 29
 Conclusions 32

CHAPTER 2. MODERN SOCIETIES AND COLLECTIVE VIOLENCE:
THE FRAMEWORK OF INTERDISCIPLINARY GENOCIDE STUDIES 37
Mihran Dabag
 Framework 38
 Genocide and the Nation State 49
 Genocide and Identity 52
 Science and Perspective 52
 Conclusions 57

CHAPTER 3. THE ULTIMATE OPPRESSION: THE URGE TO GENOCIDE   63
Brij Mohan, Louisiana State University   63
   I. The Nature of Genocide   64
   II. Children of Darkness: The Banality of Oppression   66
   III. Ambiguities of Hope: Some Alternatives   68
   Conclusions   74

CHAPTER 4. ON GENOCIDE, OLD AND NEW   77
Franco Ferrarotti, University of Rome

PART II. CONCEPTUAL APPROACHES TO GENOCIDE   89

CHAPTER 5. THE SUCCESS AND FAILURE OF "GENOCIDE"   91
Arthur S. Wilke, Professor Emeritus, Auburn University
   Disciplinary and Behavioral Legacies   91
   The Ethos of Liberalism: A Snarled Legacy   98
   "Genocide:" Lemkin's Unfinished Legacy   99
   The Flattening of Moral Life   102
   Nonacademic Challenges   105

CHAPTER 6. THE DECISIVE GENERATION: SELF-AUTHORIZATION AND
   DELEGATIONS IN DECIDING A GENOCIDE   113
Mihran Dabag

PART III. CASE STUDIES OF GENOCIDE   141

CHAPTER 7. STRATEGIES OF EXCLUSION: THE GENOCIDE OF THE HERERO
   IN GERMAN COLONIAL DISCOURSE   143
Medardus Brehl
   The Facts and the Discourse   145
   The Stream of History   148
   Scramble for Identity   151
   Coding the "Enemy"   154
   Phrases of Elimination   155
   Conclusions   158

CHAPTER 8. GLOBAL INACTION, ETHNIC ANIMOSITY, OR RESOURCE
   MALDISTRIBUTION? AN ECOLOGICAL EXPLANATION OF GENOCIDE
   IN RWANDA   163
Tarique Niazi, University of Wisconsin, Eau Claire
   Section I. Introduction   163
   Section II. Background   166
   Section III. Ecological Construction of Ethnicity and
    Ethnic Distribution of Ecology   169
   Section IV. Ecological Limits and Ecological Overshoot   179

Section V. Discussion and Conclusions 185
Conclusions 188

CHAPTER 9. THE FORGOTTEN DEAD: REPRESENTATIONS OF THE PAST
IN THE TIBETAN REFUGEE COMMUNITY IN INDIA 195
Lydia Aran

PART IV. COMPARATIVE ANALYSES OF GENOCIDE 217

CHAPTER 10. GENOCIDE AS A POSSIBLE RESPONSE TO WESTERNIZATION:
GOVERNMENT TREATMENT OF MINORITIES IN AFGHANISTAN AND IRAN 219
Raj P. Mohan, Auburn University
The Relevance of Critical Theory 220
Reactions to Westernization 221
The Hindus, Sikhs and Shi'ite Muslims in Afghanistan 224
The Baha'is and Others in Iran 226
Conclusions 229

CHAPTER 11. CONFLICT REGULATION IN CHILE AND NORTHERN IRELAND:
THE ROLE OF ELITES 233
Max Koch, University of Ulster
Introduction 233
Chile 234
Northern Ireland 238
A Comparison of the Case Studies 245
Conclusion 247

PART V. RESPONSES TO GENOCIDE 251

CHAPTER 12. WITNESSING THE CATASTROPHE 253
Kristin Platt
1. Doubts About the Survivor's Narrative 255
2. Limits of Experience 267
3. Surviving and Trauma 274
Conclusion 279

CHAPTER 13. GENOCIDE AND ME 283
Kurt H. Wolff, Brandeis University

GENOCIDE: A BIBLIOGRAPHY 289
James Jenkins, Auburn University Libraries
Reference 289
Films 291
Web Sites 291
Africa 292
Armenia 294

Asia Indonesia and the Middle East   296
Bosnia Hercegovina Yugoslavia   297
Holocaust   298
General   302

NOTES ON CONTRIBUTORS   305

SUBJECT INDEX   309

NAMES INDEX   317

FOREWORD

Erik Allardt, Professor Emeritus, University of Helsinki

In this volume, edited by Graham Kinloch and Raj Mohan, the study of genocide is portrayed as both globally sensitive and as a central issue in contemporary social science. When the field of ethnic studies proliferated in the 1960s and 1970s, its main focus concerned a rebirth of ethnic consciousness in many parts of the world, including those technologically and economically advanced. Today there is an increasing consciousness of a grim and upsetting reality - namely, the widespread presence of genocide not only in the history of mankind, but also in the contemporary international milieu.

One of the main purposes of this book is to demonstrate how frames of reference and social science theories such as those associated with sociology can contribute to a better understanding of the wide variety of genocide activity in human societies. Its point of departure, however, involves observations of how genocide and attempts to eliminate ethnically defined populations have taken place in history. Three observations concerning genocide, emphasized in different articles in the book, seem crucial:

(1) It is found in societies which can have either a high or a low formal level of educational attainment. Nazi genocide under Hitler and the Rwanda massacre in 1994 prove this point;

(2) Citizens of countries where genocide has taken place tend to be unaware of the presence of such horrific activity among them. This unawareness was fairly common in many European countries. Hence, it is perhaps under-

1

standable that Kurt H. Wolff, himself a Jewish survivor, in his contribution to this volume, "Genocide and Me," gives us his very profound and honest reaction when he reveals that he himself remained unaware of the relationship between Nazi genocide and his personal life. Even today, in educationally and economically advanced countries, only a small percentage of the population is particularly aware of what has happened to the Tutsis, Tibetans, and people of East Timor;

(3) For a long time, research about genocide was carried out primarily by historians, as noted by Mihran Dabag. This is not in all respects an unfortunate limitation. However, in all genocidal events there are unique characteristics of those who carry them out and those who suffer by them. Thus, it is very important to search for a number of factors including the biological, psychological, and sociological which could explain the presence of genocide in the history of mankind. To point out the various factors, whatever they may be, that might explain the presence of genocide could have the advantage of preventing its occurrence in the future. In this work Graham Kinloch comments on a number of general factors that could account for the rise of genocide. It becomes apparent that theories about genocide have to be interdisciplinary. This implies that there are biological, psychological, and sociological factors that could explain genocidal events.

This volume also contains a special focus on the contributions offered by two disciplines; namely, moral philosophy and comparative sociology. Nevertheless, most of the articles also reflect the importance of a multi-disciplinary approach. A systematic study of attempts to carry out genocide requires both conceptual and empirical analysis about the nature of evil. Conceptual analyses related to moral philosophy appear in many of the book's contributions, particularly in the chapters by Lydia Aran, Brij Mohan, Franco Ferrarotti, and Arthur S. Wilke. The other disciplinary keystone of the book is sociology, especially comparative sociology, in the form applied by the two editors. The chapter by Raj Mohan argues for the relevance of Critical Theory and an unmasking of deliberately self-evident insistencies on authority and possessions of the truth. The stress on Critical Theory is indeed a necessary and well-grounded emphasis, not the least because acts of genocide usually have been exercised under the mask of civilization and culture. A dreadful truth is that agents of genocide and terror often have sought to legitimize their actions on the basis of religion and religious doctrines. More than in the studies of most social phenomena, analyses of genocide definitely require applications of Critical Theory.

A central application of Critical Theory concerns studies how distributional inequities are conditioning animosities and the slaughtering of people conceived as deadly enemies. Tarique Niazi shows how the Rwandan massacre in the 1990s was an outcome of both ecological scarcities and discriminatory practices by the colonial powers during earlier periods of the twentieth century. Raj Mohan emphasizes how threat-producing Westernization as it occurred in both Iran and Afghanistan was apt to create tendencies to treat minorities in destructive ways. Max Koch, on the other hand, analyzes how successful economic policy leading to both a domestic and an international integration of elites tends to lead to peaceful conflict resolution.

Despite the importance of Critical Theory, this volume put together by Kinloch and Mohan shows the fruitfulness of applying a variety of theories in the fields of social and human science. The chapter by Medardus Brehl on strategies of exclusion successfully applies the discourse view developed by Michel Foucault and socio-cultural approaches advocated by Pierre Bourdieu and Zygmunt Bauman. Brehl's chapter deals with the genocide of the Herero in German South West-Africa, now Namibia, in 1904, but the theoretical importance of the chapter is that it shows how annihilation policies and processes of stigmatization have been conveyed by linguistic and verbal media in such a fashion that the exclusion of victims and genocide of an alien population is defined not only as legitimate action but as a downright moral duty.

Mihran Dabag's chapter concerning political generations which are strongly motivated by an urge to carry out genocides is, in a sense, an application of discourse theory and the socio-cultural approach also. Concretely, the chapter deals comparatively with the Turkish reform movement which around the turn of the 19th and 20th centuries carried out an annihilation of Armenians. It also deals with the German National Socialist movement focusing on the genocide of the Jews. It shows how these genocidal policies were carried out in the midst of society, affecting totally every area of social life. The use of the concept of generation is empirically productive and theoretically fruitful, but also raises the question whether the rise of genocidal ideologies and policies were especially typical for the second half of the 19th and the first half of the 20th century.

Nevertheless, a shocking fact is that the 20th century has been one of the worst, if not the worst period in human history in terms of the number of deaths due to genocide. UN Secretary General Kofi Annan has said, "*We have entered the third millennium through a gate of fire... The 20th century was perhaps the deadliest in human history, devastated by innumerous conflicts, untold suffering, and unimaginable crimes.*" This volume calls for a thorough and continuing analysis of the factors and conflicts which made the 20th century such a deadly era. To perform such an analysis is definitely the task for a follow-up of the thoughts presented in the book. There is now for instance only scarce information about the technology and technological policies which have made many deadly games possible. To perform such analyses is indeed a task of Critical Theory.

Most chapters in the book on genocide deal with the perpetrators and power of those carrying out genocide. There are also, however, revealing chapters by Lydia Aran and Kristin Platt analyzing the victims and survivors in the populations victimized. Platt uses a biographical approach based on well-planned interviews. The result is a very complicated picture about how traumas and present-day adjustments are interwoven in such a fashion that these traumatization processes are not linear, but determined by variances created by new life situations.

This volume introduces in a both cogent and upsetting manner a new sociological field, the sociology of genocide. It is, of course, related to numerous former studies and theories about social conflict, but the analysis of genocide contains observations and findings hitherto unknown and unanalyzed. It is obvious that the analysis of genocide contains a wealth of new insights about and contributions to general theories of social and societal conflict. Genocide represents the ultimate and most devastating consequence of social conflict.

PREFACE

Genocide, despite the major political, economic, and social advances of the twentieth century, continues to plague significant areas of the world today. Disturbing cynicism is also indicated in the political reluctance to even employ the term. In light of contemporary, pressing human rights issues and apparently endless wars of human destruction, this volume was originally designed and published as a special issue of the *International Journal of Contemporary Sociology* (Vol. 39, No. 2, October 2002), with the title *Genocide and Society*. Many of these essays and some of their titles have been revised, while a foreword, three new papers and a bibliography have been added to the current manuscript as follows:
- Foreword, by Professor Erik Allardt;
- "The Decisive Generation: Self-authorization and Delegations in Deciding a Genocide," by Mihran Dabag;
- "Strategies of Exclusion: The Genocide of the Herero in German Colonial Discourse," by Medardus Brehl;
- "Witnessing the Catastrophe," by Kristin Platt; and,
- "Genocide: A Bibliography," by James Jenkins.

We believe that the range, variety, and depth of the analyses provided by the book's chapters offer important insight into major factors behind, reactions to, and policy issues relating to this kind of agonizing human conflict.

In bringing this project to successful fruition, we are deeply grateful to the following:
- Professor Allardt for providing the book with a foreword;
- to our authors for their cooperation, patience, hard work and important contributions to this work;

● to the *International Journal of Contemporary Sociology* for permission to use the special issue as the basis of this volume; and,

● to Algora Publishing, particularly its editor Andrea Sengstacken, for their enthusiasm, help, and support in publishing this book.

Our heartfelt thanks to them all.

Graham C. Kinloch
Raj P. Mohan

INTRODUCTION

Graham C. Kinloch & Raj P. Mohan

Despite increasing global sensitivity to human rights issues and international intervention in societies experiencing severe forms of intergroup conflict, societal violence in genocidal proportions continues to plague many parts of the world, particularly Africa, Eastern Europe, the Middle East and the Pacific. Any optimism regarding improving the "human condition" in the new century, despite significant political, economic, and social advancements, appears prematurely naive and optimistic. What do these destructive trends reflect?

This volume was designed to expose readers to a wide variety of genocidal situations, both historical and contemporary, exploring major factors behind them and their possible future avoidance. Major topics include issues of definition, varying types of genocide, theoretical and methodological approaches, policy implications, detailed case studies of genocidal situations, and evaluation of particular attempts to prevent this kind of destruction generally. Our scope is intended to be as multi-disciplinary, world-wide, varied, and as practical as possible. Authors were asked to focus on a particular aspect of genocide, explore it in detail with regard to its relevance and development over time, and evaluate its implications for human rights policies both internationally and within particular contexts. We were particularly concerned with developing *new* and *practical* insights into this highly relevant and important topic.

Contributors developed a wide range of papers, focusing on a variety of theoretical and conceptual approaches to the topic, detailed case studies, comparative analyses, and exploration of related biographical experiences. The first four chapters attempt to specify some of the major factors behind the continuing occurrence of genocide: Graham Kinloch examines the term itself, its socio-logical context, relevant theories, related factors, comparative case studies, possible prevention and general policy implications, locating the source of this problem in the ubiquitous nature of ethnocentrism and intergroup competition. Mihran Dabag takes an interdisciplinary approach to understanding genocide, involving the study of "social, historical and psychological relationships and structures" highlighting the "whole of society," "multiple kinds of violence," and normative legitimations. Brij Mohan comments on continuing human destruction and relative lack of international response to such tragedies, delin-eating the "variegated and banality of the new tribal evil that threatens the foun-dation of a civil order." Franco Ferrarotti argues that "genocides are bound to re-occur ... because the roots of discrimination against minorities have not yet been eliminated." He emphasizes that many fail to comprehend that genocide is not limited to the holocaust while unfortunately many have grown accustomed to its continuing existence, not really caring or being moved by its horrifying destruction.

Conceptual issues are addressed by Arthur Wilke and Mihran Dabag. The former criticizes current use of the "genocide" term for its emotive use rather than effectively addressing "conditions for a moral life." He feels that since the term tends to harmonize with the "new social pathology model," encouraging the growth of victims, its "critical potential" for influencing international affairs has largely been lost. The latter adopts the "construct of generation" in his analysis of genocide, underlining powerful effects of ideological models, agreed identity, a "shared history," and generational attempts to "realize an expected history." From these discussions, it is clear that the term requires interdisci-plinary understanding and practical application if group murder is to be brought to an effective end.

The next three chapters involve case studies of genocide in Namibia, Rwanda and Tibet. Medardus Brehl, using German texts, reveals the "binary arguments contained in colonial strategies of exclusion" applied to the "natives" in (what was then) German South-West Africa. Accordingly, the latter were "assigned a position ... outside of all obligations and norms," thereby permitting the colonial elite to annihilate them in the name of "cultural higher devel-opment." Tarique Niazi takes an ecological approach to the former, arguing that genocidal events in Rwanda resulted from "distributional inequities in productive resources" present during the country's pre-colonial, colonial, and post-colonial development periods. According to him, these "scarcities" were used by Hutu leaders to mobilize their followers to murder the Tutsis as well as their "moderate Hutu allies." Thirdly, Lydia Aran presents a detailed analysis of the manner in which Tibetans have reconstructed and attempted to account for their "recent past." Focusing on the Dalai Lama's "actions and rhetoric," she demonstrates how he deals with his people's "shattered identity" and "struggle for survival" through his particular use of "traditional cultural codes" in representing the past in a manner which he views as in their best interests.

A comparative approach is taken by Raj Mohan and Max Koch. Applying Critical Theory, the former examines genocidal events in Afghanistan and Iran as involving the destructive cultural and ideological reactions of governing elites to the threatening economic and cultural effects of Westernization on their societies. In response, these governments have attempted to ensure their dominance by treating minorities in destructive ways. Examining elites in Chile and Northern Ireland, Max Koch concludes that even in deeply divided societies, conflict may be resolved fairly peacefully when the ruling elite is successfully integrated into the "global economy" and is able to maintain and transform its resources during periods of social change. These cases are particularly helpful in illustrating both negative and more positive situations regarding potential genocidal developments.

Kristin Platt outlines some of the major methodological difficulties involved in effecting research on the "biographical self-depictions" of genocide survivors, illuminating "sequences of stress factors," the complex nature of "traumatization processes," and survivor reactions to the "challenges of a new life." Clearly, this topic is complex, dynamic, challenging, and highly relevant to our understanding of the long-term effects of genocide. Kurt Wolff explores the effects of biographical contexts and personal experiences on his reactions to Nazism and Nazi genocide. While encountering Nazi discrimination, the loss of family members to death camps, and Fascist intolerance, his poetic, futuristic, and visionary approach to reality resulted in his avoiding becoming polemical. Consequently, during the above events he remained relatively unaware of their interconnectedness and destructive implications.

Finally, James Jenkins provides a detailed bibliography of literature on genocide, including relevant reference works, films, studies of this kind of violence in various continents and societies, along with more general works.

Bringing the above chapters together, the following major aspects of this pressing social problem tend to be highlighted:

- need to appreciate the potentially destructive effects of competitive situations on human ethnocentrism;
- importance of adopting an interdisciplinary approach to this subject, given its complexity and need for multilevel, analytical, and societal understanding;
- continuing danger posed by global "tribalism," which constantly threatens the possibility of "civil order;"
- continuous need to reduce "discrimination against minorities," as well as appreciate the general rather than specific nature of genocide and our continuing insensitivity towards it;
- crucial relevance of using this term in a practical rather than "emotive" and pathological fashion;
- applicability of the "construct of generation" to understanding genocide, revealing the major effects of generational ideology, identity, common past and expected history;
- the "binary arguments contained in colonial strategies of exclusion," justifying the genocidal treatment of the "natives" in the name of "cultural higher development;"
- relevance of historical societal inequality to understanding continuing genocidal treatment of a society's minorities;
- appreciation of how threatened minorities interpret their genocidal past using their traditional culture in a manner which aids their current endurance;
- possible negative reactions to the economic and cultural effects of Westernization on traditional societies, involving treating minorities in destructive ways to ensure the elite's continuing dominance;
- positive effects of global economic development on elite responses to conflict even in deeply split societies;
- major methodological difficulties involved in carrying out research on the "biographical self-depictions" of genocide survivors and their ongoing adjustment, illuminating the long-term, destructive effects of genocide;
- biographical contexts and personal experiences which may seriously limit an individual's awareness of and reaction to surrounding destructive developments; and, finally,
- the availability of a wide variety of available literature and documents on this crucial subject.

In general, these chapters underscore the potentially destructive effects of negative societal circumstances, both economic and cultural, on minorities in any society, expressed in the form of extreme ethnocentrism as genocide. The latter, in turn, indicate their own unique attempts to interpret their past and cope with the present. The term itself needs to be applied carefully and in a practical manner, while we all need to develop much greater awareness of and sensitivity to this major social issue. On the positive side, some societal conditions, particularly the economic, may prevent the emergence of murderous intergroup conflict even in deeply fragmented situations. Greater consciousness of the ever-present danger of potential genocide in *any* society, detailed insight into the conditions under which it emerges, and attempts to prevent its bloody consequences are clearly vital to potential social harmony in the new century. Hopefully, the above chapters will encourage a major shift in this direction. In this connection, we would like to thank each of the authors for the valuable insight they have provided into these matters.

Part I. Theoretical Approaches to Genocide

Chapter 1. The Possible Causes and Reduction of Genocide: An Exploration

Graham C. Kinloch, Florida State University

The terrible events of September 11 reflect, perhaps, a continuing lack of respect for human life in the new millennium, occasioned by ongoing political conflict on a worldwide scale. While not genocidal in proportion, such terrorist attacks remind those left alive of the ever-present possibility of human destruction on a massive scale.

There is little doubt that genocide has probably occurred since the beginning of human intergroup contact, reflected in the long-term history of societal conquest and violence, warfare, "holocaust" events and, more recently, so-called "ethnic cleansing." Particularly disturbing in all of this is the apparent lack of reaction, approaching indifference, on occasion, to such developments by both the international community and the United States, despite clear knowledge of destructive events and available intervention strategies which have proved effective in the past (Power 2002). While variously rationalized as respecting the internal affairs, independence, and local control of the regimes involved, such apathy is reprehensible during an era of supposed sensitivity to "human rights." While international organizations such as the United Nations have, on occasion, attempted to intervene in some of these destructive situations, their effectiveness has largely proved to be temporary and extremely limited.

As a result, genocide remains a burning issue during the twenty-first century, vital to a deeper understanding of global issues such as terrorism, war, international refugees, human civil rights, and the worldwide problem of social inequality. This chapter attempts to address the issue by examining the term, its general sociological context, relevant theories, related factors, comparative case studies, applicability to US society, possible prevention, and general policy implications. We begin with the term itself.

DEFINING THE TERM

The term has generally been traced back to Lemkin who in the 1940s defined genocide as "the destruction of a nation or an ethnic group," involving a "coordinated plan of different actions aiming at the destruction of essential foundations of the life of national groups, with the aim of annihilating the groups themselves" (Lemkin 1944). In a more recent work, Porter (1982: 12) defines the term as "the deliberate destruction, in whole or in part, by a government or its agents, of a racial, sexual, religious, tribal, ethnic, or political minority."

According to these approaches, the heart of genocide is *destruction*: the annihilation of *minorities* (racial, sexual, religious, tribal, ethnic, national, and political — Lemkin 1944; Porter 1982), including the "disintegration" of their institutions, culture, language, national feelings, religion, economic existence, personal security, liberty, health, dignity, and, ultimately, their lives (Lemkin 1944). This generally involves an "attack on nationhood," often resulting in the severe decline or elimination of self-government, local institutions, traditional languages, religions and cultural activities, increased economic impoverishment, depopulation, declining fertility, significant food and health declines, and various kinds of moral "debasement" typified in high levels of gambling, pornography, and alcoholism (Lemkin 1944). Major techniques effected to accomplish this national destruction include negative official ideologies (particularly the definition of minorities as non-human), the use of technology to ensure efficient death rates, and organization of state bureaucracies to maximize these negative outcomes (Porter 1982). Thirdly, genocide often occurs under conditions of war, colonization, and tribal conflict (Porter 1982). A number of analysts have also attempted to delineate major types of genocide, including the desire to eliminate rivals, increase wealth, impose terror on their enemies, and implement a highly destructive ideology (Johanssohn and Chalk 1987). In all of this, the ironic attraction of genocide is its potential solution of intergroup conflict by totally eliminating the "enemy," thereby extinguishing the "problem" (Dadrian 1999).

16

ALTERNATIVE THOUGHT

The above approaches essentially take an exclusive approach to genocide: it either occurs or fails to take place. A more flexible approach, perhaps, involves conceptualizing (potential) genocide as a *continuum*, ranging from group demographic control (e.g., forcible migration, reduced fertility, mass rape, imposed cultural assimilation), through exploitation and discrimination (e.g., life-threatening conditions, group harm) to deliberate mass death. While some may object to such an approach as "debasing" or trivializing the term (Porter 1982), such a perspective highlights the *potential* for genocide in any society, highlighting the need to monitor current and emerging events in the attempt to prevent any movement towards possible minority destruction. Sensitivity to the potentially deadly effects of minority control and discrimination may prove vital to the avoidance of mass murder in *any* society. This implies that genocide *may* occur in any society since its *potential* is universal and endemic. Accordingly, we turn to discuss its possible sociological sources.

SOCIOLOGICAL BACKGROUND

The potential for genocide may be viewed as endemic or essentially built into the foundation of any society. In this regard, Sumner's concept, *ethnocentrism*, may be particularly useful: involving a view of "one's own group [as] ... the center of everything, and all others ... scaled and rated with reference to it" (Sumner 1906), this kind of ubiquitous normative prejudice represents the basis of in-group harmony and out-group hostility and the perception of out-group members as non-human, often expressed in extreme forms of nationalism, patriotism, and chauvinism under stressful circumstances. The de-humanization of out-group members is particularly relevant to the issue of genocide in which such an ideology is vital to the justification of large-scale human destruction.

A number of social scientists have also viewed competition and conflict as built into the human social condition. In this connection, Park and Burgess' notion of the ecological cycle of intergroup "contact, competition, conflict, accommodation, and assimilation" (Park and Burgess 1921) is particularly relevant. They view human competition for resources as universal with ensuing conflict as essentially inevitable. While accommodation and assimilation tend to follow in some cases, others may involve intergroup destruction and genocidal developments instead. Consequently, reactions to inevitable competition and conflict are vital to the possible prevention of human destruction.

Another contributing factor involves the normalization of human torture, particularly in contemporary society. Often torturers go unpunished; instead, official reactions typically include denial, minimizing the abuse, blaming the victims for their presumed deviant behavior and thereby suggesting that they "deserve" such treatment, emphasizing their speedy recovery, and blaming a few of the officials involved as "bad apples" (Conroy 2000). As a whole, society tends to view such behavior with indifference and accept it as "necessary" under threatening conditions. Such avoidance of guilt tends to be enhanced by the rules, impersonal nature, and minimal individual responsibility typical of modern bureaucracies. In general, modern bureaucracies, with their highly specialized, hierarchical roles, administration by rules, blind individual obedience, self-interest and lack of responsibility in such vacuous contexts, may be viewed as major contributors to both potential and actual genocidal situations (cf. Human Rights Watch 1995; Weiss 1996).

Bringing the above discussion together, it is evident that under certain threatening or competitive conditions, inherent ethnocentrism in any society may possibly be expressed in genocidal terms, exacerbated by modern bureaucracy. We turn next to elaborate our understanding of such "conditions" by examining a number of theories which attempt to delineate major factors behind the emergence of mass murder.

THEORIES OF GENOCIDE

A broad variety of researchers have attempted to account for the rise of genocide with respect to a number of factors — biological, psychological, social psychological, and the more sociological. Some have posited that genocide is built into human "instinctual aggression," the frustration of which, intensified by "militant enthusiasm," may result in mass homicide (Lorenz 1970; 1977*). Others have argued that the human species represents an "evolutionary misfit," involving a conflict between old and new brain structures, resulting in highly destructive wars (Koestler 1978*). Still others have identified human "malignant aggression" — a form of "biologically nonadaptive" reactions to need-frustration with virulent consequences (Fromm 1975*). Such perspectives are obviously limited in their deterministic and non-contextual approaches to radical social conflict. Given the variety of human societies and types of conflict, attempting to

GENOCIDE IS NOT INSTINCTUAL

explain genocide in instinctual terms fails to take us far in understanding this complex topic.

Some researchers have taken a more psychological stance, applying psychological and psychoanalytic views to German history and the society's leaders in particular. Problematic child-rearing practices and related personality development aberrations have been used to understand the emergence of the German holocaust and Hitler as its leader (Loewenberg 1971; 1975*). Recently, Raymond has explored Hitler's behavior in terms of the "conditional love" and abuse he experienced as a child (Raymond 2000). Others have included necessary "personality preconditions" as one of the major factors behind the possible emergence of negative motives and genocidal behavior (Staub 1989). Anger and frustration may also aggravate potential hostility behind the development of human warfare (Horowitz 1976), while frustration-aggression theory may be relevant in this regard also (Dadrian 1947*). Again, while psychological and personality factors may contribute to ruinous social conflict, understanding the societal contexts in which they are reinforced is particularly crucial to the fuller appreciation of this issue.

On the group level, Rubenstein (1975*) has pointed to the importance of the First World War as one of the earliest mass military killings in Europe, representing, perhaps, unconscious attempts to eliminate "surplus populations," a practice later implemented overtly by the Nazi regime. The rise of state bureaucracy as a major tool of modern government further ensured the easy disposal of minorities with its removal of individual moral responsibility, dehumanized mentalities, high levels of role specialization, use of neutral euphemisms to denote murder, and implementation of highly efficient forms of "state murder" (Rubenstein 1975*; Human Rights Watch 1995; Porter 1982: 15). Combined with ideologies defining minorities as non-human or animals, evil, degenerate, and a major threat to state power and societal survival, thereby requiring elimination (Porter 1982; Kuper 1981; Weiss 1996; Lerner 1992), these state organizational structures proved deadly to the minority populations under their control.

Other researchers have focused on more sociological factors, concentrating on a society's external and internal factors as well as their possibly destructive consequences for minority group members. Major *external factors* have been delineated as follows (cf. Harff 1987; Kuper 1981; Porter 1982):

- colonialism;
- colonial control, manipulation, and exploitation;
- colonial terror;

- post-colonial conflict, attempted secessions, etc.;
- societal upheavals;
- external threats;
- external control, domination, manipulation, and expansion;
- high geographical isolation; and,
- low external reaction to internal genocide, including support and official denial on occasion.

In general, these factors highlight the relevance of external exploitation, control, manipulation, threats and the non-interference of others to significant levels of internal mass murder.

Major *internal traits*, on the other hand, tend to involve the following (cf. Elias 1996; Ferrarotti 1994; Fein 1979; Horowitz 1976; Lerner 1992; Porter 1982; Rummel 1994; Simpson 1993; Staub 1989):

- significant declines in state power;
- the possibility of minority retaliation against the state;
- totalitarian, non-democratic governments;
- high levels of diversity, cleavage, pluralism, and political polarization;
- a society's genocidal history and tradition;
- negative life conditions;
- high levels of internal competition — economic, labor, physical resources, etc.;
- a well developed state bureaucracy with high levels of institutional support and technology to ensure efficient levels of homicide;
- weak minority victims, including pariah groups;
- high minority resistance to state control and violence, including post-colonial strife; and,
- emergence of 'toxic ideologies,' viewing minorities as threatening the society's welfare in animalistic, disease, exclusive, and extreme terms.

According to these analysts, societies which are pluralistic, totalitarian, conflict-ridden, highly bureaucratic, competitive, discriminatory, and prejudiced are most likely to experience genocidal events.

What are the likely *consequences* of these external and internal traits and developments? These include the following (cf. Allen 1996; Kuper 1981; 1997; Nascimento 1989; Staub 1989):

- increasingly extreme, repressive and destructive control measures applied to target minorities;

- the failure of political negotiation, resulting in polarization and destructive conflict;
  - genocidal reactions against minority secession attempts;
  - genocidal/counter-genocidal intergroup dynamics;
  - accelerating attempts to vilify victims;
  - increasing bureaucratic control of minorities;
  - accompanying genocidal euphemisms and minimization of individual
  - responsibility for murdering victims; and,
  - demographic abuse of victims through rape and miscegenation.

Generally, then, genocidal-type situations tend to experience increasing state control and abuse, destructive conflict, intergroup polarization, minority vilification, demographic manipulation, as well as bureaucratic control and elimination.

Bringing the above discussion together, genocidal societies generally tend to reveal high levels of external control, exploitation, threats, and international apathy, combined with internal cleavages, bureaucratic-totalitarian governments, and high rates of intergroup competition and discrimination. Destructive consequences include increasing state control, abuse, polarization, toxic ideologies, minority vilification and elimination. External influence, worldwide apathy, and conflict-ridden minority group relations appear to represent the most powerful recipe for potential genocidal conflict. We turn next to elaborate this perspective by examining these factors with respect to particular societies.

COMPARATIVE CASE STUDIES

The discussion to follow is based on a wide range of case studies of genocidal societies, as discussed in the research literature, grouped by similar external and internal characteristics. While each country is clearly unique in a number of ways, it is possible to view them in the context of a number of general types.

Table 1 analyzes a number of genocidal societies subject to external threats, ranging from Germany to the former USSR While each situation is obviously very unique, they reveal a number of similarities with respect to the factors we have delineated in our above discussion.

21

Table 1. Genocidal Societies Subject To External Threats

Country	External Factors	Internal Factors	Consequences
GERMANY*	Major upheavals, external threats, high economic suppression & exploitation, low external reaction to genocide	Economic crises, high state bureaucracy, high state technology, extremely negative ideas, including euthanasia, high professional support for state	Threat definition of minorities, property expropriation, then concentration camps, then extermination racial purity & disease views of minorities
TIBET**	High external threat, high external control & domination, becomes China's remote defenses, low external reaction, criticism, or action	Weak victims of Chinese abuse, Local resistance to external domination, resulting in high levels of conflict	Increasing external bureaucratic control, high external destruction and domination
TURKEY***	High external threat (USSR), low external reaction to genocidal behavior	Intolerant Ottoman culture, state theocracy, weak victims with very little power	Increasing state restriction and manipulation of Armenians, high genocidal behavior
USSR****	High external threat, revolution, low external interference	Communist theory - shift from pro-nationalism to anti-nationalism, state ideology: unified, central state = new socialist nation, increasing internationalism	Deportation, resettlement, liquidation, cultural repression, national destruction
GENERAL TRENDS:	EXTERNAL THREAT	SOCIETAL REACTION AND SCAPEGOATING	GENOCIDAL DESTRUCTION IN DESIRE FOR NATIONAL PURITY

Literature:
* Black 2001; Friedlander 1995; Kenrick & Puxon 1972; Lerner 1992; Lifton 1986; Taylor 1985; Weiss 1996.
** Gilbert 1959
*** Dadrian 1999
****Deker & Lebed 1958

A number of trends are clearly visible: each society has faced a major external threat in some fashion, combined with international apathy to internal social violence and in some cases, strong economic support for the power elite in place. In the case of Tibet, the Chinese viewed the society as part of their remote defenses and were motivated to control the country accordingly. The minorities in each case tend to be very weak, while some countries have developed a powerful and efficient central bureaucratic state, supported by the professional classes in the case of Germany, used as a killing machine. Minority resistance, in some situations, only provoked further violence, while some states such as Turkey were particularly intolerant and theocratic in orientation. The impact of these societies' extremely powerful, centralized elites on the minorities subject to their control was devastating: notions of disease, racial purity, eugenics, sterilization, and national unity were used to justify their demographic control, manipulation, cultural repression, and attempted total destruction. According to these cases, a society's response to major external threats, combined with the acquiescence of other powers, may involve the extreme repression and destruction of weak minorities as scapegoats in their elite's urgent desire for survival and internal homogeneity. Under such conditions, a society may respond to major external threats by controlling and attempting to destroy the minorities under its control.

Some countries are particularly subject to external control and manipulation. These are presented in Table 2, involving Bosnia, Iraq, Kampuchea, and the Sudan. Each society has experienced extremely high levels of external control, dominance, and manipulation, often with the acquiescence of other nations. Kampuchea's geographical isolation has also served to aggravate its negative features generally. Each case, furthermore, reflects high levels of racial, ethnic, religious, and demographic diversity with these minorities lacking significant political and economic power of any kind. The bureaucratic state elite responds by attempting to impose an orderly, homogeneous state of some kind (ethnic, ideological, or religious) in an extreme fashion, vilifying particular minorities, controlling others, engaging in "ethnic cleansing" in some cases, reacting to their own failure with more violence, and, in some cases, producing new impoverished under-classes. Accordingly, the consequences of severe external interference in a society may involve genocidal attempts to impose societal unity in a diverse situation by any destructive means possible. Again, while each of these cases is clearly unique in a number of historical and societal features, the central trend delineated here appears common to all of them. Attempts to effect societal unity in countries subject to outside manipulation and consequent internal diversity may involve genocidal policies and consequences.

Table 2. Genocidal Societies Subject to External Control and Manipulation

COUNTRY	EXTERNAL FACTORS	INTERNAL FACTORS	CONSEQUENCES
BOSNIA*	Very high external control and manipulation	Serbian state ideology, high levels of political organization, support of military & media in effort, high use of economic resources	Vilification of Muslims, increasing "ethnic cleansing," increasing rape, increasing population control
IRAQ**	Very high external control, manipulation, domination, lack of external interference	High oil resources, religious diversity, orderly society ideology, weak victims, high state bureaucracy, high state efficiency, high state specialization	High bureaucratic euphemisms used in genocidal policies, high diversity and minority destruction, very high genocide levels

KAMPUCHEA***	Very high external domination and manipulation, high colonialism, high geographic isolation, high wars	High traditionalism, high rural/urban division, high forced socialism, extreme negative ideology	Extreme control of general population, very high levels of human destruction, high failure of new regime, reinforcing totalitarianism and genocidal policies.
SUDAN****	Very high external colonialism and manipulation	High racial and religious diversity, attempts to impose an Islamic state	Very high death rates, rape, famine, development of an underclass, high genocide
GENERAL TRENDS:	EXTERNAL MANIPULATION AND CONTROL	IMPOSED STATE	DESTRUCTIVE MEANS TO ACCOMPLISH THIS

Literature:
* Allen 1996; Cigar 1995
** Human Rights Watch 1995; Salih 1995
*** Kiernan 1996
****African Rights 1995

When external control and manipulation involve colonialism, negative consequences often involve pluralistic rivalries, instability, attempted secession, and civil war. State reactions to such dynamics frequently include genocidal attempts to restore order and effect societal unity while protecting their own power. These cases are outlined in Table 3 and applied to Biafra, Bangladesh, Rwanda and Burundi, and recently independent East Timor. The first two of these experienced major secession movements with accompanying genocidal state reactions in the attempt to prevent their withdrawal. Conflict, both internal and external, has plagued both of these societies. Rwanda, Burundi, and E. Timor were all subject to severe external colonial manipulation and differential support of internal groups and minorities — the Indonesian army in E. Timor and particular ethnic groups in the case of Rwanda and Burundi. Many of these situations, furthermore, were largely reinforced by external apathy and indifference. Internal developments included severe ethnic rivalries, secession movements, military governments, de-colonization violence, and external military invasions. Destructive consequences involved genocidal attempts to prevent secession, counter-genocidal violence, and genocidal attempts by colonial powers to prevent local independence taking place. Clearly, the kinds of unstable diversity produced by external colonialism, along with resulting rivalries, political instability, and civil war tends to eventuate in genocidal attempts to maintain societal order and unity. In these cases, the colonial heritage has been particularly murderous in its impact on the minorities so produced.

Table 3. Genocidal Societies Subject to External Colonialism and Manipulation

COUNTRY	EXTERNAL FACTORS	INTERNAL FACTORS	CONSEQUENCES
BIAFRA*	High external colonialism and manipulation, part of Nigeria	High ethnic, geographical, economic diversity, high ethnic rivalry	Muslim attacks on Ibos, genocidal reactions to attempted secession
BANGLADESH**	High external colonialism and domination, post-colonial developments, separation: India and Pakistan, W. Pakistan attacks	High religious diversity, increasingly militaristic government, high secession movements	Genocidal reactions to abort attempted secession, very high levels of anti-Bengali racism
RWANDA/ BURUNDI***	High German and Belgian colonialism, external support of particular ethnic groups, external tolerance of conflict	Conflict-ridden post-colonial developments, very high political instability and consequent violent conflict	Very negative effects of colonialism, both genocidal and counter-genocidal violence with very high death rates involved
EAST TIMOR****	External Dutch colonialism, Indonesian Declaration of Independence resulting in army control & exploitation of East Timor, low external reaction	1975 external invasions, internal party divisions, civil war, Indonesian repression, high army economic interests	Very high levels of external invasions and genocidal conflict
GENERAL TRENDS:	EXTERNAL COLONIALISM AND MANIPULATION	PLURALISTIC INSTABILITY AND CONFLICT	GENOCIDAL REACTIONS TO SECESSION ATTEMPTS

Literature:
* I.C.E. Case Studies 1997
** Jones 1999
*** Nyamkanzi 1998
**** Jardine 1999

Societies which have experienced limited types of genocide, according to some analysts, and have experienced direct external colonialism with subsequent competition for various resources, are outlined in Table 4. These include Australia and Brazil. As can be seen, both countries were subject to high levels of colonial settlement. In Australia's case, no treaties were negotiated with the indigenous population while Brazil's development involved the forced importation of very large numbers of African slaves. Both countries were subject to very high rates of migration, settlement, and economic development, involving increasingly racist reactions to minority populations. Some Australian aborigines were subject to genocidal treatment while black Brazilians experienced high levels of white rape and cultural assimilation. The indigenous population also suffered murderous violence and the increasing removal of their land for mining and agriculture purposes. Clearly, external colonialism tends to aggravate intergroup competition for various kinds of resources, resulting in increasing colonial domination of minorities and their genocidal treatment in some cases.

Table 4. Genocidal Societies Subject to External Colonialism

COUNTRY	EXTERNAL FACTORS	INTERNAL FACTORS	CONSEQUENCES
AUSTRALIA*	Very high external colonialism, no treaties with indigenous population	Very high rates of migration and settlement	Increasing economic competition with indigenous population, competition results in increasing violence and genocidal-type behavior
BRAZIL**	Very high external colonialism, very high importation of African slaves	Very high white racism, very high rates of physical and cultural miscegenation	High rates of white rape of blacks, large numbers of mulattos, increasing "whiteness" of population, increasing destruction of indigenous population, increasing removal of their land for mining and agriculture
GENERAL TRENDS:	EXTERNAL COLONIALISM	INCREASING INTERGROUP COMPETITION	INCREASING COLONIAL DOMINATION AND MINORITY DESTRUCTION

Literature:
* Moses 2000
** Nascimento 1989

We turn finally to consider the United States as representing a genocidal *continuum*. The society's major features and related consequences are summarized in Table 5. Here it can be clearly seen that this society possesses all the major features of the colonial society: extensive external colonial migration, very negative treatment of the indigenous population, including assumption of many of their resources, and importation of a wide variety of minorities for labor purposes, including the use of slavery in some cases. Native Americans were subject to genocidal-like treatment on occasion; and many minorities experienced "negative life conditions," while many whites adhered to extremely negative ideologies and social movements. Some minorities were subject to forced migration and starvation, sterilization, medical experimentation, lynching and other hate crimes, severe forms of segregation and discrimination, and demographic control generally. Two broad types of minority resulted: colonized (e.g., Native Americans, African Americans, Hispanics) and immigrant (other racial and ethnic groups) (cf. McLemore and Romo 1998). All of this highlights the genocidal continuum, ranging from demographic control, through discrimination, to death in some cases. While no social group has been entirely eliminated, colonized minorities have been subject to all forms of negative treatment along this continuum, some of which continue today. Such a perspective highlights the *potential* for some kinds of destructive behavior under certain circumstances, a *danger* the society needs to be aware of and prevent at all costs. Greater awareness of issues relating to possible shifts in this violent direction is also vital to reduce and avoid future intergroup conflict and destructive violence.

Table 5. US Society as a Genocidal Continuum

Country	External Factors	Internal Factors	Consequences
US *	High external colonial migration, negative impact on indigenous population, forced importation of some minorities for slavery purposes, importation of a variety of other minorities for labor purposes	Early genocidal treatment of Native Americans, colonial land and mineral desire, white manifest destiny, black slavery, negative life conditions for many minorities, negative ideologies, including eugenics, racist social movements	Early forced migration and starvation of Native Americans, high racism, eugenics, K.K.K. movement, hate crimes, minority demographic control, minority discrimination, laws against miscegenation
GENERAL TRENDS:	EXTERNAL COLONIALISM	COLONIZED AND IMMIGRANT MINORITIES	RACIAL HIERARCHY WITH GENOCIDAL CONTINUUM APPLIED TO MINORITIES

Literature:
* Churchill 1994; Power 2002; Svaldi 1989; Tolnay & Beck 1992.

Bringing together the above comparisons, it appears evident that genocidal conflict may occur in a number of situations:

- a society's response to *external threat*, expressed in the form of extreme repression and destruction of minorities as scapegoats in the state's desire for survival, dominance and societal unity;
- genocidal reactions to external *interference*, expressed in attempts to impose social unity in *diverse situations* by extremely destructive means;
- genocidal responses to the kinds of *unstable diversity* created by *external colonialism*, including sectional rivalries, political instability, and civil war, expressed in attempts to maintain societal order and unity;
- genocidal responses to the kinds of *intergroup competition* for resources occurring as the result of external colonialism; and,
- a *genocidal continuum* which exist in many *colonial societies*, ranging from demographic control, through discrimination, to death in some cases, highlighting the *potential* for group destruction.

Such a perspective underlines any society's potentially destructive reactions to external threat, interference, or colonialism as these processes may result in elite insecurity, conflict-ridden diversity, and intergroup competition, expressed in the state's genocidal attempts to maintain its survival, social order, societal unity, and political dominance of the situation as a whole. These trends emphasize that genocide may emerge in any society, depending on the situation at hand, highlighting the need to develop and implement relevant preventative measures. We turn to this topic next in our analysis.

POSSIBLE PREVENTION

Kuper (1985) has outlined a number of very helpful ideal and practical steps to be used to reduce and/or prevent genocide. Ideally, he would like to see the full removal of group inequality and their "...full incorporation into the political and other institutions of the society" (Kuper 1985: 209). Worldwide development of socialism and greater societal equality generally would also help if such societies prove more concerned with human rights and less imperialistic. On a more practical level, he emphasizes the importance of global "preventative action against genocide" (1985: 210) through international organizations such as the United Nations, more effective protection of vulnerable indigenous groups, implementing "early warning systems" as monitoring devices, thereby enabling important pro-action, increasing national rights to "self-determination," and organizing effective "humanitarian intervention" where peace is threatened in *particular situations*. Such an approach clearly underlines the relevance of societal equality, international monitoring and intervention, protection of indigenous groups, and maximizing the political independence of all groups worldwide.

Our analysis suggests the addition of the following practical steps to his very useful discussion:

- monitoring and major reduction of ethnocentric and dehumanizing ideas in all
- societies;
- monitoring and reduction of all negative and destructive ideas regarding human beings generally;
- monitoring and reduction of all negative and toxic ideologies in particular, heightening general awareness of their extremely dangerous potential;
- replacement of negative, destructive views of human nature with the more positive and constructive;
- replacement of violent role models with more positive, harmonious models of conflict-resolution; and,
- a general emphasis on non-violent images and aspects of popular culture generally.

We shall deal with the policy implications of these suggestions in more detail after bringing together our analysis as a general theory of genocide.

TOWARDS A GENERAL THEORY OF GENOCIDE

The literature reviewed in this chapter has underlined the relevance of a number of major factors to the understanding of genocide: (1) endemic ethnocentrism present in every society and social groups within it; (2) the heightening of such de-humanizing stereotypes by a variety of types of intergroup competition; (3) major impact of particular external factors which may increase a society's potential for genocide; (4) possible reinforcement of these factors by a country's particular internal features; with (5) extremely destructive consequences for the minorities within it. Such a perspective emphasizes that genocide may involve the extremely destructive effects of ethnocentrism on individuals and groups facing competitive circumstances within societies which have developed under negative external and internal conditions. These factors are summarized in Table 6. Here it can be seen that universal ethnocentrism and inevitable intergroup competition occurring under negative external conditions (major upheavals, external control, manipulation, and colonialism) and internal circumstances (high intergroup competition levels, internal crises, high state control, weak victims, minority resistance, imposed states, high state scapegoating) make the probability of genocide in both relative (i.e., genocide continuum) and absolute terms (minority destruction) high. The reduction and/or removal of these factors, combined with positive action to reduce inequality, protect minorities, and implement uniform human rights and independence, is obviously crucial to the cause of global peace in a strife-torn world.

We turn next to discuss the kinds of policy implications such a perspective implies.

POLICY IMPLICATIONS

Such a theory highlights a number of potential policy implications as follows:

1. If *ethnocentrism* is the major factors behind potential genocide, addressing this issue effectively should become a national priority, particularly in the media, politics, and education. The importance of increasing awareness of this problem on a national level is a great deal more than "political correctness" (a fashionable insult of the political right); boosting social and cultural tolerance in the context of societal

diversity and greater equality becomes vital to avoiding destructive violence on a potentially massive scale;

2. Since *competition* is endemic, unavoidable, and ubiquitous, its greater appreciation, understanding, and potential regulation is also important to preventing societal shifts towards group-based violence. Furthermore, the importance of facility group equality throughout society in a manner that facilitates rather than threatens group welfare is vital to improving the social environment in which inevitable competition, market-based and otherwise, inevitably occurs. Such equalitarianism should also results in the full societal incorporation of all groups in society, rather than just a few (Kuper 1985);

3. Dealing effectively with *external factors* implies effective international cooperation reducing global upheavals, preventing and/or regulating external threats, and facilitating a society's internal political, economic, and social independence for all of its social groups, particularly its minorities. Maximizing group independence has been found to be particularly vital to avoiding and/or reducing violence in all societies worldwide (cf. Kinloch 1999);

4. The international community could also be more effective in ameliorating and/or reducing the precipitation of *internal* crises, simultaneously protecting the independence of any society and its internal social groups;

5. Internally, state *bureaucracies and technology* could be put to more positive rather than destructive uses, combined with the development of humanitarian rather than "toxic" concepts and ideologies;

6. All of the above measures would also contribute to the development of *pluralistic equilibrium* rather than instability, reinforced greatly by the facilitation of group equality and full incorporation into the larger society; and,

7. Particularly crucial to all the above is the implementation of positive, *constructive models* and icons of peaceful, harmonious conflict-resolution in place of the typical violent, divisive, and destructive.

Table 6. Major Factors Contributing to Genocide and Its Prevention

ETHNOCENTRISM	COMPETITION	EXTERNAL FACTORS	INTERNAL FACTORS	CONSEQUENCES	PREVENTION
- ubiquitous aggravated by negative childrearing experiences resulting in negative personality traits	- resources; labor; power; cultural dominance - resulting in inevitable intergroup conflict	- major upheavals; external threats; external control and manipulation; external colonialism and manipulation; high external colonialism	- internal crises; high state technology and bureaucracy; professional and institutional support; toxic ideologies; weak victims; pluralistic instability and conflict; minority resistance; societal scapegoating; imposed uniform states; increasing intergroup competition; colonized and immigrant minorities	- destructive reactions to minorities; high state minority control; genocidal attempts to impose social unity; vilification of minorities; destructive attempts to impose unified state; genocidal state reactions to minority secession attempts; increasing colonial domination and minority destruction; genocidal continuum reflected in minority hierarchy	- reduce ethnocentrism; positive child rearing; limit competition; increase equality; reduce external threats, control, and manipulation; end external and neo-colonialism; reduce state bureaucracy and technology; remove toxic ideologies; remove minority group boundaries; increase incorporation of all groups; maximize diverse political participation; protect independence and human rights; greater international monitoring and intervention.

In general, the above policies highlight the significance of dealing effectively with ethnocentrism by increasing social equality, group independence, human rights, and constructive models of conflict-resolution, combined with their global reinforcement, in order to reduce and hopefully eliminate the possibility of genocide in an effective manner in any society. While these suggestions may appear hopelessly general and idealistic, awareness of their relevance and potentially crucial importance to worldwide peace is an important starting point.

We turn to complete our discussion with this study's conclusions.

CONCLUSIONS

In this chapter, we have attempted to examine the possible causes and effective reduction of genocide. The term implies the demographic, institutional, cultural and physical destruction of minorities and may be applied either in an exclusive or more flexible manner, i.e., only applied to death or also involving demographic control and discrimination. We located its sociological foundation in the kinds of ethnocentrism found in all societies, potentially aggravated by intergroup competition and inevitable conflict, reinforced by the dehumanizing effects of modern state bureaucracies. Attempts to account for its occurrence include biological, psychological, social psychological, and more sociological approaches. We would argue that societal contexts might exacerbate the first and second of these, implicit in the potentially destructive consequences of a number of clear external and internal factors and/or societal traits. Examining a wide range of comparative case studies of genocide, we found that such mass murder appears likely to occur in situations in which states respond destructively to external threats, interference in countries containing diverse populations, internal instability in unstable, pluralistic colonies, internal intergroup competition resulting from external colonialism, and potential genocidal reactions in colonial societies such as the United States, involving a continuum of group destruction and discrimination. Based on this analysis, we concluded that greater awareness of and intervention into ethnocentrism and intergroup competition worldwide, combined with effective global reduction and/or removal of these contributing factors, coupled with positive action to reduce inequality, protect minorities, and implement human rights and independence, would go a long way in protecting future generations from the ongoing horror of mass murder.

Despite the new millennium, modernization, worldwide development, and global economy and increased concern with universal human rights, warfare in the contemporary world appears to continue largely unabated, often with long-term genocidal consequences. Greater awareness, political accountability, and effective global intervention are crucial to the possible reduction and hopefully eradication of this continuing human scourge (cf. Power 2002). While it is far easier to concern ourselves with our own narrow, selfish, societal interests, the welfare of our planet remains in jeopardy and requires urgent attention. Appreciating potential civil rights erosions in the context of the present US terrorist crisis is crucial also, along with the urgent need to more fully understand the factors underlying terrorism generally. We can only hope that enough time, sensitivity, resources, and motivation remain to deal with these pressing social issues effectively.

NOTES

* cited in Kuper, 1981.

REFERENCES

African Rights. 1995. "Facing Genocide: The Nuba of Sudan." *www.oneworld.or/news/africa/* nuba.html.

Allen, B. 1996. *Rape Warfare: The Hidden Genocide in Bosnia-Herzegovina and Croatia.* Minneapolis: University of Minnesota Press.

Black, E. 2001. *IBM and The Holocaust.* New York: Crown Publishers.

Churchill, W. 1994. *Indians Are Us? Culture and Genocide in Native North America.* Monroe: Common Courage Press.

Cigar, N. 1995. *Genocide in Bosnia, The Policy of "Ethnic Cleansing."* College Station, TX: Texas A&M University Press.

Conroy, J. 2000. *Unspeakable Acts, Ordinary People. The Dynamics of Torture.* New York: Knopf.

Dadrian, V. N. 1947. "Factors of Anger and Aggression in Genocide." *Journal of Human Relations* 19, 394–416.

_____. 1999. *Warrant for Genocide: Key Elements of Turko-Armenian Conflict.* New Brunswick: Transaction Publishers.

Dekker, N. K. & A. Lebed (eds.). 1958. *Genocide in the USSR, Studies in Group Destruction.* New York: Scarecrow Press.

Elias, N. 1996. *The Germans: Power Struggles and the Development of Habitus in the Nineteenth and Twentieth Centuries,* edited by M. Schroter and translated by E. Dunning and S. Mennell. New York: Columbia University Press.

Fein, H. 1979. *Accounting For Genocide, National Responses and Jewish Victimization During the Holocaust.* New York: Free Press.

Ferrarotti, F. 1994. *The Temptation to Forget: Racism, Anti-Semitism, Neo-Nazism.* Westport: Greenwood Press.

Friedlander, H. 1995. *The Origins of Nazi Genocide: From Euthanasia to the Final Solution.* Chapel Hill: University of North Carolina Press.

Fromm, E. 1975. *The Anatomy of Human Destructiveness.* Greenwich: Fawcett Publications.

Gilbert, R. (ed.). 1959. *Genocide in Tibet: A Study in Communist Aggression.* New York: American-Asian Educational Exchange.

Harff, B. 1987. "The Etiology of Genocides." In *Genocide and the Modern Age, Etiology and Case Studies of Mass Death,* edited by I. Wallimann and M. N. Dobkowski. Westport, CT: Greenwood Press, pp. 41–59.

Horowitz, I. L. 1976. *Genocide, State Power and Mass Murder.* New Brunswick: Transaction Books.

Human Rights Watch. 1995. *Iraq's Crime of Genocide: The Anfal Campaign against the Kurds.* New Haven, CT: Yale University Press.

ICE Case Studies. 1997. "The Biafran War." Http://gurukul.american.edu/TED/ice/biafra.html.

Jardine, M. 1999. *East Timor: Genocide in Paradise.* Monroe: Odonian Press.

Johanssohn, K. & F. Chalk. 1987. "A Typology of Genocide and Some Implications for the Human Rights Agenda." In *Genocide and the Modern Age, Etiology and Case Studies of Mass Death,* edited by I. Wallimann and M. N. Dobkowski. Westport, CT: Greenwood Press, pp. 3–20.

Jones, A. 1999. "Case Study: Genocide in Bangladesh, 1971." *www.gendercide.org/case_bangladesh.html.*

Kenrick, D. & G. Puxon. 1972. *The Destiny of Europe's Gypsies.* New York: Basic Books.

Kiernan, B. 1996. *The Pol Pot Regime: Race, Power, and Genocide in Cambodia under the Khmer Rouge, 1975–79.* New Haven, CT: Yale University Press.

Kinloch, G. C. 1999. *The Comparative Understanding of Intergroup Relations, A Worldwide Analysis.* Boulder, CO: Westview Press.

Koestler, A. 1978. *Janus: A Summing Up.* London: Hutchinson.

Kuper, L. 1981. *Genocide: Its Political Use in the Twentieth Century.* New Haven, CT: Yale University Press.

Kuper, L. 1985. *The Prevention of Genocide.* New Haven, CT: Yale University Press.

_____. 1997. *The Pity of it All: Polarisation of Racial and Ethnic Relations.* Minneapolis: University of Minnesota Press.

Lemkin, R. 1944. *Axis Rule in Occupied Europe.* New York: Fertig.

Lerner, R.M. 1992. *Final Solutions: Biology, Prejudice, and Genocide.* University Park, PA: Pennsylvania State University Press.

Lifton, R. J. 1986. *The Nazi Doctors, Medical Killing and the Psychology of Genocide.* New York: Basic Books.

Loewenberg, P. 1971. "The Psychohistorical Origins of the Nazi Youth Cohort." *American Historical Review* 76, 1457–1502.

_____. 1975. "Psychohistorical Perspectives on Modern German History." *Journal of Modern History* 47, 229–279.

Lorenz, K. 1970. "On Killing Members of One's Own Species." *Bulletin of the Atomic Scientists,* October, 3–5, 51–56.

Lorenz, K. 1977. *On Aggression.* New York: Harcourt Brace & World.

McLemore, S. D. & H. D. Romo. 1998. *Racial and Ethnic Relations in America.* Boston: Allyn & Bacon.

Moses, A. D. 2000. "An Antipodean Genocide: The Origins of the Genocidal Movement in the Colonization of Australia." *Journal of Genocide Research* 2, 89–106.

Nascimento, A. 1989. *Brazil, Mixture or Massacre? Essays in the Genocide of a Black People.* Dover: The Majority Press.

Nyankanzi, E. L. 1998. *Genocide: Rwanda and Burundi.* Rochester, NY: Schenkman Books.

Park, R. E. & E. W. Burgess. 1921. *Introduction to the Science of Sociology.* Chicago: University of Chicago Press.

Porter, J. N. (ed.). 1982. *Genocide and Human Rights, A Global Anthology.* Washington, DC: University Press of America.

Power, S. 2002. *"A Problem From Hell": America and the Age of Genocide.* New York: Basic Books.

Raymond, N. 2000. *The Genesis of Genocide: Why the Holocaust Happened.* San Jose, CA: Writer's Showcase.

Rubenstein, R.L. 1975. *The Cunning of History.* New York: Harper & Row.

Rummel, R.J. 1994. *Death by Government.* New Brunswick: Transaction Publishers.

Salih, K. 1995. "Anfal: The Kurdish Genocide in Iraq." *www.xs4aa.nl/-tank/kurdish/htdocs/ his/ Khaledtext.html.*

Simpson, C. 1993. *The Splendid Blond Beast: Money, Law, and Genocide in the Twentieth Century.* New York: Grove Press.

Staub, E. 1989. *The Roots of Evil: The Origins of Genocide and Other Group Violence.* New York: Cambridge University Press.

Sumner, W. G. 1906. *Folkways.* Boston: Ginn & Company.

Svaldi, D. 1989. *Sand Creek and the Rhetoric of Extermination: A Case Study in Indian-White Relations.* Lanham: University Press of America.

Taylor, S. 1985. *Prelude to Genocide: Nazi Ideology and the Struggle for Power.* London: Duckworth.

Tolnay, S. E. & E. M. Beck. 1992. *A Festival of Violence: An Analysis of Southern Lynchings, 1882– 1930.* Urbana, IL: University of Illinois Press.

Weiss, J. 1996. *Ideology of Death. Why the Holocaust Happened in Germany.* Chicago: Elephant Paperbacks.

Chapter 2. Modern Societies and Collective Violence: The Framework of Interdisciplinary Genocide Studies

Mihran Dabag

If discussions on the topicality of research regarding processes of state violence and genocide are still necessary today, does this not imply that we have failed with respect to a decisive challenge raised by National Socialism, namely the imperative to ensure that such atrocities are not repeated, the commitment to a "never again"?

The fact that the study of the murder of Jews and specific other minorities in Europe can stimulate important orientations for a democratization of social structures was an important point of departure, and not only for post-1945 German politics. However, primarily on the basis of the changes in international politics following 1990, in particular the new proximity of violent clashes, it has become more clearly evident that the collective phenomena of violence cannot be treated as historical mistakes. It is not sufficient to describe the violence in the Balkans or the genocide in Rwanda as escalated reactions or as aggressive eruptions motivated by hatred.

Is it possible to determine similar or even identical courses for individual incidences of violence? What consequences does the obvious repetition and repeatability of state violence, even after National Socialism, have for measures of early recognition and prevention of grave human rights violations?

The search for explanations as to why the global society is also marked by acts of violence is currently concentrated on attempts to determine particular potential risks. Trans-state violence potential, for instance in the form of international terrorism, is not the only important factor in this context. Categorizations such as "Fallen States" or "High-Risk States," which have found their way into present-day political theory, are coming to increasingly mark certain state characteristics as presenting possible dangers to the world system. Multi-ethnic states or states with limited bureaucratic centralizations in particular are attributed as having an increased tendency towards violent conflicts. Other discussions focus on regional tendencies, which stand in opposition to leading industrial states.

The talk of "global wars" and "world order wars," and the distinction between "high-intensity" and "low-intensity" civil wars, is also testimony to current efforts to standardize global potential crises. In view of this, the question of which *specific* social or political structural characteristics impose increased risks of state violence tends to be pushed into the background. Accordingly, the reflections outlined below, which examine the relevance of the study of processes of collective violence for an interdisciplinary genocide research, based not least on an attempt to stimulate a critical analysis of the perspectives that determine the approaches of explanation involved in the study of massacre, persecution, war and genocide. An interdisciplinary approach does not convey here a mixture of theoretical methodological perspectives, but rather implies different disciplines complementing and verifying one another through their explicit disciplinary positions. It is also precisely through a confrontation with disciplinary historical perspectives that those central guiding questions need to be developed that are to be studied in detail by interdisciplinary genocide research. The object of such research, particularly its motives and motivations, emphasizes that institutions and structures of genocide should be placed within processes relating to the whole of society — and it should be viewed neither as belonging to the specific politics of an isolated perpetrator group nor as a the general phenomenon of a particular epoch.

FRAMEWORK

For a long time, research on collective violence and genocide has been restricted almost exclusively to historians. Only recently have interdisciplinary approaches been developed with contributions from sociological, social-psychological and literary research. Historical analyses of persecution, genocide, massacre and war tend to focus on unique historical contexts. The historical approach highlights an attempt to grasp the *historical results* of war and genocide, aiming at sketching an overall process and classifying the single event within the general course of history. According to this view, the Holocaust has already become the characteristic of a specific epoch. More recent debates on the relationship between genocide and modernization have also led to the assumption that there are typical patterns of events of genocide processes, creating schemes of interpretation which emphasize periodical lines and basic structures, and permit more general interpretations. In contrast to sociological paradigms, which will be sketched out later, historical approaches survey the course of "world history" and concentrate primarily on tracking down so-called "anomalies."

Historical research on societal developments has long been dominated by the postulate that every epoch has its own history and thus develops its own historiography, as well as evolutionary concepts of society and bipolar analytical categories: dictatorship versus democracy, fascism versus totalitarianism, the principle of leadership versus the party state, and especially "intentionalism" versus "functionalism." Historical research on Nazism has long highlighted the concept of the "acting leader" as the only acting subject; this concept has recently been extended by research on the "acting small groups" such as special agencies. Recent approaches to the history of everyday life that concentrate on the tacit support of individuals, especially studies based on political science, usually cause highly controversial reactions, e.g., the reaction to the so-called Goldhagen-thesis.

Apart from these basic biases, historical research is influenced by two analytical debates: the controversy concerning the singularity or comparability of genocides and the distinction between "understanding" and "explaining" the past. Apart from these, there is also a third issue: the concept of objective science itself, which prides itself on its validity and its adherence to universal categories, is challenged by perspectives related to "ethical demands," in that it restricts the perspective of "those affected" or the "perspective of the victim" and points to a collective, universal victim.

Whereas historical approaches still dominate the analysis of genocide, the sociological approach begins with a demand for a political sociology, as formulated by Irving Louis Horowitz (Horowitz 1997, Horowitz 1998). As in the case of history, a critical examination of sociological approaches to genocide research reveals fundamental difficulties in the social sciences. As a result, one is faced with a discipline that until now has been extremely cautious in its analysis of issues such as persecution, terrorism, war and genocide. It has also emphasized the dilemma of personal involvement, which supposedly hinders the creation of objective categories. Since the sociological approach to a subject requires the establishment of a sufficiently detached perspective, a positivist social science denies members of a victim group any potential for scientific objectivity — a tacit yet apparently valid assumption. The sociological perspective tends to distance itself from the concept of experience; it prefers standardized models rather than interpretation, and it is primarily interested in those social facts that illustrate the social *typology* of the individual and society. As a result, the victim as such cannot be taken into account. In contrast to its extensive preoccupation with the perpetrator,[1] sociology usually avoids the analysis of processes which create victims and with the victims themselves, since this might possibly involve emotions and ethics. In contrast to research on socially acting perpetrators, reflections on socially 'suffering' victims cannot be typified; the victim is not only a marginalized phenomenon but also an anomaly and does not exemplify the ideals or the norms of a society.

Sound sociological genocide research needs to break with these traditional concepts: instead of considering genocide to be a mere reaction to economic and technological developments, sociological research must acknowledge the status of genocide as an independent social phenomenon. In this context, however, approaches to a "sociology of violence" (Trotha ed. 1997; Gay 1993; Lichtenberger and Lüdtke eds. 1995; Röttgers and Saner eds. 1978) must also be critically examined. An analytical approach to violence that regards it as a general phenomenon pervading the entire history of mankind denies the existence of specific characteristics of violence as well as the singularity of each occurrence. For this reason, the analytical distinctions between genocide and other forms of mass extinction — for example, natural disasters, arbitrary killings, war and other symbolic or cultural acts of violence (Horowitz 1998) — made primarily by genocide researchers who use a sociological perspective must be subject to criticism. Interdisciplinary frameworks for genocide research make use of analytic models proposed by historical research on epoch-making issues (Bell-Fialkoff 1996) and systems of power (Horowitz 1997, Kuper 1981, Chalk and

---

1. The study of perpetrators' biographies and generational transmissions of the perpetrators' memories is currently booming (cf. Roberts 1998, Welzer, Montau and Plaß 1997).

Jonassohn 1990)[1], and they also incorporate influences from research on socio-logical and historical minorities (Melson 1992), social conflict (Dobkowski and Wallimann eds. 1998) and prejudice (Lerner 1992).

Comparative Genocide Research

In more recent times it appears that with the definition of conflict, in par-ticularly the establishment of an "ethnic conflict," an explanation for the courses of modern-day violence has been found. To speak of conflict is to assume opposing partners, *action and reaction*, failed communication relationships, points of escalation or turning points of actions. However, in the analysis of modern politics of violence as the result of competing group relationships or escalating conflicts, it is difficult to take into account endeavors to achieve national self-determination, nationalistic movements or national homogenization politics. To what extent, if any, in inter-ethnic or intercultural conflict, are there two opposing groups that can be defined in the same way? Can it really be assumed that ethnic conflicts result from an escalation of failed communication? To what extent is it overlooked that although the politics of violence can oppose a group, the motives are not oriented towards their real characteristics but rather against the stigmatizing characteristics assigned to them?

Ethnicity and regional culture appear to be generally considered as "critical dimensions" for the worldwide network of states. In the conception of the world as a coherent, networked structure, ethnic conflicts are classified as a danger for the whole. In particular, a disruption to relations on an economic or political level is diagnosed.

The topicality of genocide research is particularly apparent in view of the limited scope of the conflict parameter since it argues against an overhasty stan-dardization of the causes of collective and state violence in terms of inevitable causal relationships of ethnicity and conflict, exclusion and violence. Instead, it encourages a consideration of *intentions* and *strategies*, and consequently recog-nizes the need to look at the foundations of knowledge of modern societies. Not least — and this is a challenge that is particularly difficult to accept — genocide research points out that many of the foundations of knowledge in the legitimati-zations of genocide are still valid today. Indeed, it stresses that we retain and continue with this validity today through, among other things, globalization

---

1. See also Drost 1959. Drost sketches central questions of genocide research in their discussion of international signs in his problematizations of the UN convention.

frameworks. The topical nature of genocide research lies in the fact that it is still possible to conceive of genocide today.

Approaches of examinations that compare structures are therefore devoted first of all to the differentiation of genocide from other forms of collective violence: massacre and war in particular. Using the various criteria of analytical genocide research, one can restrict the term *massacre* to those acts of violence that appear to be sudden, momentary outbreaks. In this case, the murderers involved rarely exhibit systematic discipline or training. They also usually constitute a self-contained group, not necessarily divided into a planning as opposed to an executing team. The implementation and choice of methods for the realization of the plan are usually left up to those who carry it out. Apart from this, there is no long-term, intergenerational plan of extermination; the massacre generally constitutes an act of situational elimination, an outbreak of "punishment" and "revenge." Both the ideological and technical preconditions to a massacre are minimal. The victims usually belong to an easily recognizable group, but despite the massacre, the group itself is not actually in danger of being entirely destroyed. A massacre kills individuals and destroys families, but it does not exterminate entire generations. Consequently, a massacre does not interrupt the generational succession of the victim group.

Following this framework, the term *war* refers to an international and organized armed conflict between two different states. The main motives are conflict, imperialism/conquest, and the enforcement of the interests of one state against another. Today, war is still considered to be a political option, although it has recently become fashionable to replace the term by either "military" or "humanitarian intervention." The distinction between victim and perpetrator is inappropriate in the case of war; here, one speaks of friends and enemies, actors and re-actors. Accordingly, the term *civil war* describes a non-international armed implementation of violence between non-state conflict parties as a consequence of the attack of one group on another within a state-organized society with the goal of the violent enforcement of group-related interests.

Ethnic cleansing (due to its euphemistic nature, in the following I will replace this term, which has become fashionable in the context of the war in Kosovo, with the term *ethnic violence*) can be understood as the attempt of a dominant ethnic group to expel from a certain region or murder (massacre) a non-dominant ethnic group who live within the same state or confederation of states, with the intention of achieving or safeguarding sovereignty of the region through the ethnic homogenization of the population. *Ethnic violence* is therefore imple-

mented in the context of conflict with regard to the sovereignty of a certain geographical region and initially does not direct itself against the members of an
ethnic group in the whole area of the state, but rather solely against those who
live within the region in question. *Ethnic violence* does not necessarily presuppose
an ideological legitimation.

In contrast to all of these terms, *genocide* refers to the ideologically authorized and systematic extermination of a specific, defenseless part of society in
order to realize the vision of a homogenous society, culture, territory and
system of power. This is achieved by eliminating those parts of society which
are supposed to be incapable of being integrated. It is a unique, national crime
relating to the whole of society, which takes places in the course of particular
processes of national transformation. According to Raul Hilberg, one central
characteristic of this process consists of the different phases in its implementation: group definition, deprivation of rights, selection, deportation, and extermination (Hilberg 1961).

This outline makes it clear that is not the forms of violence implemented
that enable distinctions to be made between genocide, massacre, ethnic violence,
war and civil war, but rather the perpetrator groups and institutions implementing the violence, the mechanisms of publicity, ideological frameworks,
motivations and objectives of the perpetrators or the arguments of legitimation.
This brief sketch could be expanded to include numerous other typical characteristics; but they may not necessarily be found in each and every case.

In his work on discipline, Ulrich Bröckling has compiled some principles
of warfare: rigid and inflexible structures of hierarchy and military command,
propaganda used to create stereotypes of the enemy, intensive preparations
based on drill, obedience, and training, and a lack of personal emotion with
regard to the enemy, since war is not fought for personal reasons (Bröckling
1997). This assignment of typical characteristics leads to further questions, since
many of these elements also play a role in genocide: a strict allocation of roles and
disciplinary structures, planning, propaganda and the creation of a rather
complex negative mythology in order to slander the (collective) victim. Of
course, genocide is directed against an enemy within the society in question, one
who aims at subverting the national unity from within. Furthermore, genocides
are not decided or carried out on a battlefield, they are not surprise attacks;
instead they are implemented in various stages of social exclusion and
extinction. They also involve a different type of perpetrator, since the majority of
these executioners are not recruited from the military but from all walks of life,

including average citizens of both sexes and various backgrounds, from science, business and the arts.

This typological approach raises the possibility of a link between the violence of war and that of genocide. The last stages of genocide — the attempts to eliminate European Jews and Armenians — occurred during both World Wars. However, according to analytical genocide research, warfare provides the perpetrator with a kind of "screen" which promotes an atmosphere that supports mass extinction.[1] In this case, genocide appears to be reduced to issues of conquest and resource expropriation (Aly and Heim 1993, Aly 1995). Are war and genocide both characterized by the same specific type of violence, i. e., a form of violence linked to a specific authority, which originally occurred in the context of war and then became a model for subsequent genocides? Are both war and genocide reflections of the same kind of society? Did the ideologies of the two perpetrating societies — the National Socialist as well as the Young Turks — consciously fall back on militaristic arguments to justify their practices of extermination? War is usually equated with aggressive violence, whereas genocide is a desire to exterminate that derives from irregular, pathological attitudes. War is legitimized as a highly regulated kind of killing, as violence that either attacks or defends. Genocidal violence is also directed against a specific victim, but since its radical intention is to exterminate not only the (collective) victim but also his entire historical and social presence, genocidal violence is both destructive and influences the structure of the perpetrator society. The typological approach appears to weaken the differentiation between war and genocide. Nevertheless, genocidal violence must be regarded as an independent type of violence, i. e., a variety that can take many forms, one that is related to traditional forms of violence but is necessarily accompanied by a specific, clearly defined motivation — annihilation.

Thus, it is not possible to characterize the violence of a genocide as modern or anti-modern, as civilized or traditional: the violence of the National Socialist perpetrators was just as *modern*, mechanized and alienated as it was *direct*, filled with hatred, traditional and "barbaric." Initiating individual actors stand alongside employees of the "untarnished" profiteering bureaucracy. In spite of

---

1. Cf. Dadrian 1993. In the text it says on pp. 180f.: "Such crises can reach their peak in times of external war, especially global war, which will facilitate the rapid transformation of tentative ideas of massive violence into plans of action behind the screen of war. War thus emerges as the connecting link between the embryonic and implementing stages in the evolution of a genocide."

this, there are numerous examples of analytical totalizations, which by means of generalized structural characteristics of the Holocaust, have been abstracted and imposed on models of other forms of collective violence. However, such approaches, with their feature-oriented universal definitions, do not make any real contribution to genocide research: talk of "total," "ultimate," or "bureaucratic" genocide — contrasted with the less "total" or the less "bureaucratic" acts of violence — mainly serves to construct a type of hierarchy of genocides.[1]

The key focus of genocide research should therefore be on structures, self-explanations and institutions, figurations of prejudice, anti-Semitism and racism or aspects of morality and normalization. Examined *individually*, these should show detailed aspects of the planning and realization of genocide. Comparative interdisciplinary discussions of these aspects should, in addition, be related to parameters that are used *generally* for the analysis of social policy. The actual implementation of violence is not the only violent characteristic of genocide. Further characteristics are also found in the integration of genocide in forms of exclusion, deportation or murder in a society: the planning and implementation by means of societal actor groups or societal changes, which genocide processes both strive for and leave as their legacy. Thus, there is one thing genocide-research is definitely *not*: an additive series of different collective violent crimes and attempts to bring some order in this mass through wild constructions of hierarchy.

The works of comparative genocide research can usually be assigned to two basic traditions. On the one hand, there are analyses based on the first useful definition of genocide, proposed by Raphael Lemkin in 1944, or the definition proposed by the United Nations Genocide Convention, issued in 1948 (which was the result of political compromise).[17] On the other hand, there are approaches which use the National Socialist genocide as their starting point and attempt to account for National Socialist persecutions (Katz 1994). In his 1944 report on German occupation policy in Poland, Raphael Lemkin directed public attention towards a new kind of persecution, which he considered to be a new form of governmental population policy called *genocide* (Lemkin 1944). This first attempt to specify the new phenomenon and define it raised issues that characterize genocide research still today, since it primarily deals with complex theo-

---

1. The specific political or sociohistorical structures of the relevant perpetrator societies are by no means included in this ranking. The "comparison of genocides" does not therefore lead to a "system comparison" or a "structure" comparison, but rather to a counting of victims and types of killing.

retical issues and relies on juridical concepts to facilitate the early diagnosis and prevention of human destruction. Lemkin pointed out the difficulties of defining a victim group or the shift from persecution to systematic annihilation. Since he also took into account indirect genocidal measures, his work has remained valuable.

Comparative genocide studies have mostly focused on individual elements of genocide research such as the perpetrator, victim, motive, planning, implementation, and results. These studies are hardly ever compared to or examined in the light of historical and sociological case studies. Helen Fein, who sought to establish genocide as part of sociological discourse, limits the term to political crime: "Genocide is sustained purposeful action by a perpetrator to physically destroy a collectivity directly or indirectly, through interdiction of the biological and social reproduction of group members, sustained regardless of the surrender or lack of threat offered by the victim" (Fein 1990, p. 24). Is it possible to assume that a lack of effective resistance is a genocidal criterion without running the risk of distortion? Is it possible to include the attitude and constitution of the victim in a general, standardized scheme or paradigm of genocide? In her later works, Fein continued her attempts to establish a theoretical framework, trying to analyze the relationship between the victim group and the perpetrator as well as the difficulties in the formation of concepts of the collective victim: "Genocide is ... a strategy that ruling elites use to resolve real solidarity and legitimacy conflicts or challenges to their interests against victims decreed outside their universe of obligation in situations in which a crisis or opportunity is caused by or blamed on the victim ..." (Fein 1993, p. 813).

Two Canadian researchers, Frank Chalk and Kurt Jonassohn, developed the following definition of genocide as a specific political means to exert power: "*Genocide* is a form of one-sided mass killing in which a state or other authority intends to destroy a group, as the group and membership in it are defined by the perpetrator" (Chalk and Jonassohn 1990, p. 23). In their study of collective violence in the twentieth century, Michael Dobkowski and Isidor Walliman examine the role of industrialization, population growth, and resource distribution (Dobkowski and Wallimann 1998). Christina Larner and Connor Cruise O'Brien — whose work remains valuable although less widely known than others — analyze genocidal processes against the background of processes of nation-building and accompanying myths of national foundation (Larner 1981, O'Brien 1999). Other approaches also distinguish between possible variants: politicide, ethnocide, and democide (Harff and Gurr 1987, Rummel 1992).

Bernhard Taureck introduced a new interpretation by distinguishing between situational as opposed to intrinsic variants of genocide. This includes issues of identity creation and elimination for the sake of securing resources, and takes into account specific trends and strategies of modern development from colonialism to globalization — an analytical framework that focuses on representations rather than victims (Taureck 1999).

Finally, I should like to mention an approach which is not derived from comparative genocide research but from German history — the attempt by Immanuel Geiss to interpret world history as a *history of massacre* (Geiss 1992). He distinguishes between temporally and locally restricted massacres and those which are inherent in a specific system, between spontaneous or sudden and institutionalized massacres, and massacres that occur in the course of revolutions as opposed to massacres that take place during civil wars. He also introduces an intermediate stage between massacre and genocide, "genocidal massacres," which he applies to the Armenian case. According to Geiss, the term "genocide" should only be used to refer to the Holocaust.

The debate on analytical and comparative frameworks does not simply result in a discourse on legitimation but rather provokes one. It is necessary to underscore the singularity of each occurrence or form of collective violence, and this necessitates precise differentiation. However, this easily turns into a classificatory, evaluative perspective against the background of a specific analytical framework. Any comparison that tries to differentiate without any moral qualification risks becoming lost in highly problematic analytical qualifications as the complexity of collective violence and genocide is reduced to a single analytical structure.

In order to develop a typological and structural analysis, previous genocides have to provide an analytical framework: for example, the comparative approach usually contrasts the deportations of the Armenian Genocide with the National Socialist concentration and death camps (Goldhagen 1996, p. 414; Sofsky 1997) to illustrate the technological development of extermination methods. There are also additional arguments used to rank the two genocides. This approach can even lead to the denial of the Armenian genocide by official Turkish historiography — a depressing example of differential analysis. So far, comparative analyses have usually focused on the societies of the perpetrators, ignoring the victims and reducing their role to a mere analytical category.

The Perpetrator of Genocide

By now it should be obvious that genocides cannot be explained purely as general types of extermination but rather as an inherent part of complex societal processes. Genocide is not a manifestation of collective violence but is realized through a complex network of individual, collective and institutionalized structures of violence, through ideas and knowledge, acting and resisting (it was one of the central characteristics of National Socialism that resistance to it aimed to bring about the fall of the regime, but not the end of the murder of the Jews). The perpetrator is primarily characterized by determination, an intentional will. Historical and socio-psychological "profiles" of Nazi perpetrators, as exemplified in the works of Gitta Sereny, include further characteristics such as team spirit, a bureaucratic mentality based on unrestricted obedience, willingness to follow authority slavishly, and a low threshold of aggression (Sereny 1974). But is it possible to define genocide perpetrators in these terms, or are they mere products of societal and ideological conditions, influenced by a particular mentality? Despite these kinds of problems, many analyses continue to focus on perpetrators. Early approaches, largely influenced by the concept of leadership, apparently aimed at establishing a certain group of perpetrators to turn attention away from possible German collective guilt. The issue of deliberate extermination dominates contemporary scientific debates still today, even though discussions of intentionalism and functionalism have long since proved unproductive. Nevertheless, they seem to be present in questions regarding visionary, ideological or situational decision-making aspects. Consequently, the search for evidence, documents, protocols, declarations and decrees continues. Solving this problem requires a closer examination of the language, images, projections, political ambitions and visions of the perpetrators to point out that there was in fact a "reason" for killing the victim group and, even more, that the victim group was, of course, "innocent" despite this so-called "reason." This line of argumentation has to rely on the "logic" of extermination, it has to construct and explain the motives that led to a particular behavior. However, this means returning the victims to the disastrous logic of guilt and innocence, guaranteeing the continuity of the perpetrators' discourse beyond the act of extermination.

Genocide, however, is not a question of guilt or innocence. Can it actually be characterized as an enforced act between a victim and a perpetrator? One could argue that genocidal annihilation does not call for an examination of the relationship between guilt and innocence, victim and perpetrator, but for an examination of the extinction of a group which has previously been deprived of its rights. In fact, the question of the perpetrators' "intentions" is usually answered by focusing on traditional patterns of behavior rather than concentrating on particular aspects of the actual decision-making involved. Up to now, explanatory models have provided numerous motivations based on sociological, ideological and economic reasons. Does it appear too difficult to consider annihilation as the main objective?

When analyzing genocidal processes, it appears impossible to either comprehend a single or dominating motivation or to speak of complex combinations of motives. Nevertheless, we can observe the undisputed results of previous genocides today: successfully homogenized societal structures. Collective violence, massacres and genocides of the previous century have succeeded in destroying what they intended to destroy. They constituted an integral part of major societal transformations. The modern authority of the state has not only accompanied but also shaped the modernizing processes that have led to the realization of nation states. In the face of an increasing escalation of annihilating acts, pointing towards an overall development and structure of the perpetrators and their institutions, it appears appropriate to assume an "intention" and "program" of extermination. Thus, the term "genocidal intention," which I consider important at this point, does not assume there are inevitable or even cyclical historical processes, nor does it seek any one particular explanation, be it the paradigm of totalitarianism, the principle of leadership, or general concepts of world history, such as fear of falling back into an uncivilized state. There have always been alternatives to genocide: genocide is not the last step in an evolutionist, escalating process.

GENOCIDE AND THE NATION STATE

An examination of *epochs* characterized by specific types of violence, e.g., *the age of religious wars*, or *the age of colonial conquests*, does not make any sense as long as it only results in a cyclical perspective, highlighting a kind of violence that is typical of the twentieth century. However, the analysis of *genocide and the modern age* becomes useful as soon as violence against specific groups is no longer considered a unique "accident" of world history but part of the development of our current society (Platt 1998). During the Enlightenment, most European societies realized that people demand a government they can identify with, and that the future belongs to those societies that have settled the identity of people and state, religion and culture, language and territory, origin and history amongst themselves. However, the articulation of principles such as freedom, education, and progress was also accompanied by certain duties, rights, and legal forces. The departure of God as the creator of the world and His replacement by evolution and history allowed man to assume his position as the center of the world. At this point, history turned into win and lose, give and take, power and powerlessness, past and future. The Enlightenment was the first vision of the European modern age, not only a new beginning after the break-up of old structures, but also a deliberate intervention in the development process. This vision constituted a radical departure for the sake of creating a new society for subsequent generations (Dabag 2000).

When Ziya Gökalp wrote his poem *Turan* in 1911, the Young Turks had already seized power and brought parliament under their control (Dabag 1998): The movement of Young Turks had grown out of secret groups in the Ottoman Empire, which had been fighting for modernizing reforms — particularly a constitutional system — since the 1820s. But at the turn of the century the strategies of the movement were institutionalized in a stable network of intellectual and paramilitary groups. The aims of the Young Turks were no longer freedom, democracy and progress: they had one goal of overriding importance — identity. By the end of the nineteenth century, the reform process had been replaced by the visions of a "new life" and a "new order," which were subordinate to the implementation of the "national life." They aimed at the political implementation of the unity of all Turks along the lines of a territorial and in particular culturally and linguistically legitimized vision: *Turan*. The term *Turan* first of all reveals a shift in orientation: Arabic and Persian elements of history and culture were rejected and replaced by a Turkish identity (Turkism) with a territorial North-East-orientation, i. e., to the Turkish peoples of the Russian Empire. The concept of *Turan* embraced the Turkish speaking peoples of Central Asia, Iran, and Afghanistan all the way to the Great Wall of China. The historic basis for the link between Turan and a territory belonging to the "Tur" or "Turk" people has not yet been established, nor have its exact historic borders between Hungary, Finland and China. In his epic *Kizilelma*, Ziya Gökalp had the female protagonist, the "noble" maiden Ay Hanim, who was supposed to be the ancestor of numerous generations, say the following: "The people is like a garden, / we are supposed to be its gardeners! / First the bad shoots are to be cut / and then the scion is to be grafted".[1]

Genocidal policy is primarily focused on designing new generations as a conscious creative act and on providing for the development of new, different generations. The definition of a particular victim group is supported by widespread stereotypes and preconceptions or reveals a history of persecution. The atmosphere of annihilation, however, is primarily influenced by a sense of fulfilling a national duty, one which might be considered difficult: carrying out an important, honourable duty for the sake of a new beginning and the emergence into the modern age, in the face of a menacing threat to the "national body."

Moving beyond the sphere of any traditionally accepted moral code, annihilation is itself turned into a moral issue. The perpetrator does not turn into a beast or a callous monster. He surmounts any moral conflict by strongly believing that he is carrying out an important, necessary task. The perpetrator is not motivated by hatred, contempt or racism, but by a determination derived from a normative claim to authority. This claim has not been imposed by terror and is felt both by the circle of perpetrators and "average citizens."

In his reflections on the strategies involved in legitimizing the annihilation of the Herero people in South-West Africa in 1904, Medardus Brehl proves the presence of a similar pattern of argumentation: "Genocide is turned into a contribution to creating a future mankind as well as into moral behaviour and into an element of moral maturity. The perpetrators are not considered to commit a crime but to carry out useful, morally justified and hard work..." (Brehl 2000, p. 27).

Systematic mass extinction cannot be considered a specific phenomenon of the modern age. Comparative genocide research, which follows up this kind of thought, runs the risk of reducing genocide to an international crime. In contrast, genocide constitutes a national crime occurring in the context of specific nationalizing processes of transformation, aiming at the implementation of an inner normative order. Genocide does not involve solving a conflict, but is rather the realization of a "noble" and "sacred" goal, the realization of a *new future*.

---

1. This poem was published in several magazines: Genç Kalemer No. 4 (23 May 1911); reprinted in: Gökalp, Ziya: Kizil Elma, Istanbul 1914/15. The translation was made according to a later edition of the complete works: Siirler ve Halk Masallari. Ziya Gökalp Külliyati 1, ed. by Fevziya Abdullah Tansel, Ankara ³1989, p. 5. "Fatherland for the Turks is neither Turkey, nor yet Turkestan; / Fatherland is a great and eternal country: Turan" (Astourian 1999, p. 32). Compare Tekin Alp's free rendering for a translation into German in: Österreichische Rundschau 46, 6, 1916, pp. 284–297, here p. 285.

GENOCIDE AND IDENTITY

The fact that the scholarly treatment of collective violence raises the issue of individual and collective concepts of identification is not due to the extreme nature of modern violence such as persecution, war and genocide. The killers and bureaucrats as members of the group of perpetrators are not only connected by ideology and hierarchical structures of an unfathomable system of command. The exertion of violence and its authorization are also closely related to the construction of collective identity in the perpetrator society. Thus, the study of genocide and identity raises two issues: for the victims, suffering from genocide implies a multitude of discontinuities, injuries, and losses. The experience of extreme physical and psychological violation not only leads to long-term traumatic effects which are passed on to following generations, but also to the radical destruction of their identities. This kind of destruction, however, is not a mere side effect of genocidal violence, but rather its primary objective. In the case of a genocide, racial and ideological stigmatization are directed towards the destruction of all aspects of identification (e.g. history and language, family and profession, belief and traditions) since it aims at complete annihilation, which goes beyond the physical extermination of the victim's presence, extinguishing both the past and future. This leads to the second issue of genocide and identity: extermination plans also provide for the creation of identity within the perpetrators' societies. The elimination of a specific part of the population, and thus the erasure of different expectations, systems of reference and concepts, is intended to strengthen and unify the future identity of the perpetrating society.

SCIENCE AND PERSPECTIVE

In German discussions, the debate concerning the uniqueness and comparability of genocide has turned out to be particularly effective in distorting scholarly preoccupation with forms of collective violence. Interestingly enough, there appears to be no motivation within this discussion to deal with competing analyses of genocidal occurrences. Similarly, the debate on the relative number of casualties plays a rather marginal role: in German scholarly discourse, the victim as such has become subject to comparison and controversies. Thus, attempts are being made to establish a hierarchy of the victims of National Socialist persecutions. Before discussing this debate, it is important to assess the specific kind of alienation which affected Jewish identity due to the segregational measures as well as racial and ideological definitions involved in National Socialism. This alienation was completed by specific patterns of interpretation, in particular by the image of the nameless, anonymous victim, and it hinders the commemoration of remaining victim groups as well as an appropriate commemoration of the Jewish victims. The attempt to deal with the history of Jewish everyday-life by assigning names and identities to the largely anonymous victims promotes the understanding of the processes of persecution and murder, but it also has a side effect: it actually conceals a central aspect of the Holocaust — the negation of individuality. This approach exemplifies the possibilities of playing down the actual events. Historiography still sticks to its emphasis on the anonymous, almost uncountable and appalling number of victims. The request to commemorate other victim groups implies a concern with the peculiarity of the Jewish victim group rather than its overwhelming numbers. This does not call for research on totalitarianism, fascism or dictatorial leadership. Preoccupation with the peculiarities of Jewish victims requires an examination of the attitudes that lead to the formation of a society of perpetrators: Anti-Semitism and the National Socialist ideology, prejudice and envy, racism and "seduction." Considering the scholarly controversy connected with the Goldhagen debate, it appears to be even more difficult to face the complexity and variety of motives that facilitated the extermination of the Jews than it is to study the broad societal basis which supported and guaranteed its planning and implementation.

In post-war research, the racial criteria according to which National Socialists established their specific hierarchies of persecution have resulted in projections onto the victim group, which have had to be internalized by the latter as a precondition to their participation in scientific debates. Research on genocide should neither be reduced to a debate regarding different victim groups such as Jewish and Polish victims, victims among the German civilian population and victims of the National Socialist persecution, nor to a mere addition of increasing numbers of separate victim groups that make up the general figure of "six million Jews, Sinti, Roma, Homosexuals." In contrast, comparative genocide research focuses on comparable aspects of the ideological and bureaucratic systems of the perpetrating societies. By addressing different forms of collective violence, genocide research provides an approach which acknowledges the distinct singularity and peculiarity of each victim group. Occasional reproaches of victim groups for demanding exclusive commemoration cannot be used by researchers to justify avoiding current occurrences of collective violence. Since there are no basic analytical categories which permit detailed case studies without inciting a debate on singularity and comparability, dealing with the persecution of the Sinti and Roma as well as with the victims of socialist totalitarianism and Stalinist terror has become an extremely explosive subject. A possible analytical category could be established by falling back on the concept of collective violence, which implies different forms of realization: massacre, war, genocide.

There is another aspect worth mentioning to complete this theoretical framework. With regard to the debate on singularity and comparability, it is important to bear in mind the strategic aspects of each discourse. Anyone who addresses the issue of singularity and comparability is not interested in fundamental aspects of the theory of history, but rather seeks to position himself within a framework of theoretical concepts that are closely linked with denial and relativism.

Does the choice between an *explanatory* and an *understanding approach* imply a choice between two scientific theories, that is between two analytical procedures? Considering historiographic works, is it even possible to speak of conscious decisions between explaining and understanding? Almost any introduction to National Socialism and the Holocaust tries to approach the actual events rather than explain them: no attempt to renounce all explanatory approaches, however, has ever been made. Dan Diner has presented a detailed account on the motivations that underlie explaining vis-à-vis understanding approaches to genocidal processes (Diner 1991). Surprisingly enough, most reflections on the theory of history that deal with the paradigm of explaining and understanding, which in fact constitutes a central theoretical borderline in the case of genocide research, do not even refer to the controversy on genocide (Goertz ed. 1998). The debate on explaining and understanding basically affects different forms of the process of historical recognition, analytical frameworks, as well as the structuring and hierarchical arrangement of event, pattern, interpretation and projection. In the context of this debate, the study of history places itself within its own developmental process: it scrutinizes the character of interpretation and arrangement of its statements as well as preconditions influencing its interpretation.

Analyzing occurrences of violence illustrates the fact that this debate on perspective, too, is not limited to simple questions of method and procedure, but that it primarily demands consideration of the validity of the resulting statements. This has consequently led to the debate on different ways of reducing the

Holocaust to a mere historic event, by means of historical analyses with no political, moral and pedagogical obligations. In addition, issues such as the generalization of analytical categories as well as the assumption of continuity are examined. In fact, especially as far as the analysis of genocidal processes is concerned, the study of their history needs to reflect on its traditional periodical concepts, in particular the paradigms of continuity and discontinuity, singular or universal structures of event. Paradoxically, the analysis of genocidal processes appears to be hindered and restrained by these basic issues, although the Holocaust initiated the debate on the theoretical paradigms of historical research. In coming years, the debate will no longer be limited to a warning about reducing the Holocaust and other genocidal processes to mere historical events or whether it is even possible to do so. Due to the fact that new forms of collective persecution and violence demand scientific study, the analysis of collective annihilation will increasingly have to take into account the difficulties and implications of scientific categorization. An approach that posits a contrast between an understanding and an explanatory interpretation is thus inextricably linked to the discussion on the singularity or comparability of genocidal processes. It should be noted that both debates on perspective are primarily concerned with warnings, the definition of their own point of view as well as assigning of other points of view to other perspectives. The debate seems to resemble a ball in a gaming machine, not permitted to touch the edges in order to remain in the game.

It is not possible to use theoretical considerations to solve the problem of how to account for the singularity of each occurrence and still formulate comparative statements that are relevant to current research, nor can the complex and multi-causal nature of genocidal processes be adequately explained in a theoretical context. After all, these issues do not appear in the context of theoretical reflections, but in connection with case studies. Consequently, genocide research can only begin to meet these requirements if its comparative statements concentrate on structural elements of the perpetrating society (Dabag 1998, pp. 152–153). General comparisons as well as the comparison of casualty figures cannot be the subject of serious genocide research. Similarly, it must be clear that monocausal patterns are not sufficient to explain genocide. Genocide research can make an important contribution by demonstrating that the paradigms of totalitarianism, fascism, or dictatorship can be used to describe perpetrating societies. The analysis of processes of persecution, violence, and murder, however, must be kept separate from the analysis of a particular political system since they are not inevitable but independent processes.

Finally, there is a third perspective relevant to genocide research — that of the victim. The fact that there appears to be no acceptance of survivors' recollections and that they have not been truly integrated into the historiography of world history is due to the nature of public and academic discourse after 1945. The discussion has mainly focused on the perpetrator. There are two reasons for this: first, the preoccupation with an identifiable perpetrator has been preferred to a concern with anonymous victims who, because of their sheer numbers, appear to lack any tangible substance, and second, the discourse has continued to be determined by the terminology and argumentation of the perpetrators. The victim was turned into a mere witness: a victim who stood for the experience of extermination, but was denied the status of a legitimate eyewitness to the actual events in court proceedings against the perpetrators (Platt 1998b, Platt 2000, Platt 2002),[1] since his testimony was "not assigned any authenticity, i.e. congruence with an experience of violence which was considered too complex, too absolute and radical, and at the same time too simple and unstructured," as Kristin Platt puts it (Platt 2002, p. 46). The witness was reduced to the status of mere evidence, and as such had more value dead than alive. The victim does not participate in the discourse on genocide, since he "gives evidence of the excluded — and the excluding — [the survivor] represents an experience, which cannot be shared, which is selective rather than representative, but not finished either" (Platt 2002, p. 46). The victim's testimony belongs to the past. Each articulation of the victim's perspective is misinterpreted as an attempt to turn the opposite number into a perpetrator, since the identity of the victim can only be maintained in connection with its perpetrating counterpart. The victim's experience is misunderstood as an attack, as a demand for the confession of one's guilt. The fact that genocide research has to face the victim's perspective is both a central precondition and a theoretical innovation. It is related to approaches to the history of everyday life and oral history and permits concern for psychological and socio-psychological issues. It also takes into account the central characteristic of genocidal processes, i.e., that genocide goes beyond the victim's death to cause long-term traumatic effects as well as creates successfully homogenized structures in the perpetrating society. Taking into account the victims' per-

---

1. Cf. Also Kristin Platt's chapter in this volume.

spective not only implies assigning them a place in historiograph
including factors such as trauma, memory, and testimony as fundar......
lytical categories.

CONCLUSIONS

Genocide research, as research on a systematic social policy, is also
research on social, historical and psychological relationships and structures.
Genocide research has the task of creating awareness of general structures of
knowledge and politics that involve the possibility of genocide, but is also concerned with presenting detailed individual studies on less well-researched acts
of collective violence. This is accompanied by a clear differentiation of genocide
from other forms of collective violence as well as an exact setting of the
descriptive, empirical and comparative tasks. An interdisciplinary, structure
comparative genocide research should take into account the following aspects
when considering the term genocide:

(a) Genocide is always a crime that relates to the whole of society. Its
causes can be traced across generations. Its structures demonstrate general characteristics of modern societies. Nevertheless, planning and implementation are
only to be understood as specific national processes. For the researcher this
means that no generally valid universal model of the course of genocide can be
defined. Every genocide is singular from a historical and social point of view: the
individual forms of each deprivation of rights, each act of persecution and
genocide are different.

(b) Genocides are the result not only of a variety of causes but also multiple kinds of violence. We cannot reduce genocides to an — ultimate — form of
murder, for instance in the form of an extermination massacre or an extermination camp. Genocide is realized in a number of stages of differing violence:
exclusion, stigmatization, and deprivation of rights.

(c) Goals and characteristics of individual genocides should be viewed
from a specific historical point of view. However, persecutions and violence are
legitimized with arguments that belong to general norms of modern reality: stability, balance, the restoration or protection of identity, talk of an inner enemy.
The contemplation of a genocide is integrated into the creative planning of the
future of a society — legitimized as "safeguarding" or "saving," legitimized by
reference to general patterns of progress and civilization.

The relevance of the parameters of the analysis of genocide for the discussion of present-day conflict situations and the potential violence that will possibly come to determine the 21st century, relates to the modern-day foundations of knowledge: patterns of identity, norms and values of membership, patterns of unity and stability. The critical convergence towards the setting of paradigms of the present, efforts to develop new forms of learning and communication as well as endeavors to foster and produce sensitivity towards intercultural tolerance are to be understood as obligations that play a central accompanying role in the analysis of processes of genocide.

It might initially seem surprising that (potential) perpetrators do not allow themselves to be deterred by the legal consequences of their actions. However, in the legitimizing justifications of state violence it becomes clear that the consequences of (as well as the conviction for) one's one actions are consciously accepted by the perpetrators planning a genocide. As genocide is realized not primarily for one's own generation but rather for the following generations, i.e., for the future of the perpetrator society, the (potential) perpetrators are able to explain their own actions outside of the valid norms and values as right, or even as moral.

Also against this background, considerations to view not only genocide itself but also the denial of genocide as punishable offences under international law should be taken seriously, in order to include the successor generations of the perpetrators in the processes both of moral reappraisal and of social responsibility.

The fields of activity of the Permanent International Criminal Court in the Hague (ICC), constituted on March 11, 2003, on the basis of the Rome statute adopted on July 17, 1998, which could mean an institutional breakthrough for a protective system against genocide and human rights violations, stretch far into the societies.

However, it is possible that tasks of recollection alone, in a society radically homogenized following a genocide, could also place the victims themselves back in a social discourse. For this reason it should at least be considered whether a general recognition of other genocides (such as the genocide of the Armenians, which continues even today to be officially denied by Turkey), in addition to leading to the punishment of the perpetrators, could not also have an influential effect on the prevention of further plans for genocide. The punishment of the perpetrators has not, as yet, succeeded in banishing genocide from legitimizable political strategies. But perhaps the insistence on recollection can, at least in the societies in question, halt the possibility of continuing perpetration.

Thus, the genocide in Rwanda has shown that it is very difficult to speak of prevention of grave human rights violations when we only concentrate on the final stages of the murders, and do not consider the stages leading up to them. The decision to murder a minority that is declared as impossible to integrate is made only at the end of different stages of ideologization, of definition and segregation.

The conceptualization of models of prevention and protection, early recognition and control of systematic politics of violence must therefore start where the focus is on developing group and community rights. Where the concern is with finally developing and implementing alternatives to the national model that declares itself as the general model and which through specific representation considerations is only conceivable as a homogenous structure and deems everything else as a non-transparent zone and a danger. Not least, prevention cannot be conceived of without the requirement that the international community must finally recognize the voice of the victim: as the witness of persecution as well as the voice of a right to one's own accepted position, an accepted political place in the world society.

Translated into English by Sarah Mannion MA (Cantab)

REFERENCES

Aly, Götz 1995. *Endlösung. Völkerverschiebung und Mord an den europäischen Juden*, Frankfurt/Main: S. Fischer.

Aly, Götz and Heim, Susanne 1993. *Vordenker der Vernichtung. Auschwitz und die deutschen Pläne für eine neue europäische Ordnung*. Frankfurt/Main: Fischer TB.

Astourian, Stephan H. 1999. "Modern Turkish Identity and the Armenian Genocide." In *Remembrance and Denial. The Case of the Armenian Genocide*, ed. by Richard G. Hovannisian, Detroit MI: Wayne State University Press, pp. 23–49.

Bell-Fialkoff, Andrew. 1996. *Ethnic Cleansing*. New York NY: St. Martin's Griffin.

Brehl, Medardus. 2000. "Vernichtung als Arbeit an der Kultur. Kolonialdiskurs, kulturelles Wissen und der Völkermord an den Herero." *Zeitschrift für Genozidforschung* Vol. 2, No. 2, pp. 8–28.

Bröckling, Ulrich 1997. *Disziplin. Soziologie und Geschichte militärischer Gehorsamsproduktion.* Munich: Wilhelm Fink 1997.

Chalk, Frank and Kurt Jonassohn. "The Conceptual Framework." In *The History and Sociology of Genocide. Analyses and Case Studies*, ed. by Frank Chalk and Kurt Jonassohn. New Haven CT: Yale University Press, pp. 3–53.

Chalk, Frank and Kurt Jonassohn eds. 1990. *The History and Sociology of Genocide. Analyses and Case Studies.* New Haven CT: Yale University Press.

Dabag, Mihran. 1998. "Jungtürkische Visionen und der Völkermord an den Armeniern." In *Genozid und Moderne. Strukturen kollektiver Gewalt im 20. Jahrhundert*, ed. by Mihran Dabag und Kristin Platt. Opladen: Leske + Budrich, S. 152–205.

_____. 2000. "Genozid und weltbürgerliche Absicht. Perspektiven." In *Weltbürgertum und Globalisierung*, ed. by Norbert Bolz, Friedrich Kittler and Raimar Zons, Munich: Wilhelm Fink, S. 43–70.

_____ and Kristin Platt, eds. 1998. *Genozid und Moderne. Strukturen kollektiver Gewalt im 20. Jahrhundert.* Opladen: Leske + Budrich.

Dadrian, Vahakn N. 1993. "The Secret Young-Turk Ittihadist Conference and the Decision for the World War I Genocide of the Armenians." *Holocaust and Genocide Studies*, Vol. 7, No. 2, pp. 173–201.

Diner, Dan 1991. "Die Wahl der Perspektive. Bedarf es einer besonderen Historik des Nationalsozialismus?" In *Vernichtungspolitik. Eine Debatte über den Zusammenhang von Sozialpolitik und Genozid im nationalsozialistischen Deutschland*, ed. by Wolfgang Schneider. Hamburg: Junius 1991, pp. 65–75.

Dobkowski, Michael N. and Isidor Wallimann. 1998. "The Coming Age of Scarcity. An Introduction." In *The Coming Age of Scarcity. Preventing Mass Death and Genocide in the Twenty-First Century*, ed. by Michael N. Dobkowski and Isidor Wallimann, New York NY: Syracuse University Press, pp. 1–20.

Dobkowski, Michael N. and Isidor Wallimann, eds. 1998. *The Coming Age of Scarcity. Preventing Mass Death and Genocide in the Twenty-First Century.* New York NY: Syracuse University Press.

Drost, Pieter N. 1959. *The Crime of State*, 2 Vols. Leiden: Sythoff.

Fein, Helen 1990. "Genocide. A Sociological Perspective." *Current Sociology* 38: 1, 1990, pp. 1–126.

_____. 1993. "Revolutionary and Antirevolutionary Genocides. A Comparison of State Murders in Democratic Kammpuchea, 1975 to 1979, and in Indonesia, 1965 to 1966." *Comparative Studies in Society and History* 35: 4, 1993, pp. 796–823.

Gay, Peter. 1993. *The Cultivation of Hatred. The Bourgeois Experience.* New York, NY: Norton.

Geiss, Imanuel 1992. "Massaker in der Weltgeschichte. Ein Versuch über die Menschlichkeit." In *Die Schatten der Vergangenheit. Impulse zur Historisierung des Nationalsozialismus*, ed. by Uwe Backes, Eckhard Jesse and Rainer Zitelmann, Frankfurt/Main: Ullstein, pp. 110–135.

Goertz, Hans J. ed. 1998. *Geschichte. Ein Grundkurs*. Reinbek: Rowohlt.

Gökalp, Ziya 1911. "Kizil Elma." *Genç Kalemer* No. 4 (23 May 1911) .

_____. 1914. *Kizil Elma*. Istanbul 1914/15.

_____. 1914. *Kizil Elma*, Istanbul: Hayriye Matbaas 1914.

_____. 1989. *Siirler ve Halk Masallari*. Külliyati 1, ed. by Fevziya Abdullah Tansel, Ankara: Türk Tarih Kurumu Basimevi.

Goldhagen, Daniel Jonah. 1996. *Hitler's Willing Executioners. Ordinary Germans and the Holocaust*. New York NY: Knopf.

Götz Aly and Susanne Heim. 1993. *Vordenker der Vernichtung. Auschwitz und die deutschen Pläne für eine neue europäische Ordnung*. Frankfurt/Main: VERLAG 1993.

Harff, Barbara and Ted Robert Gurr. 1987. "Genocides and Politicides since 1945: Evidence and Anticipation." *Internet on the Holocaust and Genocide* 13, pp. 1–7.

Hilberg, Raul. 1961: *The Destruction of European Jews*, Chicago IL: Quadrangle Books.

Horowitz, Irving Louis. 1997. *Taking Lives. Genocide and State Power*. New Brunswick, NJ: Transactions Publ. (first 1976).

_____. 1998. "Wissenschaft, Modernität und autorisierter Terror." In *Genozid und Moderne. Strukturen kollektiver Gewalt im 20. Jahrhundert*, ed. by Mihran Dabag and Kristin Platt. Opladen: Leske + Budrich, pp. 320–337.

Katz, Steven T. 1994. *The Holocaust in Historical Context*, Vol. 1: The Holocaust and Mass Death before the Modern Age. Oxford, NY a.o.: Oxford University Press.

Kuper, Leo. 1981. *Genocide. Its Political Use in the Twentieth Century*. New Haven CT: Yale University Press.

Larner, Christina. 1981. *Enemies of God: The Witch-Hunt in Scotland*. London: Chatto & Windus.

Lemkin, Raphael. *1944. Axis Rule in Occupied Europe. Laws of Occupation – Analysis of Government – Proposals for Redress*. Washington DC: Carnegie Endowment for International Peace.

Lerner, Richard M. 1992. *Final Solutions. Biology, Prejudice, and Genocide*. Pennsylvania State University Press.

Lichtenberger, Thomas and Alf Lüdtke, eds. 1995. *Physische Gewalt. Studien zur Geschichte der Neuzeit*. Frankfurt/Main: Suhrkamp.

Melson, Robert F. 1992. *Revolution and Genocide. On the Origins of the Armenian Genocide and the Holocaust*. Chicago IL/London: The University of Chicago Press.

O'Brian, Conor Cruise. 1999. *On the Eve of the Millennium*. Toronto: Stoddart Publishing.

Platt, Kristin. 1998a. "Genozid und Moderne. Strukturen kollektiver Gewalt im 20. Jahrhundert. Einleitung." In *Genozid und Moderne. Strukturen kollektiver Gewalt im 20. Jahrhundert*, ed. by Mihran Dabag and Kristin Platt. Opladen: Leske + Budrich, pp. 5–38.

_____. 1998b. "Gedächtnis, Erinnerung, Verarbeitung. Spuren traumatischer Erfahrung in lebensgeschichtlichen Interviews." Bios. Zeitschrift für Biographieforschung und *Oral History* 11: 2, pp. 242–262.

_____. 2000. "Historische und traumatische Situation. Trauma, Erfahrung und Subjekt. Reflexionen über die Motive von Zerstörung und Überleben." In *Gewalt. Strukturen, Formen, Repräsentationen*, ed. by Mihran Dabag, Antje Kapust and Bernhard Waldenfels. Munich: Wilhelm Fink 2000, pp. 257–275.

_____. 2002: "Über das Reden, die Redenden und die Gefährlichkeit der Erfahrung von Gewalt. Einleitung." In *Reden von Gewalt*, ed. by Kristin Platt. Munich: Wilhelm Fink, pp. 10–58.

_____, ed. 2002. *Reden von Gewalt*. Munich: Wilhelm Fink.

Roberts, Ulla. 1998. Spuren der NS-Zeit im Leben der Kinder und Enkel. Drei Generationen im Gespräch. Munich: Kösel.

Röttgers, Kurt and Hans Saner, eds. 1978. *Gewalt. Grundlagenprobleme in der Diskussion der Gewaltphänomene*. Basel / Stuttgart: Schwabe.

Rummel, Rudolph J. 1992. *Democide. Nazi Genocide and Mass Murder*. New Brunswick/London: Transaction Publ.

Sereny, Gitta 1974. *Into that Darkness. From Mercy Killing to Mass Murder*. London: Deutsch.

Smith, Roger W. 1998. "Pluralismus und Humanismus in der Genozidforschung." In *Genozid und Moderne. Strukturen kollektiver Gewalt*, ed. by Mihran Dabag and Kristin Platt. Opladen: Leske + Budrich, pp. 309–318.

Sofsky, Wolfgang. 1997. "Gewaltzeit." In *Soziologie der Gewalt* (Special Issue of the Kölner Zeitschrift für Soziologie und Sozialpsychologie No. 37), ed. by Trutz von Trotha. Opladen/Wiesbaden: Westdeutscher Verlag, pp. 102–121.

Tansel, Fevziya Abdullah, ed. 1989. Siirler ve Halk Masallari. Ziya Gökalp Külliyati 1. Ankara: Verlag ³1989.

Taureck, Bernhard H. F. 1999. "Genozide – unerklärlich und doch zu verhindern." Neues Deutschland (17./18.07.1999), p. 13.

Trotha, Trutz von ed. 1997. Soziologie der Gewalt (Special Issue of the *Kölner Zeitschrift für Soziologie und Sozialpsychologie* No. 37). Opladen/Wiesbaden: Westdeutscher Verlag.

Welzer, Harald / Montau, Robert / Plaß, Christine 1997. "Was wir für böse Menschen sind!" *Der Nationalsozialismus im Gespräch zwischen den Generationen*. Tübingen: Edition Discord.

Chapter 3. The Ultimate Oppression: The Urge to Genocide

Brij Mohan, Louisiana State University

"A genocide begins with the killing of one man — not for what he has done, but because who he is. A campaign of 'ethnic cleansing' begins with one neighbor turning on another. Poverty begins when even one child is denied his or her fundamental right to education. What begins with the failure to uphold the dignity of one life, all too often ends with a calamity for entire nations," said Kofi Annan, as he received the centennial Nobel Peace Prize with a call for humanity to fight poverty, ignorance and disease (Annan 2001).

Social psychologists tend to posit human aggression in a variegated instinctual-institutional context, thereby mystifying inexplicable human behaviors. While analytical philosophy has often neglected this phenomenon, continental academics, particularly Freudo-Marxists, have extensively explored the heart of darkness with, understandably, limited success. The human condition has been a subject of immense inquiry and introspection. However, scientific explorations still pose daunting challenges. As a mega tribe of human animals, humankind has evolved into a stage of development when cultivated attributes tend to be regressive in nature. What is the net result of a nuclear bomb? Why do we blow ourselves up in a fit of insane passion? Why are pogroms, genocides, and ethnic cleaning still with us? Why do we kill each other in the name of a belief system, including God? The discussion to follow involves an attempt to outline some of the major factors which appear to perpetuate the forces of human depravity, its allies and their destructive consequences.

I. THE NATURE OF GENOCIDE

We begin by discussing the nature of human aggression. What is ultimately behind the ongoing occurrence of genocide among human beings? Is the answer embedded somehow in human nature? "The fateful question for the human species seems to me to be whether and to what extent cultural development will succeed in mastering the disturbance of their communal life by the human instinct of aggression and self-destruction," concluded Sigmund Freud (Freud, 1961: 92). The *discontents* seem to foster much of human self-destruction in the name of dubious developmental delusions of this *civilization*. Has "cultural development" mastered the *death instinct* of our communal life? Exploration of this question will offer unsettling answers to unlock both human aggression and cultural-communal developments. The tale of human survival through destruction is a classic dualism that has sealed the fate of humanity. To demystify this paradox is to unravel the nature of human destruction.

The particular nexus involved encompasses a range of individual and institutional patterns (of carnivorous nature) that involve both predatory and defensive behaviors. The evolution of this formulation is grounded in the history and anthropology of human social development. Neolithic hunters and food gatherers were not predators; they became corrupt, violent and rapacious when they began to settle down as owners of private property. In other words, the rise of a civil society heralded the demise of Rousseauean "primitive innocence."

Can "there be a human ancestor, a pre-historical Adam who is responsible for man's "fall"? — asks Fromm (1973: 153). He cites S.L. Washburn, who believes that this "Adam" was essentially *the hunter*. However, "the motivation of the primitive hunter was not pleasure in killing, but the learning and optimal performance of various skills, i.e., the development of man himself" (Fromm, 1973: 158). Norman Brown's observation, in light of the conflicting debate between Freudians and Rousseaueans (followed by Marxists) on the origins of aggression, appears to go deeper into the ontogenesis of the human development: "If there is a class which has nothing to lose but its chains, the chains that bind it are self-imposed, sacred obligations which appear as objective realities with all the force of a neurotic delusion," observes Norman Brown (quoted by Becker, 1975: 38). If the problem is "innate,"

> both benignity and malignancy tend to be products of the quality of social transformation that changed the primitive society for better or worse. In other words, the evolution of the "anthropological Adam" is a consequence of phylogenesis that

transformed human society. Unbuilding a malignant, destructive human creature into a creative and peaceful being is thus a theoretical possibility if controlled social forces can be rationalized to deconstruct a new culture of tolerance, understanding and sharing.

Ideas and methods are two different constructs. However, they can both be flawed and utopian. The task before us is to enshrine ideas of change within a framework of values, knowledge and methods that nourish humanity and its hopes. Individual and societal values and interests, however, define these two sets of forces with varied interests and interpretations. This evolution of conflict sustains human strife in a destructive mode.

"Men rode in blood up to their knees and bridle reins.... Indeed, it was a just and splendid judgment of God," wrote a Crusader after a massacre of Muslims on Temple Mount (quoted by Van Biema, 2001: 49). Carnage and exultation have marked humanity's journey from its darkest caves to our neon enclaves in the process of evolutionary development. Savants and savages have coexisted in a mysterious alliance eluding the existential dualism of this puzzling human paradox.

Human monstrosity has no parallel in the entire domain of creaturely evolution. Advancement and scientific development do not necessarily correspond with collective rationality. Nothing can be worse than genocide and war. It is an irony that both of these monstrosities should have occurred most hideously in the 20th century, the epoch of our modern growth, marking the demise of hope as well. It is not easy to deal with this issue since human nature represents phenomenal opposites; consequently, a universally acceptable definition is neither intended nor possible. An attempt is nevertheless made to conceptualize the nature of human depravity in all its vile intent and content.

Erich Fromm wrote about malignant destructiveness and necrophilia as being hideous, sinister and monstrous, regardless of its apparent magnitude and "rectitude" (Fromm, 1973). This is both banal and lethal. You run into a wolf in a sheep's clothing. His act of destruction goes unnoticed but this man is a "conscious *artist*" capable of committing murder while maintaining a stealth identity. You come across this type at least once in a lifetime. Others masquerade as experts of death and tend to make a cult out of perversities. Note the villainy and sadism in the following statement:

> We calculated in advance the number of casualties from the enemy...we did not reveal the operation to them until they were there and just before they boarded the planes.... One group of people did not know the other group.... They were overjoyed when the first plane hit the building, so I said to them, Be patient.... Due to my expe-

rience in the field, I was thinking that the fire from the gas in the plane would melt the iron structure of the building and collapse the area where the plane hit and all the floor above it only. This is all that we had hoped for" (Bin Laden, quoted by Elliott, 2001: 46-47).

The above discussions all highlight the complexity and ambiguity of human aggression and the nature of genocide.

II. CHILDREN OF DARKNESS: THE BANALITY OF OPPRESSION

What are the effects of modern societal contexts on the apparent ubiquity of genocide? One of the great tragedies of modern times involves the increasing familiarity and apparent acceptance of violence and destruction at the societal level. "Power is preserved by the same Virtues by which it is acquired," wrote Hobbes ([1651]1985: 711). Somewhere in the evolution of this power acquisition, Hobbes' "robust child" forgot the rules of the game. When virtue is used and sacrificed, acquisitions generate grievance and protest by others. Blatant power cannot remain an end in itself for it needs its own justification. Civilizations have fallen as they failed to justify the cause of their existence. Man remains a social delinquent. From the insane destruction of the World Trade Center to the Nepalese Royal palace and the killing fields of Cambodia, the stench of human debris benumbs spirits that beg for answers about the tragic fate we mortals share with and inflict on each other. Global family violence is an apotheosis of a dysfunctional family that thrives on its perversities and perpetuates a progeny of amoral, sometimes cruel, creatures who seek perfection in the art and science of killing each other. No other species on earth has this distinction.

A conscious pogrom targeted toward a particular ethnic, racial or religious group, based on ignorance, willful malice and murderous intent, leads to genocide, an obscene word that did not exist before Winston Churchill in August 1941 called it a "crime without a name." The Final Solution came to symbolize the finality of human destruction at its best. After Raphael Lemkin described this as "genocide" in his treatise *Axis Rule in Occupied Europe in 1944*. Webster's *International Dictionary* immediately editorialized this phenomenon as "Genocide" (Urquhart 2002: 12).

There have been six cases of recorded genocides in the 20th century: "the mass killings of Armenians by Turks in 1915, of Jews (and other groups such Gypsies) by Hitler, of Cambodians by the Khmer Rouge, of the Kurds of North Iraq by Saddam Hussein, of the Tutsi of Rwanda by the Hutu, and of Croats,

Muslims, and the Albanians of Kosovo by the Serbs" (Urquhart 2002: 12). Barbarity, territoriality and necrophilic leadership (in the Frommian sense) characterize these human tragedies. Is the tragedy Shakespearean or Chekhovian? We do not know, yet.

Totalitarian beliefs and systems have given a new character to the issue which Hannah Arendt viewed as perverse, pervasive and patently chameleon (Arendt [1951]1973). Arendt succinctly depicts this with remarkable precision in the view that a system has emerged "...in which all men have become equally superfluous" (Arendt, in Baehr 2000: 139-140). The contemporary superfluity of people (Power 2002) is perhaps the most serious crisis that humankind has ever confronted. We have become immune to the stench, ubiquity and horrors of radical destruction. While monumental tragedies do get attention, relatively regional and local atrocities are hardly ever taken on par with genocidal behavior. Also, it depends on the historical significance of the victims. Gypsies were victims of the Holocaust but no museum has ever been built to memorialize their suffering.

Human territoriality, arrogance and ignorance have played havoc with humanity's benign impulses. It is hypothesized that the banality of this malaise is deeply rooted in constructs and contexts that incubate and transform innate vulnerabilities into manifest destruction: impersonal aggression. I argue that humanity's fate is sealed into this tragic impasse unless a radically new culture of sharing and caring is deconstructed. This may well be a utopian hope but all other alternatives are doomed to be disastrous and suicidal. Human destructiveness is instinctually self-annihilating. As a learned behavior, this trans-generational-culture is too deeply implanted in the collective psyche for any possible reform. History lends support to this grim realization. In brief, we are all implicated in a collective culture of death.

This may be an overly pessimistic scenario given the banality and triumph of human illusions. The notion of "ambiguity of hope," as Erich Fromm would have us believe, lies in the foggy vacuum of desires and despair: "Optimism is an alienated form of faith, pessimism an alienated form of despair" (Fromm 1973: 483). There are good reasons to have "rational faith" and "rational despair" (Fromm 1973: 483). Fromm's radical humanist stance holds some clues to the fundamental issues that imperil humanity:

> This humanist radicalism goes to the roots, and thus to the causes; it seeks to liberate man from the chains of illusions; it postulates that fundamental changes are

necessary, not only in our economic and political structure but also in our values, in our concept of man's aims, and in our personal conduct (Fromm, 1973: 485).

In his premise that root causes warrant fundamental liberation, continental philosophers, especially the Frankfurters, have underscored the Freudo-Marxist explanation for human brutality against humans. Again, Fromm has a point: "Exploitation and manipulation produce boredom and triviality; they cripple man and all factors that make man into a psychic cripple turn him into a sadist or a destroyer" (1973: 483).

As I began writing this piece, a former Bosnian Serb general was found guilty of genocide for his role in massacre of about 8,000 Muslims in Srebrenica in 1995. This ruling marks the first genocide in Europe since the persecution of Jews and Gypsies during World War II. Graham Jones filed this report on CNN:

> LONDON, England (CNN) — It is now remembered as the worst atrocity in Europe since World War II. In a five-day orgy of slaughter at Srebrenica in July 1995, 7,500 Muslims were systematically exterminated.... What made it worse was the genocide took place in what had been designated a U.N. "safe area" three months earlier. A judge at The Hague tribunal was later to describe what happened in Srebrenica as "truly scenes from hell written on the darkest pages of human history" (Jones 2001).

The civilized world simply overlooked the mayhem in Rwanda. Ted Koppel went to the Congo (DRC) and telecast a series of horrifying spectacle of poverty, ravages of war, and abject isolation (Nightline, ABC TV, January 21-25, 2002). And war criminals are still at large in the history books. An Irish historian once told me that Churchill might well be declared a war criminal if history were rewritten. Humanity's record is dismal when the art and science of mass murders is reviewed without prejudice.

Civility, it appears, is a façade. We remain a manipulative, aggressive, territorial and self-serving species. We wage wars and justify mass murders in the name of religion, nation, and peace. Our trivializations empower the forces of war and destruction; euphemisms breed a culture of ambiguities that impart a dubious character to death and aggression.

III. AMBIGUITIES OF HOPE: SOME ALTERNATIVES

Where should we go from here? What does it mean to be human? Ernest Becker summarizes the crux of the human condition:

Man is an animal....It is man's ingenuity, rather than his animal nature, that has given his fellow creatures such a bitter earthly fate" (Becker, 1975: 1/5).

The history of civilization is fraught with hope and hopelessness, pride and shame, and ignorance and arrogance. Our existence lies within the mist of freedom and un-freedom — a human condition that is both alienated and fulfilled at the same time. The rise and fall of civilizations has offered no serious lesson to the contemporary rulers of the world. Nor has the advancement of knowledge benefited from the humility of Aristotelian discourse. We have invented a pretentious culture of new science, which plays god at the dictates of corporate interests. The consequence of this perversity is that we no longer believe in the meaning and purpose of the Enlightenment. We remain slaves of our old habits while modernity's claims over progress sound hollow.

Sure, the concentration camps have been outlawed. Slavery has been abolished. The third world is free from the old-fashioned colonial yoke. Finally, democracy seems to have won, as free market and globalization continue to ascend hand in hand. But it is too soon to call this victory. The illusory nirvana of capitalism is shattered by the fall of Enron. Wall Street does not offer a true measure of progress. One must discard the old vocabularies of success, discount the new illusions of hope and rethink both in light of our continued struggle for survival as a human race.

It is hard to construct a schema — a typology — of human destruction that befits the context of our collective developmental stage. Civilization, a façade at best, appears naked the moment one of its artifacts goes astray. We still burn books, people and their collectivities whenever our passions are challenged. Spouses kill each other and the magnitude of child abuse within homes and churches is scandalous. When priests and preachers become suspects, faith melts into fear. Put simply, potential destruction pervades all primary and secondary institutions beyond regions and cultures. In other words, the global dimensions of human perversity call for a wider context to unravel its nature and complexity.

The evolution of human destruction marks development of human processes in different stages from the animism through the superstitious, religious, theological, and rational to the more human. Unfortunately, the human psyche is not developmentally linear in the sense that occult and superstitious structures still prevail in the post-Enlightenment era. These ambiguities create overlapping, conflicting and even dehumanizing perceptions and realties. With Rousseau, Becker writes, the early Establishment "laid the basis for nothing less than a fully 'secular' theodicy..." (Becker, 1968: 31). I will argue that new tribalism destroyed the rise of a secular theodicy and our advanced superstitions continue to play havoc with the fate of humanity (Mohan, 1993). Humanity is hurt when a Buddha is callously bombarded to ruins. We all lose when two oppressed groups — Israelis and Palestinians — brutalize each other in the name of security and territorial imperatives.

A new vision that liberates humanity from the darkness of its own shadows must be a high priority. The idea of a world society sounds utopian but if the alternative is global fragmentation, its significance cannot be overstated. The notion of world citizenship is both challenging and intriguing at a juncture when human evolution is fraught with explosive contradictions. I venture to postulate three planks of this new vision:

1. Triangulate world conflicts and institutionalize universalism;
2. De-globalize oppressive structures of control; and
3. De-utopianize the techno-hubris (Mohan, 2002).

The proposed triune of global equality and justice is premised on the notion that polarities of conflicts, power structures and social development are detrimental to world peace. The world remains treacherous as long as civilized nations ignore and abet global oppression. Samantha Power reveals how "vital national interests" have determined the United States to stand idly by genocidal societies (Power 2002a).

Inequality and injustice alienate both victims and oppressors from the essence of what makes people human. This state of pervasive inhumanity is a global malaise, which does not fit into any DSM classification. Yet a massive neurosis of conscience constitutes a crisis of civility that has escaped humanity since the inception of civil society.

There are two plausible explanations: 1) modern civilization is the root of human aggression; and 2) "primitive innocence" is a romantic fiction. There is hope in the first thesis; the latter one is indicative of a bleak origin lurking behind a dark future. In either case, we remain doomed by this historical apocalypse. Civilization cannot be reinvented easily especially when the ideologies of the Enlightenment have failed to liberate humankind. On the other hand, if the seeds of aggression were inherent in human origin, we have not yet advanced in our evolutionary process to eschew our self-destructive instincts. Our innate character deprives us of a possible escape from this sordid human reality.

Beside mutual understanding and acceptance, we must learn to co-exist. But how does one compromise with genocide? No one has answered this

70

question clearly. Relativism and its post-modern versions offer some pragmatic alternatives but its imperatives are seldom actualized. Secularism, equality, and global justice make no sense in a world that is hopelessly divided into North and South, the one white, rich, powerful and the other black, poor and powerless. The butterfly theory which promises a hurricane at the flutter of a few wings is a soothing, self-fulfilling metaphor. The reality is that colorful butterflies of hope are ruthlessly crushed under the boots of oppression. In the oceanic depths of our nature there lies a hydra which raises its ugly head each time human aspirations attempt to fly away on the wings of hope. The reality is that global inequality and injustice perpetuate a cycle of oppression, its allies and apologists without any hope of relief. Globalization of the economy has unleashed a new dynamic which sustains this infrastructure in the name of democracy, boosting only corporate interests. Oppressed people live in oppressive conditions under the shadows of rapacious human creatures.

One must accept the notion of civil co-existence as the cornerstone of any organized society. A rule of law with optimal secular bonds will go a long way to ensure a climate conducive to acceptable harmony amongst diverse groups. To expect that a socialist or capitalist utopia will unilaterally and unconditionally establish a free society is to fall prey to delusions. The human creature is a flawed being. It is very doubtful that Marx would prevail over Darwin. The latter's triumph is written all over the global walls.

Genocidal behavior, the epitome of unabashed destruction, is an indicator of a primordial-developmental crisis: the individual has failed to grow from his/her endowed trappings. Likewise, society itself remains implicated in sustaining a culture that breeds ghoulish responses to vulgar inequalities. Is it, then, culture which incubates the seeds of oppression?

There were no genocidal acts in caves. As homo sapiens grew as a species and their organization became more complex, conflicts and contradictions became a part of their cultural baggage. Caves were free of otherwise ominous corruption despite the inhospitality of environmental conditions that helped evolve a social system. What we view today as "conscious *artistry*" is a product of civilizational malaise where religion, ideology and ethnicity have yielded dysfunctional outcomes. This cultural dysfunctionality has broken down the human bonds that connect us with each other on a simple benign human level. Our greed, avarice, and anxieties nourish a culture that breeds malignant control agencies and mechanisms.

It is arguable whether some cultures are less prone to cruelty than others. A point however is made regarding how one instance of cultural chaos becomes imminent in a particular time frame. Bernard Lewis argues that underlying "much of the Muslim world's travail may be a simple lack of freedom" (Lewis, 2002: 43-45). V.S. Naipaul has also written extensively about the cultural crisis of both the Muslim and Hindu civilizations (Naipaul 1977: 1999). Muslim civilization, Lewis concludes, "has fallen low" under the bulldozer of Western economic domination.

> If the peoples of the Middle East continue on their present path, the suicide bomber may become a metaphor for the whole region, and there will be no escape from a downward spiral of hate and spite, rage and self-pity, poverty and oppression, culminating sooner or later in yet another alien domination — perhaps from a new Europe reverting to old ways, perhaps from resurgent Russia, perhaps from the expanding superpower in the East" (Lewis, 2002: 45).

The apparatuses of totalitarian control, domination and annihilation vary in purpose and design with a singular motive: alienate, exploit and, if necessary, exterminate unwanted, inconvenient or expendable people. Absolute destruction is quintessentially a human monstrosity typical of a chaotic mundane, political and social environment. Arendt sums up the outcome of this new development:

> Just as the victims in the death factories or the holes of oblivion are no longer "human" in the eyes of their executioners, so this newest species of criminals is beyond the pale even of solidarity..." (Arendt, in Baehr 2000: 139-40).

When designed as disingenuousness, destruction assumes a totalist structure and becomes the pervasive reality of a diabolical order. It is doubtful if a single force or factor can be attributed to its dynamic; it is however, apparent that its genesis and manifestation betray simplified theories and explanations. Also, manifestations of human destructiveness are not isolated social-psychological phenomena. When an entire village of *dalits* is set afire by a rapacious higher caste in India, it is difficult to isolate criminality from mythologized institutional terror. Slavery, like the caste system, may well be analyzed as the most heinous system of explicative control. A decadent cultural legacy thus serves as an engine of death manufactured in different hues, patterns and shapes.

The emerging new tribalism is fraught with miscalculations. Ethnic cleansing resurrects the genocidal ghosts that seemingly vanished after the War. A new world conflict — shall we say the Third World War? — is shrouded in the fog of post-ideological nihilism. It is unsettling to see that the United

Nations' special commission is still not calling the systematic extermination of African Muslims in Darfur a genocide.[1]

New tribal conflicts masquerade as ideologies of a flawed past that sustains its atavism. Fanaticism, intolerance and pathologies of hate simply reinforce a culture of death that hounds humanity at the expense of hope. Elie Wiesel is right: "To defy them, first we must understand them" (Wiesel 2002). He says:

> Previous centuries suffered from tribal and religious wars and from national extremists, but our last century was ravaged by ideological and secular hatred.... Never have man-made ideologies ... given Death so much power... The fanatic who kills in God's name makes his God a murderer.... *To stem fanaticism, we must first fight indifference...We fight indifference through education; we diminish it through compassion. The most efficient remedy? Memory*" (Wiesel 2004: 5; emphasis added).

Ten years after Rwanda, we are reminded of the promise so many of us had committed to: "Never Again!"[2] This is humanity's monumental failure. "The children of Enlightenment sometimes have an inadequate understanding of the possibilities of the Endarkenment" (Morrow 2003: 74). The urge to genocide is a hellish impulse to be unlearnt and sublimated if humanity's claim to civility has any significance (Mohan 2003; 2004; 2004a; 2005; 2005a). There is a need for *Enlightenment II* which would transform human ingenuity into universal creativity.

> "Nothing can cure the soul but the senses, just as nothing can cure the senses but the soul."
>
> — Oscar Wilde.

---

1. The United Nations commissions accepts that there is "killing of civilians. Torture, enforced disappearances, destruction of villages, rapes and other forms of sexual violence, pillaging and forced displacement...It is clear that most attacks were deliberately and indiscriminately directed against civilians" (quoted by Nat Hentoff 2005: 7B).

2. Sudan's war on the people of Darfur "is not about religion, as it is elsewhere in Sudan," reports Nicholas Kristof. "It is largely about race and ethnicity.... Meanwhile, the world seemed to spend more time observing the 10th anniversary of the Rwandan genocide and solemnly vowing 'never again' than actually doing something to prevent a recurrence in Darfur" (Kristof 2004: 50).

CONCLUSIONS

In this paper, we have attempted to delineate some of the potential factors behind human aggression; emphasized the apparent acceptance of genocidal techniques which has made many people in this modern age relatively immune to the horror and destruction involved in this kind of behavior; and outlined platforms involved in a new vision that should help humanity move in a more positive global direction. Cultural decadence, political corruption, new tribalism and a surfeit of religious bigotry have nourished a ghoulish culture of death that breeds fanatic intolerance, pathological hatred and political terrorism. As a consequence, avarice, violence, and chauvinism — the true axes of genocide — eclipse hope for peace, prosperity and development. The new ordnance and old habits simply add despair to the bleak human destiny. Our analysis has highlighted the complexity and ambiguity of human aggression and genocide, reinforced by modern euphemisms regarding death and destruction, requiring a new vision to liberate humanity from this. Unless nations, societies and cultures of the world rebuild a new culture, chaos will prevail and pessimists will win against all notions of civility and order. This calls for the road not yet taken: a new vision to refill "the river of blood"[1] with the milk of humanity.[2]

REFERENCES

ABC-TV. 2002. The heart of darkness. *Nightline,* January 21-25.

Annan, Kofi. 2001. http://www.nobel.no/eng_lect_2001b.html

Arendt, Hanna. [1951]1975. *The Origins of Totalitarianism.* New York: A Harvest Book.

Baehr, Peter. 2000. *The Portable Hannah Arendt.* New York: Penguin Books.

Becker, Ernest. 1968. *The Structure of Evil: An Essay on the Unification of the Science of Man.* New York: The Free Press.

_____. 1975. *Escape from Evil.* New York: The Free Press.

---

1. In an anti-immigration speech in April 1968 in Britain, the conservative Enoch Powell said: "It is like watching a nation busily engaged in heaping up its own funeral pyre. Like the Roman, I seem to see the River Tiber foaming with much blood" (quoted by Dionne 2002: 9B).
2. Chapter largely based on Mohan, B. (2002). The age of evil: ambiguities of hope, *International Journal of Contemporary Sociology,* 39, 2:153-168.

Berkeley, Bill. 2001. *The Graves Are Not Yet Full: Race, Tribe and Power in the Heart of Africa.* New York: Basic Books.

Elliott, Michael. 2001. The Bin Laden tape. *Time,* December 24: 45-49.

Freud, Sigmund. 1961. *Civilization and Its Discontents.* New York: W.W. Norton.

Fromm, Erich. 1973. *The Anatomy of Human Destructiveness.* New York: Fawcett Crest.

Hobbes, Thomas. [1651]1985. *Leviathan.* New York: Penguin Classics.

Jones, Graham. 2001. "Srebrenica: 'A triumph of evil.'" August 2, Posted: 4:28 AM, EDT (0828 GMT, CNN).

Lewis, Bernard. 2002. "What went wrong?" *The Atlantic,* January, 289, 1: 43-45.

McDowell, Patrick. 2002. "Muslim nations fail to define 'terrorism'." *The Advocate,* April 3: 12A.

Mohan, B. 1993. *Eclipse of Freedom: The World of Oppression.* Westport, CT: Praeger.

_____. 2000. The rise and fall of social practice: Epistemologies of change. *International Journal of Contemporary Sociology,* 37, 2: 140-157. Professor D.P. Mukerjee Memorial Lecture delivered to the XX Conference of *The Indian Association of Social Sciences,* Tata Institute of Social Sciences, Bombay, June 2-4.

_____. 2000a. Metaphysics of oppression: Human diversity and social hope. Paper delivered to the Second Diversity Conference, University of South Carolina, Atlanta, GA, November 11-14.

_____. 2002. Toward an international society: Social work education for world citizenship. Congress of the International Association of Schools of Social Work, *Social Work Education and Citizenship in a Globalizing World.* Montpellier, France, July 15-18. Published in *The Hong Kong Journal of Social Work,* 2003, 37, 1: 29-39.

_____. 2003. 20/21 Visions of social development: Globalization, Violence and Counter Terrorism. 13th International Symposium on "Toward democratic pluralism: Challenges for social development in the 21st century," Inter-University Consortium for International Social development, Bombay December 29, 2003-January 1, 2004.

_____. 2004. Qualitative research and social transformation: Notes toward a theory of logical humanism, First Brazilian International Conference on Qualitative Research, March 24-27, 2004 in Taubaté, São Paulo, Brazil.

_____. 2004a. Redefining *Social:* Evolution of a construct — From oxymoron to interdisciplinarity, The 3rd Annual Hawaii International Conference on Social Sciences, June 16 (Wednesday) to June 19 (Saturday), 2004, Sheraton Waikiki Hotel, Honolulu, Hawaii. social@hicsocial.org

_____. 2005. Demise of civility: The future of human society. Global Social Work 2004, International Association of Schools of Social Work Congress, Adelaide, Australia, October 2-5.

_____. 2005a. *Fallacies of Development* (forthcoming).

Morrow, Lance. 2003. "The real meaning of Evil." *Time,* February 24: 74.

Naipaul, V.S. 1977. *India: A Wounded Civilization.* New York: Penguin Books.

_____. 1998. *Beyond Belief: Islamic Excursions Among the Converted Peoples.* New Delhi: Viking.

Power, Samantha. 2002. *"A Problem from Hell": America and the Age of Genocide.* New York: Basic Books.

_____. 2002a. Genocide and America. *The New York Review,* XLIX, 4: 15-18.

Ratnesar, Ramesh. 2002. "Season of revenge (World)." *Time,* April 8: 24-37.

Urquhart, Brian, 2002. Shameful Neglect. *The New York Review of Books, April 25,* XLIX, 7: 12-14.

Van Biema, David. 2001. "Jerusalem at the time of Jesus." *Time,* April 16: 49.

Wiesel, Elie. 2002. "How can we understand their hatred?" *Parade,* April 7: 4-5.

CHAPTER 4. ON GENOCIDE, OLD AND NEW

Franco Ferrarotti, University of Rome

Once in a while, at least in Europe and among intellectually fairly well-equipped people, one notices, as regards genocide, some sort of saturation-reaction that is loosely expressed as follows: "Why are we still talking about genocide today? The Holocaust belongs to the past. It is over. Let's move on. Enough, already." Unfortunately, the Holocaust still looms large and disturbing, perhaps at the unconscious level, in people's minds. It is not something to look back at in the distant past. Magazines and newspapers cannot help reminding their readers that anti-Semitism and anti-minority discrimination practices generally are about to manifest again. The past is painfully slow to disappear.

Referring to synagogue destructions in Europe, *Time Magazine* asked (June 17, 2002) in a somewhat melodramatic vein:

> How bad is it? The recent upturn in anti-Semitic incidents arouses fears that Europe is reverting to an ugly past.... Jews and Jewish interests are being attacked because they are Jewish.... In France, in April alone, 400 acts of violence took place against Jews.... But once you face that terrible fact, you have to start asking yourself: Why them? Why now? What's changed?

No clear cut answer is available. Undoubtedly, the cultural and political scenery has changed. But has the basic idea connected with the syndrome of Eurocentrism changed? The European educational system carries within itself a built-in assumption of an indisputable European cultural superiority relative to other cultures and ethnic groups. Political regimes have changed. Democracy appears well-established throughout Europe. A conscious effort has been made by some scholars such as Ernst Nolte (1965) to blur the tragedy of the Holocaust, dilute it little by little, to compare it with other historical tragedies from Genghis Khan to Stalin, yet the shadow of the Holocaust remains.

I

The first major reason for this involves the fact that the Holocaust's real nature has not been understood. It does not concern the Jews only. As I have remarked in *The Temptation to Forget* (1994), the extermination of the gypsies or nomads — the Rom — was statistically even more thorough than that of the Jews. The simple fact is that the persecution of the Jews should be understood as a special instance within the broader category of intolerance for minorities and the historical elimination of the "different," generally. This phenomenon goes well beyond racism as it is usually conceived. What remains to be seriously considered is that the mass murder of the Jews by the middle of the twentieth century had attained an exemplary, paradigmatic value as an attempted "final solution." The Holocaust is striking and original in the technical efficiency, cold-blooded, bureaucratic organization and businesslike bookkeeping of the whole operation.

This aspect of the Holocaust should not be overlooked. History has recorded many gruesome mass murders and wide-reaching criminal operations conducted against harmless and defenseless populations, such as the Soviet Gulag. Were they, however, as methodically as a modern-day industrial extermination?

Despite the efforts of E. Nolte, (1965) S. Romano (1999), and other commentators, the Holocaust raises a question that transcends a specific historical situation and certainly cannot be explained away, as, quite unexpectedly, Arno Mayer (1988) also attempted to do in his *Final Solution*, resorting to the notion of Hitler made angry by defeats on the Russian Front. They cite the Crusaders, the Inquisition, and Stalin's purges. Moreover, while classical sociologists such as Herbert Spencer emphasized that industrial societies would be more rational and radically different from traditional military countries, the Holocaust has proved beyond a doubt that rational planning can be used to serve a criminal purpose of massive proportions. The Holocaust has taught us that technology per se could be nothing but perfection without purpose and that a contemporary society can be technically advanced and humanly barbaric.

To understand the essence of the Shoah, or Holocaust, it is necessary to move beyond the mere counting of victims (important as this is to keep their memory alive), and economic considerations such as the confiscation of Jewish estates, to the religious meaning of this event. In the Nazi doctrine as revealed in the official statements and texts of Hitler's "Beweging" and *Gauleiter*, notions of individual responsibility and moral conscience are denied in the name of "total, cadaveric, obedience" to the *Fuhrer*. No principles like the Enlightenment's call for *liberté, egalité, fraternité*, are admitted; the only ethical obligation involves complete service to the Aryan race as the *Herrenvolk* or "People of the Lords." The rest of mankind must accept a subordinate position as slaves or be exterminated. The white Aryan race is the only Nazi God. Jewish monotheistic religion, like Christian monotheism, were enemies to be destroyed and replaced by the new neo-pagan, Nazi, secular religion.

Contrary to the view of Hitler's persecution of the Jews as an unfortunate turn at the end of his career, in *Temptation to Forget* (1994), I believe I have demonstrated that he had already thought of eliminating them while writing his *Mein Kampf*. While anti-Semitism exists throughout German history and European thought, to concentrate on the confused generalities of Nazi doctrine and minimize anti-Jewish persecution as if dealing with a *faute de mieux* occurring after military setbacks on the Russian eastern front would be a serious misunderstanding. No doubt, Nazism and its pedagogy of "education to death" contains a conglomerate of world visions, from Julius Langbehn (1936), author of the *Spirit of the Whole*, who later converted to Catholicism, to Martin Heidegger, a passionate theorizer of the *Heimat*, not far from the cult of *Blut und Boden* ("Blood and Soil").

These are not exceptions: Wilhelm Dilthey has remarked in his *History of Hegel's Youth and Posthumous Fragments* (1986: 112-115) that:

> according to Hegel, after Abraham, Jewish history becomes more religious and more estranged from men and nature ... life for the Jews was characterized by a radical separation and constant contrasts, by the passivity of the popular masses and by unhappiness.... For Hegel, the destiny of the Jewish people is the destiny of Macbeth, who separated himself from nature, befriended alien persons and in order to serve them he had to disregard and eventually kill whatever is sacred to human nature ...

Hegel is certainly not alone in his condemnation of the Jews. From Machiavelli, who sees Europe as the product of individual virtues while Asia and the Orient generally mean stagnant despotism, to Bossuet (1976), who ignores China in his *Discours sur l'histoire universelle* and only makes passing mention of the Arabs, and to Voltaire who, in spite of all his proclaimed cosmopolitanism, portrays

Europe as the ultimate outcome of human history and development, the *nec plus ultra* of civilization in his *Essai sur les moeurs et l'esprit des nations* (1828) and *Le siecle de Louis XIV* (1976), cosmopolitanism coincides with a single cultural tradition and ethnic group — European.

In this regard, the Holocaust was no improvisation. In the first draft of *Mein Kampf* (1943) Hitler refers to the Jews as parasites, as insects to be exterminated. He attributes to the World War I defeat of Germany to a "series of symptoms of the disease and its germs." Nobody can deny that very early in his political career, Hitler pointed to the Jews as carriers of a deadly bacillus eating away at Germany. Even in purely literary and philosophical fields, according to Hitler the Jews produced "literary garbage, artistic trash and absurdity in the world of theatre." I have noted in *My Temptation to Forget* that even prior to 1914, Hitler maintained that German Jews had spread "the putrid virus of Marxist ideas" and asks himself why the country at that time did not have a "responsible government which should have put ten to fifteen thousand Jews, corrupters of the German people, under poison gas — the same gas which hundreds of thousands of German workers ... had to ensure on the battle-field." Ten to fifteen thousand — the figures mentioned by Hitler as desirable to solve the Jewish question are still relatively modest given the millions exterminated by 1945. However, the method or technology to be cold-bloodedly applied, *sine ira ac studio*, as an impersonal, bureaucratic routine explicitly involved poison gas.

II

The second reason behind the general reluctance to take the Holocaust seriously has to do with the extent to which we have become accustomed to it. We are unable to view this phenomenon from a critical distance because it is not really over. The Holocaust continues today and we are unable to see it clearly because our eyes are blurred by the sleep-walking of everyday life. Developed, democratic countries, self-appointed sentinels of human rights and noble values, appear unable to take adequate risk and necessary action to block and eventually suppress genocide as it continues to be conducted in many parts of the world today.

Affluent European and North American societies have many excuses at hand: genocide occurs at a distance in foreign lands, some with names that are difficult to pronounce. Besides, nobody appears to care very much, including various churches, the United Nations, and the United States, the pl remaining superpower and champion of democracy. Even United Europe, with the sad experience of the former Yugoslavia on its doorstep, has largely been looking away. In this regard, despite public pronouncements that genocide should "never again" be permitted, along with a good deal of triumphalism regarding the ascent of liberal, democratic values, the last decade of the twentieth century was one of the grimmest and most deadly: in 1994, Rwandan Hutus slaughtered eight thousand Tutsi daily for one hundred days without external intervention. It is significant that genocide occurred *after* the Cold War; *after* the establishment of human rights organizations; *after* the invention of modern, instantaneous communication technologies; and *after* the foundation of the Holocaust Museum in Washington, DC (Power 2002).

At the present time, democratic, technically developed, industrially advanced, affluent nations appear unmoved by recent genocidal destruction. They know everything about them and cannot feign ignorance. Global electronic communication ensures instantaneous transmission of current events. Indeed, since the Vietnam War, television reporting spare none of the details, regardless of how chillingly horrifying they might be. Nevertheless, television hardly acts as humanity's good conscience; rather, it appears to serve as a viable substitute or stimulant for dormant consciences. The fact is that we watch television reports comfortably seated in our living rooms, viewing disturbing events at a distance. After scenes of mass graves, hunger and torture, television immediately switches to something more amusing, including advertisements for helpful, enjoyable products.

We cannot rely on television to be an ethical sentinel, important though its reports are, for the simple reason that the mass media do *not* mediate — they seduce us with synthetic images but the profound *meaning* of what we view escapes us since we are mesmerized and tied to the *immediate* present. No perspective or logical sequence is permitted or easily detected. Consequently, knowledge of recent genocides, from the Khmer Rouge to Rwanda and Kosovo, might be denied in good faith, particularly since their actual reality is too general, remote, and savage to appear real to us. While events such as the Holocaust might be accepted as part of past history, present destructive events are largely overlooked (Power 2002).

What about the United Nations? Why is it that this organization, the sole timid beginning of world government, cannot act or speak out in the name of humanity against all past and present genocides occurring in the world today?

Some secretary generals have spoken out on occasion; however, their pronounce-ments are invariably little more than bland recommendations. Various member-states, furthermore, given their specific interests and use of veto power, effec-tively block UN long-range, decisive initiatives. While paying lip-service to human values and solidarity, these countries continue to decide policy on the basis of their narrow national interests reminiscent of the 1815 Vienna Congress.

When genocides occur, diplomatic *savoir faire*, supplemented occasionally by food and medicine aid shipments to suffering victims, remains sadly inade-quate. Often, such humanitarian aid may actually reflect attempts to appease troubled moral consciences, a kind of *faute de mieux*, rather than effective inter-vention. Even the language of genocide reflects attempts to describe and organize mass murders as if they were normal bureaucratic exercises. In this regard, the Holocaust set the tone and blueprint for terminology such as "special treatment," "population relocation," "rational redistribution of resources," and "ethnic cleansing." Such linguistic perversion moves well beyond Orwell's *1984* (1977) ideas, representing the total subversion of meaning, typified in Nazi con-centration camp signs such as "This is the Door through which the Just Ones Enter" and "Work Makes Us Free."

In this manner, genocides both old and new acquire a *meta-historical* dimension: genocide, since it implies the extermination of those who are "dif-ferent," calls into question the *concept of identity*. On the one hand, forgetting one's roots can be dangerous for individuals and their cultures; on the other hand, worshiping memories may be a precursor to group discrimination and mass murder (Todorov 1995). Eliminating memories of the past, however, fails to solve this dilemma, making it impossible to understand the present and prepare for the future. To make a *tabula rasa* of our memories invites the dictator's omnip-otent delirium. Currently, the world is approaching a situation of global *syn-chronic presence*, in which various memories and cultural traditions appreciate their inter-dependence. Perhaps the time is ripe for the elaboration of *cultural co-traditions* to guarantee humanity's survival.

III

At the present time, with an after-war in Iraq which appears to be more tragic that the war itself, the danger of a clash among civilizations with religious underpinnings becomes real. The failure of what used to be called "melting pot" and "global village" seem both evident and inescapable. There is not only one fundamentalism. Islamic fundamentalism is faced by a corresponding Western fundamentalism that is based on an "American Syndrome," that is to say the belief that the West, and only the West, holds the key and can determine the orientation of human destiny. No wonder that, actually, perhaps as some sort of tropismatic reaction, throughout the world there is a passionate search for one's own roots, the evaluation or indeed the re-discovery of the vivid explosions of those little realities and "little homelands" which almost never coincide with the official maps. These are the "natural concrete communities," as Adriano Olivetti (1947) called them. After the "melting pot," the "salad bowl," and beyond. This is not to idealize a mythical community of the golden age, but to take good note of the uncrossable frontier which big, formal organizations must take into account. The latter's rigidity does not permit the flexibility which is needed today. Their complexity and "distance" makes motivation levels fall. They are perverted from means into ends. They become apparatuses at once omnivorous and useless. To say, as has been said, that the "enterprise is born in the heart of society whereas now it is in the heart of history" simply means a frantic refurbishing and restoration. The problem today is not simplistically reduced to that of giving a "shot of soul" to organizational apparatuses that have lost contact with real society and given rise to neo-feudal privileges or parasitic returns. Today's problem is that of resuming contact with the roots of true legitimacy.

At the basis of these turmoils there is a reflux of ethnic self-awareness, a desire, perhaps too long suppressed, for cultural and political autonomy, which comes close to the proud expression of a national identity, but also a racial one, which does not tolerate alien elements or foreign masters. However, there is also an intolerance which couples the contemporary disturbances which shake the former USSR today, to say nothing of the United States. The world has become small. When one says the planet Earth is now "unitary," one is no longer making an ideological prophecy or moral choice. One is confining oneself to a statement, stressing a reality which on a planetary scale proves a still mysterious, but potent, law of interconnection.

Never before was it so true that no man, country, social class, is an island. Is this perhaps the melting pot, real at last? It is fair to doubt this. The North American sociologists who hoped by coining the phrase to exorcise the conflicts and real racial struggles in the Bronx and Brooklyn, but also in Watts, Los Angeles in B. A., were guilty of uncritical optimism. They mistook their hopes for the fact of experience (for a happy exception, cf. Alfred McLung Lee 1967). They believed that contact, duly multiplied and sanctioned in the name of the more perfect Union, would have produced a basically harmonious society, a variegated, "halfbreed" world, generally quiet and peaceful, a melting pot. They were wrong. These were hopes betrayed and desires as rash as they were frustrated. Re-reading today one of their most honest, complete statements is moving: "American culture is a synthesis of different contributions from interpreters and critics of American life committed to the common idea of American democracy." There is a very widespread, indeed a dominant, belief that American culture is exclusively linked to the Anglo-Saxon tradition. In fact, American ideology and culture are naturally indebted to German influences, especially in the fields of science, music, and philosophy; and to French influences, from the founding fathers' Enlightened education to the French alliance in the war of independence, etc. "The Scots, the Irish, Scandinavians and Jews — these and other national, racial and religious minorities have made irrefutable contributions to the common culture. The 'coloured minorities' — that is, the American Indians, Hispanic Americans and Black Americans — have made substantial contributions.... And yet, despite our American records and its interpretations, we have repudiated the old values and placed a growing value not on individuality but rather on conformism" (Margaret Just Butcher 1971).

More precisely, the growing value has gone to reward individuality in the sense of the dominant Anglo-Saxon culture. C. Wright Mills' analysis of the power elite leaves no doubt of this. By attending the same schools and gaining diplomas and degrees from the same "prestigious," that is, expensive, universities, by marriage, friendships, membership of the same exclusive clubs, the lords of politics, the economy and war consolidate and perpetuate an oligarchical dominion — if not a caste one — of the white, Anglo-Saxon, Protestant elite — the famous WASPS. The melting pot has not occurred. Coming in contact, even through the praiseworthy legislation directed at racial integration, especially in infancy at school, ethnic groups have not only not been fused or mingled. On the contrary, they have withdrawn and entrenched themselves in defensive positions, hostile and intransigent. We see a feverish, often hit-and-miss search and re-evaluation of one's own identity and roots. Instead of the melting pot there is at best the salad bowl, in which every ingredient, every leaf not only does not reject, it exalts, its own specific individuality.

Once the anthropological hopes had been dashed, the path of technology was tried. For some years, the ideas of Marshall McLuhan of a "global village" had polarized the concern of social analysts. The world now, it was thought, was a single "cable society." It was possible at once to maintain a planetary perspective and enjoy the proximity and warmth typical of a village community. Electronics, the media and informatics abolished the celebrated "friction of space" which had worried the classical economists, primarily Adam Smith, so much. At home, quietly sitting in an armchair in his drawing room, the "bon bourgeois" suddenly, instantly was promoted into "citizen of the world." Localism and globalism went hand in hand. The transmission of data instantly and through space made them co-present and united them.

Harold Adam Innis was certainly more important than Marshall McLuhan, and the latter moreover recognized him and considered him his teacher. But Innis, a difficult, compressed writer, was not destined for the international reputation of his brilliant, enterprising and contradictory pupil — from time to time Thomist and materialist, humanist and technologist, writer of books on the end of the book, and the coming of the new orality. McLuhan has not been fully understood. His real "message" was probably to be sought in his considered distrust of traditional culture and of intellectuals seen as a priestly caste, double-locked into their "separate room," put at the same time yearning for absolute control over the world. Everyone thought that McLuhan criticized the world of mass communications from an old-style humanistic viewpoint, as one might logically expect from a spiritualistic Thomist. But this was not so. McLuhan did not criticize the media. He explored them. He held out his ear and announced its return to a dominant position after centuries of supremacy by the eye, and after a whole Graeco-Roman-Judaic-Christian civilization dominated by visual perception.

Arthur Kroker (1984) grasped McLuhan's intention well. "His intention lay in the creation of anti-environments, on the basis of which the silent massage of the media could be felt." The medium sends messages, but every message is also essentially a "massage" of the mind, a new way of perceiving and understanding, and so a new way of coexisting, acting and interacting. The intellectual used to discussing everything and never committing himself, or without experiencing anything personally, gets his warning here. In his basic *The medium is the message*, where he definitively shows the way in which the content becomes irrelevant once a given hot or cold technology has been established to communicate it, McLuhan (1967) stresses that it is impossible to understand the new technological situation without experiencing it personally, from without. It is not enough to describe it, however accurately: one must live it, existentially. He says: "All the media work on us and transform us completely. They are so pervasive in their personal, political, economic, aesthetic, psychological, moral, ethical and social consequences that they leave no part of us untouched, unaffected, unaltered. Any understanding of social and cultural change is impossible without a knowledge of how the media work as environments."

These are the reasons which, regarding the world we are called on to live in, lead me to consider seriously McLuhan and his probably mistaken hypothesis of the "global village." The socio-anthropological thesis of the melting pot is too openly apologetic as regards the existing social and political order to deserve an in-depth analysis. It has been completely worked out for those countries which welcome immigrants driven out by poverty or political persecution. These countries, euphemistically defined as "welcoming countries" are so anxious to welcome that they do not hesitate to mangle. Their embrace is so fraternal it tends to clamp shut in a suffocating vice. Their greatest concern seems to be that of welcoming, assimilating, integrating, "digesting." The stranger appears to them acceptable only insofar as he is malleable, docile, plastic, ready to renounce his identity and forget his roots. The alternative for him is extermination.

References

Bossuet, J. B. 1976. *Discourse on Universal History* translated by E. Forster. Chicago: University of Chicago Press.

Butcher, M. J. 1971. *The Negro in American Culture*. New York: New American Library.

Dilthey, W. 1986. *Storia della Giovinezza di Hegel e Frammenti Postumi*. Naples: Guida.

Ferrarotti, F. 1994. *The Temptation to Forget: Racism, Anti-Semitism, Neo-Nazism*. Westport: Greenwood Press.

Hitler, A. 1943. *Mein Kampf*, translated by R. Manheim. Boston: Houghton Mifflin Company.

Kroker, A. 1984. *Technology and the Canadian Mind*, New World Perspective. Montreal

Langbehn, J. 1936. *Lo Spirito del Tutto*. Brescia: Morcelliana.

Mayer, A.J. 1988. *Why Did the Heavens Not Darken?: The "Final Solution" in History*. New York: Pantheon Books.

McLuhan, M. 1967. *The Medium is the Message*. New York: Bantam Books.

Mclung Lee, A. 1967. *Race Riot*. New York: Octagon books

Nolte, E. 1965. *Three Faces of Fascism: Action Française, Italian Fascism, National Socialism*, translated by L. Vennewitz. New York: Holt, Rinehart and Winston.

Olivetti, A. 1947. *L'Ordine Politico della Comunità*. Ivrea.

Orwell, G. 1977. *1984*. San Diego: Harcourt Brace Jovanovich.

Power, S. 2002. "Genocide and America." *New York Review of Books*, March 14.

Romano, S. 1999. *An Outline of European History from 1789 to 1989*, translated by L. Gunzberg. New York: Berghahn Books.

Spencer, H. 1923. *The Principles of Sociology*. New York: Appleton.

Time Magazine, June 17, 2002.

Todorov, T. 1995. *Les Abus de la Mémoire*. Paris: Arlea.

Voltaire, 1828. *Essai sur Les Moeurs et L'Esprit des Nations*. Paris: Librairie Universelle de P. Mongie.

_____. 1976. *Discourse on Universal History* translated by E. Forster. Chicago: University of Chicago Press.

PART II. CONCEPTUAL APPROACHES TO GENOCIDE

CHAPTER 5. THE SUCCESS AND FAILURE OF "GENOCIDE"

Arthur S. Wilke, Professor Emeritus, Auburn University

Once the term "genocide" or its synonyms (e.g., mass killing, extermina-
tions, etc.) are expressed, an abhorrent condition is acknowledged. Often the
expression comes after the fact, after genocidal acts have taken their toll. Such
acts are variously incorporated into collective memories (cf. Halbwachs
1980[1950]) and their contemporary uses and, less frequently, in judicial acts
(e.g., international tribunals) of retribution.

DISCIPLINARY AND BEHAVIORAL LEGACIES

What do disciplinary pursuits (cf. Schmidt 2000), such as corporate sociology, bring to occurrences of genocidal acts, those periodic, undifferentiated
mass killings of people due to a categorical identity (e.g., Jews, Gypsies, ethnic
Albanians, Tutsi, etc.)? At this time, not much. Periodically, various commen-
taries direct criticisms and insights at political leaders and the intelligentsia for
current and past acts of omission in responding to genocidal acts or for not
responding to them in a timely fashion. These concerns are often expressed with
an air of resignation or an exhortation that in moral-ethical terms is known as
emotivism.

While there isn't much to show in stopping the machinery that unleashes
genocidal acts or transforming callous as well as benign nonresponsiveness, the
fashioning and use of "genocide" has served as a blueprint for the ever expanding

arrays of "problems" and cultural workers drawn from the growing ranks of the professional middle class (PMC) (Ehrenreich and Ehrenreich 1979). These disciplined workers (Schultz 2000), now under the umbrella of a generic, but snarled array of notions to which the label liberalism (cf. Mills 1962; Gottfried 2002; Piccone 2000) is applied continue (cf. Gerth and Landau 1963) to labor on specialized, provincial topics. The notion of "genocide" has been a paradigmatic case for an orientation that I'll label *the new social pathology model.*

The old social pathology model (Davis 1975; Mills 1943) was grounded on a notion that modernizing developments such as industrialization had unfortunate consequences. Some people, "outsiders" such as immigrants, were viewed as disproportionately contributing to social ills such as poverty and crime. These deplored conditions were traced not to the intrusiveness of industrialization, but to other pathologies that were located "in" people which, collectively speaking, was portrayed as "their" culture. Outsiders exhibited, it was held, wrong, inappropriate, or nonexistent values and beliefs, and a lack of familiarity with norms. The appropriate cultural attributes were ones that were consonant with the demands of industrialists and others desiring maximum labor discipline, often at the lowest possible cost.

The "solution" to outsider "problems" entailed the recruitment and self-promotion of an army of cultural healers (case workers, educators, clergy, motivational speakers, public opinion leaders, etc.) who sought, in effect, to change the hearts and minds of the dysfunctional outsiders. Accompanying this shift in surveillance and related activities was the growth in repressive tactics directed against the predominantly poor outsiders. Moral crusades, public health measures and suburban developments aided in concentrating those who were deemed the vectors of deviance and disorder. Not only, then, did the outsiders require "treatments" that would better integrate them into things such as the required practices of the dominant economic institutions, but they served as a ready source of moral examples for constituencies that were being encouraged to see their comparatively beneficial status as due primarily to possessing "correct" cultural attributes and meritorious achievement.

In the contemporary era, the social pathological model has been redesigned and redeployed. The same kinds of cultural healers are present. Drawn from the ever expanding ranks of the PMC, these healers are increasingly found supporting and participating in welfare activities of the expanding managerial state (Gottfried 1999). What is different are the nature and scope of social ills that come under the oversight of the managerial state. No longer is the "outsider" the only source of social pathology. Now, those formerly considered "insiders" are ~~ treated. Though in past social pathological framing, the "insiders" who were lumped into an amorphous but seemly invisible social category, that of the "majority," now the very same are seen as harboring the pathologies that are at the root of discordant conditions such as inequalities linked to (alternative) life styles, ethnicity, gender, race. Despite disputes over whether a century or more old social ills or "problems" (e.g., crime, drugs, poverty, sexuality) should be framed as defects of "outsiders" or manifestations of defects in the majority, the latter orientation is ascendant. In the extreme, the new social pathology model seeks to consider social ills such as crime as due to long established patterns of discrimination (e.g., against blacks, gays, the poor, women) and antecedent prejudicial beliefs and attitudes directed against the "outsiders."

This movement from outsider to insider pathology was aided by work undertaken to respond to genocide, especially the Holocaust. After World War II, the unfolding display of documented acts of genocide, especially undertaken under the auspices of the Nazi Germans, served as a springboard to identify imbedded pathologies. An exemplar of this type of work, undertaken under the auspices or with the support of organizations such as the American Jewish Congress and out of character with the author's early work, was Theodor Adorno's, *The Authoritarian Personality* (1959). The "majority" population was surveyed for clues to the existence of a cultural-cum-individual, prejudice, anti-Semitism, located in the deep recesses of the human psyche.

Once this framework was established and extended to other cultural-intra psychic prejudices, direct indicators, though still used, are not always required. With identified and deplored pathological conditions conflated with the term "prejudice" (thus a negative connotation), in the extreme, documentation could be set aside. The existence of an actual or putative discrimination could be taken as "caused" by a prejudice. More intriguing, in instances where condemned pathological prejudices is stipulated, denial on the part of the accused, is taken as evidence of the workings of a deep-seated, unconscious mind. The observer-judge and, in some instances, "victims" make *ex cathedra*-like pronouncements. The gravity of the topic and the identity of the speaker is used to quiet opposition.

The increased domain of victims increases the range of possible topics and conditions to which cultural therapists respond. In addition, criticism of a select number in the therapeutic ranks energizes support for new victims. Past cultural therapeutic overlords through past actions of commission or discredited framing

[margin annotation: Political Correctness]

of pathological conditions (e.g., treating blacks, Jews, etc. as pathological), and use of questioned procedures (e.g., limited positivistic ones) provide polemical conditions that galvanize struggles over who should control the agenda and methods of particular disciplines. Of late, support of procedures that valorize victim testimony contribute not only to a growth in the "jargon of authenticity" (cf. Adorno 1973[1964]) used by victims as well as cultural therapists who position themselves to become conduits, promoters and apologists while advancing treatments. In the extent case of "genocide," this notion became subordinated in the 1967 to 1973 period, the date of the two Arab-Israeli wars, to the term "Holocaust" (Finkelstein 2000). The emergence of the Holocaust coincided with the emergence of a wave of "new victims" in the US (Best 1999:95). Victims and their advocates highlighted that finally such people were "receiving the recognition, sympathy, and support they deserve[d]...." Among the specific categories of new victims, many of which "involve[d] direct exploitation by a victimizer..." and which enjoyed, and continue to enjoy, varying degrees of acceptance involve those who have been subject to:

> marital rape, acquaintance rape, date rape, elder abuse, sibling abuse, peer abuse, work abuse, emotional abuse, telephone abuse, verbal abuse, clergy abuse, satanic ritual abuse, sexual abuse, sexual harassment, hate crimes, serial murder, freeway violence, bullying, stalking, drunk driving, and UFO abductions (Best 1995:95).
>
> In keeping with the culture-cum-psyche emphasis, other new victims are identified as well as found giving testimony to suffering from ... sexual addiction, love addiction, food addiction, eating disorders, post-traumatic stress disorder (PTSD), multiple-personality disorder (MPD), false-memory syndrome, credit-card dependency, and codependency (Best 1999:95).

The proliferation of victims has seen the shift in the use of critical perspectives such as social constructionism (cf. Hacking 1999) from treating now intolerable conditions (e.g., notions of "race" or "woman") as "constructions," asserting that received notions of such inevitable conditions should be changed to criticisms regarding the constructed character of new victims (Best 2001; Murray, Schwartz and Lichter 2001). Some of these disputes have become stylized politically in the "culture wars" as battling factions seek either to maintain their favorite victims and their problems, such as those listed above, or challenge these and promote their own list of pathologies and victims such as the right to life of "human" fetal victims, equal treatment of evolution and creationism in the schools, and family values. Though there are disputes, there tends to be a convergence among the disputants. Credentialing, a feature of membership in the cultural therapists of the PMC is increasingly sought and recognized. All use, selectively, some form of empirical demonstration and documents from official and academic sources. All routinely debunk proponents of challenged victim constructions as well as opponents to their own causes, cultivating a suspicion that inheres with ideological thought (Mannheim 1952[1925]. This is done through exposing underlying assumptions or the failure of opponents to employ data that meets the positivist canons of scientific validity and reliability. And all seek to privilege capable victims' testimonies as to the harm experienced or what was occurring when an adverse action or event was underway.

Victims and their pathologies are not only limited to cultural therapeutic overlords. They can be caricatured in entertainment as is seen on US television programs such as *The Jerry Springer Show* or *Montel*. This not only signals some outer limits as to victims and claims, with mostly seemingly poorer people being put on display in moral dramas fashioned as counterparts to freak shows of the past. Like televised professional wrestling matches, these are known to have at least some contrived character to them. But unlike carnival hawkers and some revival organizers of the past who put shills in the audience, today the shills may be performers paid to put on a show. In a postmodern world, in which virtual and empirically accurate representations are often not clearly distinguished nor determinable. Even if the differences are highlighted and such events are unmasked, this may do little more that promote popular snobbery: "taking a petty, superficial, or irrelevant distinction ... and running with it" (Epstein 2002: 15). This augers well with social pathological thought which, as Mills (1943) noted, exhibits a non-too critical, pedestrian quality and a tendency to merge empirical and normative concerns. This shall be taken up after I address the ethos of liberalism that is reproduced in the victim-cultural therapy relationship and the success and failure of Raphael Lemkin's program for bringing genocide into the center stage of social and intellectual life.

While various certified victims are dramatized in the mass media, genocide has dominated in movies, of which several of the prominent exemplars are *Judgment at Nuremberg* (1961, Stanley Kramer, director) and *Schindler's List* (1993, Steven Spielberg, director). These seem to resonate more than films such as *The Killing Fields* (1984, Roland Jaffe, director) dealing with the mass killings undertaken by the Pol Pot regime in Cambodia in the 1970s. Rwanda is not a likely setting nor, I conjecture, is Kosovo.

To compound matters, even among some testifying to their victimage in Nazi Germany, there are frauds (cf. Finkelstein 2000; Maliszewski 2002). Simultaneously, in the extreme, there are deniers of the existence of the Holocaust (cf. Finkielkraut 1998[1982]), activities which in some European countries are subject to legal sanctions. For proponents of Holocaust victimage, these actions along with desecrations of synagogues and cemeteries are treated as dangerous conditions that require extended therapeutic-educational actions to alert people to impending dangers, possibly of future Holocausts, as well as vigilant policing (Finkelstein 2000). Meanwhile, momentum, for example in behalf of some victims (e.g., women) in hate crime legislation (Jenness and Grattet 20001) seems to have proceeded without extensive lobbying on the part of organized special pleaders. This indicates that the fashioning and acceptance of victims energizes others than the victims or their proponents. Once the cause of victims gains a certain level of attention, things such as legal remedies, in addition to the established cultural-therapeutic activities such as courses and curricula in Holocaust studies and women's studies, seem to be attractive to lawmakers and undertaken, in some instances, on their own initiative.

While the trend is to expand the categories of victims, disputes still arise over what should count as the collective memory. This is currently seen in Poland regarding Auschwitz. Should the sites of the grim horrors of World War II be refurbished as a reminder of the nature and character of the Nazis operations of gas chambers and crematoria or should these be left to slowly deteriorate, retaining a ghostly aura of a terrible time that should signal contemporary disapproval (Williamson and Davis 2001)?

While the nature of collective memories and their uses can entail contested terrains, uses that attach to biographies, as suggested in the notions of *Holocaust piety* (Finkelstein 2000) and what Zygmunt Bauman has labeled, the *ghost of the holocaust*, produce an array of other cultural and even political practices that go well beyond the boundaries of a perpetrator's act and the victim. The personal embrace and dramatization of the Holocaust, either as a survivor or as one who was spared the fate of extermination, even generations removed, colors how some conduct their personal lives as well as their contributions to collective memory and contemporary practices. For survivors and survivors by proxy, the memory of the Holocaust becomes an obligation, at times a burden as these contemporaries struggle in maintaining a commitment to a collective identity that incorporates recollections of extensive acts of eradication. At once this is a part of a fashioned "heritage," but one which entails an ambiguous program action. Does one give testimony to some kind of horror, apologize for being a survivor or descendent, or rally contemporaries to not forget the Holocaust just as others, in the US, to "not forget the Alamo?" Or does memory plunge people into problems with the nondiscursive (cf. Langer 1951[1942])? Not only are there no words that capture the experience of annihilation, where the discursive does exist, as in reports of people facing the inevitability of death, there is an uneasiness. Despite the dread, people continued to live, live until they died. And while there is no experiencing of death, of nothingness, for survivors, the nondiscursive may be a part of life to which lingualization is inadequate. Rituals dealing with death often give a nodding recognition of this while signaling that are limits to how much of this can persist in the world of survivors. Given the scale of genocidal acts and the denial of survivors to deal with the victims not only is estranging from what is commonly taken as collective life, but renders the victims and their survivors as doubly "different." One can sense that some will sense that something extraordinary about genocide needs to be added. Whether such a quest can be satiated is dubious thus leaving unfinished business in the construction of collective memory. This may be what has contributed to writers such as Adorno 1995[1966] to sense that with the Nazi Holocaust there was a kind of end of history. Things like art that stylized nondiscursive aspects of life seemed, to commentators such as Adorno, to be overwhelmed by the collective shadow of the Holocaust. Such a loss, however, may have been more challenging for Adorno's life work than in a world with which Adorno's life work sought to assist in illuminating and liberating from the destroying life ways found in daily living as well as many intellectual practices.

Though the use of "genocide" as an indicator and call to action has not found its ways into the conventional practices of the command posts of the political establishment in the US, its study has been incorporated into the cultural apparatus of a growing, though at times contested, managerial state. Analytic stances and popular movements in behalf of victims, energized by the popularization of the Holocaust, have merged together and been amplified through the diverse, at times, competing activities. This has provided the overseers who practice cultural therapy in various venues such as higher education, an opportunity not only to expand domains of interest, but promote programs and policies that extend the reach of the managerial state. This reach is enhanced by the growth of actual and virtual or imaginary surveillance (cf. Foucault 1979[1978, 1975], the nature and character of which are fashioned and mystified in a number of disciplinary pursuits, including the social sciences. Treatments or solutions undertaken by cultural therapists range from moral exhortation to such things as clinical-educational, multi-cultural, multi-racial awareness and sensitivity rituals. How efficacious such activities are and how they contribute to the reproduction of differences, victims and further responses that justify the managerial state and its supporting agencies is beyond the scope of this essay.

The Ethos of Liberalism: A Snarled Legacy

The benevolent cultural therapeutic overlords working in response and behalf of victims promote policies and procedures that are justified as being for people's "own good" to promote a "more inclusive" social order. The watchwords are "diversity," "tolerance," "individual rights," notions that are drawn from the now generic, but snarled claims known as liberalism. Augmented by an embrace of the social pathological framework, analyses that are undertaken are pedestrian or left unexamined (Mills 1943; Adorno 1973[1964]).

> Liberalism entails the specific, personal freedom of the individual, even the self-imposed obligation, to make *no* unconditional commitments to *any* organization. All loyalties to movements or organizations, parties or states are, for the liberal, conditional upon his own principles and conscience (Mills 1962: 24).

The intelligentsia practicing cultural therapy embrace this as a part of the "freedom" enjoyed in selecting objects of study, often denying that they operate under external constraints. If there is a recognition, the "choice" that is exercised often takes the form of "bad faith," indicating the conditions are inevitable, not subject to intellectual or political resistance. Meanwhile, comfort is sought in identifying others, more often the comparatively powerless, who similarly engage in an alternation between deterministic fatalism and imaginative portrayals and ascriptions of choice with regard to the self and others.

The practitioners fashioning conditions as well as cultural therapeutic practices promote choice through challenging a determinism in the "majority" that is signaled by some expression of absolutism. The foundation for this derives from the methodological approach of cultural relativism that asserts an often denied truism, that there's recognized variability in human affairs. After all, travelers have long reported on seeing people in different places doing different things. In instructional settings, for example, this approach is used to "teach" (i.e., overturn) a presumed absolutism in the guise of ethnocentrism that is encountered or presumed to exist when students are introduced to the varying patterns and practices of distant and even non so distant others. Aside from highlighting variability, this introduction promotes a confusing, if not incoherent, espousal of tolerance and diversity.[1] For the "majority" who presumably exhibit ethnocentric and other pathological attributes, tolerance and appreciation of diversity should be elected in order to cure defects both in the individual and in collective life. Meanwhile, the cultural therapists retain the right to judge and reward those complying with the espousal of victim rights, tolerance and diversity without any guarantee of reciprocity.

To erode the "majoritarian" pathologies, assertions and demonstrations are made that undercut their viewpoints. The life ways or cultures of distant others are illustrated as being "as good as" or "better than" that of the targeted majority. Often the rejection of the majority's views on how a person ought to live introduces the specter of moral relativism: one way of life or culture is "as good as" any other or there is some kind of equivalence in the world of diversity. This however comes with caveats. Presumably perpetrators of genocidal acts would not be accorded tolerance for their diverse ways, though the basis for this view would very likely not be elaborated. The rightfulness for this would very likely derive from the identification of imputed pathological cultural conditions and a moral sentiment, cultivated in the expression of a term like "genocide," that would subordinate moral reasoning for emotivism. This will be elaborated upon later.

"GENOCIDE:" LEMKIN'S UNFINISHED LEGACY

The term "genocide" was a carefully crafted term that made its appearance in 1944 (Lemkin 1944). It's author, Raphael Lemkin (1901–1959), opposed state sponsored killing and the barrier to prosecution, state sovereignty. "Genocide" was selected as a most egregious instance of such killing. Though "genocide" was

---

1. One of the snarls in the liberal ethos centers in appeals to tolerance and diversity. Strategically located operators in the PMC often have license to exercise a sleight of hand. Tolerance and diversity are at once attributes to be extended to distant others, but not those subject to this instruction, students. Students are expected, if not commanded, to not only vocalize but behave in ways giving evidence of tolerance and the promotion of diversity. The result, to use Marcuse's (1965) apt but oxymoronic-appearing phrase, a form of *repressive tolerance*. Such practices are sustained not through a careful explication of concerns and notions, but by the warrant that PMC membership in institutions such as higher education confers. Tolerance and diversity are advanced by the intolerance that is warranted by priestly identities and practices of dominant status validation.

embraced in the 1948 draft of the United Nations' *Convention on the Prevention and Punishment of the Crime of Genocide*, endorsed by a requisite number of nations in 1950, its endorsement and implementation has been uneven. The US approved the *Convention* in 1986 with implementing legislation passed in 1988. Most recently, further implementation via the establishment of an International Criminal Court has seen the US withdraw its support.

Based on Lemkin's notion and Article 2 of the Convention, genocide is a family of criminal acts undertaken by corporate actors (i.e., nations) and their agents "committed with the intent to destroy, in whole or in part, a plurality of people and/or their life-ways based on categorical ascriptions or affiliations (e.g., race, ethnicity, religion, etc.)." Proscribed and punishable acts include:

> (a) *Killing members of the group; (b) Causing serious bodily or mental harm to members of the group; (c) Deliberately inflicting on the group conditions of life calculated to bring about its physical destruction in whole or in part; (d) Imposing measures intended to prevent births with the group; (e) Forcibly transferring children of the group to another group* (italics added, Power 2002, p. 62).

Article 3 of the Convention specifies the following as punishable acts: "(a) Genocide; (b) Conspiracy to commit genocide; (c) Direct and public incitement to commit genocide; (d) Attempt to commit genocide; (e) Complicity in genocide" (cited in Power, 2002: 62, italics added).

The prosecution of genocide has not been uniform during the past half century and has been a notion that officials, such as many in the US, have been reluctant to aggressively certify and invoke in dealing with foreign affairs. Some, such as former Secretary of State Henry Kissinger, implicated in some foreign proceedings prosecuting perpetrators of genocide and the object of an unofficial brief accusing him of being a war criminal (Hitchens 2001), vigorously oppose political actions on the part of the United Nations to pursue war crimes (Djordjevic 2000).

Lemkin's uniquely fashioned term "genocide" was embraced by the United Nations, imbedded in the collective memory of contemporaries, and used, as noted above, in various ways. Two features of Lemkin's notion of "genocide" are of interest. First, even though his notion would assist in closing a loophole in prosecuting perpetrators of state sanctioned mass murder, Lemkin's intent was much broader, something of interest to contemporary social observers. Second, the term "genocide" was fashioned in a way that its expression not only sustains the snarled legacy of liberalism, but to promote sentiments whose nature and expression reduce contributions for the nurturing of robust moral lives.

Lemkin had a more inclusive notion of genocide. "Genocide," he wrote, meant "a coordinated plan of *different* actions aiming at the destruction of essential foundations of life of national groups, with the aim of annihilating the groups themselves" (Lemkin 1944:40 and quoted in Power 2002:43, italics added). Lemkin went on:

> Genocide has two phases: one, destruction of the national pattern of the oppressed; the other, the imposition of the national pattern of the oppressor. This imposition, in turn, may be made up the oppressed population which is allowed to remain, or upon the territory alone, after removal of the population and colonization of the area by the oppressor's own nationals (quoted in Power 2002:43).

"Genocide," then, was not only killing people, but their collective bases of existence, in a shorthand term, their culture. While the specifics of this notion are not detailed, Lemkin's notion would apply to many contacts involving foreign peoples, the most dramatic instances being colonial intrusions and promoting conditions for the maintenance and growth of world markets ranging from commodities to manufactured goods. This has been a province of some social scientists, particularly anthropologists. Such inquirers face the dilemma of at once being but one set of organized agents that make contact with foreign peoples while at the same time questioning the consequences of such contact. It remains an unsettled condition that can energize polemical disputes over what should be studied, what methods are to be privileged, and who should be the gatekeeper. Operationally, actual practices entailing foreign field work, teaching junkets and the like, a part of the program for cultivating appreciation and tolerance for a multi cultural world leaves many things murky. For example, it is often unclear what and how this cultivated awareness is to affect not only those people under study, but those undertaking to produce or subjected to various research findings concerning these distant others. At times, a "radical," anticolonialist stance is cultivated, however its scope and adequacy seems suspect, especially in an environment which makes such findings and claims elective, a matter of individual "choice." In matters that bear on things that are often portrayed as entailing moral-ethical dimensions, this does not auger with the "form[s] of life" (Wittgenstein 1958[1953]) with which most contemporaries are engaged. This is something to be revisited later.

The second feature of Lemkin's creation, the term "genocide," is that what he designed the term to do compromises his project. Once, as we see, it is like the opening of Pandora's Box. Certain ensuing cultural productions such as "victims," as in the Holocaust, are unleashed and reproduced in other programs to pursue grievances. Lemkin carefully crafted "genocide" so that its use would entail both indicative and evocative moods. Encountering something described as "genocide" is to provoke a sentiment of revulsion, disgust, horror. Without a carefully marshaled program of action, such use frequently also calls up an imperative mood in which targeted populations such as students are, following the practice of many cultural therapists' programs, subject to exhortations that "something," possibly on their part, "ought to be" done. Such *pastiche*, in effect "add ons" to be crafted into a lecture, a chapter, possibly a course on "ethics" that become event or topic specific, plunging people into a labyrinth of "theories" and obtuse, vicarious considerations of how such targeted people report on how they "ought to" behave if, for example, they were guards at Auschwitz. This imaginative reverie does not comport with the "form[s] of life" which people live, no less the foundation for substantive programs for moral living. And pursued in a world that celebrates individual "choice," what ensues, other than a sense of virtue on the part of cultural therapists and yet further calls for managing human affairs including oversight of discourse on things such as ethics, is ambiguous.

The Flattening of Moral Life

Lemkin's formulation of "genocide" and repeated in the numerous conditions cited by a growing array of victims conveys indicative, evocative and imperative moods. Describing occurrences has "genocide" or "child abuse" call up a pathological framing of the contributing behavior, something, presumably can be treated by various cultural therapists. This distinguishes this growing army of practitioners from those who would frame the same underlying events as an evil that are inevitable, responded to in another world or require miraculous, if not, magical interventions. The expressions convey the inappropriateness of the behavior by calling up bodily states. Such sentiments are also wrapped around appeals to what "ought to be." In sum, the behavioral-cum-moral stance being cultivated is one of emotivism. Determinations and expressions of right and wrong are attributed to feeling states. For cultural therapists, attention is directed at looking for clues to such sentiments or minimally, in a world of flattened affect (cf. Jameson 1991[1984] where people communicate less in face-to-face interactions, some signal of their emotional response (e.g., declarations on some report which are prefaced by a self-referencing claim such as, "I am horrified about...." How such "horror" looks is left to the imagination of the receiver, an imagination that correctly or incorrectly envisions if the report is actual or simply an effort to use a ritually appropriate expression).

Emotivist conditions prevail because many of the forums in which reported events such as "genocide" are reported are delimited. In a classroom, for example, a little time may be set aside to provide a report and queries may be made such as "What do you think about this?" or "How do you *feel* about this?" In most instances, "I feel this is terrible!" signals an appropriate appreciation. To go deeper than this, to query how people frame this, where this interfaces in their biographies, or to assess an existential situation pales next to diffuse calls for engaging in expressive public condemnations or efforts to urge officials to act. Masked in a language of "choice," "importance" and "necessity," these exercises tend to disenfranchise or recruit some to limited programs of special pleading, not that these are inconsequential.

If moral living entails addressing "What is a good life?" and "How ought one behave?," skirmishes that call for the irrigation of sentiment or some rituals of imaginary activity are not only problematic, but may warrant investigation to assess their contribution to such concerns. This approach recognizes that moral affairs entail an array of behaviors and reasons (Cf. Aiken 1962), reasons and behaviors that augur with the "form[s] of life" (Wittgenstein 1958[1953]) with which people are familiar. One becomes proficient at becoming a baseball player not, as social science talk would have it, by knowing the rules (norms) of the game, believing in the existence of the game and valuing of conferring importance of the game. These are elements involved in playing and appreciating the game. However, to become competent one also practices. And even then there are gradations: some players are far more proficient at playing the game than others.

The social science contribution to the moral life is often far removed from this. Cultural therapists with a pathological bent are on the look out for clues that reveal things such as values, beliefs and norms (rules) are absent, wrong or inappropriate. By providing the "right" ones, if possible, will signal the efforts of these PMC participants in "solving" the problem. However, this talk gets mired, though at times accurately reported, in the "ritual of the 'is' and 'ought'" (Kovesi 1979). In addition, as agents of the managerial state, there is a tilt toward conducting moral talk in accord to a narrow reading of Thomas Hobbes (1588–1679). Hobbes, the author of *Leviathan* (1651) sought to provide a nonreligious rationale for the state. In an unsupervised "state of nature" people were "short, mean and brutish." Their saving grace was reason that led them to subordinate themselves to external power. This popular portrait is reproduced in many ways (e.g., Errol Morris directed 1988 documentary, *The Thin Blue Line*, in which the view is expressed that civil life is possible primarily by police vigilantly patrolling the forces of chaos). For cultural therapists armed with notions of humans having no *a priori* attributes, being *tabula rasa*, an overseeing state is not only necessary for order, but for facilitating the growth and development of "reason." This becomes a warrant for required education, even though in practice the development and exercise of reason is abstracted, flattened and left in policy and practice to choice, a key element in the liberal ethos. In practice, then, many human and educational activities are portrayed as if human affairs are like a naive shopper with requisite resources who proceeds to "choose" items to put into the shopping cart. This looks quite different than what occurs when one follows people shopping. Available resources, habits and efforts to dislodge practiced behaviors are occurring. Even when this halcyon portrayal is viewed inadequate, word magic therapies are proposed where supplying the right rules (e.g., displaying the Ten Commandments or providing the "basic concepts" [i.e., terms] of the field), right value expressions and indications of right beliefs, as if these are unproblematic, will reconstitute the human in an appropriate way. This is less a program for analysis than it is one for "fitting in."

In the wake of World War II genocide, social psychologists developed experiments that in effect confirmed Hannah Arendt's (1969[1963]) observation of what she termed, "the banality of evil." The famous Milgram (1963) experiment demonstrated that many naive subjects would follow commands in effect, according to the drama, execute someone. Zimbardo, et. al. (1973) showed how role playing in a contrived prison setting became all-consuming. Those playing guards became aggressive and vicious while those who were prisoners became withdrawn. This and other selected findings and vignettes have made up moral commentary still in evidence in many academic settings. Orne's (1962) insight that such experiments are based on exploiting misplaced trust wherein things such as "science" are conventionally accepted as nonharmful has, with exceptions of entities such as Institutional Review Boards, still not been digested. People, such as those subjected to these findings and moral exhortations, are treated as exhibiting similar flaws of character and in need of the guidance of cultural therapists. These are exercises in what Marcuse (1955) labeled "surplus repression."

Mannheim (1952[1925]) suggested that an ideological climate existed where suspicions were raised and the practice was to impute interpretations to people's interests and social circumstances. This seems operating in the programs of cultural therapists as Kinloch and Mohan (*International Journal of Contemporary Sociology* 2000) have recently dramatized. However, raising suspicions (cf. Kinloch and Mohan 2000) has not resulted in what Mannheim envisioned, overturning or deconstructing the social practices, just as this essay will not lead to toppling dominant practices that, with exception of a few thin "radical" polemics, tend less to analyze the conditions of collective life, but aid in its reproduction. At the margins this has been true for some time in part because many of the corporate practitioners in the therapeutic state are more preoccupied with producing texts (cf. Agger 1989) that affirm identities, status, and tokens of "meritorious" performance. Corporate practitioners either deny the existence of or do not work in behalf of a "public" engagement with materials (cf. Lemert 2000; Agger 2000) nor sufficiently "surrender and catch" (Wolff 1976, 2000) to arm people with resources to probe the existing order of things in less that a facile fashion.

NONACADEMIC CHALLENGES

Genocide and victimage are being addressed in challenging and imaginative ways. Three examples of work highlighting this are reviewed here.

The first is the appropriation of the term "Holocaust" by Mike Davis in his work, *Late Victorian Holocausts: El Nino Famines and the Making of the Third World* (2001). Davis sets out to show that colonialist practices exacerbated natural calamities. In the face of privation, despite appeals by missionaries, the world market for foodstuffs and the implementing of developments ignored not only the plight of millions, but efforts to dispute the dominant "modernist" practices. Tens of millions died, many unnecessarily. The imperatives of the world market and the need to finance this participation ruled other options out. Lemkin's notion that genocide entails "organized" efforts that impose repression and destruction of established ways of life seems apt. Lemkin's unknown identity and role in working to bring genocide to the forefront, ignored until recently, may signal ruling out political and intellectual options or simply the lack of resources to deal with the knotty implications of these notions, notions by no means which are unambiguous.

The second author of interest is Sven Lindqvist. In *Exterminate All the Brutes* (1996), Lindqvist builds on a phrase found in Joseph Conrad's, *Heart of Darkness*

(1990[1902] that is expressed by a central character in dealing with the natives in the Belgium Congo. Lindqvist searches the literature of the late 19th century, looking for items that likely influenced Conrad. He found a rich trove of writings, including those of Hebert Spencer, that not only recognized what was occurring to the Congo natives but endorsed and framed as inevitable these developments. His next work, *A History of Bombing* (2001[2000]) highlights not only the expansion of air power and bombing, but how these were developed and practiced, constituting what Lemkin would identify as acts of genocide — organized acts designed that are designed to destroy established ways of life. Whether it is Churchill's instruction to bomb workers' homes in Germany in World War II or the US bombing of dikes and other infrastructural items in North Vietnam, the machinery of war, which Lemkin so early noted, was dangerous.

Michael De Landa's, *War in the Age of Intelligent Machines* (1991) shows not only how successive waves of military hardware are advanced as bringing decisive closure to a range of conflicts. The record is poor, however, as institutionalized practices persist along with a continued record of unfulfilled promises. What De Landa illuminates is the circulation not only of suspect specifications of zero-sum (for a winner there's a loser) conflict situations such as the prisoner's dilemma, but from the outset, the aim of such modes of thought: to automate decision-making. Two things are of interest. First, data become the currency of the real, whether it is the feedback from missile siting mechanisms or the automated instructions to buy or sell on the stock market. Second, automated data gathering and responses are promoted to remove humans from engaging in key activities and judgments. While much of these efforts have yet to bear fruit, if ever, the effort is to render many, including inhabitants of the PMC, into *dromomaniacs* (Virilio 1986[1977] — increasingly unanchored people on the move awaiting for some kind of leadership or solution, entailing human or, increasingly, nonhuman attributes. The embrace of a burdenless technological revolution, already heralded with anthropomorphized constructions of "smart bombs" and "smart classrooms" not only renders conditions sanitary, but the role of not just the underdogs of social life but many of the overlords in the PMC as incidental, superfluous. In effect, it is an embrace of practices that are, as Lemkin envisioned, genocidal but without physical death.

Contemporaries face challenges from the nature, use and apologetics involving technology as well as practices of cultural therapists that extend victimization. Actual injuries along with victimization that is limited primarily to identity and cultural politics is a concern addressed in Lani Guinier and Gerald Torres in The Miner's Canary (2002). The metaphor of the miner's canary is used to suggest that in many instances, the fate of the vulnerable canary victim, death by lethal gas, is a signal that on the horizon this may be the miner's fate. The task is at once to develop sensitivities to victims, turning these signals and experiences into a general awareness. Instead of emphasizing who a victimized speaker is, the twofold ask is to mobilize people and illuminate the world, an unfulfilled promise of disciplines such as sociology, but now left for fashioning a "public sociology" (Agger 2000) or some perspectives that are for people (cf. Wilke 2000) as they grapple with the uncertainties and problematic formulations that ensue from not just problems of living, but the suffocating operations of an intrusive managerial state. And while there may be a recognition that conditions of mutual indifference (Geras 1998) exist, as Milgram and Zimbardo also acknowledge, resistance to this drift of the times may render Geras's (2002) minimalist agenda which he calls "multivious care" workable and desirable. Eschewing the command posts of the dominating military-economic order and numerous apologists in the PMC, Geras returns to celebrating what humans do and can do. It no longer seems, if it ever was, a lack of knowledge that hampered responding to various external constraints and events, including genocide, but rather following the seductive siren songs of unexamined formulations, unexamined for their contribution, if any, to collective and moral life and which, it appears have tolerated broad-based attacks on masses of people while at the same time asserting that they have been complicit in their own fate. Extending business as usual with identity and cultural politics and the undemocratic programs of apologists of cultural therapy renders everyone into miner's canaries. Doing different things politically, intellectually and morally in this context doesn't seem a herculean task. Will a new direction guarantee escape? No. But neither will business as usual.

REFERENCES

Adorno, Theodor W. 1973[1964]. *The Jargon of Authenticity*. Trans. by Knut Tarnowski and Frederic Will. Evanston, IL: Northwestern University Press.

_____. 1959. *The Authoritarian Personality*. With Else Frenkel-Brunswick, Daniel J. Levinson and R. N. Sanford. New York: Harper & Brothers.

_____. 1995[1966]. *Negative Dialectics*. Trans. By E. B. Ashton. New York: Continuum.

Agger, Ben. 1989. *Reading Science: A Literary, Political and Sociological Analysis*. Dix Hills, NY: General Hall.

_____. 2000. *Public Sociology: From Social Facts to Literary Acts*. Lanham, MD: Rowman and Littlefield.

Aiken, Henry David. 1962. *Reason and Conduct: New Bearings on Moral Philosophy*. New York: Knopf.

Arendt, Hannah. 1969[1963]. *Eichmann in Jerusalem: A Report on the Banality of Evil*. New York: Viking.

Bauman, Zygmunt. 2000. "The Holocaust's Life as a Ghost." pp. 7–18 in *Social Theory After the Holocaust*, edited by Robert Fine and Charles Turner. Liverpool: Liverpool University Press.

Best, Joel. 1999. *Random Violence: How We Talk About New Crimes and New Victims*. Berkeley: University of California Press.

_____. 2001. *Damned Lies and Statistics: Untangling Numbers from to Media, Politicians, and Activists*. Berkeley: University of California Press.

Conrad, Joseph. 1990[1902]. *Heart of Darkness*. Mineola, NY: Dover Publications.

Davis, Mike. 2001. *Late Victorian Holocausts: El Nino Famines and the Making of the Third World*. London and New York: Verso

Davis, Nanette J. 1975. *Social Constructions of Deviance: Perspectives and Issues in the Field*. Dubuque, IA: W.C. Brown.

De Landa, Manual. 1991. *War in the Age of Intelligent Machines*. New York: Zone Books.

Djordjevic, Djordje. 2002. "War Crime Tribunals: The Prospects for International Justice," *Radical Society* 29 (April): 1, 61–69.

Ehrenreich, Barbara and John Ehrenreich. 1979. "The Professional-Managerial Class," pp. 5–45 in *Between Labor and Capital*, edited by Pat Walker. Boston: South End Press.

Epstein, Joseph. 2002. *Snobbery: The American Version*. Boston and New York: Houghton Mifflin.

Finkelstein, Norman C. 2000. *The Holocaust Industry: Reflections on the Exploitation of Jewish Suffering*. London: Verso.

Finkielkraut, Alain. 1998[1982]. *The Future of a Negation: Reflections on the Question of Genocide*. Trans. by Mary Byrd Kelly and introduction by Richard J. Golsan. Lincoln, NE: University of Nebraska Press.

Foucault, Michel. 1979[1978, 1975]. *Discipline and Punish: The Birth of the Prison*. Trans. By Alan Sheridan. New York: Vintage Books.

Geras, Norman. 1998. *The Contract of Mutual Indifference: Political Philosophy After the Holocaust.* London and New York: Verso.

Gerth, Hans and Saul Landau. 1963. "The Relevance of History to the Sociological Ethos." Pp. 26–34 in *Sociology on Trial,* edited by Maurice Stein and Arthur Vidich. Englewood Cliffs, NJ: Prentice-Hall.

Gottfried, Paul Edward. 1999. *After Liberalism: Mass Democracy in the Managerial State.* Princeton, NJ: Princeton University Press.

_____. 2002. "Reply to James Kalb," *Telos* (Winter): 122, 120–26.

Guinier, Lani and Gerald Torres. 2002. *The Miner's Canary: Enlisting Race, Resisting Power, Transforming Democracy.* Cambridge, MA and London: Harvard University Press.

Hacking, Ian. 1999. *The Social Construction of What?* Cambridge, MA and London: Harvard University Press.

Halbwachs, Maurice. 1980[1950]. *Collective Memory.* New York: Harper and Row.

Hitchens, Christopher. 2001. *The Trial of Henry Kissinger.* London and New York: Verso.

International Journal of Contemporary Sociology. 2000. Special issue edited by Graham C. Kinloch and Raj P. Mohan on non-traditional approaches to the social sciences. Vol. 37 (October) No. 2.

Jameson, Fredric. 1991[1984] *Postmodernism or, The Cultural Logic of Late Capitalism.* Durham, NC: Duke University Press.

Jenness, Valerie and Ryken Grattet. 2001. *Making Hate a Crime: From Social Movement to Law Enforcement.* New York: Russell Sage Foundation.

Kinloch, Graham C. and Raj P. Mohan (Eds.). 2000. *Ideology and the Social Sciences.* Westport, CT and London: Greenwood Press.

Kovesi, Julius. 1978. "Against 'The Ritual of 'Is' and 'Ought'," *Midwest Studies in Philosophy.* III, 5–16.

Langer, Suzanne. 1951[1942]. *Philosophy in a New Key: A Study in the Symbolism of Reason, Rite and Art.* Cambridge, MA: Harvard University Press.

Lemert, Charles. 2000. Series Editor's Foreword, "The Necessary Truth-Telling of a Public Sociology." Pp. ix-xv in *Public Sociology: From Social Facts to Literary Acts.* Lanham, MD: Rowman and Littlefield by Ben Agger.

Lemkin, Raphael. 1944. *Axis Rule in Occupied Europe: Laws of Occupation, Analysis of Government, Proposals for Redress.* New York: Carnegie Endowment of International Peace, Division of International Law.

Lindqvist, Sven. 1996. *Exterminate All the Brutes.* Trans. By Joan Tate. New York: New Press.

_____. 2001[2000]. *A History of Bombing.* New York: The New Press.

Livingston, Donald W. 2002. "Lincoln Symbols": A Review of Barry Schwartz's, *Abraham Lincoln and the Forge of National Memory* (Chicago, IL: University of Chicago Press, 2000) in *Telos* (Winter): 122, 156–68.

Lovejoy, Arthur O. and George Boas. 1973[1935]. *Primitivism and Related Ideas in Antiquity.* New York: Octagon Books.

Maliszewski, Paul. 2002. "A Holocaust Fantasy." (A review of Stefan Maechler's, *The Wilkomirski Affair: A Study in Biographical Truth.* New York: Schocken Books. 2001 and Blake Eskin's, *A Life in Pieces: The Making and Unmasking of Binjamin Wilkomirski.* New York: Norton. 2002. The Wilson Quarterly XXVI (Summer): 3, 109–111.

Mannheim Karl. 1952[1925]. "The Problem of the Sociology of Knowledge. Chapter IV." Pp. 134–90 in *Essays on the Sociology of Knowledge* by Karl Mannheim and edited by Paul Keckskemiti. London: Routledge & Kegan Paul.

Marcuse, Herbert. 1955. *Eros and Civilization: A Philosophical Inquiry into Freud.* Boston: Beacon Press.

_____. 1965. "Repressive Tolerance," pp. 81–117, in *A Critique of Pure Tolerance* by Robert Paul Wolff, Barrington Moore, Jr. and Herbert Marcuse. Boston: Beacon Press.

Milgram, Stanley. 1963. "Behavioral Study of Obedience," *Journal of Abnormal and Social Psychology* 63, 127–34.

Mills, C. Wright. 1943. "The Professional Ideology of Social Pathologists," *American Journal of Sociology* 49 (September): 3, 165–80.

_____. 1962. *The Marxists.* New York: Dell.

Murray, David, Joel Schwartz, and S. Robert Lichter. 2001. *It Ain't Necessarily So: How Media Make and Unmake the Scientific Picture of Reality.* Lanham, MD: Rowman & Littlefield.

Orne, M. T. 1962. "On the Social Psychology of the Psychological Experiment: With Particular Reference to Demand Characteristics and their Implications," *American Psychologist* 17, 776–83.

Piccone, Paul. 2000. "Ten Counter-Theses on New Class Ideology: Yet Another Reply to Rick Johnstone." *Telos* (Winter): 119, 145–55.

Power, Samantha. 2002. *A Problem From Hell: America and the Age of Genocide.* New York: Basic Books.

Schmidt, Jeff. 2000. *Disciplined Minds: A Critical Look at Salaried Professionals and the Soul-Battering System that Shapes Their Lives.* Lanham, MD: Rowman and Littlefield.

Virilio, Paul. 1986[1977]. *Speed and Politics: An Essay on Dromology.* Trans. by Mark Polizzotti. New York: Semiotext(e).

Wilke, Arthur S. 2000. "People Before Sociology, Sociology for People: Recovering the Obvious." *International Journal of Contemporary Sociology* 37(October): 2, 128–39.

Williamson, Elizabeth and Bob Davis. 2002. "Burden of History: Auschwitz Repairs Force Tough Debate Over Preservation." *The Wall Street Journal.* Vol. CCXL (August 14) No. 32, pp. A1 and A8.

Wittgenstein, Ludwig. 1958[1953]. *Philosophical Investigations.* Trans. By G. E. M. Anscombe. New York: MacMillan.

Wolff, Kurt H. 1976. *Surrender and Catch: Experience and Inquiry Today.* Dordrecht and Boston: D. Heidel.

_____. 2000. "Toward a Conception of Sociology." *International Journal of Contemporary Sociology* 37(October): 2, 117–127

Zimbardo, P. G., C. Haney, W. C. Banks and D. Jaffee. 1973. "The Mind Is a Formidable Jailer: A Pirandellian Prisoner." *New York Times Magazine* (April 8), pp. 38–60.

Chapter 6. The Decisive Generation: Self-Authorization and Delegations in Deciding a Genocide

Mihran Dabag

The concept of genocide research commonly conjures up images of studies that attempt to provide a general overview of diverse forms of persecution and genocide, ambitiously endeavoring to produce statistics on victims or maps highlighting geographical frequencies of human rights violations. On the one hand, such studies can be justifiably dismissed, as they are a long way from providing a detailed analysis of the causes of individual acts of genocide. On the other hand, the approaches of cultural history and cultural anthropology make it clear that, as yet, few research concepts have been developed that as key categories enable genocide to be studied from an interdisciplinary perspective.

The concept of generation, which constitutes the main focus of the following analysis, should not only facilitate the examinations of social, historical and psychological questions. It should also be particularly valuable in strengthening an approach that tends to be disqualified as an "intentionalist perspective." In order to understand the causes and course of an act of genocide (this will be elucidated in greater detail below), motivations and constructions of consensus should be seen as centrally important.

Raul Hilberg in particular pointed out, that the Holocaust was realized across different phases and by means of different perpetrator groups (Hilberg 1961). It affected all social groups and every area of social life. Genocides are carried out in the midst of a society, they are realized by means of the formation of a *perpetrator society* (Dabag 2002, pp. 181 and pp. 183–184).[1] With this category, my aim is first of all to highlight the social integration of the individual. I will stress that there is no "external being," no position "between" perpetrators and observers, between those who profit and those who become victims. In this way, National Socialist politics was able to create an unambiguous separation of positions within society. Second, such a category allows references to be made to the institutionalized networks involved in the realization of deportations and murders (Hilberg 1992).

But how is a perpetrator society formed? In the following, this question will be analyzed with the help of an *individual aspect*. The point of departure for this is the observation that both within the Young Turkish leadership as well as the National Socialist movement, genocide was legitimized as belonging to the *politics of a specific generation*. In this context, in the following, four aspects will be considered: the requirement of shaping new generations; the integration of this requirement into generational knowledge and generational discourse; the importance of the construction of generation for the legitimization of genocide; and the construction of *second generations*. With the help of examples and by applying the concept of *political generation*, these aspects should enable a characterization of the specific convergence of genocide research with the structures and processes of genocide and collective violence.

The Creation of New Generations

The following analysis focuses on the term "generation" as a model of self-explanation in contemporary understanding of political movements and groups at the beginning of the 20th century. Wilhelm Dilthey defined this idea of a political generation, which is central in German history of philosophy, as a "generational unity" characterized by a *consciousness* of community (Dilthey 1875).

With regard to generation, the *self-perception* of a group of individuals as a "generation" who share a *social period in time* and see a historical *area of experience* as shared is of central importance. In the following discussion the concern is not with an attempt to outline historical connections as developments in the course or rivalry of political generations, which are comprised of individuals growing up at the same time. Instead, the focus will be on *self-explanations* as generation and aspects of the definition of shared experiences, i.e. the construction of a specific social and temporal closeness, of a shared present and shared expectations.

---

1. See also my chapter on "Modern Societies and Collective Violence" in this volume.

The recognition of the importance of a specific generational consciousness is derived from different studies from the area of historical and cultural studies, which currently re-examine the enforcement of particular social-historical mentalities. In this context it is not coincidental that above all, attempts are made to reassess aspects of the mentality in Europe before the First World War (Wohl 1980, Eghigian and Berg 2002). The political power of movements has again come into the field of vision, particularly in the framework of debates on globalization and transnationalization, on new national and world orders. Does the transition to the 20th century mark a decisive turning point towards models of identity and nation, which *willfully* caused two world wars, countless subsequent wars and genocide? The re-emerging ethological discussions also address social-historical behavioral dispositions. Through this, particularly in the European context, it can be established that the important models of analysis drawn out in social psychological works — such as in David Riesman's study *The Lonely Crowd* (Riesman 1952) or in the social psychological studies of Anselm Strauss — were only partially developed, and particularly in the research on historical mentality, were not put to any extensive use.

Thus, although the term "generation" is used in a historical context in Germany (Schulz and Grebner 2003), the conditions of its construction are not examined. Generation is understood as "natural" cohorts of age and experience, which due to this given mutuality, share political ideas, social values and action norms. This has been demonstrated, for example, by Detlev Peukert (1987) and Ulrich Herbert (1996) with regard to the history of the Weimar Republic or National Socialism. However, what conceptualization of mutuality, identity and political action is behind the framework of political action that is understood as the action of or for a generation?

In his study on the "Generation of 1914," Robert Wohl (1980) reflected that great historical events — wars, revolutions, plagues, famines, or economic crises — could have a constitutive significance for historical generations because it is great historical events like these that would move the individual to place himself in history and society and thus in "his generation" (p. 210). In this way, the understanding as a generation initially follows one constituting idea (pp. 2–3): "Historical generations are not born; they are made. They are a device by which people conceptualize society and seek to transform it" (p. 5). With an analysis of the "militarization" in families of soldiers, Marcus Funck illustrated that in order to explain the preparedness for killing, it is necessary to describe not only cross-generational values, but also to search for the motivations of generational transfer (Funck 2002). The relation between conceptions of identity and conceptions of community has been outlined particularly clearly by Omar Bartov and Michael Geyer in terms of the history of National Socialism (Bartov 2000, Jarausch and Geyer 2003). Omer Bartov drew attention to certain elements of glorification and secular elements of sacrification which can be seen as aspects of the formation of German identity in the German Reich and in National Socialism, which reached across generations (Bartov 2000).

Outlines of a "theory" of historical-social generations are to be found in the work of Wilhelm Dilthey (1875) and Karl Mannheim (1965), François Mentré (1920) or José Ortega y Gasset (1933, 1937).[1] In the areas of literary history or history of art they can also be identified in the writings of Julius Peterson (1930) and Wilhelm Pinder (1928). Academic interest does seem to reflect the time of political-social relevance and explosiveness of the term, which in 1900 claimed to be a leading term of political models.

It was Sigmund Freud in particular who stressed that the construction of a generation is considerably dependent on transferences — seen not as the handing down from one generation to the next, but as the "taking over" by the new generation itself. For according to Freud, the "continuity in the mental life of successive generations" (Freud 1950, p. 158) is only to be understood in part as the passive inheritance of specific dispositions. "For psycho-analyses has shown us that everyone possesses in his unconscious mental activity an apparatus which enables him to interpret other people's reactions ... An unconscious understanding such as this of all the customs, ceremonies and dogmas left behind by the original relation to the father may have made it possible for later generations to take over their heritage of emotion" (Freud 1950, p. 159).

Beyond the definition of *generational contexts*, generation enables the analysis of specific individual integrations in (the relevant interpretations of) history, society and identity. Interpretations, attributions of meaning and objectives are explained in self-perception as being part of a generation that is independent of the ideas of identity and society of the parents' and grandparents' generations; they are oriented further towards desires and goals that are created for future generations.

The identification as a historical-political generation fulfills a particular task of integration. Generation appears to be a "flexible concept" (Wohl), as

---

1. For a more detailed analyses of Ortega's concept of generation see: Mariás 1970 and Spitzer 1973.

membership seems at first glance to require no particular social
However, there are in fact strict boundaries for membership (and in re
a national understanding, in which the task of creating national identity and
national consciousness has priority over the creation of state structures). Generation describes *young* actors. It is spoken of in a political context when the goal is
to characterize actors, an active group.

In the self-definition as a *political generation*, a particular continuity can
therefore be found. For the self-description as a "generation" construes a social
actor in society, who categorizes himself in a succession of generations, in a
genealogy, but whose actions strive to break with previous experiences. Interestingly, the political generation is a political self-conception which lays claim to
lying outside of history or having to place itself there.

In order to elucidate this brief outline I would like to stress at this point
that the definition of a generational context takes on a particularly important
role in the consideration of culprit groups in genocide: the explanation of
belonging to a new level of actors — to a group of actors with specific tasks —
took on an important position in political self-explanations. The model of being
a generation — and not just a political grouping, not merely a specific movement
— should be seen as an important element of formation. Independently of the
actual years when its members were born, the definition as a generation, brought
about by a declaration of community through mutual experience, allows not
only continuities to be defined: it also provides a framework for the demand of
breaks. These breaks are to signify a fundamental change in political and social
relationships in order to realize an ideal future that has been promised in the
past. The concern is with a break that brings together the history of expectation
and promise. The self-conceptualization is of a "historically acting generation,"
which authorizes itself to exterminate by means of a break in order to realize a
future promised in the past. At the same time it also fulfills a historical task, and
defines a moment of truth, of proving one's worth. The generation that authorizes itself, through such a violent bringing together of promise and fulfillment in
order to shape the "future" by destroying a presence, I describe here as a "decisive
generation."

The constitution of such a "generation" of self-appointment also takes on a
central role in Hitler's *Mein Kampf*, as can be shown by a cursory reading. Here,
generation is depicted as a *direct actor* in society. The text states: "For if a generation suffers from faults which it recognizes, even admits, but nevertheless, as
occurs today in our bourgeois world, contents itself with the cheap excuse that

there is nothing to be done about it — such a society is doomed" (p. 406).[1] The demand for action targeted at the present is oriented directly towards the well-being of the coming generation: "Anyone who refuses to see these things supports them, and thereby makes himself an accomplice in the slow prostitution of our future which, whether we like it or not, lies in the coming generation" (p. 255).

In both volumes of *Mein Kampf* there are a multitude of examples for the depiction of a generation as a decisive social creator. In this way, the new generation stands in much greater contrast to the "generation of our present notorious weaklings" (p. 402), the "generation of hothouse plants" (p. 409) or the "generations of rabble without honor" (p. 177).

The construction of a generation enables a direct address in political discourse, it invites a direct achievement of solidarity. The goal of the National Socialist movement was not to enter "into politics in order to play a part in parliamentary benefices and ministerial posts, but much more in order to conquer the empire and win power in general," according to Joseph Goebbels in the 1932 work *Kampf um Berlin* [Battle for Berlin] (Goebbels 1934, p. 37).

Inherent in the political definition of a generation is not only the habitus of a particular time, the "idealism" of an "excited generation," as Albert Speer noted in his memoirs (Speer 1969, p. 32).[2] It also includes an attempt to define a new political-social level of actors. In this way, the formation as a generation fulfills yet another function as the racial-national definition of a people. In contrast to the forming of a "people," it is not the primary basis for the framework of a new society, but it is the basis for the framework of a specific achievement of solidarity. Indeed, I would even go so far as to say that it directly prepares the inverse morality and determination of a perpetrator group.[3]

---

1. See also p. 460: "For otherwise the next generation in turn could, with the same right, squander its strength on such purely formal work within the party, instead of recruiting new adherents and thereby new forces for the movement." p. 527: "Of them no notice was taken whatever, for it was realized that the doglike submissiveness of the political formations of an old outlived generation would never be capable of serious resistance."

2. Albert Speer, Erinnerungen. Frankfurt am Main u.a. 1969, p. 32.

3. The "determination to act" and the conviction that determined acting will lead to success is an important aspect in genocidal projects (Dabag 1996, p. 187). In the very beginning of *Mein Kampf* Hitler wrote: "obstacles do not exist to be surrendered to, but only to be broken" (p. 18–19). All that matters is to be determined, in other words, to be willing to be successful; and in the end, the will will be victorious (p. 20–21).

In political speeches and works, "generation" is understood as a ation, which is primarily determined by a historical experience, that is through a *shared* historical experience. In the conception of such an identical — and identifiable — unity, Karl Mannheim saw a typical model inherent in German thinking: for the generation provides a special, quasi natural "storing ... in historical-social spaces" (Mannheim 1965, p. 36)[1]; thus a simultaneously biological, historical and social unity. The self-definition as a generation links together experience, values and identity, and elucidates from this: election and mission. The politically and socially acting generation does not follow any bureaucratic rules: its action norms are oriented towards action and example, as suggested by Max Weber for the charismatic rule. Its authority is based in terms of the charismatic rule context on the devotion to exemplary nature and heroic power.

In order to briefly consolidate this, let us look at the movement of the Young Turks. This so-called Turkish reform movement at the end of the Ottoman empire was responsible for the decision, the planning and the carrying out of the murder of the Armenians, who for centuries had lived in the Ottoman Empire as an integrated although despised and suffering community.[2]

The Armenians did not pose a danger to the Young Turks on account of their actual economic or educational standing in the Ottoman Empire.[3] The

---

1. Mannheim states that the question of generations gained a "specifically German" face among others from Dilthey (p. 26). While in the context of French discussions the biological limitations of generations and the intention of discovering a *general law* of the historical rhythm" take on a central role (p. 25), the French-positivist thinking category would be compared to a German "historical-romantic" one, in which no longer the "quantitatively measurable" but rather the "qualitatively experiencable" is addressed (p. 28f).

2. For a more detailed analysis further see Dabag 1996. On the Millet system, the specific societal system in the Ottoman Empire and its ordering of Muslims and non-Muslims, see: Bat Ye'or 1985.

3. It is not only a particular characteristic of the analyses on the Ottoman Empire which take into account the genocide of the Armenians or also the explicit analyses of the genocide that the history of the deportations is derived from the construction of a "neighborhood in conflict over centuries." Here it should at least be briefly emphasized that the theory of the traditional enemy neighbors (who would only need a little civil rationality in order to solve their conflict) always lends itself to the elucidation of specific escalations in the form of a pogrom or a massacre. For the analysis of war and genocide this dismissal of the extermination intentions and the denial of the essential ideological features should be judged critically.

danger the Turks faced was related to their present — their present in a phase of newly defining Turkish-national, modern Turkish identity. This identity of the absolute and the total was accompanied by a reconstruction of ancient Turkish elements and a racial definition of all that was Turkish.

The very name *İttihâd ve Terakki* (unity and progress) reflects the pretensions of this Turkish national movement. Its history can be traced from 1860 by means of the works of national reformers as well as the formation of political secret societies. Ultimately, with the so-called revolution of 1908, the movement changed the balance of power in the Ottoman empire decisively: the program of *İttihâd ve Terakki*, "unity and progress," refers to the most important political and social goals, with the particular aim of creating a strong, united country, which, through a national renewal, would also be able to gain a new position in the world.

German military and diplomats were contemporary witnesses of the euphoria which the Young Turks spread, and often allowed themselves to feel a certain amount of fascination for it. General Field Marshal Colmar von der Goltz,[1] for instance, spoke of "the work of the educated part of the Ottoman youth — especially the young officers," whose "moral rights" (Goltz 1913, p. 7) to political actions were realized where "centralization, sluggish bureaucracy and endless filling-in of forms have always prevailed" (Goltz 1913, p. 17). They could not believe that the "decomposition, decay, depravity" of Turkey could not be due solely to a specific decline of the military system, and considered that the "interesting thing from a popular psychological point of view is to search for these causes" (Goltz 1913, p. 7).

---

1. Wilhelm Leopold Colmar Freiherr von der Goltz (1843–1916), in military service from 1861, worked from 1878 to 1883 as a lecturer on military history in Berlin. In June 1883 he became military advisor of the Turkish Sultan and made a significant contribution to the reorganization and modernization of the Turkish army. In the First World War von der Goltz was for a short period initially General-Governor in the occupied Belgium. As early as 1914 he became advisor to the Turkish Sultan Mehmed V. and supreme commander of the Turkish 1. army in Mesopotamia. The circumstances of his death on the 29th April 1916 are unclear: according to official accounts he died of a typhus infection, but unofficial reports suggest that he was the victim of a poison attack.

Chief of General Staff Hans von Seeckt[1] characterized this breakdown even more clearly. In a 1918 essay on *Die Gründe des Zusammenbruchs der Türkei* [The reasons for the breakdown of Turkey], Seeckt, from 1917 acting Chief of Staff of the Ottoman army, determined that "the inner weaknesses [of Turkey] in their entirety, call for the history of culture and custom of the new Turkish empire to be written".[2] "Only a few moments of the destruction are still mentioned. The upper levels of society had become unwarlike; the main reason being the increasing mixing with foreign elements,"[3] explained Seeckt of a "long-standing unculture." He portrayed the Armenians and the Jews as being particularly responsible for this. In July 1918 he sent a telegraph to the General Staff in Berlin stating: "It is an impossible state of affairs to be allied with the Turks and to stand up for the Armenians. In my view any consideration, Christian, sentimental and political, should be eclipsed by a hard but clear necessity for war."[4]

In the literature, the Chief of Staff is popularly described as "monarchistically minded" (Angermeier 2001, p. 177). His concentration on state and the national future (Angermeier 2001, p. 177) are often outlined and surprise is expressed that the Prussian military could be interested in the tasks of the army in times of peace. For Hans von Seeckt, war was actually not the modern crossroads: it proves one's worth, but does not represent ultimate fulfillment.[5] Without wishing to glorify war, Seeckt sees it as a necessary element of society. For him, war is an institution that ensures stability and promised unity. The duties of the military are therefore not solely to lead a war, but rather to build or

---

1. Hans von Seeckt (1866–1936) entered Prussian Army Service as early as 1885. From 1899 with the Imperial General Staff, in 1913 Seeckt was made head of the General Staff of the II Army Corps in Berlin. During the First World War he led operations at the Eastern Front and in the Baltic States. In 1916 Seeckt became General Staff Commander of the Austrian-Hungarian army and in 1917 took over the General staff leadership of the field army in Turkey. From 1916 to 1926 Seeckt, who had led the military department of the German delegation in the peace negotiations in Versailles, functioned as head of the newly established "Troop office in the Imperial Defence ministry." In the Reichstag elections of 1930 Seeckt was a candidate for the Deutsche Volkspartei (DVP) and won a seat in parliament. Between 1933 and 1935 he frequently visited China and functioned there as military advisor to Marshal Chiang Kai-shek (1887-1975).
2. Hans von Seeckt, Die Gründe des Zusammenbruchs der Türkei, Herbst 1918 (vom 04.11.1918), BMA Freiburg N 247/50.
3. Seeckt, Die Gründe des Zusammenbruchs der Türkei.
4. Hans von Seeckt, note from 30.07.1918 (Konstantinopel), PA-AA/R 11054, 1918-A-32652.
5. For the way in which Seeckt differs from many contemporary interpretations cf. Brehl 2002.

educate a society. But Seeckt also sees the military's role in times of peace to bring about the "necessary adaptation of industry in times of peace to its tasks in times of war."[1] Therefore the initial seeming resistance to glorifying war is still accompanied by an identification of military and society and the definition of specific tasks: "We Germans cannot make run our politics like France, England, Italy, America, Russia can or have to run theirs, but rather we are forced to pursue German politics, forced by the land on which we live" (Seeckt 1933, p. 5), according to Hans von Seeckt. He attempts to make it clear here that the previous political frameworks were characterized by the "severe neglect of history and the requirements of the German land" (Seeckt 1933, p. 6). For Seeckt, future means: German unity as a renewal of state, as recovery, as an awakening of new vitality, as territorial unity, as power political centrality. Seeckt claimed that it was particularly necessary to steer away from the "foreign infiltration," from "foreign infiltration of German industry," as Germany should not become a "colonial area of international capital," and "an economic rule of foreigners" would give rise to "a gradual bleeding dry of the Volkskraft [national power]" (Seeckt 1929, p. 33).

Without looking in any greater detail here at how the figure of the foreigner who swamps and infiltrates society actually represents a central tenet of anti-Semitism, it should be briefly pointed out that in modern (particularly sociologically oriented) studies that see ethnic mélanges as the cause of long-lasting conflicts,[2] it is often forgotten that the violence-based, genocide-based exclusions of the 20th century were not the result of a specific modern principle or a dialectic of movement and counter-movement. Rather, they were the result of a national homogenization policy, they used a natural law of the rise and fall of nations and cultures to legitimize their actions. In maintaining the pattern of fundamental dynamics of inclusion-exclusion,[3] the specific representation principle of the concept of nation, which claims homogeneity as a prerequisite for governability and stability, is forgotten.

The decisive "historical" actions of the Young Turkish reformers, their readiness to radically reshape social structures, were at any rate treated with no lack of admiration by contemporary German observers and military. Particularly

---

1. Seeckt, Die Gründe des Zusammenbruchs der Türkei, p. 179.
2. "It is *inevitable* that he conflict in Bosnia-Herzegovina lasted the longest, because there is a mélange there that can hardly be solved" according to Richard Münch (2003, p. 271) [italics, MD].
3. Cf. the critique of thoughts of exclusion/inclusion in Platt 2003, in particular p. 18ff.

notable in the politics of the Young Turks, who from 1908 organized themsel\
terms of a double structure (movement and party), was the establishment of centralized professional associations and interest groups — and the closure of all
organizations that were not connected to the movement. From 1908 a dense
network of paramilitary subsidiary organizations had emerged, the so-called *Icrat-
i Hususiye*. The founding of occupational associations, youth organizations or
women's groups, attempted not only to create a strong, strictly organized foundation, but also tried to prepare the emergence of a new, modern social differentiation: the emergence of a Turkish working class, the restructuring of Turkish
public employment and civil service. But above all the aim was to integrate as large
a population as possible into the atmosphere of national rebirth: in the "new life,"
yeni hayat, declared by Turkism. In this regard, the organizations for intellectuals,
among them the organizations *Türk Derneği*, the *Türk Ocağı* ("Turkish Hearth"), the
literary circles and their periodicals, such as *Genç Kalemler* ("Young Feathers") or
Türk Yurdu ("Turkish homeland"), took on an important function.

The most important goal of the Young Turks was the idea of a homogenous
state reborn out of the return to ancient Turkish roots. However, the unity of all
Turks, that greatly implored *tevhîd-i etrâk*, was still to be achieved. For not only
was an "alienization" by Jews, Greeks and Armenians still in effect, as well as old
elite groups, particularly the military,[1] but also Islamite positions which
opposed the Turkish nationalization at least until the end of 1912.

The self-definition of being a *decisive* actor at a particular point in history
was conjured up in the aforementioned publications, particularly Young Turkish
newspapers and periodicals. However, autobiographical and biographical works
played a particular role in the creation of an ideological foundation: as early as
1908 a commission was set up by the party to promote and control the formation
of these biographies of the movement and individuals.[2] The political biography
is not solely an attestation of the individual creations of one person. Rather, it

---

1. Finally a group of officers had formed under the description of "Rescuing officers,"
   Halâskâr Zâbitân, in order in 1911/12 to force the adherence to the constitution, a reform of
   government as well as free elections. The opposition attempt failed not least to the
   problem of the war in the Balkans. When on 23rd January 1913 the government showed
   its readiness to leave Edirne to the Bulgarians, a Young Turkish unit, under the leadership of Enver stormed the Hohe Pforte and killed the Defence Minister. With this coup
   of January 1913 the Young Turks again placed themselves at the top of the government.
2. Consulate report Saloniki 13th November 1908 to Alois Freiherr Lexa von Aehrental,
   Wien. Haus-, Hof- und Staatsarchiv PA XXXVIII 410, here cited according to Ohandjanian, ed. 1995, p. 3245.

has a particular function as representative evidence for the emerging generation. The biography places the individual in the course of history, it locates him in relation to tradition and culture, places him in a Volksgemeinschaft [people's community]. In view of the numerous impressive biographical examples of Young Turkish authors, it seems safe to conclude that the Young Turks had shown foresight in recognizing the significance of the biography of the political actor as an element of formation.[1]

The biographical notes and fragments of the Young Turkish leaders — Talat, Enver und Djemal Pascha — share a common feature: they describe disappointments and moments of failure, biographical goals through which one was deceived; but in striving for these goals, clarity had been achieved, that insight of having to take the future into one's own hands. The construction of initiation situations is given particular importance. With regard to an episode from his time training at a military school, Enver Pascha wrote: "Tears welled up in my eyes and I repeated my constant prayer: My God protect the Turkish people and ensure that I too serve my fatherland."[2] A comparable structure can also be found in Hitler's *Mein Kampf*. Hitler too constructs a moment of initiation. At the end of the First World War, temporarily blinded by a gas injury, Hitler reflects on the situation of the German Reich as well as his own personal biography: "I knew that all was lost. Only fools, liars, and criminals could hope in the mercy of the enemy....In the days that followed, my own fate became known to me. I could not help but laugh at the thought of my own future..." (p. 206). But this situation, where the crisis of the nation coincides with the crisis of the individual, is depicted by Hitler as a moment of insight, an instant of decision-making and resolve: "At last it became clear to me that what had happened was what I had so often feared but had never been able to believe with my emotions....There is no making pacts with Jews; there can only be the hard: either - or. I, for my part, decided to go into politics"[3] (p. 206). The political biography makes political actions visible and understandable, both on an individual and on a representative level.

---

1. It is particularly interesting that the model of the national hero construed in the biographies is carried further in the reflection through the German Oriental literature: thus the figure of the Turk as a hero of conscience, who struggles for his national identity, is encountered in numerous popular literary works, see for example: Marquardsen-Kamphövener 1916.
2. From the German version of the autobiographical fragments of Enver Pascha in: Hanioglu ed., p. 273. See as a further example, also in German: Enver Pascha 1918.
3. In the German edition of *Mein Kampf* the final sentence of this passage reads »Ich aber beschloß, Politiker zu werden.« ("But I decided to become a politician.")

"Thank the Lord, Germanic democracy means just this: that any old climber or moral slacker cannot rise by devious paths to govern his national comrades, but that, by the very greatness of the responsibility to be assumed, incompetents and weaklings are frightened off. But if, nevertheless, one of these scoundrels should attempt to sneak in, we can find him more easily, and mercilessly challenge him: Out, cowardly scoundrel! Remove your foot, you are besmirching the steps; the steps front of the Pantheon of history are not for sneak-thieves, but for heroes!," wrote Hitler in *Mein Kampf* (p. 91) with regard to the specific constitution of a new national hero, who although actively serving the community, did not enter into the "Pantheon of history" as an individual. Parallels can also be drawn here to the work of Ziya Gökalp. As a sociologist and programmatic thinker of the Young Turks, Gökalp gave this generation, whose members saw themselves neither as revolutionaries nor as reformists, but rather as renewers and creators, a theoretical foundation. He wrote: "When a nation is in danger, it cannot be saved by one individual. Only the nation itself can be its own savior" (Gökalp 1913, Berkes ed., 1959, p.68).

With the self-declaration as a generation, a perception of society was drawn up in which social stratifications no longer play a role, in which the sharing of experience and duties are the only things that count (Dabag 2000). An important argument in this context, to define a "young generation" as political actors, is presented by the possibility of relating this to generational knowledge and generational discourse.

Generational Knowledge and Generational Discourse

The formation of a unified, total, modern society as outlined in the political aims and objectives of the Young Turkish or the National Socialist movement, was masterminded not only by the generations of the movement itself, but also has more general contexts. It is found in generally accepted considerations of history and society. In writings, links to Plato's "emotional society" are constructed: "communion in pleasure and pain bind the city together..." (Plato 1940, V. 462, p. 152). References are also found to Hegel's thoughts on alienation: "But civil society tears the individual from his family ties, estranges the members of the family from one another, and recognizes them as self-subsistent persons. Further, for the paternal soil and the external inorganic resources of nature from which the individual formerly derived his livelihood, it substitutes its own soil and subjects the permanent existence of even the entire family to dependence on itself and contingency" (Hegel 1952, p. 76).

In the construction of a generation of the same experiences and a restricted knowledge, such references are explicitly defined: they play a central role in declaring the patterns of action and behavior as proven, but they also serve to verify the knowledge not by way of theories, but through personal references — the construction of "fathers" of the movement. For the Turkish national movement, important references for developing a series of quotations were presented by the likes of Plato or Herder, who had played an important role in the literature on the philosophy of history at the turn of the century in Germany. In addition, the works of the first generations of national "awakening"[1], above all, by Friedrich List, Albert Sorel, Gabriel de Tarde, Charles Seignobos und Lucien Levy-Bruhl, provided a strong focus (Akçura 1912). The production of such reference points is interesting in that the immediate concern is not with the construction of knowledge, but rather with attestations, delegation situations are developed, the references become "testaments."

In this vein in 1922, following his return from Malta,[2] Ziya Gökalp wrote some autobiographical fragments, entitled *Felsefi Vasiyetler*, "Philosophical testaments," in which he constituted three different delegations: an initial election by his father (Babamin Vasiyeti), an election by a philosophical teacher (Hocamin Vasiyeti,) and a third by a political master (Pîrimin Vasiyeti; [*pir*, Eng: sage]).[3] Gökalp's path is determined by a handing over. "One evening, when I came home

1. On the characterization of the first influential reformers Ahmed Cevdet Paşa (1822-1884), Ahmed Vefik Pasa (1823-1891), Ibrahim Sinasi (1828-1871), see: Dabag, Jungtürkische Visionen, p. 164ff.

2. Directly after the armistice agreement of the 30th October 1918, efforts had begun on the part of the Allies for a prosecution of those responsible for the genocide. However, the British government began to increasingly doubt that a proper prosecution would be carried out by the Ottoman authorities and demanded the extradition of those chiefly responsible, in order to put them before and set up court of justice. Approximately 140 Young Turkish functionaries were taken to Malta where they were to await their trial. The plan to examine the genocide of the Armenians before a court of law was, however, never realized; the perpetrators imprisoned on Malta were — after the Turkish government had assured that sentence would be passed on them in Turkey — passed back to the Turkish authorities on 30th October 1921. The expected sentencing failed to materialize. On the 31st March 1923 a general amnesty was finally passed in Turkey.

3. The testimonies were published: Babamin Vasiyeti, in: Küçük Mecmua No 17, 1338 (1922/23); Hocamin Vasiyeti, in: Küçük Mecmua Nr. 18, 1338 (1922/23); Pîrimin Vasiyeti, in: Küçük Mecmua No 19, 1338 (1922/23).

from school, I found him [the father, M.D.] very sad and depressed. ... 'I have to tell you some very sad news ... that our most important teacher and the greatest man of our nation, Namik Kemal, is dead!' I had grown up with the words of Namik Kemal, particularly with his unpublished and banned works, but I had not known that he was a great teacher and a great man. In a sad voice my father told me the story of his battles, about his ideals, the injustices from which he had suffered, the heroic resistance that he had shown, and finally he said. 'And now you will follow this man. You will become a patriot like he was, and a defender of freedom.' ... From this moment on the love of freedom was awoken in my thoughts ... In me the ideals of freedom, fatherland, nation came alive. My soul was suddenly moved by a spirit ready to act.... My father had not been able to realize his plans. But his words remained in clear letters buried in my soul as a holy testament" (Gökalp 1922/23a).

The construction of delegation — father, philosophical teacher, political teacher — with which an individual's own political position is explicitly anchored in a generational transmission process, creates a second line of continuity which stands for the "true and essential nature" of a political order. It remains effective in spite of the alienation and must now be once again turned into reality. The concern is with a continuity that finds its expression in the fathers, the family, the culture. However, the realization (and therefore these delegatory settings cannot be read solely as the expression of patriarchal relationships, and not merely as the expression of authoritarian relationships) requires a break with all that which currently exists. It demands an action carried out outside of the continuity of the present. Furthermore, the reality that is handed down is not "tradition" or a specific morality of a tradition; it is the "ideals" *mefkûre* that are handed down and need to be realized. The ideals can be distinguished from moral values as they do not describe "external" values, but rather "internal" ones, where emotions and knowledge coincide (Gökalp 1923, p. 33–34, Gökalp 1968, p. 29). "The ideals are the teachers of the present, the creators of the future, the reality of the past" (Gökalp 1913, Gökalp 1918, p. 68, Berkes ed. 1959, p. 70), according to Gökalp, whose works can be characterized as didactic essays: published in the broad organs of the Young Turks, the essays are always devoted to a specific theme — nation and patriotism, nationalism and Islamism, ideals and morals, teaching, language — whose derivations he justifies for example with Fichte or Tarde. For instance in the essay *Mefkûre*, "ideal," he addresses the question of the first phase of the "shaping" and the second phase of the "growing" of a seed, a national character of a people. The ideal is therefore

sacred thinking of a nation. It is born in times of crisis, just as the Ger-
l emerged in light of the Napoleonic conquest. In this context it is the
ideal that binds the nation and the individual within its national personality. It
is also the connecting link between passing down and civilization, between
knowledge and the "heart" of the individual. The question of the ideal, i.e. the
emergence of a national consciousness of the ideals, is a question of determining
identity. The determination of identity and ideal is, according to Gökalp, the
central "historical mission" of a nation.

"The basic attitude from which such activity arises, we call — to distinguish it from egoism and selfishness — idealism. By this we understand only the
individual's capacity to make sacrifices for the community, for his fellow man.,"
and "The purest idealism is unconsciously equivalent to the deepest knowledge,"
according to Hitler in *Mein Kampf* (pp. 298–299). In his political construct of biography he develops similar sequences of the awakening of ideals: first there is the
teacher, personal experiences of crisis, and war.

No shared discourse can be construed from the apparent parallels in the
ideological frameworks of the Young Turks and National Socialists.[1] Importantly, though, similar *mechanisms* can be identified, namely the attempt at a legit-
imatizing construction of a national plan of creation through the (apparent) link
to existing knowledge discourse. Thus, the picture of an ideal community of the
familiar, the historical, social and biological common bond was a central component of world views at the beginning of the 20th century. The basis for picking
this out as a central theme was certainly not found solely in cultural anthropology, historicism, and social Darwinism.

When analyzing the formation of this broad layer of perpetrators in an act
of genocide it is interesting to note that the self-declaration, to represent a new
generation of uniformity — which in its uniformity will overcome its alienation
— also contains a shared *task*. To carry out this task allows — indeed demands
— a natural morality. As early as 1885, in his *Foundations of Sociology*, Ludwig
Gumplowicz had established a natural morality of generations. This work, as
Franz Oppenheimer stressed in 1926, emphasizes the importance of the collective, in contrast to which the primacy of the individual and the ideas, "above
all those, result in morality and rights" (Oppenheimer 1926, p. xvii), are a priori
negated. Gumplowicz therefore represents the broad search for the natural

---

1. The contemporary correspondences between Young Turks, National Liberalists and
   Popular Nationalists in Germany have as yet been very insufficiently researched.

aspect of forging communities and forming states. The narrower group of social Darwinistic authors, in comparison, seem to understand this too narrowly: "for man is also subject to the laws of nature.... This omnipotence of nature and the processes that it drives forward impress its spirit deeply in him, he can hardly imagine any other means of existence. And this means seems to him to be right and just, as the rational and the moral one.... What is natural appears to him for that very reason to be rational and moral — and unnatural is a synonym for all that is irrational and unmoral. Thus the forces of nature have educated the ethical feeling of man, the norms of nature — also in social life — have changed and condensed themselves in his soul into a moral idea. By nature, the older and the old take over the leadership of the coming generation — and the honor and respect that they are given by the younger generation reflects our idea of morality. That which has come into being through nature, that which is in accordance with nature, that is moral. And therein, in that which has become natural, in that which is in accordance with nature, lies the eternal, definite and unalterable foundation of all ethics and morality..." (Gumplowicz 1926, p. 202).

The anthropologization of ethics and morality, which was seen so widely at the turn to the 20th century, is accompanied in the nationalist literature by a historicization: historical developments of this morality are outlined. For example, in addition to the historical context, Alfred Rosenberg outlines the second extension of the identification of national and social being: the construction of a call to act from this very election to be moral. "The moral side of man is therefore based on the fact that man knows to let a categorical moral law rule in him, and also feels the possibility in him to obey this law. Otherwise all moral laws would be laughable and Christ and Kant would have to have been pretty stupid people. "Should" and "could" presuppose each other: without freedom there is no feeling of responsibility, no morality, no spiritual culture," according to Rosenberg in *Mythus des 20. Jahrhunderts* (Rosenberg 1934, p. 326).

To briefly round off these arguments I would like to suggest that an important structure of argument of the totalitarian movements was that they declared their goals not to be new, but as proven, as clearly confirmed by historical and social experience, by science and knowledge. What is "new," however, is their demand for realization and the construction of a decisive moment. It is much more the state of being backed into a situation where there is no other alternative, where actions are absolutely necessary. It rests with the generation of the present, according to the self-explanation, to achieve a historical change, which is necessary if not even overdue. The focus for this generation is on a fundamentally new future, the concern, according to the ideological aims and objectives, is with the future as a whole. The aims and objectives achieve a confinement in which for the survival of the nation, for the strengthening of national identity, there is no alternative other than the extermination of this internal foreign body.

The Importance of the Construction of Generations for the Legitimization of Genocide

According to the theologian and historian Adolf v. Harnack in a lecture in 1917, "It is however the last purpose of historical work, namely *intervening in the course of development*, more precisely: confronting it. Intervening in history — this means repelling the *past*, where it is reaching into the present and restraining it, it means in addition: doing the right thing in the *present*, and finally it means — preparing the *future* prudently" (Harnack 1917, p. 8). In order to conceive of a genocide, in order bestow upon secret organizations and functional units the task of carrying it out, in order to be certain of a broad consensus in the population, an explanation based on traditional prejudices and racism did not suffice. The perpetrators of a genocide, who over a lengthy period of time, daily, for months on end, systematically and pitilessly murder, have a clear goal, an unambiguous task — and they perceive themselves in a positive light.

A central tenet of this self-perception is the model of being the chosen one: to achieve a task that others cannot manage; a task that is carried out for others, which follows a greater good. The individual perpetrator sees himself as part of a broader community that shows solidarity in its will and its readiness for the act. The model of a generation of "chosen ones," which due to its decisiveness and determination is in the sole position of being able to fulfill this task, also introduces the factor of time[1] — indeed it leads to a radical tightening of the temporal scope to the lifespan of one generation. Thus, for example, in October 1937, in an *Address in front of propaganda leaders*, Hitler explained that he himself did not have much longer to live and that it was therefore necessary to "solve the problems that need to be solved (Lebensraum! [living space]) as soon as possible so that this is achieved in one's own lifetime. Later generations would no longer be able to achieve this." (Domarus 1973, p. 745). The conviction of the necessity of solving the tasks within one's own lifetime — and with it in the lifetime of one's own, decisive generation — which becomes apparent here is found repeatedly in Hitler's

---

1. See for this aspect also Schmidt 2002, p. 57.

writings and speeches. In a secret speech held during a meeting in the Imperial Chancellery on 5th November 1937 (Hoßbach 1937), which Hitler wanted to be understood as his "testamentary legacy in the case of his demise" (Hoßbach 1937, p. 749), he determined the years 1943/45 to be the latest possible time for action, as time was pressing. He ascribes this urgency in particular to the fact that "the movement and its leaders are getting older" (Hoßbach 1937, p. 752).

There are numerous examples that show that this pattern of argument is not found solely in the discourse of the National Socialists. For instance, Otto Hofmann, Group Leader and General Lieutenant of the Waffen-SS and Head of the Race and Settlement Main Office pointed out in his concluding remarks to the conference of SS leaders in the area of race and settlement in September 1942: "But I believe that large tasks are still awaiting us in the areas lying further to the east. We must achieve this in the 20 years that we still have to live. For I doubt very strongly whether the generation that follows us would approach these tasks with the same determination and relentlessness." This construction was described by Hans Blumenberg as an attempt to speed up the future and with this to unite lifetime and world time in the realization of a delusional plan (Blumenberg 1986, p. 80).

The argument of being a "chosen one" even allows for the fact that the specific moral standards according to which one acts will later be condemned, and also: that the individual himself will be condemned. But the task in hand demands this specific "difficult act," according to many self-portrayals. For the task is a historical one, the goal is about the future, and these two things cannot be measured using normal standards. The Turkish writer and feminist Hâlide Edib Adivar, herself a prominent representative of Turanism, reported in her memoirs of an encounter with Talat Paşa, one of the main planners of the genocide of the Armenians. "I saw Talat very rarely following the deportations. I remember one day well, when he … said in an unyielding tone of voice, 'You see, Halidé Hanum. I have a heart just as good as yours, and at night I am kept awake thinking of the human suffering. But that is a personal matter, and I am here on Earth to think of my people, and not about my own sensitivities…. I am convinced that a nation, as long as it does its best for its own interests and is successful, will be admired by the world and judged as moral. I am ready to die for that which I have done, and know that I will die for it'" (Adivar 1926, p. 387).

Perhaps this aspect of generational "election" takes on a particularly central role if one tries to formulate explanations for actions of the lawyers and police officers in the *Einsatzgruppen* [Mobile Killing Units] of the National

...ialists, the special commandos and special task forces. It is interesting in this regard to look at how legitimizations of actions were outlined. For instance, a statement by the Protestant priest and former Superintendent Paul Blobel, cruel leader of an *Einsatzgruppe* in the area of Kiev, reads as follows: "I have to say that our men who took part in it were more at the end of their tether than those who were shot to death there" (Grabitz 1986, p. 29).

One of the central aspects of *why* a whole society is successfully integrated into a genocide is that the idea of an extermination comes to be considered as conceivable, that it appears to be not only necessary, but also possible. In this vein, terms and concepts are introduced with which people are able to communicate about this extermination, models are presented within which the extermination becomes conceivable. Perhaps most significantly, it becomes possible to interpret one's own actions as moral.

Such a model, which focuses on the readiness to act in genocide through motives such as election and higher morals, is represented by that of the historically decisive generation. The individual perpetrator, who declares himself to be the carrier of a generational duty, does not have to answer to the norms of a higher moral code or of a later justice. His responsibility is the heroic act, the sacrifice for the generation.

To quote once again from *Mein Kampf*: "First of all, it was not permissible to take this [Jewish, M.D.] question frivolously; it had to be understood that the fortune or misfortune of generations would depend on its solution; yes, that it could, if not had to be, decisive for the entire future of our people. Such a realization, however, obligated us to ruthless measures and surgical operations. What we needed most was the conviction that first of all the whole attention of the nation had to be concentrated upon this terrible danger, so that every single individual could become inwardly conscious of the importance of this struggle. Truly incisive and sometimes almost unbearable obligations and burdens can only be made generally effective if, in addition to compulsion, the realization of necessity is transmitted to the individual" (p. 249). The forming of a generation of chosen ones serves to form a level of actors, which not only symbolizes a new chapter in history but also deliberately opens it. In order for this acting and actively decisive generation to be able to bring about such a break, in order for it to begin its history anew, it removes itself in its ideological aims and objectives from the continuity of history — and this also implies: it is removed from historical responsibility! The self-declarations create a freedom that should be mea-

132

sured not according to the standards of the present, but rather only in terms of the future results.

Construction of "Second" Generation

Finally, in the framework of legitimization ideologies outlined here and the aspect of explanation of a historically decisive generation, let me add a few thoughts on what happens *afterwards*. An important task for genocide research is to extend its research questions beyond the historical end of the direct killings. This requires a consideration of survivors, questions of trauma, memory and transmission. The focus is on analyzing consequences and changes for the perpetrator societies.

However, here one is faced with the challenge having to seek continuities in the self-definition of a generation at the very point where the subsequently constructed society was striving to ensure an absolute break, a radical new beginning, a new start. A generation that understood itself as a "betrayed generation" and speaks of the abuse of its goals and dreams. For once again, a generation is set up that acts as a social and political actor to mark the beginning of a new history. And the absoluteness of this beginning again places the generation outside of historical continuity.

It is therefore interesting in this regard to consider to what extent the generations following 1945 represent aspects of a continuation in their very arguments for a new beginning. For this new beginning was very deliberately characterized as a revision of the past through the self-description of a new generation. It was possible to emphasize with this self-definition that the revision applied to *all* valid political and social perspectives.

Thus, once more a generation became the actor in an historical hour, once again it stands detached from the torments of the past, rigidly orientated towards the future. Once again a generation claims to be the product — and also the victim — of historical circumstances. This provokes the question of whether this generation, which is aiming to make a completely fresh start in a homogenized society, is not fulfilling the very goal of the fathers' generation. Is this new beginning not the very result of the actions of the father's generation, who saw their task as fundamentally changing the basic conditions of society? Something which, incidentally, not only the National Socialists and the Young Turks, but also all perpetrators of genocide right up to the present day have succeeded in doing?

Thus, it is to be considered whether the science of history, which looks today at the concept of generation and examines "generation-forming political key events" (Fogt 1982, p. 4), perhaps overlooks mechanisms involved in the construction of a generation and accepts its powerful self-explanations without discussion. For even if the thinking in terms of a "zero hour" prevented the continuation of historical identity, it still did not allow an absolute break with regard to historical experience.

Thus, in the literature portraying the military, political and intellectual leadership histories at the beginning of the 20th century, the term "undecided generation" (Stolberg-Wernigerode 1968) is also found. However, generations at the turn to the 20th century actually appear to have decided upon a specific German, national path at the very point where they defined themselves as a political generation.

Conclusion

Genocide is particularly provoking as a violent crime because it is not the soldier armed with long-range weapons who does the killing, and it is not the dehumanized psychopath removed from any social ties. Rather we are confronted with the forming of a perpetrator society: i.e. a society in which the genocide is set as a high, central task; in which extremely broad system of acts of cooperation emerges; in which the individual consciously assumes a responsibility and acts upon it.

The task of the murder is integrated in a consensually shared hierarchy of values. A central role here is given not only to the ideological aims and objectives of the party, but there are also ideological models at work, discourse on the connection to particular perceptions of history. The goal of these models is to make murder appear to be a normal constituent of everyday life. For genocide cannot be implemented merely by setting up special troops — it only becomes possible when a consensus is successfully achieved with regard to the extermination. When the members of such special troops come from all levels of society. The planning of a genocide is not merely represented by decrees and laws. However, the systematic nature of its implementation becomes clear, for instance, when a German-Russian phrasebook provides a translation for the question, "where is the gasification?" (Ledebur, ed. 1941).

I have outlined here the construct of the generation with regard to the question of how genocide is made possible as a means of accelerating an assumed process of history or to realize an expected history. The main focus in this context was on the self-description as a generation and its function as an element of formation. In the aims and objectives of the Young Turks and the National Socialists, a political generation was understood in a political-social action context in which the decision to undergo a mutual action was justified by an agreement of identity and of a shared history. Perhaps this mutuality, which emerges by means of the self-description as a generation, should be recognized as a field of discourse. It appears to be of particular importance that with the idea of "generation," a genealogical concept is brought into politics.

This finally leads me to present-day Turkey. From the generation of the "chosen ones," a political elite has emerged in Turkey, which from 1920 has controlled the fates of Turkey and never waned in its endeavors to homogenize the Turkish state. What should the approach be to a "second generation" in a society that constructs monuments to the perpetrators? A society that was not even prepared to confront the genocide of the Armenians through its model of a "generation of breaking with the past." What goal, what purpose, therefore, can institutionalizations of a national model legitimizing genocide have if not this: to include the possibility of violence in the future; to hold on to traditional creative visions and to preserve genocide as a possible course of action.

The questions which result from the observations outlined here therefore highlight that analyses of genocide research always have to be taken beyond the factual processes of events. Research on structures and processes of genocide needs to discuss the foundations of knowledge of modern societies. In so doing it needs to place a particular emphasis on the political models in which common bond and unity, stability and ability to work, modernity and identity are conceived.

(Translated into English by Sarah Mannion, MA (Cantab))

REFERENCES

Adivar, Halidé Edip. 1926. *Memoirs of Halidé Edip*. New York, NY: Century / London: James Murray.

Akçura, Yusuf. 1912. *Üç Tarzi Siyaset*. Istanbul: Matbaa-i Kader 1327 (1912) (first published in 1904 in the Numbers 24–34 of the periodical *Türk*).

Angermeier, Heinz. 2001. Deutschland als politisches Rätsel. Gegenwartsanalysen und Zukunftsperspektiven repräsentativer Zeitgenossen des 20. Jahrhunderts. Würzburg: Königshausen und Neumann.

Bartov, Omer. 2000. *Mirrors of Destruction: War, Genocide and Modern Identity*, Oxford: Oxford University Press.

Bat Ye'or. 1985. *The Dhimmi. Jews and Christians under Islam*. London, Toronto: Associated University Presses (first printed in french: Paris 1980).

Berkes, Niyazi, ed. 1959. *Turkish Nationalism and Western Civilization. Selected Essays of Ziya Gökalp*. London: Allen & Unwin.

Brehl, Medardus. 2002. "Krieg der Codes". In *Reden von Gewalt*, ed. by Kristin Platt. Munich: Wilhelm Fink, pp. 196–226.

Dabag, Mihran. 1996. "Katastrophe und Identität." In *Erlebnis-Gedächtnis-Sinn. Authentische und konstruierte Erinnerung*, ed. by Hanno Loewy and Bernhard Moltmann. Frankfurt am Main/New York, NY: Campus, pp. 177–235.

_____. 1998. "Jungtürkische Visionen und der Völkermord an den Armeniern". In *Genozid und Moderne. Strukturen kollektiver Gewalt im 20. Jahrhundert*, ed. by Mihran Dabag and Kristin Platt, Opladen: Leske+Budrich, pp. 152–206.

_____. 2000. "Genozid und weltbürgerliche Absicht. Perspektiven". In: *Weltbürgertum und Globalisierung*, ed. by Norbert Bolz et al. Munich: Wilhelm Fink, p. 43–70.

_____. 2002. "The Realm of Perspectives: Some Reflections on An Interdisciplinary Approach to Genocide Studies". *International Journal of Contemporary Sociology* 39, 2: 177–197.

_____ and Platt, Kristin, eds. 1998. *Genozid und Moderne. Strukturen kollektiver Gewalt im 20. Jahrhundert*. Opladen: Leske+Budrich.

Dilthey, Wilhelm 1875. "Über das Studium der Geschichte der Wissenschaften vom Menschen, der Gesellschaft und dem Staat" (1875). In: Dilthey, Wilhelm, *Gesammelte Schriften* Vol. 5, Stuttgart: Teubner 1982, pp. 36–41.

Domarus, Max. 1973. Hitler. Reden und Proklamationen 1932-1945. Kommentiert von einem deutschen Zeitgenossen, I, 2: 1932–1938. Wiesbaden: Löwit.

Eghigian, Greg and Berg, Matthew Paul, eds. 2002. *Sacrifice and Nationale Belonging in Twentieth-Century Germany*, Arlington, TX: Texas A&M University Press.

Enver Pascha. 1918. *Um Tripolis*. München: Bruckmann.

Fogt, Helmut. 1982. *Politische Generationen. Empirische Bedeutung und theoretisches Modell.* Opladen: Westdeutscher Verlag.

Freud, Sigmund. 1950. *Totem and Taboo. Some Points of Agreement between the Mental Lives of Savages and Neurotics* [1912/13]. Authorized Translation by James Strachey, New York NY: Norton & Company.

Funck, Marcus. 2002. "The Meaning of Dying: East Elbian Noble Families as 'Warrior-Tribes' in the 19th and 20th centuries." In: *Sacrifice and Nationale Belonging in Twentieth-Century Germany,* ed. by Greg Eghigian and Matthew Paul Berg. Arlington, TX: Texas A&M University Press, pp. 26–63.

Goebbels, Joseph. 1934. *Kampf um Berlin. Der Anfang.* Munich: Eher (first published 1932).

Gökalp, Ziya. 1913. Mefkûre, in: *Türk Yurdu,* Jg. 5, Istanbul (1913), H. 32;

_____. 1922/23a. "Babamin Vasiyeti". *Küçük Mecmua* No 17, 1338 (1922/23).

_____. 1922/23b. "Hocamin Vasiyeti". *Küçük Mecmua* Nr. 18, 1338 (1922/23).

_____. 1922/23c. "Pîrimin Vasiyeti". *Küçük Mecmua* No 19, 1338 (1922/23).

_____. 1923. *Türkçülügün Esaslari* [1923]. Istanbul: Türk Kültür Yayini 1978.

_____. 1968. *The Principles of Turkism,* translated and edited by Robert Devereux. Leiden: Brill.

_____. 1976. Türklesmek, Islâmlasmak, Çagdaslasmak ve Dogru Yol, Istanbul: Inkilâp ve Aka.

_____. 1996. *Türklesmek, Islâmlasmak, Muasirlasmak.* Istanbul: Kamer Yayinlari [first printed 1918 in Ottoman script].

Goltz, Colmar Freiherr v.d. 1913. *Der Jungen Türkei Niederlage und die Möglichkeit ihrer Wiedererhebung.* Berlin: Paetel.

Grabitz, Helge. 1986. *NS-Prozesse. Psychogramme der Beteiligten.* Heidelberg: Müller (first 1985).

Graf zu Stolberg-Wernigerode. 1968. *Die unentschiedene Generation. Deutschlands konservative Führungsschichten am Vorabend des Ersten Weltkriegs.* München/Wien: Oldenbourg.

Gumplowicz, Ludwig. 1926. *Grundriß der Soziologie.* Innsbruck: Wagner (first published 1885).

Hanioglu, M. Sükrü, ed. 1989. *Kendi Mektuplarinda Enver Pasa.* Istanbul: Der Yayinlari.

Harnack, Adolf v. 1917. *Über die Sicherheit und die Grenzen geschichtlicher Erkenntnis* (lecture given in committee meeting of the German Museum on the 6th February 1917 in Munich). Munich: Oldenbourg.

Hegel, Georg Wilhelm Friedrich. 1952. *Philosophy of Right / Philosophy of History,* ed. by Robert Maynard Hutchins. Chicago, IL/London/Toronto/Geneva: William Benton.

Herbert, Ulrich. 1996. *Best. Biographische Studien über Radikalismus, Weltanschauung und Vernunft 1903-1989.* Bonn: Dietz.

Hilberg, Raul. 1961. *The Destruction of European Jews.* Chicago, IL: Quadrangle Books.

_____. 1992. Perpetrators, Victims, Bystanders. The Jewish Catastrophe 1933–1945, New York, NY: HarperCollins.

Hitler, Adolf. 1999. *Mein Kampf* [1925/27]. Translated by Ralph Manheim. Boston, MA/ New York NY: Houghton Mifflin.

Hoßbach, Friedrich. 1937. "Niederschrift über die Besprechung in der Reichskanzlei am 5. November 1937" [Hoßbach-Protokoll]. In: Domarus 1973, pp. 748-756.

Jarausch, Konrad R. and Michael Geyer. 2003. *Shattered Past: Reconstruction German Histories.* Princeton/Oxford: Princeton University Press.

Ledebur, Ferdinand Frhr. v., ed. 1941. *Wehrmacht-Sprachführer Deutsch-Russisch*, Berlin: Junker und Dünnhaupt.

Mannheim, Karl. 1965. Das Problem der Generation [1928/29], in: *Jugend in der modernen Gesellschaft*, ed. by Ludwig von Friedeburg. Berlin: Kiepenheuer & Witsch, p. 23-48.

Mariás, Julián. 1970. *Generations. A Historical Method.* Tuscaloosa, AL: Univ. of Alabama Press 1970 (first: spanish 1967).

Marquardsen-Kamphövener, Else. 1916. *Der Smaragd des Scheichs. Erzählung aus dem Erwachen der Türkei.* Munich: G. Müller.

Mentré, François. 1920. *Les générations sociales*, Paris: Bossard.

Münch, Richard. 1998. *Globale Dynamik, lokale Lebenswelten. Der schwierige Weg in die Weltgesellschaft.* Frankfurt am Main: Suhrkamp.

Ohandjanian, Artem, ed., 1995. *Österreich-Armenien 1872-1936. Faksimilesammlung diplomatischer Aktenstücke* (photocopies). Vienna: Ohandjanian 1995, here: Volume 4: 1897–1909, p. 3245.

Oppenheimer, Franz. 1926. "Zur Einführung". In Ludwig Gumplowicz, *Grundriß der Soziologie.* Innsbruck: Wagner (first published 1885), p. vii-xxiv.

Ortega y Gasset, José. 1933. "Im Geiste Galileis" (1933). In Ortega y Gasset, José: *Gesammelte Werke*, 6 Vols., Stuttgart: DVA 1996 (first published 1978). Vol. 3, S. 386-567.

_____. 1937. "Das Generationsproblem". In Ortega y Gasset, José: *Das Wesen geschichtlicher Krisen* [1937], Stuttgart: DVA 1943, p. 11-36.

Petersen, Julius. 1930. *Die literarischen Generationen*, Berlin: Junker und Dünnhaupt.

Peukert, Detlev J. K. 1987. *Die Weimarer Republik. Krisenjahre der klassischen Moderne.* Frankfurt am Main: Suhrkamp.

Pinder, Wilhelm. 1928. *Das Problem der Generation in der Kunstgeschichte Europas* [1928], Köln: Seemann 1949 (first Leipzig 1928).

Plato. 1940. *The Republic of Plato.* Translated and with an Introduction by A. D. Lindsay. New York, NY: E. P. Dutton.

Platt, Kristin. 2003. "Unter dem Zeichen des Skorpions". In *Feindschaft*, ed. by Medardus Brehl and Kristin Platt. Munich, p. 13-52.

_____. ed. 2002. *Reden von Gewalt.* Munich: Wilhelm Fink.

Riesman, David. 1952. *The Lonely Crowd. A Study of the Changing American Character*. New Haven, CT: Yale University Press.

Rosenberg, Alfred. 1934. *Mythus des 20. Jahrhunderts. Eine Wertung der seelisch-geistigen Gestaltenkämpfe unserer Zeit*. Munich: Hoheneichen-Verlag (first published 1930).

Schulz, Andreas and Gundula Grebner. 2003. "Generation und Geschichte. Zur Renaissance eines umstrittenen Forschungskonzepts". In *Generationswechsel und historischer Wandel* (=Historische Zeitschrift, Beiheft 36), ed. by Andreas Schulz und Gundukla Grebner, München: Oldenbourg 2003, pp. 1–23.

Seeckt, Hans von. 1929. *Die Zukunft des Reiches. Urteile und Forderungen*. Berlin: Verlag für Kulturpolitik.

_____. 1933. *Deutschland zwischen West und Ost*. Hamburg: Hanseatische Verlags-Anstalt.

Schmidt, Rainer F. 2002. *Die Aussenpolitik des Dritten Reiches 1933-1939*. Stuttgart: Klett-Cotta.

Speer, Albert. 1969. *Erinnerungen*. Frankfurt am Main u.a.: Ullstein 1969.

Spitzer, Alan B. 1973. "The Historical Problems of Generations." *American Historical Review* 78, p. 1353–1384.

Wohl, Robert. 1980. *The Generation of 1914*, London: Weidenfeld and Nicolson.

PART III. CASE STUDIES OF GENOCIDE

Chapter 7. Strategies of Exclusion: The Genocide of the Herero in German Colonial Discourse

Medardus Brehl

Recent research has emphasized that incidents of genocide are implicit in processes of social transformation and can only be understood as processes related to society as a whole (Dabag 1999, p. 9, Dabag 2002, p. 177, Platt 1998). When focusing on the social dimension of genocidal processes with regard its perpetrators, the question of the past history of modern political violence, mechanisms behind the exclusion of victims and strategies of legitimization of annihilation policies presented to society are particularly salient. Within the preparatory phases of modern genocide policy, measures of stigmatization of the victim group supported by processes conveyed by linguistic media are of decisive importance. In this context, in definition and exclusion strategies, updatable discursive patterns handed down across generations are adopted, which claim validity as historical, cultural or ideological knowledge (Platt 2003a). Analyzing those patterns that are effective in general social discourse represents a central interest of interdisciplinary genocide research: the de-construction of knowledge structures against the background of which genocide is conceived and appears to be legitimate (Brehl and Platt 2003, p. 10).

The genocide of the Herero, perpetrated by the German colonial power in 1904 in the then colony of Deutsch-Südwestafrika [German South-West Africa, now Namibia], involves major patterns of exclusion and strategies of legitimization apparent in the extensive contemporary literature on this event, many of which have not yet been considered in any great detail. In general historiography and even in works with a clear focus on German colonialism, the annihilation of the Herero long appeared only as a peripheral event, not anchored in the developments of German history from the point of view of the history of mentality, ideas or discourse. To gain any consideration at all, this flood of contemporary publications on the "Herero War" — be they campaign reports, diaries, (popular) historiographic accounts, novels, or books for children or young adults — were interpreted as apologetic "propaganda." However, such a procedure leads to a misleading delimitation of the legitimizing constructions from the discourse generally accessible in a society. Under such circumstances it is hardly possible to formulate any opinions regarding the relationship of these constructions to contemporary knowledge and speech conventions. As Klaus Vondung showed in his analysis of German literature of August 1914, the term "propaganda," used regularly to qualify German colonial literature (Warmbold 1988), only ostensibly breaks the impasse apparent here: "Propaganda is dependant on man's rooted ideas and prejudices and, if need be, can channel, intensify and functionalize them" (Vondung 1980, p. 16). To follow Klaus Vondung, before using the term propaganda, before taking refuge in such an abstract concept, it would be advisable to examine these "rooted ideas of man" and develop categories in order to locate them analytically.

In the following discussion it is assumed that contemporary depictions of the "Herero War" emerge from a background of a specific socio-cultural knowledge and must be understood in the context of societal discourse. I use the term "socio-cultural knowledge" in the sense of its previous deployment in the literary sciences, but at the same time my aim is to render it more precise and expand upon it as a method of text analysis. Following Michel Foucault's discourse theory, the literary expert Michael Titzmann defines "cultural knowledge" as the "all of the propositions that members of a culture hold to be true or that a sufficient number of texts of culture render true" (Titzmann 1989, p. 48). However, the assumption of a homogeneous state of knowledge among all "members of the culture" seems improbable, for as Pierre Bourdieu has convincingly shown, within one particular "culture" there are different, competing cultural conventions with "subtle differences" providing social distinctions (Bourdieu 1984). For this reason, cultural-sociological considerations are added to Titzmann's basic definition to expand the term "socio-cultural knowledge." While the attribute "socio-cultural" often refers only generally to appearances of structure, an examination of "socio-cultural knowledge" applied precisely in the field of discourse theory, cultural sociology and literary history can contribute important aspects to the analysis of inter-generational states of knowledge, their transmission, updating and reconstruction. The attribute "socio-cultural" in this context highlights the difficulty of distinguishing social norms, cultural values, patterns of interpretation and linguistic-discursive conventions from one another in the modern age. Rather, it must be assumed that world view, social structure and cultural-aesthetic conventions increasingly overlap and integrate one another in the construction and representation contexts of *reality frameworks*. The relevant contexts of the contemporary publications on the events of the years 1904-1908 should be sought less in the *real* events than in the socio-cultural knowledge, the socio-cultural and discursive framings which determine per-ception and re-presentation: texts do not depict *facts* but rather contribute to the construction of *reality*.

Accordingly, the following analysis does not focus primarily on historical *events* in the former colony of German South-West Africa in 1904/05 and debates concerning political or military strategy, but rather on the *stories* that are told about this event, as well as the knowledge of a universal "history" in which the event is classified, according to which it is interpreted, and which function as a framework of legitimization for the genocide of the Herero. In these legiti-mization patterns, different constructions operating across strategies of unam-biguous inclusion and exclusion can be perceived.

THE FACTS AND THE DISCOURSE

The events of the years 1904/1905 in South-West Africa — from 1884 the first so-called "Schutzgebiet" [protectorate] and only German colony, for which an extensive settlement program was to be drawn up (Bley 1996) — provide a complex picture of different structures of violence (Drechsler 1980, Bridgman 1981, Gewald 1999). During the nights of January 11 and 12, 1904, the Herero had begun their rebellion against the German colonial power, involving the destruction of the rail line Swapokmund-Windhuk, attacks on telegraph lines, the farms of German settlers and the murder of the adult German males encoun-tered there. The number of those killed is estimated at 123. The timing of the rebellion was well chosen insofar as Governor Theodor Leutwein was away in the south of the colony with a large proportion of the co-called "Schutztruppe" (colonial army) in order to quell what was termed the "local unrest" of the Bond-elwarts-Nama. To end the "Herero rebellion," Leutwein initially pursued a strategy of negotiation and de-escalation, but this was not marked by success, particularly as he found no support from the settler societies. On February 9, Leutwein was informed by Berlin that he was no longer to lead military operations and that the Great General Staff in Berlin had itself taken over the leadership of the Herero campaign. The command was transferred to Lieutenant-General Lothar von Trotha, who during the battles in German East-Africa (1894) and in China (1900) had established a reputation of military intransigence. Trotha was convinced that the battles in the German South-West area were part of a race war which could only be resolved with "floods of blood and floods of gold." His goal was to destroy the Herero in a decisive battle. After several smaller skirmishes, on August 11, 1904 a battle took place at Waterberg between the German troops and the Herero, who had moved there together with women and children (approx. 80,000 men, women and children). The latter were defeated and forced to the East in the arid Omaheke steppe, pursued by the German troops.

On October 2, von Trotha published a proclamation that read as follows: "I, the Great General of the German soldiers, send this letter to the people of Herero. The Herero are no longer German subjects. They have murdered and stolen ..., and now, through cowardice, no longer want to fight. I say to the people: ... the people of the Herero must ... leave the country. If they do not, I will force them to do so with the Groot Rohr [big canon]. Within the German borders any Herero with or without rifle, with or without cattle, will be shot, I will no longer shelter women or children. I will force them back to their people or let them be shot. These are my words to the people of Herero. The Great General of the Mighty Kaiser" (Gründer ed. 1999, p. 152). In the following days the few wells on the edge of the desert were blocked off by the Germans. Herero who approached these wells were shot or forced back. Only a few succeeded in fleeing across the desert into British Bechuanaland. The lifting of the shooting order by the German Emperor in December, 1904 could not stop the annihilation of the Herero, particularly as von Trotha retained command until December, 1905. Before the battles began, the number of living Herero within the German "Schutzgebiet" (protectorate) was estimated at 80-100,000; in 1911 only 15,130 Herero were counted (Bridgman 1981, pp. 164–165).

How, then were these events portrayed and legitimized in the eyes of the German public in the colonial literature? First of all, as already mentioned, it should be emphasized that the "Herero rebellion" was a contemporary discourse event. Many of the authors of these early publications belonged to the colonial milieu as officers or members of the "Schutztruppe" [colonial army], as farmers, settlers or as employees of the colonial administration. Their books were published by appropriate colonial or military publishers — for instance, the *Deutschen-Kolonial-Verlag* (Berlin), the publishers *Reimer* (Berlin), *Süsserot* (Berlin) or *Mittler & Sohn* (Berlin). This has often led to the assumption that the contemporary literature on the wars against the Herero and Nama, and indeed the whole of German-language colonial literature, solely served the interests and views of a small, narrowly-defined group. However, contrary to this assumption of a closed circle in the case of the "colonial literature," one which can only be identified with a particular social and political interest group, there also exists a large number of texts on the "Herero war" that were not written by authors with a colonial background and were not published and read in the context of principally colonial political interests. These publications reveal that these events as they were depicted in publications geared to a public interest in colonies were also accessible to broader circles of the Wilhelminian bourgeoisie. Thus, the accounts and interpretations of the events of the years 1904 to 1908 in publications that were directed at a broad bourgeois readership concur to the greatest possible extent with those of texts from genuine colonial authors. The most prominent example in this regard is Gustav Frenssen's 1906 novel *Peter Moors Fahrt nach Südwest. Ein Feldzugsbericht* [Peter Moor's journey to Southwest Africa. A campaign report]. This was one of the most successful contemporary publications on the "Herero war" and its high circulation alone makes it representative. Second, in the first decade of the 20th century, Frenssen was among some of the most famous, internationally recognized and discussed German authors and is even said to have been nominated for the 1912 Nobel Prize for literature (which then however went to Gerhard Hauptmann). These were not the words of an unknown, a colonial soldier dabbling in writing or a farmer, colonial officer or commissioned author, but rather a recognized first-class author whose name had a good reputation in bourgeois circles: Frenssen was the author of *Jörn Uhl* (1901), the first genuine bestseller in Germany, which in its year of publication already sold 130,000 copies (in comparison, Thomas Mann's *Buddenbrooks*, also published in 1901, only sold a little more than 1000 copies in the same period). *Peter Moors Fahrt nach Südwest* was tipped to have a similar success to that of *Jörn Uhl*. The novel was received with enthusiasm by critics at home and abroad, and developed in a short time into an international bestseller. In its first year of print, the novel was in its 63rd thousandth print, and by 1945 there were more than half a million copies printed. In 1908, English-language editions appeared in Great

Britain and the USA. In addition the novel was translated into Danish, Dutch, Afrikaans and Swedish. Annotated editions for teaching in schools appeared in Germany, the USA and Sweden. The significance of this text for providing a picture of the events of 1904 to those in bourgeois-conservative and national-liberal circles can hardly be overestimated.

In his text, which followed the genuine narrative form of the educated middle class represented by the "Entwicklungsroman" [novel showing the development of a character], Frenssen developed two aspects, which also appear, albeit implicitly, in numerous other published portrayals of the "Herero war": he abstracts the events in South West Africa and reasons for annihilation of the Herero from the colonial context and categorizes them in the process of a general, cultural evolution based on historical mythology, as well as in the construction of a collective German identity. Frenssen places the narrative perspective with a soldier of a sea battalion taking part in the campaign, who has no insight into military strategy and initially also cannot see the scope of these events from the point of view of (world) politics. The "insight" into the general relevance of the events is then transferred to the first-person narrator of the novel himself; the reader is required to follow the protagonist step-by-step in this process of discovery.

THE STREAM OF HISTORY

Towards the end of the novel, when the Herero have already been forced back into the desert, a conversation between the protagonist and his commanding Lieutenant is depicted, which reveals the novel's major message. The Lieutenant justifies the annihilation of the Herero with the words: "These blacks have earned their death before God and Man, not because they murdered two hundred farmers and rebelled against us, but because they have not built any houses or dug any wells....God has allowed us to triumph because we are the more noble and forward-striving....The world belongs to the more virtuous, to the bolder. That is God's justice" (p. 200). This short passage condenses three strands of discourse to justify the annihilation of the Herero. First, the argument that the annihilation is an act of retaliation is rejected; the portrayal is therefore separated from the actual, concrete, contemporary historical context. In the place of the concrete reference of the event is an argument borrowed from discourse from the philosophy of history, already formulated by Kant, Herder, and

Schiller and which at the latest in Hegel's *Vorlesungen zur Philosophie der Geschichte* (Lectures on the philosophy of history), published between 1822 and 1831, experienced a setting claiming validity: The "blacks," according to the text, do not contribute anything to the development of mankind and to the advance of the process of history. Using this argument, Frenssen is following an idea virulent in the universal historical frameworks since the Enlightenment of a single, universally valid history; a history in the centre of which stands the active man (Dabag 2000, pp. 64ff.) — where the term "man" is associated with completely exclusive ideas, for instance white skin color, education, etc. — and which is geared towards a particular, strongly defined goal: Herder's "general humanity," Kant's world society of rational citizens of the world, Schiller's "intelligent thinkers" and "educated men of the world." A common feature of these different approaches is that the history of the peoples who are said to contribute nothing to carrying out nature's plan, are fundamentally viewed in an episodic manner, as Kant formulated in the *Idee zu einer allgemeinen Geschichte in weltbürgerlicher Absicht* [Idea for a universal history with a cosmopolitan purpose] (1783). The significance and value of each individual history is measured solely according to its contribution to the carrying out of this assumed general process of history. The virulence and influence of this idea around 1900 should not be underestimated, as Kristin Platt convincingly showed in an analysis of texts on the philosophy of history by Theodor Vischer, Heinrich von Treitschke and Wilhelm Dilthey (Platt 2003b). In Frenssen's novel, this model of the history of philosophy is now supported with, in the greatest sense of the word, a "religious" argument, which for its part is interwoven with arguments that can be traced back to social or cultural evolutionist discourse. According to the text, it is God's will that the "more noble," "more forward striving" and "bolder" will be victorious and the inferior will be defeated. By means of inversion, a proposition of the Sermon on the Mount is cited here: according to Frenssen, who before his literary successes had already had a career as a protestant country parson, it is "God's justice" that the world belongs to the "virtuous" who use violence and eliminate the "inferior blacks," while according to Matthew 5:5 it is known that those who will "inherit the earth" are "the meek," i.e., those who do not use violence. It should first be emphasized at this point that the novel categorizes the events in German South-West Africa as exemplary in the development of a universal process of history made generally valid, which is aimed at the cultural progress of mankind. The annihilation of the "blacks" is described as a necessary and justified element in carrying out of this historical process, as an acceleration of the inevitable death of the peoples at the edge of history.

It can be demonstrated that Frenssen's arguments are not the only ones that follow inherited knowledge and previous patterns of speech — numerous contemporary texts on the same events resemble his arguments to the point of being interchangeable. The model of legitimization outlined is made explicit in Adolf Fischer's essay *Menschen und Tiere in Deutsch-Südwest* [People and animals in the German South-west], published in 1914, which tells the story of Southwest Africa from prehistoric times as one of a slow death of land, animals and men, which reached its conclusion in the years 1904-1908: "It was the battle between old and new times....From the South and North, pressure was effected on the coloured and the wild. They were annihilated or pushed back into the frontier area. The German was not to blame. He was the coincidental heir of the field that had long lain before him in the throes of death. The same strength that brought him [i.e. the German, M.B] to power swept away the old, weak, strange people in Africa" (pp. 92-93). While the German colonial rulers are placed in the role as executers of a plan of history, Fischer characterizes the peoples of South-West Africa through their readiness to consent to the necessary fate that history had determined for them. He therefore judges the fate of the Herero as distressing, as they died "fearlessly before the gullets of fire of modern times or in the horrendous draught of the desert," while the Nama, according to Fischer, should have sought to "be defeated honourably" two hundred years earlier — their "fate" at the beginning of the 20th century he therefore judges as a "delayed death" devoid of any tragedy (p. 92).

In this context, another passage from Frenssen's *Peter Moor* is significant, in which it is described how during the pursuit of the Herero, a group of "helplessly languishing" old men, the wounded, women and children are seized in a desert, still living but already covered in flies. These stand *pars pro toto* for a people that is meant for death but who cannot die, who then, according to Frenssen, are "helped to their deaths" (p. 162). What may initially seem to be a euphemistic turn can be read as a metaphor of a specific idea of humanity inherent in the evolutionary interpretations of universal historical frameworks, in which the killing of the "native" is recoded into a philanthropic act of mercy.

Scramble for Identity

In addition to the classification of the idea of a universal historical process, legitimizing the "elimination of native peoples," there is a second model which holds a central position in contemporary talk of the "Herero war": the idea of a necessary battle for individual and collective identity linked with the question of existence and proving one's worth in an enemy environment — thus a battle for existence justifying the use of radical violence.

Even from a cursory reading of colonial texts the link with patterns of speech through individual and collective identity is apparent. Indeed, the colonies are frequently outlined as the ideal place for realizing collective identity. In his account of the pursuit of the Herero from the posthumously published papers of a "Schutztrupper" [colonial soldier] called Otto Eggers, for example, the military doctor Philalethes Kuhn states: "Each country has its own special soul-building energy. Countries with harsh conditions make for energetic, capable inhabitants, they force the people living in them to apply all the tension within them, bring it to life, in order to make a living" (Kuhn 1907, p. 34). Identity is directly coupled here with a "struggle for existence" — which the more effective, the worse the conditions. In barren South-West Africa, the text continues, there is "an immense energy" which lies in its "inhospitable nature," as it provides the "floor for a capable, strong national tradition of folklore." "Struggle for existence" and "withstanding in the battle for existence" are ultimately outlined as a prerequisite for realizing and retaining collective identity: the country is "bad enough for the Germans to be able to stay German" (p. 35).

The overlapping of territory, struggle for existence and identity described here is just as clear as it is paradigmatic for colonial frameworks of individual and collective identity. Also the program formulated in this construction becomes the engine for narration in numerous novels on the "Herero war." The question of existence and of holding one's own in an enemy environment is also a central aspect in Frenssen's *Peter Moor*, whereby the question of the existence of the individual is coupled inseparably with the existence of the collective. Frenssen uses the narrative structure itself to exemplify the "question of existence" and shifts the process of gaining insight into an — again generally valid — paradigmatic framework "into" the protagonist of his novel. He later characterized the macrostructure of the novel in his *Lebensbericht* [Life report] of 1940 as a sequence of "two, perfectly equal waves," each consisting of the motives "departure, in the bush, distress (catastrophe), peace." The second wave outshines "the first in terms of the power and the host of pictures" (Frenssen 1940, p. 144). The association of the narrative schema described by Frenssen with the building principle of a double course in the tradition of the court Arthurian novel (departure — first adventure cycle — crisis — second adventure cycle — successful solution) is not coincidental and falls back on a handed down literary form, which models the maturation process of a protagonist and his journey to community, whereby at the same time a programmatic aspect of *Peter Moor* would be defined. The novel is divided into two sections of more or less equal length, with the first half describing the departure of the protagonist as a volunteer of a sea battalion to South-West Africa on the occasion of the "rebellion of the natives." The motivation for this is initially outlined as exclusively subjective: as an escape from the confinement of the workshop of his father, a blacksmith, whose journeyman had predicted that the young Moor would stand at the anvil until he was grey. The *Journey to Southwest Africa* then turns into torture for *Peter Moor*. The encounter with foreign parts is characterized as unnerving and destructive for the individual, the inhospitable wilderness and unfamiliar climate rips at the physis, and the "mass of blacks" threaten the existence of the isolated "whites." The first part of the novel ends with the themes of desperation and illness, but at the same time proposes a solution: the overcoming of the crisis of the individual by his integration into the collective. The moment of insight into this principle is described as kind of epiphany: "And there, in the shadow of a veranda, stood a German woman; she had a small child in her arms. How we looked at her! ... Like the Three Kings, who coming out of the desert and dismounting their horses, saw Mary with her child." (p. 111). Here, in an "oasis of Germanness" in the middle of the "desert," the shattered protagonist returns to "full health" (p. 116). The whole of the second part of the novel serves to confirm the view that the individual can only find himself if he makes his contribution to the establishment of the Volksgemeinschaft [people's community]. This framework is supported by the portrayal of the characters. With a few exceptions, the actors remain anonymous — even the name *Moor* can only be found twice in the whole novel — they are characterized by rank, occupational group, or, as Frenssen calls it, "Stammeszugehörigkeit" [tribal membership]: the General, the Lieutenant, the doctor, "a linen weaver from Upper Silesia," "a chimney sweep from Berlin," the Swabian, the Bavarian, a Boer. Even the few who are given names are awarded no sharper contours than their nameless comrades-in-arms. By defining characters through social and regional assignments and typecasts they, on the one hand, become universally valid "models," open to general identifications. On the other, they appear not as individuals but rather as — initially potential — parts and function bearers within a collective. The threat by the "existential" other (here depicted in the sense of Carl Schmitt[1]), the overcoming or substitution of the class war by race war allows the Silesian, Bavarian, Holsteiner, linen weaver, chimney sweep, simple soldier, officer and General to become a homogenous Volksgemeinschaft [people's community]. The novel outlines this mechanism not only for the colonial context but also as a generally valid paradigm binding for "the whole world." Towards the end of the novel, the protagonist lets his gaze wander broodingly over the wide steppes: "I had often thought during the campaign: 'what a crying shame.... This thing is not worth good blood!' But then I heard a great song that sounded across the whole of South Africa and across the whole world and it gave me a sense of the thing" (p. 201). With this *insight* the path is made clear for the establishment of a homogenous body of people in identity with itself and with the territory that this people makes into its "Lebensraum" [living space]. Significantly, towards the end of the novel the barren steppe turns into a garden, grass springs up from the soil that had been previously described as infertile and the thorn bush sprouts "snowy white petals" (p. 203): The homogenous community of "whites" also generates a white territory.

As a prerequisite for community and identity, colonial texts demand a radical exclusivity of antagonists; antagonists between whom any understanding, any comprehension is impossible. Any convergence between "black" and "white" is projected as an existential and fatal overstepping of the boundaries which — for both sides — would lead to a loss of identity, in colonial terms: to a "bastardization," or "Verkafferung" ["going native"] and thus ultimately to decline. This setting of a radical exclusivity is accompanied by the dissolving of semantic selectivity between the terms "other," "stranger" and "enemy." The terms serve no possible differentiation purposes; they do not even provide a series of comparisons, but are used virtually synonymously. The effect, though, is clear; anything that is not identical to oneself becomes — or in terms of the inner dynamics of this construction — "is" a priori an enemy. With the dissolving of semantic selectivity the dividing line between one's own existence and that of the threatening enemy is strengthened and manifest: "position" and

---

1.."The political enemy ... is simply, the other, the foreigner, and for his being it is sufficient that, in a particularly existential sense, it is something different and something foreign..." (Schmitt 1996: 27).

"negation" are described as exclusive entities, between which, metaphorically speaking, gapes a no-man's land of lack of identity (Brehl 2003).

CODING THE "ENEMY"

The claimed existential difference between two races stated is described by Frenssen quite conventionally in the context of colonial discourse, using antithetical constructions that overlap and penetrate one another: a fundamental different racial quality, coded through the terms "black" and "white," causes an irreconcilable antagonism between "culture" and "wilderness" and a contrast between "order"[1] and "amorphous mass." The positive connotations of the positions "white," "culture" and "order" are thereby under constant threat by the negative connotations of their antitheses. The model of the opposing natures of order and amorphous mass runs through the whole novel: the "white troops" stand in "row and rank," their "black drivers" on the other hand advance "wildly and screaming" (p. 117). Upon the first encounter with "blacks," still during the crossing, the text reads: "as it came across both boards, creeping like a cat, sliding like a snake, black and long and half naked ..." (p. 28), and during a battle in which the protagonist takes part, "blacks" are described as follows: "Then I too saw something foreign advancing. It lay in huddles and kneeled and slid between the bushes. I didn't see any individual, only a mass." (p. 84). The use of the German neuter form of the personal pronoun (es — "it") as the collective singular describes the "blacks" — or to be precise, "the black" — as a formless threat that cannot be more closely identified.

The difference described between (white) culture and (black) wildness is at the same time also the point of departure for the formulation of the "white" task to cultivate the wilderness. In this manner, books and letters become symbols and insignia of the capacity for culture: they are the only things that the "blacks" leave behind after the plundering of the white farmers and thus the "natives" — according to the logic of the text — equally prove their incapacity for "culture" and the existential threat they pose to it.

The use of biological and cultural arguments in order to contrast "blacks" and "whites" is a basic model of the colonial construction of reality and identity

---

1. For the relationship between models of order and annihilation projects in the modern day see the standard work of Zygmunt Bauman: Bauman 1989.

present in almost all colonial publications. Thus, Maximilian Bayer, officer of the "Schutztruppe" [colonial army] during the war in South-West Africa from 1904–1907, stated that the "natives" of South-West Africa are "from their whole nature" not "suitable ... to get along with the white race" as "their aversion to cultural work is too great" (Bayer 1907, p. 6). Although Beyer still explained the "aversion of the natives to cultural work" with relative caution and limited specificity from their "whole nature," Kurd Schwabe interpreted the war from 1904 to 1906 as a "period of great race wars, at the beginning of the last furious resistance of non-culture against culture." He claimed to recognize the origin of these *race wars* in the fact "that the views of the natives on state, religion and economy ..., are *hostile to culture*" (Schwabe 1906, p. 22).

What are the implications of such a crossing over of biologistic and culturalistic models (antagonism between the "races" and antagonism between "culture" and "wilderness")? Initially, the contrast depicted between "blacks" and "whites" is not interpreted as one based, for instance, on history or experience, but more as one that is determined by "nature." Accordingly, the stated "antagonisms" are de-historicized. At the same time they are characterized as existential, which not only emphasizes their irreconcilability but also their non-negotiable nature: for the "natives" of Africa, according to the logic of the texts, have not — due for instance to a possibly negotiable conflict of interest — become enemies of culture (and therefore of the "whites"), but were rather born as enemies of culture. The contrast between "black" and "white" is turned into a simple question of existence. In *Peter Moor*, this construct is consistently realized linguistically: while the word "Herero" is not used in the whole of the novel, there is universal and synonymous talk of "blacks" and "enemies"[1] or "the enemy people."

PHRASES OF ELIMINATION

In the context of the constructions outlined, the question of the means and methods with which the colonial works depict or legitimize the fight against the "born enemies" for one's own existence are particularly significant. In texts from colonial military discourse, a structure of argument is notable which is used to

---

1. Even the description of the first encounter of the protagonist with Herero states: "On this morning, as I happened to be walking around the railway station building, I saw the first enemies, a prisoner and his woman" (Frenssen 1906: 43).

describe the enmity of the "natives" as non-negotiable and consequently exceptions to the rules valid for the fight against "civilized enemies" are legitimized. In
his short volume *Kriegführung in Süd-Afrika* [Warfare in South-Africa] published in
1900, the former commander of the "Schutztruppe" [colonial army] Curt von
François, for instance, claimed that the rules of the European war are invalid in
the "native war" because the "natives" themselves would not observe these rules.
The goal of the "natives," according to François, is not so much to "drive the
opponent from the battlefield ... as to annihilate him." (p. 18). As a consequence,
the "annihilation of the enemy" (p. 44) also needs to become the maxim of the
European military command against the "natives."

It is significant that François places the military command in the colonies
fundamentally outside the rules that should be valid for wars against "civilized
peoples" and justifies this with the military command of the "natives." This construction is no exception — indeed it follows discursive conventions regarding
war, and particularly colonial war, which prevailed around 1900 — and this is
precisely how it becomes accessible. Thus, in the course of the first Hague Peace
Conference in 1899, analogous arguments were offered to abandon the ban on so-
called dumdum bullets in the special case of a colonial war. While rules were
being drawn up for the "humanization" of war between "civilized powers,"
simultaneous attempts were being made to establish exceptions to their validity.
The structure of this argument is as simple as it is drastic: because the "natives"
do not know and therefore do not adhere to the rules of war between civilized
peoples or the corresponding international legal agreements, they are not under
their protection. However, the consequences of this are far-reaching: the "wild
peoples" of Africa, through a circularly structured argument, are excluded from
the "universe of general obligations" (Fein 1993, p. 813), the status of their exclusivity is established.

Just beneath the surface of the directives issued by General Lothar von
Trotha in August 1904 for the attack on the Herero at Waterberg, there lies a
palimpsest of the program for the "native war" outlined above. In the aforementioned book *Der Krieg in Südwest-Afrika 1904-06* [The war in South-West Africa
1904-06], Kurd Schwabe quotes Trotha's directives for the attack against the
Herero as follows: "as soon as the Deimling unit is gathered, I will attack the
enemy simultaneously with all units, in order to annihilate him....All forces are to
be used to annihilate the fighting enemy" (p. 265). While von Trotha speaks
explicitly of an "annihilation of the fighting enemy," and with this initially
appears to completely follow the formula coined by Carl von Clausewitz of the

"annihilation of the enemy forces"[1], in his "annihilation orders" cited above from the 2nd October 1904 a certain shift takes place: this proclamation was addressed unmistakably to the "people of the Herero." This address can be read five times in the short passage — any differentiation of status (combatant or civilian), gender or age is made equal. As is also the case with Frenssen's wording of "enemy people" quoted above, Clausewitz's program of "annihilation of the enemy troops" is re-coded into an "annihilation of the enemy people."

Reading these contemporary texts shows that the realization of the program of "annihilation of the enemy people," the genocide of the Herero, required no further retrospective legitimization but rather appeared — according to the knowledge about the evolution of history as well as the knowledge about the battle between exclusive entities — a priori to be legitimate, even necessary and heroic. The official description of the "Herero campaign" published by the department for military history of the Great General Staff states that with the "annihilation of the Herero people" carried out with great resolve, the "reckless energy of the German leadership" was allowed to appear in "a glorious light."

It is noticeable that in contemporary portrayals of the events there is rarely any attempt to deny the extermination of the Herero or to justify it as an act of desperation from the point of view of military strategy. The lifting of the order to exterminate by the Emperor and Reichskanzler [Imperial Chancellor], for example, is not even mentioned in any of the texts. On the contrary, annihilation is the goal aspired to, since it seems to make sense in itself and is also forward-looking. It is a tool in carrying out nature's plan of history and is portrayed as a legitimate means in the clash with an enemy who is threatening one's own existence and standing in the way of the construction of a homogenous, white collective in identity with the individual, community and territory. This highlights what Mihran Dabag has convincingly described as a characteristic feature of a genocide policy: genocide is a method "of creating identity, identity in the society of perpetrators, and is to contribute to the safeguarding of their future" (Dabag 2002, p. 186). Precisely with the aspect of forward-looking, of safeguarding one's own existence across generations, which is attributed to the annihilation, and in the resolve to consistently carry this out, colonial texts show

---

1. However, Clausewitz had used the expression "annihilation" explicitly with a double connotation: "Annihilation of the enemy forces is the means to a goal.... Different points of view that are possible in this case. 1 only annihilate to the extent that the object of the attack requires, 2. or as much as is possible ..." (Clausewitz 1914: p. 556).

models of argument that point prospectively to the great genocides of the first half of the 20th century: the genocide of the Armenians in the Ottoman Empire and the Holocaust.

CONCLUSIONS

From the re-constructed patterns of distinction found in the texts, it is apparent that a scenario of unambiguous, irreconcilable antagonisms is depicted in colonial discourse: black versus white, nature versus culture, wilderness versus civilization, desert versus arable land, heathenism versus Christianity, order versus amorphous mass, unproductiveness versus productivity, stagnation versus progress, ahistoricity versus history, decline versus future — these are the binary arguments contained in colonial strategies of exclusion. According to this logic, the "natives" are not only forced out solely due to the validities of general obligations and norms, but rather their exclusivity is established: they are assigned a position which is *a priori* outside of all obligations and norms. In colonial discourse, the colonized population is therefore conceived as naturally "bare life" without protection or rights, as "Homo Sacer" in the sense of Giorgio Agamben (Agamben 1998). In this context it should be pointed out that efforts made following 1907 to construct an "Eingeborenenrecht" [native law] in reaction to the "Herero war" are not to be judged as an attempt to compensate the unlegislated area in which the "natives" found themselves, as for instance through a law especially tailored to them. In my opinion this approach needs to be primarily understood rather as an element of fixing their position outside the standardized legal system: the "native law" means codifying the placing of the native "Homo Sacer" in his own unlegislated area beyond generally valid norms; it means judicialization of his lawlessness.

Following this logic, the killing of the "natives" appears in the colonial texts to be in no way a moral, ethical or even a legal problem. On the contrary, the annihilation of the "bare life" is portrayed as a contribution to the moral maturation of the people who, through carrying it out, are working for culture, history and identity. This is highlighted at the end of *Peter Moors Fahrt nach Südwest*: "We need to continue to be tough and kill for a long time to come; but at the same time we must endeavor, as individuals and as a people, to have high thoughts and carry out noble deeds, in order to contribute our part to the future brotherhood of mankind" (p. 201). Genocide is stylized as a contribution to the generating of a future humanity, to moral behavior and to an element of moral maturation. As Mihran Dabag has expressed it, "the annihilation is itself turned into a moral issue" (Dabag 2002, p. 221) The perpetrators see themselves not as committing any crime but rather as carrying out a task that — following the arguments of the texts — is meaningful, morally justified and difficult, which accelerates an inevitable, historical process of cultural higher development and contributes to the construction and safeguarding of the identity of the colonizers. The conventionality of these lines of argument and the wide circulation of the texts mentioned, as well as their close relation to the socio-cultural knowledge of this time, therefore allow one thing to be concluded with certainty: the arguments inherent in them were broadly relevant and accessible to society as a whole.

Thus an examination of contemporary discourse on the Herero reveals a complex system of exclusion strategies to be considered in terms of the question of why and how the genocide of the Herero was conceivable and possible: The categorization of the event in universal contexts (history, culture, nature) and with this in planning for the future; the categorization in discussions on the construction, safeguarding and stabilization of the identity of the colonizers; a strategy of the promise of Volksgemeinschaft [people's community], proving one's worth and recovery, strength, and connected to this an integration of the colonial discourse into the national discourse of the German Empire; strategies of de-individualization of the victim group (through the depiction of a "black mass" which threatens the identity of the "whites"); and finally, strategies of deregulation, the freeing from norms and the setting of a new norms, thus the placing of the extermination policies in direct relationship to the general normative system of society. The linguistic and argumentative patterns, which in accounts of the genocide often overlap and merge into one another, allow the extermination to appear necessary and legitimate, as it is to contribute to the enforcement of principles which were granted a universal validity.

This analysis of linguistic patterns of exclusion represents an important aspect of interdisciplinary genocide research. Such an analysis makes it clear that genocides are not planned on the fringe of a society or carried out against the express will of its majority. An act of genocide becomes conceivable and legitimizable — this has been shown not least by the 1994 genocide in Rwanda (Verwimp 2001; Semujanga 2003) — if the strategies of excluding the victim group and the preparation of their extermination converges with the basic paradigms of social knowledge and is directly related to the concepts of identity, the normative system and general politics of the society as a whole.

Translated into English by Sarah Mannion, MA (Cantab)

REFERENCES

Agamben, Giorgio. 1998. *Homo Sacer. Sovereign Power and Bare Life*. Stanford, CA: Stanford Univ. Press (first publ.: Torino 1995).

Bauman, Zygmunt. 1989. *Modernity and the Holocaust*. Ithaca, NY: Cornell Univ. Press.

Bayer, Maximilian. 1907. Der Krieg in Südwestafrika und seine Bedeutung für die Entwickelung der Kolonie. Vortrag gehalten in 52 deutschen Städten. Leipzig: Engelmann

Bley, Helmut. 1996. *Namibia under German Rule*. Hamburg/Münster/New Brunswick, NY: LIT (first publ.: Hamburg 1968).

Bolz, Norbert, Friedrich Kittler, and Raimar Zons, eds. 2000. *Weltbürgertum und Globalisierung*. Munich: Wilhelm Fink.

Bourdieu, Pierre. 1984. *Distinction. A Social Critique of the Judgement of Taste*. Cambridge, MA: Harvard Univ. Press (first publ.: Paris 1979).

Brehl, Medardus. 2003. "(Ein)Geborene Feinde. Der Entwurf existenzieller Feindschaft im Kolonialdiskurs" in *Feindschaft*, edited by Medardus Brehl and Kristin Platt. Munich: Wilhelm Fink, pp. 157–177.

Brehl, Medardus and Platt, Kristin 2003. "Einleitung" in: *Feindschaft*, edited by Medardus Brehl and Kristin Platt. Munich: Wilhelm Fink, pp. 7–11.

_____. eds. 2003. *Feindschaft*. Munich: Wilhelm Fink.

Bridgman, Jon M. 1981. *The Revolt of the Hereros*. Berkeley, CA/Los Angeles, CA/London: Univ. of California Press.

Clausewitz, Carl von. 1914. *Vom Kriege. Mit einer Einführung von Graf von Schlieffen*. Berlin: Behr (8. Ed.).

Dabag, Mihran. 1996. "Katastrophe und Identität. Verfolgung und Erinnerung in der armenischen Gemeinschaft," in *Erlebnis–Gedächtnis–Sinn. Authentische und konstruierte Erinnerung*, edited by Hanno Loewy and Bernhard Moltmann. Frankfurt am Main/ New York, NY: Campus, pp. 177–237.

_____. 1999. "Genozidforschung. Leitfragen, Kontroversen, Überlieferung." *Zeitschrift für Genozidforschung* 1 (1), pp. 6–35.

_____. 2000. "Genozid und weltbürgerliche Absicht. Perspektiven," in *Weltbürgertum und Globalisierung*, edited by Norbert Bolz, Friedrich Kittler and Raimar Zons. Munich: Wilhelm Fink, pp. 43–71.

_____. 2002. "The Realm of Perspectives: Some Reflections on an Interdisciplinary Approach to Genocide Studies." *International Journal of Contemporary Sociology* 39 (2), pp. 177-197.

_____ and Platt, Kristin, eds. 1998. *Genozid und Moderne. Strukturen kollektiver Gewalt im 20. Jahrhundert.* Opladen: Leske+Budrich.

Drechsler, Horst. 1980. *Let Us Die Fighting : The struggle of the Herero and Nama against German Imperialism (1884–1915)*. London: ZED Press (first publ.: Berlin (east) 1966).

Fein, Helen. 1993. "Revolutionary and Antirevolutionary Genocides. A Comparison of State Murders in Democratic Kampuchea, 1975 to 1979, and in Indonesia, 1965 to 1966." *Comparative Studies in Society and History* 35 (4), 796–823.

Fischer, Adolf. 1914. *Menschen und Tiere in Deutsch-Südwest*, Stuttgart: DVA.

François, Curt von. 1900. *Kriegführung in Süd-Afrika*. Berlin: Reimer.

Frenssen, Gustav. 1906. *Peter Moors Fahrt nach Südwest. Ein Feldzugsbericht.* Berlin: Grote.

_____. 1940. *Lebensbericht.* Berlin: Grote.

Gewald, Jan-Bart. 1999. *Herero Heroes. A Socio-Political History of the Herero of Namibia 1890-1923.* Athens, OH: Ohio Univ. Press.

Günder, Horst, ed. 1999. "... da und dort ein junges Deutschland gründen." Rassismus, Kolonien und kolonialer Gedanke vom 16. bis zum 20. Jahrhundert, ed. by Horst Gründer. Munich: dtv.

Kant, Immanuel. 1783. "Idea for a Universal History from a Cosmopolitan Point of View." In *Immanuel Kant: Philosophical Writings*, edited by Ernst Behler, New York, NY: Continuum 1986.

Kuhn, Philalethes. 1907. "Ein Ritt ins Sandfeld von Südwestafrika" in: Deutsch-Südwestafrika – Kriegs – und Friedensbilder. Selbsterlebnisse geschildert von Frau Margarete von Eckenbrecher, Frau Helene von Falkenhausen, Stabsarzt Dr. Kuhn, Oberleutnant Stuhlmann. Leipzig: Weicher, pp. 34-46.

Loewy, Hanno and Moltmann Bernhard, eds. 1996. *Erlebnis–Gedächtnis–Sinn. Authentische und konstruierte Erinnerung.* Frankfurt am Main/New York, NY: Campus.

Platt, Kristin. 1998. "Genozid und Moderne: Strukturen kollektiver Gewalt im 20. Jahrhundert. Einleitung" in: *Genozid und Moderne. Strukturen kollektiver Gewalt im 20. Jahrhundert*, ed. by Mihran Dabag and Kristin Platt. Opladen: Leske+Budrich, pp. 5–37.

_____. 2003a. "Unter dem Zeichen des Skorpions. Feindmuster, Kriegsmuster und das Profil des Fremden," in *Feindschaft*, edited by Medardus Brehl and Kristin Platt. Munich: Wilhelm Fink, pp. 13–52.

_____. 2003b. Über das Vorübergehende in der Geschichte: Gestaltung, Tod und Vernichtung in der Begründung historischer Kontinuität. Unpublished manuscript.

Presentation given at the conference "Die Machbarkeit der Welt" ("The feasibility of the world") in the Catholic Academy "The Wolfsburg," Mülheim/Ruhr, 27-29 November 2003.

Schmitt, Carl. 1996. Der Begriff des Politischen. Text von 1932 mit einem Vorwort und drei Corollarien. Berlin: Duncker und Humblot.

Schwabe, Kurd. 1906. *Der Krieg in Südwest-Afrika 1904-1906.* Berlin: C. A. Weller.

Semujanga, Josias. 2003. *Origins of Rwandan Genocide*, Amherst NY: Humanity Books (first pbl.: Paris 1998).

Titzmann, Michael. 1989. "Kulturelles Wissen–Diskurs–Denksystem. Zu einigen Grundbegriffen der Literaturgeschichtsschreibung." *Zeitschrift für französische Sprache und Literatur* 99 (1), pp. 47–61.

Verwimp, Philip. 2001. "Bauernideologie und Völkermord in Rwanda." *Zeitschrift für Genozidforschung*, 3: (1–2), pp. 47-80.

Vondung, Klaus. 1980. "Propaganda oder Sinndeutung?" in Kriegserlebnis. Der Erste Weltkrieg in der literarischen Gestaltung und symbolischen Deutung der Nationen, edited by Klaus Vondung. Göttingen: Vandenhoeck, pp. 11-37.

Warmbold, Joachim. 1988. *Germanica in Africa. Germany's Colonial Literature.* New York, NY: Peter Lang (first pbl.: Frankfurt a.M. 1982).

Chapter 8. Global Inaction, Ethnic Animosity, or Resource Maldistribution? An Ecological Explanation of Genocide in Rwanda

Tarique Niazi, University of Wisconsin, Eau Claire

Section I. Introduction

Rwanda witnessed 800,000 of its citizens slaughtered by fellow Rwandans in three months between April and July of 1994 (Mamdani 2001). As the victims were predominantly Tutsis and victimizers Hutus, the conventional explanations of ethnic animosities came in handy to explain this tragedy (see Berkeley, 2001; Mamdani, 2001). But some commentators, such as Percival and Homer-Dixon (1995), went beyond the conventional explanations to trace the roots of the Rwandan massacre, among others, to demographically induced environmental scarcity. Yet, Percival and Homer-Dixon (1995) conceded that "although environmental factors were significant development issues, environmental scarcity had at most a limited aggravating role in the recent conflict" (p. 1). Other observers (e.g., Silliman and King, 1996) have questioned their assumption that, they argue, implies to blame the victims for both environmental degradation and violence, while giving a pass to the larger social forces that actually have created what Tsing (1993) calls "Malthustans" — environmentally degraded areas where population and resources are at least temporarily out of balance.

Olson (1995), however, takes on the larger social forces to explain the Rwandan tragedy. She rejects the twin theses of demographic pressure and ethnic hatred as an explanation of the mass murder in Rwanda, and instead spots the political vested interests behind what she seems to think was an orchestrated tragedy:

"The massacres and the war were planned, led, and conducted not by poverty-stricken subsistence farmers ....Without the support of foreigners to train and arm the regime's militia, and without the silence and seeming unconcern by foreigners to the violence between 1990 and 1994 and to the 1994 massacres, it is doubtful the old regime would have chosen and depended on violence to stay in power" (Olson, 1995, p. 13). Although Olson forcefully challenges the neo-Malthusian explanation of the Rwandan massacre, she blames it on "exogenous" forces. Her analysis, together with many others' (e.g., Melvern 2000, O'Halloran 1995, Omaar and Waal 1995), does not penetrate deep enough to uncover the "endogenous" factors that could have been at the dark heart of this tragedy, beyond describing the obvious — "vested political interests."

Even those commentators (e.g., Mitchell 1997, Percival and Homer-Dixon 1995) who do explore endogenous factors, such as demographically induced environmental scarcities as a partial explanation of the Rwandan tragedy, overlook the social distribution of ecological resources as a likely causal force (Huage and Ellingsen, 2001) behind the Rwandan massacre. Percival and Homer-Dixon (1995), rather, deny the presence of what they call "structural scarcities" — environmental scarcities caused by the unequal distribution of ecological resources. Many scholars of Africa (e.g., Clay, Kampayana, and Kayitsinga 1988, Clay and Kampayana 1989b, Clay and Johnson 1992, Uvin 1996), however, offer evidence to the contrary by demonstrating that land resources were unevenly distributed in Rwanda. Of them, Clay, Kampayana, and Kayitsinga (1988) especially focus their research on "inequalities rooted in the distribution of land holdings and on the attendant polarization of relatively large landholders ... on the one hand, and near-landless households ... on the other" (p. 2). These scholars, however, also fall for neo-Malthusian explanations of the Rwandan tragedy by attributing the uneven distribution of land resources to "population pressure" that, according to them, led to the fragmentation of family holdings to the disadvantage of large-sized families (Clay and Johnson 1992, Clay, Kampayana and Kayitsinga 1988). Andre and Platteau (2002), however, show that large-sized families were less dependent on their small land holdings, as compared to the households of large-holdings. The members of large-sized families had diversified their income base by seeking off-farm jobs.

Historical evidence also does not support neo-Malthusian explanations of the Rwandan tragedy. In the pre-colonial and colonial era, for instance, ecological resources — forests, pastures, farmland — were abundantly available, but they were made scarce by Tutsi monopolization of such resources (Keane, 1995; Waller, 1993; Dorsey, 1994; Newbury, 1993). In the pre-colonial era, this monopolization of resources was used to construct "ethnicities" around ecological resources (see Keane 1995, Dorsey 1994) — i.e., forests for the Twas, land for the Hutus, and cattle for the Tutsis. The term *Twa* literally means a forest-dweller; *Hutu*, a farmer or cultivator or agriculturist; and *Tutsi*, a cattle-owner (Destexhe 1995, Keane 1995, Waller 1995). Then, these "ethnicities" were reinforced by the racist policies of German and Belgian colonizers (Mitchell, 1997), who later used them as criteria for distribution of natural and social resources — from land, cattle, and pastures to education and employment. Such monopoly-induced resource scarcities in the pre-colonial and colonial era, however, contradict the prevalent thesis that resource scarcity, especially land shortage, in Rwanda was a function of demographic pressure.

Also, in the post-colonial era, resource scarcities were created by distributional inequities committed by the Hutu governments, respectively led by Presidents Kayibanda (1962–1973) and Habyarimana (1973-1994). Both governments respectively initiated in the 1960s and the 1970s land resettlement programs, called Payasannat (Waller 1993), which redistributed land to the Hutu majority, especially the Hutus from the north. Similarly, the Habyarimana government's campaign for "intensive farming" helped the north, which was Habyarimana's home region, to the neglect of the south and the east — regions that were predominantly inhabited by the Tutsis and the Hutus opposed to the Habyarimana government. The Payasannat and the campaign for intensive agriculture also created ecological scarcities in productive land and land productivity by what Catton (1988) calls "overshooting" — over harvesting natural resources — the fragile agro-ecosystem of uplands, swamps, pastures, and forests. Later, the Hutu elite used ecological scarcities (such as land) and their ethnic distribution (e.g., land for Hutu farmers) as an incentive for their followers to kill the Tutsis (Uvin, 1996; Prunier, 1995). "All these people who were about to be killed had land and at times cows. And somebody had to get these land and those cows after their owners were dead ... this was not a negligible incentive" (Prunier 1995, p. 142). More than half of Rwanda's Tutsi population was eliminated, first in the early 1960s and again in 1973, thus freeing up vast tracts of land for cultivation in the eastern region (Uvin 1996).

It follows from the above review of literature that ecological scarcities in land resources were a function of distributional inequities of the pre-colonial (1500–1897) and colonial era (1897–1962), which were, however, worsened by the distributionist and productionist policies of the post-colonial era Hutu governments (1962–1994). This chapter examines the role of skewed distribution of key ecological resources, such as land, in the eruption of lethal violence in Rwanda. A three-part argument will be offered to show how ecological scarcities, caused by distributional inequities, contributed to the Rwandan massacre. First, in the pre-colonial and colonial era, ecological resources were used to determine "ethnicity" that was, then, used as the basis for resource distribution in each of the three eras — pre-colonial, colonial, and post-colonial. Second, the distributionist and productionist polices of the post-colonial Hutu governments contributed to ecological overshoot, creating land scarcities, on the one hand, and social divisions between the Hutus and the Tutsis, and between the northern and southern Hutus, on the other. Third, Hutu leaders, especially from the privileged north, used ecological scarcities in land resources as an incentive for their followers to kill the Tutsis.

To pursue this three-part argument, this chapter will be divided into five sections. Section I introduces the question; Section II will offer the background of the Rwandan massacre; Section III will give a historical account of ecological construction of "ethnicity" and ethnic distribution of ecological resources; Section IV will describe ecological limits and their overshoot; and Section V will discuss the case and offer conclusions.

SECTION II. BACKGROUND

In the colonial era (1916–1962), the Belgians favored the Tutsi minority over the Hutu majority in distribution of material and non-material resources — from land and cattle to jobs and educational opportunities (Waller 1993). The Belgian colonists institutionalized these discriminatory practices into daily life by classifying Hutu and Tutsi along artificially invented ethnic identities (Keane 1995). For the first time, the Belgians issued ethnic identity cards in order to distinguish Hutus and Tutsis, which, however, also led to reinforcing the ethnic divide between them. The Hutu majority resented such discriminatory practices and held the Belgian colonists and their Tutsi allies responsible for their perpetuation (Dorsey 1994). Eventually, their resentment built into what came to be known as the "Hutu Revolution" of 1959, in which 10,000 Tutsis were killed and 120,000 fled to nearby Uganda, Burundi, Zaire, and Tanzania (Watson 1991).

In the post-colonial era (1962–1994), Hutu governments introduced a system of "reverse discrimination" to undo a wrongful past, albeit by revisiting it. The Hutu governments, respectively led by Presidents Kayibanda (1962–1973) and Habyarimana (1973–1994) launched in the 1960s and 1970s the Payasannat — a land resettlement program — to redistribute land among Hutu farmers. Most of the redistributed land was pastureland occupied by Tutsi herdsmen. The Payasannat, thus, displaced over 80,000 farmers and their families, predominantly Tutsis, leading to a mass exit westward into previously unsettled areas (Uvin 1996).

Despite the Payasannat, there was not enough land to go around as Rwanda's total land area is 26,340 square kilometers — smaller than Maryland (FAO 1996). In response to the limitations of land, the Habyarimana government turned to "intensive" agriculture to increase farm and food production, and, thus, ease social unrest by supplying people's basic needs. Instead of helping ease social unrest, the Payasannat, however, worsened it by entailing two destructive outcomes for Rwandan ecology and society. First, conversion of pastures into farmland left the soil impoverished of organic fertilization, as the national livestock of 800,000 heads of cattle (Dorsey 1994), its primary source, became scarce. Second, the Payasannat contributed to the further deepening of already worsened social divisions between the Hutus and the Tutsis, as it was practically converting Tutsi pastures into Hutu farms (Mitchell 1997).

Beyond these substantial measures, the Hutu government also took certain symbolic initiatives that contributed to the deepening of social divisions. One such initiative that later proved lethal in carrying out the Tutsi extermination was the reintroduction of ethnic identity cards. As in the colonial past, the post-colonial Hutu governments also required the Rwandans to register by "ethnicity," and carry "ethnic identity cards" for personal identification (Destexhe 1995, Keane 1995). Later, these cards came in handy to Hutu bands that used them in identifying and tracking down their Tutsi victims of the 1994 massacre.

Two additional factors further sharpened the impact of distributional inequities and their ethnic edges. First, the coffee market crashed in the 1980s, which once accounted for 90% of Rwanda's export earnings, causing its income to decline from $144 million in 1985 to $30 million in 1993 (Uvin 1996). Coffee plantations also provided cash income, although as meager as 32 sterling pounds per household per year (Chossudovsky 1995), to 400,000 farmers, who constituted half of the nation's total strength (Uvin 1996). So, with the collapse of the coffee market, the Rwandan economy went bust. Second the World Bank's Structural Adjustment program led to 60% devaluation of the Rwandan currency (Uvin 1998, Chossudovsky 1995), which left common Rwandans depleted of their purchasing power. The massive devaluation compounded the impact of rural poverty that already was worsened by land scarcity, falling productivity, and a slump in the coffee market.

Thus, failed in its efforts to seek legitimacy in economic growth, the Habyarimana government started on a divisive path — favoring the Hutus over the Tutsis, and the Hutus from the north over those from the south — a region that had become a formidable base of its opposition (Mamdani 2001, Keane 1995). These divisive policies further hardened the oppositional forces among the Tutsis and the Hutus in the South. In 1990, Tutsi refugees based in Uganda banded together into what they called Rwandan Patriotic Front (RPF), and launched a succession of incursions into the northern part of Rwanda in an attempt to remove the Habyarimana government (Keane 1995, Destexhe 1995). By 1993, the RPF war with the Habyarimana government's armed forces, commonly called Rwandan Armed Forces (RAF), led to the displacement of 900,000 Rwandans, who constituted 12% of the national population (Uvin 1996). The RPF incursions, however, came as an ugly reminder to the Rwandans, especially the Hutus in the north, of their domination by the Tutsi minority, who feared in the RPF incursions Tutsis' renewed attempt to recapture power.

Habyarimana capitalized on Hutu fears, and allowed them to form into militant organizations, such as Interahamwa, a militia, and the Coalition for Defense of Rwanda (CDR), that soon began to target the RPF's Tutsi "collaborators" within Rwanda. Habyarimana's death in the shooting down of his plane on April 6, 1994 handed Hutu militant leaders a prefect pretext to whip up mass frenzy against the Tutsis and their moderate allies among the Hutus in the south to avenge the death of their president. They lethally used the incentive of land for rural peasants to kill the Tutsis and thus claim their vacated land (Uvin 1996, Prunier 1995).

The above overview of the Rwandan conflict crystallizes three elements: First, a history of unequal resource distribution eventually was reversed in the post-colonial Hutu-dominated period (1962–1994), making the "victims" into "victimizers" (Mamdani 2001). Second, the Hutu government introduced the Payasannat — a land distribution program — that led to converting Tutsi pastures into Hutu farms (Mitchell, 1997). Third, the impact of the Payasannat, as will be spelled out below, was worsened by ecological limits and ecological over-shoot resulting from intensive agriculture (Waller, 1993). All these factors deepened the pre-existing ethnic divide in society as their impact was distributed along ethnic markers that were constructed around ecological resources and later socially reinforced by German and Belgian colonizers.

In the following section, I shall discuss how ethnic identities were constructed in the pre-colonial era (1500–1897), and how they were reinforced in the colonial era, first by German colonizers (1897–1916) and then by Belgian colonists (1916–1962). Both German and Belgian colonists, however, favored the Tutsis over the Hutus for natural and social resource distribution in land and cattle to educational and job opportunities.

SECTION III. ECOLOGICAL CONSTRUCTION OF ETHNICITY AND ETHNIC DISTRIBU-TION OF ECOLOGY

Ecological Construction of Ethnicity

Since the 15th century when the Twas, the Hutus, and the Tutsis began to live side-by-side, their "ethnicities" were ecologically constructed. Those who dwelled in the forests were called Twas; those who owned cattle, Tutsis; and those who farmed land, Hutus (Keane 1995, Waller 1993). Over time, the ecological construction of social identities was internalized by the Twas, the Hutus, and the Tutsis. These identities, Keane (1995) argues, were still fluid, and one could move from one category of, say, Hutus to another of Tutsis. Later, German and Belgian colonizers "racialized" these identities "according to individuals' degree of beauty, their pride, intelligence, and political organization. The colonizers established a distinction between those who did not correspond to the stereotype of a 'Negro' (i.e., the Tutsi) and those who did (i.e., the Hutu). The first group, 'superior Africans,' were designated Hamites (named after Ham, who was Noah's son), or 'white coloureds' who represented a 'missing link' between the 'Whites' and the 'Blacks' ... Any quality attributed to an African group must be read as a sign of interbreeding with 'non-Negro' cultures ... the 'Hamites' descended from the first 'white' excursions into Africa and degeneration took place as a result of interbreeding" (Keane 1995, pp. 38–39). This racialization of the Twas, the Hutus and the Tutsis persisted into the post-colonial era, despite their shared nationality and the same language. All Rwandans speak the same language, Kiyarwanda, and share the same nationality, Banyarwanda, yet they are distributed into three major "ethnic" groups — the Twas, the Hutus, and the Tutsis. According to 1994 census, of the 7.5 million Rwandans, 90.4% are Hutus, 8.2% Tutsis, and 4% Twas (United Nations 1996).

Ever since their racialization by German colonizers, however, the Hutus and the Tutsis have been regarded as separate "ethnic" groups. Also, Belgian colonists, who took over from the Germans in 1916, treated these two groups as distinct. They made the Tutsis racially superior to the Hutus by identifying them as "Black Caucasians," "African Aryans," and more "European-looking" than Hutu (Keane 1995). By their racist policies, Belgians systematically extended Tutsi domination and exploited Hutu inferiority (Mitchell 1997). In pursuit of these policies, Belgians required Rwandans to register by "ethnicity." Claim to natural resources, however, remained the basis for claiming a desirable ethnicity. Belgian determined cattle-ownership as a criterion for ethnic categorization of the Rwandans: People with ten or more cows were Tutsis; those with fewer, Hutus (Mitchell 1997).

The colonists, later, used these artificially created ethnicities as marker for resource distribution. Based on their presumed ethnic superiority, Belgians showered Tutsis with better employment and educational opportunities (Waller 1993), making them a class of haves, and the Hutu majority a class of have-nots. In the pre-colonial era (1500–1897), resource distribution was based on an exploitative relationship between Hutus and Tutsis. The Tutsi minority exploited the Hutu majority by having it toil on farms and pay tributes to Tutsi chiefs. In return, Tutsi chiefs would provide protection and allow Hutus' access to pastures and cattle ownership. This access would even lift the Hutus from their inferior status of being Hutus (i.e., cultivators or farmers) to become Tutsis (i.e., cattle-owners or herders).

In the colonial era (1897–1962), this exploitative relationship was stripped of reciprocity, setting aside the traditional patron-client relationship between Tutsi patrons and Hutu clients. Blessed by German and Belgian colonists, Tutsi chiefs began to demand that Hutus work for them and pay tributes in physical labor, farm produce, and personal loyalty to Tutsi chiefs without expecting anything in return. This exploitation led to a gradual build-up of resentment among Hutus, which culminated in a series of riots in 1959, claiming the lives of more than 10,000 Tutsis and sending 120,000 to fleeing to the neighboring countries of Burundi, Tanzania, and Uganda (Watson 1991).

Ethnic Distribution of Ecology

Hutus and Tutsis, thus, inherited a history of bitter relationship marked by their struggle over natural resources — forests, land, cattle — that were made scarce by their inequitable distribution. In the pre-colonial and colonial era, it was the Hutu majority that found itself on the receiving end of inequitable resource distribution. In the post-colonial era, it was the Hutu majority that turned on the Tutsi minority, depriving it of its natural and social resources – from pastures and cattle to educational and employment opportunities. It was this history of skewed resource distribution and consequent resource scarcity that fueled an ethnic war that erupted into its most violent form in the post-colonial era. A temporal description of this struggle is given below to show the 500-year old exploitative relationship between Hutus and Tutsis.

Pre-Colonial Era (1500–1897): Tutsi Domination of Hutus

Historical accounts show that Twas — literally meaning those who dwell in the forests — were the first to inhabit what is now Rwanda (Destexhe 1995). By these accounts, they can be described as the "First Nation" or the "First People," or the "Native Rwandans." Twas moved to what is now Rwanda between 2000 BC and 1000 AD, and lived by hunting and gathering in the forests (Waller 1993). Their descendants still dwell in the forests, and live by hunting and gathering.

In the 15th century, independent lineages of Kiga hill dwellers and highly centralized Hutu state systems based on agricultural production and animal husbandry began to expand (Dorsey 1994). They concentrated on clearing the land for cultivation. Their society was organized in small monarchies, based on clans of related families. Their social and cultural life was geared toward preserving and promoting the interests of these clans and their alliances. This population of cultivators is often presumed to be Hutu (Destexhe 1995, Keane 1995), who now form almost 90% of the population.

As Table 1 below summarizes, almost simultaneously Tutsi herdsmen from the north and east from Karagwe, entered the area. Initial contact between Hutus and Tutsis was peaceful and remained so until the end of the 15th century, when Tutsi began to enter Rwanda in greater numbers (Dorsey 1994, Waller 1993). Tutsi expansion and incorporation began from a small nuclear area near Lake Muhazi in the east, the cradle of Rwanda. By the 16th century, Tutsis had established their dominant position, when they absorbed central region of

Rwanda into their kingdom that was seated in Kigali (Destexhe 1995, Dorsey 1994, Waller 1993), now Rwanda's capital.

Table 1. Pre-Colonial Tutsi Domination (1500 to 1897)

15th Century	16th Century	19th Century
Tutsi entered into Rwanda that was previously inhabited by forest-dwelling Twas, and Hutu farmers.	Tutsi hegemony over Hutus and Twas was established through military means and mythical lores.	Umawami Rwagbugiri refined patron-client relationship between Hutus and Tutsis, and thus consolidated Tutsi domination of Hutus.

Source: Destexhe (1995); Keane (1995); Dorsey (1994); Waller (1993).

In the 17th century, Tutsis launched a series of invasions against formerly independent Hutu areas in the north and west, which resulted in a further expansion of Rwanda's boundaries (Waller 1993). These military successes gave Tutsis absolute control over the social, economic and political systems of the pre-colonial era. Their dominant military and economic power was the backbone of Tutsi monarchy, which was founded on Tutsi lineage.

Tutsis reinforced their power in society by developing an oral mythology that featured Tutsi domination over Hutus and Twas as ordained by God, and the omnipotence of the Tutsis and their Mwami (i.e., king) to oversee all walks of life (Destexhe 1995, Dorsey 1994). Above all, the Tutsi Mwami was perceived to control even human "fertility" (Keane 1995). These myths helped break down the resistance, although momentarily, by Hutus and Twas to Tutsi control over the country. Despite being a numerical minority, Tutsi writ was extended to all regions of the country, except its northern and western regions (Waller 1993). Tutsis also developed a complex administrative structure to govern the country. The most innovative part of their administration was a "patron-client" relationship between Hutus and Tutsis (Keane 1995). Under this relationship, Hutu clients were tied to their Tutsi patrons, who could deny their Hutu clients access to pasture, or to cattle, or to military protection, if they would fail to provide them free labor and a portion of crops in tribute. The Tutsi Mwamis also manipulated a complex web of spies, and thus not only maintained their power, but also developed a capacity for political intrigue and paranoia that remains to this day throughout Rwandan society.

In the 19th century, umwami Kigeri Rwabugiri set out to introduce political reforms aimed at consolidating Tutsi power over Rwandan society. As part of his reforms, Rwabugiri refined the traditional patron-client relationship that had facilitated Tutsi exploitation of the Hutus and lesser nobility (Dorsey, 1994). Rwabugiri appointed chiefs to rule frontier regions of the kingdom whose functions were divided into land chiefs (with authority over Hutus) and cattle chiefs (responsible for Tutsi tribute). In each province was appointed an army chief (Dorsey, 1994). With this triumvirate — land chiefs, cattle chiefs, and army chiefs — Tutsis established a centralized power operating from Kigali. With oral myths, ruthless administration, and an exploitative patron-client relationship, the Tutsi minority was able to rule over the Hutus and the Twas.

Colonial Era (1897-1962): Continuation of Tutsi Domination of Hutus

Tutsis continued to dominate Hutus even under the German and Belgian colonization of Rwanda (Keane 1995, Destexhe 1995). Both colonizers elected to rule the Rwandans indirectly through Tutsi monarch and a hierarchy of Tutsi chiefs and sub-chiefs. As Table 2 below summarizes, Rwandan colonization was preceded by the arrival of German explorers in 1894 (Dorsey 1994, Waller 1993).

Table 2. Colonial Era (1897-1962): Continuation of Tutsi Domination of Hutus

German Colonists: 1897–1916	Belgian Colonists: 1916–1962	Fall of Tutsis: 1950–1962
Germans first arrived in 1894, and colonized in 1897. Germans imposed Tutsi chiefs on the north of the country. Popular uprising began in 1911 in the north against Germans and was militarily crushed. Uprising left Hutus bitter towards Germans and especially toward their Tutsi allies.	Belgians expelled Germans, colonized Rwanda and began to rule indirectly through Tutsi monarchs. Hutus were removed from all positions of authority. Hutus were blocked from higher education except priesthood.	In the 1950s, Belgians switched their support from Tutsis to Hutus. Half of Tutsi chiefs and sub-chiefs were replaced with Hutus. In the 1960-62 violence, 20,000 Tutsis were killed and 120,000 fled the country. In 1961, Tutsi monarchy was abolished. On July 1, 1962, Rwanda became an independent country with a first-ever Hutu government.

Source: Destexhe (1995), Keane (1995), Dorsey (1994), Waller (1993).

In the same year the European powers, meeting at the Congress of Berlin, divided Africa among themselves. Rwanda, along with Urundi, now Burundi, was declared to form part of German East Africa (Destexhe 1995). In 1897 the Rwandan Mwami (king) agreed to his country becoming a German protectorate. The Germans imposed Tutsi chiefs on the north of the country. Two years later the first French Catholic missionaries arrived from Uganda (Linden 1977). Within a few years they had set up six missions placed strategically around the country. The Catholic Church fully accepted the racially based interpretation of society that regarded the Tutsis as inherently superior to the Hutus (Linden 1977, Lamarchand 1970).

In 1911 Hutu resentment against the Germans, the Tutsi chiefs, and the Catholic church led to a short-lived popular uprising in the north, near

173

Ruhengeri, which was militarily crushed (Destexhe 1995, Waller 1993). It, however, left northern Hutus embittered towards German colonizers, and especially towards their Tutsi allies. During the First World War, the German forces in Rwanda, after defeated by the Belgians, were expelled from the country. Although the Belgians took over Rwanda under a League of Nations Mandate, they continued the German policy of indirect administration, and reinforced ethnic divisions within the population still further. Hutus were removed from all positions of authority within society, and blocked from all higher education except training for the priesthood. By 1959, the Tutsis occupied 43 of the 45 chiefdoms and 549 of the 559 sub-chiefdoms (Keane 1995). Belgians used chiefdoms and sub-chiefdoms to reinforce Tutsi domination. Earlier, through the custom of "ubuhake," the right to own cattle was effectively assured to the Tutsis, with the Mwami (i.e., Tutsi King), as the ultimate owner of all the cattle (Keane 1995). Thus, "Power was in the hands of the Tutsi pasturalists and hard labor was the lot of the agriculturalists, the "Hutu negroes" and the Twa.... As a result, the term Tutsi became synonymous with a rise in social position" (Keane 1995, p. 40). Tutsi chiefs used their powers within the traditional and colonial systems, whereby the old system of "patron-client" relationship gave way to outright exploitation and repression: Hutu peasants who had given labor and support to their patrons in return for access to cattle, pasture, and security now provided it just because they had to, with no expectation of receiving anything in return.

Gradually, Hutus began to develop resistance to this restructured system of outright exploitation and repression by their Tutsi chiefs and Belgian colonists. Their resistance, in part, also, was inspired by global trends toward decolonization in the 1940s, which helped them to see an end to their exploitation and colonization (Mamdani 2001). As subsequent events showed, their vision was not far from becoming a reality. With the creation of the United Nations in 1945, Rwanda-Urundi was designated as a Belgian "Trustee Territory." The UN insisted on plans for national independence and on the introduction of elected advisory structures (Destexhe 1995). In the 1950s the Catholic Church and the Belgian administration abruptly switched their allegiance from Tutsis to Hutus, and tried to push through reforms (Waller 1993). There were several reasons for this change of policy. A new generation of colonial and church leaders, many of whom had fought against ethnic elitism in Europe in the Second World War, was uncomfortable with the feeling that their organizations were sustaining similar racist policies in Rwanda (Waller 1993).

And as the world polarized around the two great super-powers of the Cold War, and the "winds of change" began to sweep throughout Africa, Tutsis were perceived to be supporting ideas of radical pan-Africanism that were seen as a threat to Western interests. So the church and the administration were only too keen to accept the "democratic" and pliant alternative offered by the emerging Hutu elite. "Thus, by the end of the 1950s, an ethnic awareness had certainly developed among the Rwandan elite. This confusion of a social problem with an ethnic problem during the period leading up to independence was attested to in an important document produced in 1957 by nine Hutu intellectuals, the 'Bahutu Manifesto: A Note on the Social Aspects of the Indigenous Racial Problem in Rwanda.' It is an expression of the first open opposition to Tutsi domination, drawing its inspiration from democratic and egalitarian ideas ... It seems to be more a plea for democracy than a call to revolution although it does contain a denunciation of colonialism by the Hamites (Tutsis) over the Hutu" (Keane 1995, p. 42).

In 1959 Hutu leaders insisted on fundamental change, and the Tutsi leaders resisted. There was tension and then violence, initially against the Tutsi chiefs and then progressively against the wider Tutsi population (Destexhe 1995). With Belgian support, more than half of the Tutsi chiefs and sub-chiefs were replaced by Hutus within the space of a few months (Destexhe 1995). Between 1960 and 1962 the violence spread: 10,000 Tutsis were killed, and another 120,000 fled to neighboring countries as refugees, where they remain to this day (Watson 1991). In 1961 the monarchy was abolished by a constitutional coup d'état mounted by the newly empowered Hutu elite, with the support of the Belgian authorities (Dorsey 1994). The population voted for independence, which was granted on July 1, 1962. The UN Trust Territory became two separate states: the Republic of Rwanda and the Kingdom of Burundi.

Post-Colonial Era (1962-1994): Hutu Majority Takes Over Rwanda

Having won independence, Hutus formed the first government — made up of all Hutus without a single Tutsi represented on it (Destexhe 1995). Kayibanda, a Hutu, was elected the first president of what was now the Republic of Rwanda. As Table 3 below summarizes, over subsequent decades, the Tutsis were targeted for inequitable distribution of natural and social resources — in pastures and cattle to education and employment opportunities.

In the 1960s and the 1970s, the Hutu government sponsored a resettlement program, known as the Paysannat, which displaced over 80,000 farmers and their families culminating in a mass exodus westward into previously unsettled areas. As the Payasannat was converting pastures into farms, it led to the impoverishment of the soils on the one hand, and embitterment of Tutsis, who owned pastures and cattle, on the other (Mitchell, 1997). As a matter of fact, the payasannat was turning Tutsi grazing lands into Hutu farmlands (Mitchell, 1997).

To further marginalize and demoralize the Tutsis, all Rwandans were asked to register by "ethnicity" (Destexhe 1995) — a leaf taken right out of the colonizers' book. This enforced ethnic classification was used in apportionment of natural and social resources (Mitchell 1997). But the most devastating use of this apparently "symbolic" measure was the "genocide" of Tutsis in 1994, when ethnic identity cards came in handy to Hutu bands in identifying and killing their Tutsi victims. "As the stereotypes of physical characteristics do not always provide sufficient identification — it was the identity cards demanded at the roadblocks set up by the militias that acted as the signature on a death warrant for the Tutsis" (Destexhe 1995 p.31).

Table-3. Post-Colonial Era (1962-1994): Hutu Majority Takes Over Rwanda

Hutu Government Formed	Tutsi Resistance Began	Habyarimana Government Reacts
In 1962, Hutu majority formed their government. Paysannat (land distribution program) launched in 1960s-1970s that displaced 80,000 Rwandans. Ethnic Identity Cards were introduced. Ethnic quota in education and jobs introduced: 85% Hutus and 15% Tutsis.	In 1961-67, Tutsi attacked northern Rwanda from their refugee bases in Uganda. In 1972, Tutsis were barred from education in retaliation against Hutu killings in Tutsi-governed Burundi. Hutus resented economic advantage of President Kayibanda's home region, and more so Tutsi influence with his government.	In 1973, General Habyarimana took over as President, and put President Kayibanda under house arrest. In 1990-92, Tutsi RPF attacked Rwanda, setting off civil war. In 1993, Arusha Accords was signed. Coffee prices crashed. Structural Adjustment program worsened rural poverty. In 1994, President Habyarimana's plane shot down in Kigali. Anti-Tutsi violence broke out, killing one million Tutsis.

Source: Destexhe (1995), Keane (1995), Dorsey (1994), Waller (1993).

The Hutu government's anti-Tutsi policies evoked militant response from the Tutsis who had become refugees in neighboring Uganda and Burundi during the 1959 "Hutu Revolution." The militants among these refugees mounted a series of attacks against the northern part of Rwanda between 1961–1967, which earned them a demeaning moniker of the Invenzi — i.e., the "cockroaches that have to be crushed" (Keane 1995, Destexhe 1995). In the face of Tutsi attacks, the Hutu majority feared that Tutsis would once again subjugate them, if their attacks were successful. The subsequent killings of their fellow Hutus in 1972 in Burundi, where Tutsis constitute majority and lead the government, lent credence to Hutu fears. The Hutus in Rwanda responded to these killings with violent reprisals in Rwandan schools, in which many Tutsis were murdered, and many barred from continuing their education (Destexhe 1995).

While the Rwandan government was unsuccessfully grappling with the military offensive posed by the militants among Tutsi refugees and the lethal reprisals within Rwanda, it came under further pressure by Hutu victims of Tutsi attacks. Hutu victims were from the north, particularly in Ruhengeri and Gisenyi, who began to accuse the Kayibanda government of kowtowing to the Tutsis within Rwanda (Waller 1993). They also resented the economic advantage gained by President Kayibanda's home region of Gitarama in the south, which caused a deep rift between the Hutus from the north and the south (Destexhe 1995). Since the Tutsi attacks of 1961-1967, the Kayibanda government now had a dual challenge of regional split and Tutsi militancy. Taking advantage of the government's inability to meet these challenges, the army chief of staff, Juvenal Habyarimana, moved in July 1973 to sack President Kayibanda, and installed himself as president. With his presidency, Habyarimana, also shifted the power base from Gitarama, the home region of the deposed President Kayibanda, to his home region of the northwest. This shift in power soothed the Hutus in the north, but alienated those in the south (Destexhe 1995).

Since his takeover as president, Habyarimana enforced a one-party system based on his National Revolutionary Movement for Development (MRND). He continued discriminatory policies of the past government toward the Tutsis (Mitchell 1997) — in land redistribution, education, and employment opportunities. He also pumped foreign assistance into his home region — the northwest — alienating the south. Soon, the south became a hotbed of oppositional forces represented by both the Tutsis and disaffected Hutus. Nature was not behind either in fomenting disaffection against the Habyarimana government. In 1989, the southwest was gripped by a devastating famine, further deepening the split between the government and its south-centered oppositional forces (Destexhe 1995).

Tutsi refugees based in Uganda took advantage of the groundswell of mass despair with the Habyarimana government, and once again started a military campaign to dislodge it (Keane 1995). On October 1, 1990, as many as 4,000 of them, mostly deserters from President Museveni's army in Uganda, attacked northern Rwanda from their Ugandan base. Banding themselves into a military outfit, the Rwandan Patriotic Front (RPF), they were led by Fred Rwigyema, who demanded that President Habyarimana step down. After a series of important successes during the first week of the war, the RPF met resistance from government troops that were supported by France, Belgium, and Zaire (Keane 1995). The war, thus, turned into a protracted guerrilla conflict that continued well into the early 1990s. Between November 1990 and July 1992 the rebels gradually took a strip of land along the length of Rwanda's border with Uganda.

In July 1992, a ceasefire was negotiated in Arusha, Tanzania, but it failed to hold. When power-sharing arrangements were finally agreed in January 1993, the extremist Hutu Party (the Coalition for Defense of Republic (CDR) emerged, and together with elements of the MRND, responded by killing political opponents and Tutsis in Gisenyi and Ruhengeri (Destexhe, 1995). As a result, in February 1993, the RPF — now 12,000-strong — a three-fold increase from its initial strength of 4,000 in 1990 — renewed its attacks and doubled its territory in three days (Mitchell, 1997). But the RPF military successes engendered a huge refugee crisis as 900,000 people (12% of the Rwandan population) had to seek refuge far from their homes (Destexhe 1995).

The disastrous outcome of this civil war was further compounded, when three factors drove the national economy to a total collapse. First, the World Bank and IMF initiated the Structural Adjustment program that led to a massive devaluation of the Rwandan currency — knocking off 60% of its value — which left common Rwandans depleted of their purchasing power (Uvin, 1998; Chossudovsky, 1995). As a matter of fact, the structural adjustment program affected all segments of the population, except for the Rwandan Armed Forces (RAF) that had grown from a force of about 5,000 in 1990 to around 35,000 in 1992 (Waller, 1993).

Second, the crash of coffee prices in the 1980s left half of the nation's farmers (400,000) without a steady source of cash income, although a pittance of 32 sterling pounds per household per year, whose impact was far more deeply felt in the rural hinterland of the country (Destexhe, 1995). Rural residents, being 93% of the population (NCA, 1991), were devastated by the crash of the coffee market. The impact of the coffee market's crash was compounded by the stagnant food production that grew at the rate of 0.6% a year between 1976 and 1983, and then, at the rate of 0.2% a year between 1984 and 1989 (NCA, 1991). This massive decrease in farm production rendered the Rwandan subsistence economy unsustainable. According to World Bank data, the growth of GDP per capita declined from 0.4% in 1981–86 to -5.5% in the period immediately following the slump of the coffee market, i.e., 1987–91 (Chossudovsky 1995). It seemed there was too little left in the land and the soil to extract any more. The reason, however, was quite obvious: Decades of ecological overshoot that was fueled by distributional inequities in resource appropriation. In the following section, I shall discuss how the Rwandans over harvested their natural resource base, creating ecological scarcities to their lethal disadvantage.

SECTION IV. ECOLOGICAL LIMITS AND ECOLOGICAL OVERSHOOT

The social impact of distributional inequities of pre-colonial, colonial, and post-colonial era was manifested in regional disparities and ethnic animosities that eventually tore apart Rwandan society. Similarly, the ecological impact of these inequities was reflected in the destruction of Rwanda's natural resource base, especially during the post-colonial Habyarimana government. The post-colonial Hutu governments of Presidents Kayibanda and Habyarimana pursued distributionist and productionist farm policies that caused what Catton (1988) calls "overshoot" — i.e., over-harvesting of natural resources. Contrary to the claims of many commentators, such as Percival and Homer-Dixon, (1995), these limits were not reached due to population density, however. As Catton (1988) argues, it is the "per capita activity," — not the population density — that causes the overshoot to occur. Also, in the case of Rwanda, as will be spelled out below, it was the land use pattern that worsened ecological limits, creating a wide-spread land scarcity that was later used as an incentive for Hutus to kill Tutsis (Prunier, 1995). Below, I shall discuss ecological limits in three quantifiable indicators — land, soil, and water — to show how their overshoot ended up in eco-logical scarcities, especially those that manifested in land shortage.

Land Limits

Rwanda is limited by land supply, both in quantity and quality. As Table 4 below shows, Rwanda's reported area is 26, 340 square kilometer (smaller than Maryland), while its land area is 24, 950 sq km. Most of its agricultural land of 17, 758 square kilometer is naturally irrigated (i.e., rain-fed). Artificial irrigation is negligible, as only 40 square kilometer of farmland is under irrigation (FAO, 1995).

Table 4. Land Distribution

Total Area	Land Area	Irrigated land
26,340 sq km	24,950 sq km	40 sq km

Source: FAO (1995)

Rwanda's land limits become even more severe when it comes to the quality of land and resultant land use patterns. As Table 5 below shows, Rwanda's total arable land is 29%. Of the remaining land, 11% is under permanent crops, 18% under meadows and pastures, 10% under forests, and 32% for other purposes (FAO 1995). Virtually, all available land is under cultivation (Clay, Kampayana and Kayitsinga 1988), except for two sub regions — the Nyabarngo and Akegera Park. Another indicator of land shortage was the dwindling base of forestland that dropped from 30% to just 7% in the early 1990s (Dorsey 1994). The revised estimate in 1996 shows a positive development of increase in forest growth up from 7% to 10% (FAO 1995). But this growth, although interpreted as good news, had a downside in adverse ecological outcomes.

Table 5. Land Use Pattern

Arable Land	Permanent Crops	Meadows/Pastures	Forests/Woodlands	Other
29%	11%	18%	10%	32%

Source: FAO (1995).

Soil Limits

Rwandan soils are severely deficient in organic matter, a deficiency that further worsens land limits. Because of this deficiency, the Rwandan soils cannot absorb much of the artificial fertilizers, which, if applied, are rapidly leached away (NCA 1991). Some of its soils, such as volcanic soils, are fertile, but other on slopes or in the south are marginal. Because of soil limits, Rwanda is divided into 12 agro-ecological zones, defined by climate characteristics and compatible farming practices (Clay and Lewis 1990). Upland farming that is widespread in Rwanda poses biggest challenge in soil erosion, however. On the steepest slopes, intense rainfall erodes more than 11 tons of soil per hectare per year. In aggregate terms, soil erosion comes to 12 million tons a year (NCA 1991). The government's Payasannat program had speeded the process of soil erosion by encouraging the settlement of hillside areas on the one hand, and low-potential valley-bottom areas and pastures on the other. The conversion of pastures into cropland also led to a decrease in the production of organic fertilizer, causing soil fertility to decline even further (Clay and Lewis 1990).

These soil limitations are, however, unevenly distributed across regions. The northwest region has high-potential productive land that is claimed by more privileged Hutu farmers, who grow higher-value products. Similarly, in the east of Lake Kivu, there are the giant peaks (a maximum of 14,000 feet in the Virunga region) that traverse the entire region from north to south. This is a region of ancient volcanoes, which are now covered with thick tropical woodlands that merge into an undulating plateau, with altitudes of 4,500 feet to 6,500 feet (Dorsey 1994). The hills and valleys in this region are scattered with eucalyptus trees and banana groves, as well as patches of luxuriant pastures. The region is quite fertile and used for herding and the cultivation of food crops (Dorsey 1994).

Water Limits

Rwandan agriculture is not limited by land and soil alone. Its major challenge comes from water deficit. As a land-locked country, Rwanda's surface water supply is marginal. Its only substantial but variable source of water is seasonal precipitation that varies between 40 and 50 inches a year (Engleman and LeRoy 1993). This variability in precipitation punctuates a given year by a long dry season, which extends from May/June to mid-September; a short rainy season from mid-September to January; and a much longer rainy season from the end of January to the beginning of May. An interruption of the cycle causes crop failure, drought, and near-famine conditions. The famines of 1916 and 1943 caused 50,000 and 36,000 deaths respectively (Dorsey 1994). Droughts are, therefore, listed as the most serious natural hazard to the Rwandan economy. One response to the drought conditions could have been irrigated farming; but water scarcity gets in the way, due to which the total irrigated land, as has been noted before, is no more than just 40 square kilometers (FAO 1995). As opposed to droughts, intense rainfall, on the other hand, produces second-order natural limits to agricultural production: On steep slopes, it erodes 12 million tons of soils per year (more than 11 tons per hectare per year) that washes into Rwanda's rivers (NCA 1991).

Ecological Overshoot

Since independence, the Rwandan governments have pursued an economic agenda that led to the over-harvesting of Rwanda's natural resource base, especially its arable land area, by expanding agricultural operations on to marginal land, such as highland, swamps, and pastures. The government's

Payasannat initiative, aimed at land resettlement, was in fact an answer to the limited supply of productive land, which was increased by 13% between 1981 and 1991 with the resettlement of marginal land (World Resources Institute 1994) According to an estimate, 76% of all rural communes (households) moved to hillside and valley-bottom areas, which both are considered ecologically unviable to sustain agricultural operations (Lewis, Clay and Dejaegher 1988).

The new settlements were subjected to additional ecological stresses, as settlers had clear-cut forests, drained wetlands, and turned pastures into farmland. As a result, the forest cover dwindled from 30% to 7% in 1990 (Dorsey 1994), creating a combine of ecological and social impact in soil erosion and scarcity of timber and fuel-wood. In response to social needs for timber and fuel-wood, the government started a reforestation program by planting the fast-growing eucalyptus tree (Uvin 1996). As eucalyptus matures as fast as in a year time, its enthusiastic plantation, 80% of the entire woodlots (Waller 1993), did supply timber and fuel needs at a faster rate, but at an ecological cost to farmland, nevertheless. As a fast-growing species, eucalyptus tends to dredge the soil of its nutrients from far and deep, leaving little or nothing for nearby vegetation or plantation (Shiva 2002). In Rwanda, too, this Australian native tree species, despite having met part of timber and fuel needs, had cost in other important farm and food supplies.

The ecological impact of cutting down forests, draining wetlands, and cultivating pastures was equally devastating. Combined with farming on steep slopes, deforestation multiplied the risk of soil depletion and soil erosion that, as noted before, had now reached 12 million tons a year (NCA 1991). Similarly, drained wetlands increased the risk of flooding and thereby contributed to further soil erosion. Above all, conversion of pastures into farmland deprived the already impoverished land of a precious source of organic fertilization from the nation's livestock of 800,000 heads of cattle (Dorsey 1994).

Sensing the limitations of the Payasannat — the land resettlement program — the government shifted its attention from "extensive" agriculture to "intensive" agriculture –i.e., growing more crops from a given unit of land. The drive for intensive agricultural was, however, successful in the northwest region that has relatively high-potential productive land, which enabled the region's farmers to grow higher-value crops (Uvin 1996). As the northwest was President Habyarimana's home region, its farmers also were beneficiaries of generous government funds (Waller 1993) that further helped the region's growth potential. On the other hand, the south had no such luck in land quality or the gov-

ernment's lavish attention. Conversely, the southern region was severely challenged by ecological scarcities in land productivity, water deficit, and frequent
droughts followed by crop failures and famines, which together contributed to
the failure of the government's campaign for intensive agriculture (Andre and
Platteau 2002). As a matter of fact, the region was shaken by droughts and consequent crop failures in the 1980s and 1990s. Broadly, the government's land
resettlement program and farm intensification drive failed to achieve its
intended goals: Increase in food production. On the contrary, the total increase
in food production over the seven-year period from 1976 to 1983 was just 4.3% —
an average of 0.6% a year (NCA 1991). For the following five years, from 1984 to
1989, increase in the total food production was just 1% — an average of 0.2% a
year (NCA 1991). As a subsistence economy, Rwanda's falling farm production
adversely impacted its per capita Gross Domestic Product (GDP) growth rate
also, which dropped from 0.4% in 1981–86 to -5.5% in 1987–1991 (Chossudovsky,
1995). On the other hand, farm growth was unevenly distributed across regions,
with explosive implications. Because of higher land productivity in the north,
the government's farm intensification drive was far more successful in the north
than the south. As a result, it further deepened the regional disparities between
the north and the south, making the south even more attractive for oppositional
forces (Kamukama 1993).

An important component of the government's campaign for intensive agriculture was its "single-crop bias" that turned out to be even more disastrous for
the Rwandan economy (Chossudovsky 1995). The government's singular focus
was on coffee production, which accounted for 90% of its export earnings (Chossudovsky 1995). The singularity of the government's focus on the commodity
and its earning potential turned the Rwandan economy into a single-crop
economy to the disadvantage of farmers. With the collapse of the coffee market
in the 1980s, 400,000 Rwandan farmers, half of the nation's total strength,
ripped up 300,000 coffee plants to clear the land for food crops (Lewis, Clay and
Dejegher 1998, Clay and Johnson 1992). As coffee plantation had an ecological
pay-off in coffee mulches that farmers would use as organic fertilizer, its clearing
for food crops left the soils unfertilized and food crops unsustainable (Clay and
Johnson 1992). Ever since food crops began to fail, and the country witnessed
worst famines in the late 1980s and the early 1990s (Uvin 1996). Another sad
reality of coffee production was the distribution inequity in pricing that verged
on outright exploitation of coffee farmers by the government, which would buy
the commodity from farmers at a lowest-possible price, and sell it in the interna-

tional market at internationally competitive prices. Farmers had no share in the export earnings either, to which the Habyarimana government and its 7,000 cronies in Kigali would exclusively help themselves (Waller 1993). The government's policies of "extensive" and "intensive" agriculture, thus, brought about an ecological breakdown, the devastating impact of which was witnessed in soil depletion, soil erosion, deforestation, lack of organic fertilization, and consequent massive drop in farm and food production.

The argument that the ecological breakdown was due to population pressure (Percival and Homer-Dixon 1995) seems superficially plausible, but it does not hold up under scrutiny. First, The Rwandan population has been actually decreasing at an alarming rate of about 6% a year between 1990 and 1995 (United Nations 1996). Second, population was unevenly distributed along ethnic lines. The most densely populated area was Ruhondo in Ruhengeri with 820 people per square kilometer of arable land, which was predominantly inhabited by the Tutsi minority (Waller 1993). On the other hand, Rusomo and Kibungo areas had as little as 62 people per square kilometer of arable land. So, with this kind of skewed distribution of land resources along ethnic lines, the sole reliance on aggregate population density rate would mask the distributional inequities in disaggregate terms. Third, even the national average of Rwanda's population density is much lower than its former colonizer, Belgium: Belgium has 322 people per square kilometer as opposed to Rwanda's average population density of 271 people per square kilometer in 1991 (Waller 1993). Fourth, Rwandan population provided much needed stewardship to its natural resources. Under the Umuganda (i.e., donation of individual adult labor for community projects) tradition of community labor, which started in the 1970s, all Rwandan adults would have to donate a day of labor for community projects, such as anti-erosion ditches, trenches for gravity-fed water systems, reforestation, and even road projects. Through Umuganda, the area of woodlots was doubled in just six years between 1980 and 1986, and it was slated to be doubled again by 2000 (Waller 1993). Without Umuganda, the state of the environment and soils, forests, and roads would have been far worse. So, "more people" do not mean "more trouble," as Grosse (1994) concludes. Fifth, larger families were less dependent upon their smaller land holdings for living than households of larger-holdings (Andre and Platteau 2002), as large-sized families would seek off-farm jobs.

Contrary to the Malthusian arguments, land scarcity in Rwanda was, thus, not caused by population density. Instead, it was a function of two factors: first, the government's ethnically driven distributionist policies did violence to both the fragile agro-ecological base (i.e., uplands, swamps, pastures, forests) and its human dependents — Tutsi herdsmen and Twa forest-dwellers on the one hand and the Hutus in the south on the other. These policies led to the worst kind of deforestation and soil degradation, which in turn caused excessive damage to land productivity. So, it was these distributionist policies that caused a decline in "productive land," and also damaged "land productivity," creating the need for more land in the process.

Second, the government's productionist policies (aimed at intensive agriculture) were driven by its regional bias to develop the north and northwest region at the cost of the rest of the country, especially the south and the east (Uvin 1996). These policies also moved northern Hutus to settle in the south and claim the land abandoned by the Tutsis who became refugees in neighboring countries. The refugees' return under the Arusha Peace Accords was seen as a threat to these new claimants to the land abandoned by Tutsi refugees (Waller 1993).

These two factors created ecologically destructive and socially divisive outcomes by widening regional disparities and deepening social divisions. Later, consistent with its divisive approach, the Habyarimana government and its militant allies in the Hutu militia Interahamwe and the Coalition for Defense of the Republic (CDR) used ecological scarcities in land as an incentive for the Hutus in the north to kill the Tutsis and their moderate Hutu allies in the south (Uvin 1996, Prunier 1995).

SECTION V. DISCUSSION AND CONCLUSIONS

Discussion of the Case

The case of Rwanda suggests that distributional inequities in land resources played a major part in sowing social divisions in the pre-colonial, colonial, and post-colonial era. The distributionist and productionist policies of the post-colonial Hutu governments, however, further worsened social divisions and ecological scarcities that were later used by Hutu leaders as an incentive for their followers to kill the Tutsis.

In the pre-colonial era (1500-1897), Rwanda was first inhabited by Twas, who dwelled in the forests. They were, later, joined by the Hutus, who farmed the land. The last to come were the Tutsis, who owned cattle. Over time, the "ethnic identities" of these groups were built around ecological resources — forests for the Twas, land for the Hutus, and cattle for the Tutsis. Once these identities came into vogue, they became the basis for ecological resource distribution that was highly skewed. Twas, who at 1% of the population, were marginal in number but in occupation of 30% of the forestland, were gradually pushed out of their forest dwellings. Hutus who needed farmland for farming and Tutsis who needed pastures for grazing would forcibly clear-cut forests to convert them into farm fields and pastures. As a result, the forests had, over time, dwindled from 30% to just 7% (Dorsey 1994). Similarly, the dominant Tutsi group would coerce the subordinate Hutu group into giving up their farmland for pastures (Newbury 1993). This happened both in the pre-colonial and colonial era, when the Tutsi minority was the dominant group and the Hutu majority, a subordinate group. The Hutu majority resented their subordination to the Tutsi minority that continued to exploit Hutu labor and resources for about 500 years (Newbury 1993).

Toward the end of the Belgian colonial rule in the 1950s, the Hutus experienced democratic empowerment, as Belgian colonists switched their support from the Tutsi minority to the Hutu majority. The transition that followed this re-alignment of support was not peaceful, however. In 1959, riots erupted in which ten thousand Tutsis were killed and 120,000 of them fled the country to become refugees in the neighboring nations of Burundi, Uganda, Zaire, and Tanzania (Watson 1991). In 1962, Rwanda won its independence from Belgians, and an all-Hutu government was installed.

Since independence, the Hutu governments (1962–1994), respectively led by Kayibanda (1962–1973) and Habyarimana (1973–1994), initiated two programs, aimed at land resettlement and intensified farming, that eventually contributed to the further widening of regional disparities and deepening of divisions between the Hutus and the Tutsis. The Payasannat — a land redistribution program — displaced 800,000 farmers (Waller 1993). It was followed by a campaign for intensive agriculture to increase farm and food production, which also was the government's response to land scarcity that was primarily caused by its distributionist policies. The ecological outcome of the government's distributionist policies was even more damaging. As under the government-launched Payasannat, Tutsi pastures were converted into Hutu farms, the livestock became scarce, depriving the soils of the most important source of organic fertilizers. Similarly, the farmers who settled the unsettled areas in the hillside, swamps, and pastures caused severe damage to the soil by accelerating its erosion. One manifestation of this widespread ecological damage was the stagnant food production that grew at the rate of 0.6% a year between 1976 and1983, and 0.2% a year between 1984 and1989 (NCA 1991). The impact of these policies was further compounded by a set of economic blows that came from a crash in coffee prices and 60% devaluation of the Rwandan currency necessi- tated by the World Bank's Structural Adjustment program (Chossudovsky 1995). The crash in coffee prices was, however, hard to absorb as coffee accounted for 90% of the government's foreign exchange earnings, and upon which depended half (400,000) of the nation's farmers for cash income, even though a pittance at 32 sterling pounds per household per year. The impact of these economic factors was the worsened economic condition for rural residents — 93% of the nation's population — which left them in an even deeper mire of poverty.

Having, thus, failed in its efforts to seek legitimacy in economic growth, the Habyarimana government started on a divisive path — favoring the Hutus over the Tutsis, and the Hutus from the north over those from the south — a region that had become a formidable base of its opposition. These divisive pol- icies further hardened the oppositional forces among the Tutsis and the Hutus in the South. In 1990, Tutsi refugees based in Uganda banded together into what they called Rwanda Patriotic Front (RPF), and launched a succession of incur- sions into the northern part of Rwanda in an attempt to remove the Habya- rimana government. By 1993, the RPF war with Habyarimana's Rwanda's Armed Forces (RAF) led to the displacement of 900,000 Rwandans, who constituted 12% of the national population (Uvin 1996). The RPF incursions, however, came as an ugly reminder to the Rwandans, especially the Hutus in the north, of their domination by the Tutsi minority, who feared in the RPF incursions Tutsis' renewed attempt to recapture power.

Driven by these fears, Hutus from the privileged north and the northwest rallied around their government and its leader, Habyarimana, who planned to cash in on their fears. Habyarimana allowed some elements within his gov- ernment, and his political outfit, National Revolutionary Movement for Devel- opment (MNRD), to found a Coalition for Defense of the Republic (CDR), which raised a militia called Interahamwe — meaning those who stand together — to ratchet up anti-Tutsi frenzy and thus direct people's frustration from the government's failings to their Tutsi scapegoats. The April 6, 1994 shooting down of the Habyarimana's plane in Kigali, Rwanda's capital, provided a perfect pretext for militant Hutus to take up machetes against the Tutsi minority, whom they suspected of killing their president. This frenzied war continued for three months — from April to July, 1994 — in which a million Tutsis were hacked to death (Keane, 1995). Ironically, their killers turned a technology of subsistence — the machete — into a weapon of mass destruction. They were primarily motivated by their hunger for land, which Hutu leaders skillfully whetted in inciting them to mass violence against the Tutsis (Uvin 1996, Prunier 1995).

CONCLUSIONS

In the colonial and pre-colonial era, distributional inequities led to the Tutsi monopoly of natural and social resources –from farms, forests, pastures, and cattle to personal security and even the possibilities of lifting oneself from an "inferior" status of being a Hutu (i.e., a farmer) to a "superior" one of a Tutsi (i.e., a cattle-owner). The Tutsi monopoly of resources created their artificial scarcity for the Hutu majority, a scarcity that was later exploited by a hierarchy of Tutsi chiefs and sub-chiefs. In the colonial era, the Tutsi monopoly of resources degenerated into an outright exploitation of Hutu labor and land resources, unencumbered by the obligations of a reciprocal "patron-client" relationship that existed in the pre-colonial era. The Tutsi chiefs, having set aside the patron-client relationship, now demanded that the Hutus provide labor and farm produce in tribute without expecting anything in return.

In the post-colonial era, the government's distributionist and productionist policies created disastrous outcomes for Rwandan society and its ecological base. In social terms, these policies widened regional disparities between the north and the south, and deepened social divisions between the Hutus and the Tutsis. In ecological terms, these policies over harvested the fragile natural resource base of the country by settling the uplands, clear-cutting the forests, draining the wetlands, and converting the pastures into farmland. These ecological outcomes were not without social consequences either, as the depleting forest cover was pushing the Twas out of the forests; conversion of pastures into farmland was limiting the avenues of subsistence for Tutsi herdsmen; and farmers from the north were crowding out farmers in the south.

These ecological and social outcomes were driven by land scarcities, which together hastened the collapse of the Rwandan subsistence economy, shattering the legitimacy of the Habyarimana government in the process. Thus, stripped of

its legitimacy, the Habyarimana government, together with its Hutu beneficiaries in the north, began to practice a socially divisive agenda of pitting the
Hutus against the Tutsis. In particular, their militant organizations — interahamwe and the Coalition for Defense of the Republic (CDR) — whipped up
mass frenzy against the Tutsis and their moderate allies among the Hutus in the
south. The killing of President Juvenal Habyarimana on April 6, 1994, handed
Hutu leaders a perfect excuse to translate the mass frenzy against the Tutsis into
their mass murder.

In summary, the case of Rwanda supports four specific conclusions: First,
it was the skewed distribution of ecological resources — forests, land, cattle —
that eventually culminated in the Rwandan Holocaust. Second, ethnicities built
around ecological resources were socially reinforced in the colonial and post-
colonial era to justify such skewed resource distribution. Third, distributional
inequities in land resources led to ecological scarcities by settling fragile agro-
ecosystems of uplands, swamps, pastures, forests and woodland. Fourth, ecological scarcities in land resources were used as an incentive for the Hutus to kill
the Tutsis.

In addition, the case of Rwanda supports the following general conclusions:

First, ecological scarcities do not flare into social conflagration on their
own; instead, it is their instrumentality grounded in distributional inequities
along ethnic markers that comes in handy to social actors, who in turn employ
them to advance their agenda. This reciprocity between natural and social forces
forms into what Catton and Dunlap (1980) call "ecological-sociological
complex."

Second, resource-dependent societies are highly sensitive to "inequitable"
resource distribution, which could put such societies at the highest risk of
erupting into lethal violence. In such events, an "equitable" distribution of
resources is the only "humanitarian intervention" that can keep "unjust" societies from becoming "genocidal."

These conclusions are even more relevant to post-genocide Rwanda,
which has been run by the Tutsi-dominated Rwanda Patriotic Front (RPF) government since July 1994 when it seized its control. On August 25, 2003, the
RPF's candidate, Maj. Gen. Paul Kagami was "elected" president of the country
with 95% of votes cast. His opponent Faustin Twagiramungu, a Hutu, polled as
few as 3.5% votes. In a country where Hutus now make up 85% (down from
90%) of its 8.5 million population (2 million Hutus are still refugees in neigh-

boring countries), Twagiramungu's tally of votes has raised many eyebrows. The European Union, Human Rights Watch and Amnesty International have found the presidential elections flawed. Similarly, the RPF claimed 70% of parliamentary seats in legislative elections held in September 2003, while Hutu-dominated Mouvement Democratique Republicain (MDR) — or Democratic Republican Movement — was banned early in 2003. The MDR's successor party — ADEP-Mizero — also was "nipped in the bud" by the Tutsi-dominated government that denied it "legal status" on charges of "foreign funding."

Besides, the RPF and its leader Paul Kagami are engaged in muzzling dissent under the garb of national integration. The Kagami government labels dissent as "divisionism," a term of discredit that is used as euphemism for "racism." The Rwandan Constitution, passed in May 2003, outlaws "ethnic divisionism." But it is the Hutu opposition parties and Hutu political candidates who are being charged with "ethnic divisionism." The Kagami government outlawed the Hutu-dominated MDR and sent into exile the two major Hutu candidates for president in the August 2003 presidential elections on charges of fanning "ethnic divisionism." To promote national integration, the RPF government has forcibly merged Hutu and Tutsi identities into a "Rwandese identity" — i.e., "we are all Rwandese." This coercive merger of ethnic identities has led to the invention of alternative terms, which are far more negatively emotionally charged, to distinguish Tutsis from Hutus and Hutus from Tutsis. "Rescape" is one such term that people use to refer to Tutsi survivors of the genocide, but it is now widely employed for all Tutsis. So is "genocidaire" that Tutsis use for Hutu dissidents.

As the foregoing account reveals, inequities are once again on the rise in post-genocide Rwanda that increasingly resembles the Tutsi domination of Hutus in the pre-colonial and colonial era, which spanned over 500 years. If the past is any guide, Rwanda's inequitable present mirrors a future fraught with horrors. Post-genocide Rwanda sends forth an urgent call for a preemptive humanitarian intervention in a global effort to help remake it into a just and fair society for all ethnic groups.

NOTES

*The author would like to thank his mentor and benefactor, Dr. William R. Freudenburg, Dehlsen Endowed Chair of Environmental Studies Program at the University of California, Santa Barbara, for his continued support to his past and present research work.

REFERENCES

Andre, Catherine and Jean-Philippe Platteau. 2002. "Land Relationship Under Unbearable Stress: Rwanda Caught in the Malthusian Trap." *Journal of Economic Behavior and Organization.* (forthcoming)

Berkeley, Bill. 2001. The Graves Are Not Yet Full: Race, Tribe, and Power in the Heart of Africa. Basic Books.

Catton, William. 1980. *Overshoot: The Ecological Basis of Revolutionary Change.* Urbana, Chicago, IL: University of Chicago Press.

Catton, W. and R. Dunlap. 1980. "A New Ecological Paradigm for Post-Exuberant Sociology." *American Behavioral Scientist* 24: 41-9.

Chossudovsky, Michel. 1995. *IMF-World Bank Policies and the Rwandan Holocaust.* Penang, Malaysia: Third World Network Features.

Clay, Daniel C. and Nan Johnson. 1992. "Size of Farm or Size of Family: Which Comes First?" *Population Studies* 46(2): 491-505

Clay, Daniel C. and Laurence A. Lewis. 1990. "Land Use, Soil Loss, and Sustainable Agriculture in Rwanda." *Human Ecology* 18(2): 147–161.

Clay Daniel C. and Theobald Kampayana. 1989b. *Inequality and the Emergence of Non-farm Employment in Rwanda.* Paper presented at the Annual Meeting of the Rural Sociological Society, Seattle, 1989.

Clay, Daniel C., Theobald Kampayana, and Jean Kayitsinga. 1988. *Inequality and the Emergence of Non-farm Employment in Rwanda.* East Lansing, MI: Michigan State University. Agricultural Surveys and Policy Analysis Project (ASPAP).

Destexhe, Alain. 1995. *Rwanda and Genocide in the Twentieth Century.* New York: New York University Press.

Dorsey, Learthen. 1994. *Historical Dictionary of Rwanda.* London: The Scarecrow Press, Inc.

Engelman, E. and P. LeRoy. 1993. *Sustaining Water: Population and the Future of Renewable Water Supplies.* Washington, DC: Population Action International

FAO (Food And Agriculture Organization Of The United Nations). 1995. Country Tables: Basis Data on the Agricultural Sector. Rome: FAO

Grosse, Scott. 1994. *More People, More Trouble.* Draft Paper, Department of Population Planning and International Health. University of Michigan.

Hauge, Wenche and Tanja Ellingsen. 2001. "Causal Pathways to Conflict." In Paul F. Diehl and Nils Petter Gleditsch (eds.) *Environmental Conflict*. Boulder, CO: Westview

Kamukama, Dixon. 1993. *Rwanda Conflict: Its Roots and Regional Implications*. Kampala: Fountain Publishers.

Keane, Fergal. 1995. *Season of Blood: A Rwandan Journey*. London: Viking

Lamarchand, Rene. 1970. *Rwanda and Burundi*. New York: Praeger.

Lewis, L. A., Daniel Clay, and Y. M. J. Dejaegher. 1988. "Soil Loss, Agriculture, and Conversation in Rwanda: Towards Strategies for Soil Management." *Journal of Water and Soil Conservation* 43(5): 418–421.

Linden, Ian. 1977. *Church and Revolution in Rwanda*. Manchester: Manchester University Press.

Mamdani, Mahmood. 2001. When Victims Become Killers: Colonialism, Nativism, and the Genocide in Rwanda. Princeton University Press.

Melvern, Linda. 2000. A People Betrayed: The Role of the West in Rwanda's Genocide. London: Zed Books.

Mitchell, Tara. 1997. *Rwanda and Conflict*. Washington, DC: International Conflict and The Environment (ICE).

National Commission on Agriculture. 1991. National Commission on Agriculture. Kigali, Rwanda: Republic of Rwanda.

Newbury, Catharine. 1993. The Cohesion of Oppression: Clientship and Ethnicity in Rwanda, 1860-1960.

O'Halloran, Patrick J. 1995. *Humanitarian Intervention and the Genocide in Rwanda*. London: Research Institute for the Study of Conflict and Terrorism.

Olson, Jennifer. 1995. "Behind the Recent Tragedy in Rwanda." *GeoJournal* 35(2): 217–222.

Omaar, Rakiya and Alex de Waal. (1995). "Genocide in Rwanda: US Complicity by Silence." *Covert Action Quarterly* 52(6).

Percival, Valerie and Thomas Homer-Dixon. 1995. *Environmental Scarcity and Violent Conflict: The Case of Rwanda*. Washington, DC: American Association for the Advancement of Science and University of Toronto.

Prunier, Gerard. 1997. *The Rwandan Crisis: History of a Genocide (1959-1994)*. London: Hurst Publishers.

Silliman, Jael and Ynestra King. 1996. "Introduction." In Jael Silliman and Ynestra King (eds.) *Dangerous Intersections: Feminist Perspectives on Population, Environment and Development*. Cambridge, MA: South End Press.

Tsing, Anna Lowenhaupt. 1993. In the Realm of the Diamond Queen: Marginality in an Out-of-the-Way Place. Princeton University Press.

United Nations. 1996. *World Population Prospects*. New York: United Nations

Uvin, Peter. 1998. *Aiding Violence: The Development Enterprise in Rwanda*. Kumarian Press.

_____. 1996. "Tragedy in Rwanda: The Political Ecology of Conflict." *Environment* 34(3): 7–15.

Shiva, Vandana. 2002. *Water Wars: Privatization, Pollution, and Profit.* Cambridge, MA: South End Press.

Waller, David. 1993. *Rwanda: Which Way Now? An Oxfam Country Profile.* Oxford: Oxfam.

Watson, Catherine. 1991. *Exile From Rwanda: Background to an Invasion.* Washington: US Committee for Refugees.

World Resources Institute. 1994. *World Resources 1994-1995.* New York: Oxford University Press.

CHAPTER 9. THE FORGOTTEN DEAD: REPRESENTATIONS OF THE PAST IN THE TIBETAN REFUGEE COMMUNITY IN INDIA

Lydia Aran

I

Tibet is a huge, landlocked, sparsely populated country in Central Asia, bordered by massive mountain ranges containing the world's highest peaks.[1] The northern part of the country is arid and almost uninhabitable except by nomads. The central and south Tibet contain wide and fertile valleys, which have been the home of Tibetan civilization for over a thousand years. Due to its remoteness, physical inaccessibility, dramatic landscapes and unique religious civilization, Tibet has for long stimulated Western imagination and even now its image often reflects a mythologized and romanticized rather than a realistic version of its society and culture (Bishop 1989 and 1993, Lopez 1998, Schell 2000, Dodin and Rather 2001). From the seventh to the mid-ninth century Tibet was a powerful kingdom during which time Buddhism was brought from India, Indian script was adapted to the Tibetan language, and the first monastery in Tibet was founded by Indian masters, laying foundations of the unique Tibetan Buddhist civilization. Since mid-seventeenth century, Tibet has been ruled by a succession of Dalai Lamas,[2] religious-political leaders, inheriting the office by reincarnation, a line of which the 14th Dalai Lama, now in exile in India, is the latest link. The traditional Tibetan regime is often described as theocracy, but, in contrast to other theocracies in which the ruling clergy competes for power with other sectors, in traditional Tibet, politics and religion were indivisible *in principle* and their unity was seen as part of the Tibetan national identity.

Following its submission to the Mongols in the thirteenth century, Tibet's status vis-à-vis China has varied at different times and in any case cannot be unambiguously defined in terms of modern political concepts. Though at times de-facto independent, for most of the time Tibet was linked to China by formal tributary relations, characterized by symbolic and ceremonial rather than political subordination.[3] It was only in the eighteenth century, when rivalry with England and Russia increased Tibet's strategic importance to China, that it tightened its control of Tibet, annexing some of its eastern provinces, supervising its foreign relations and interfering in its domestic affairs, including the appointment of the Dalai Lama.[4] There is no doubt, however, that whatever its legal status vis-à-vis China, Tibet has always had its own territory, language, a unique system of government, and its own church, which for centuries exerted influence on the beliefs of its neighbors, including China. Tibet has its own unique civilization, whose roots are derived from India, one of whose religions, the Buddhism, it adopted and preserved in a creative blend with indigenous beliefs and customs. Racially and ethnically Tibetans are of non-Chinese (i.e. non-Han) stock, and they differ from the Chinese in looks, customs, temperament, dress, food and way of life. Tibetan culture, including a rich literature, arts and architecture, has been until recently only superficially affected by China.

With the fall of China's imperial regime in 1911, Tibet became de-facto independent for forty years. In 1950, following the Communist victory and the establishment of the People's Republic of China (PRC), the People's Liberation Army (PLA) invaded ("liberated," in Chinese terms) Tibet, and in 1951 the Dalai Lama and his government signed away Tibet's independence in exchange for the Chinese formal undertaking to preserve its religion and traditional government. For a few years the Chinese honored the agreement and the Tibetan elites, including the Dalai Lama, cooperated with them. However, revolts which broke out in East Tibet reached Lhasa in 1959, where a popular uprising ended with the Dalai Lama's flight to India and replacement of the old regime by a military provincial government, directed by the Chinese Communist Party (CCP). In 1965 the Tibet Autonomous Region (TAR) has been set up on the territory formerly under direct rule by the Dalai Lama's government.

Tibet is not just a country, it is a civilization. Unlike modern civilizations, in which religion is only one component of culture, Tibetan Buddhism prescribes conduct and provides meaning in every area, including politics. It is a powerful religious-cultural- ideological system that provides not only a set of beliefs and practices but, above all, a comprehensive vision of life that orders and makes sense of experience. The grass-root Tibetan resistance to Chinese occupation had less to do with the question of legal or political independence than with the threat to the basic codes, which have regulated their lives for centuries. Armed with their commitment to their religion and culture, which, among other things, made them immune to material inducements, the Tibetans have resolutely resisted the Chinese efforts to make them into atheist communist Chinese — and paid the price.

The 1950 invasion and subsequent occupation of Tibet caused a massive loss of life, imprisonment, torture and deportation of the Tibetan people, as well as almost total destruction of the infrastructure of the Tibetan religious and cultural life. During the peak years of the Cultural Revolution (1966–76), 90–95 percent of the Tibetan cultural heritage was destroyed and hundreds of thousands of monks, nuns and laymen murdered, tortured, humiliated and driven to suicide by Red Guard gangs. According to the Dalai Lama's Government estimate, 1,207,487 men, women and children, i.e. about 20% of Tibetan population worldwide,[5] lost their lives as a direct result of the Chinese invasion and occupation of Tibet. 173,138 are reported to have died in prisons and labor camps; 156,758 were executed; 343,151 died of starvation during the two famines of 1959–62 and 1968–72; 92,731 died as a result of torture; 91,002 committed suicide; and 432,707 were killed in battle. These figures, calculated on the basis of testimonies by survivors, cannot be independently verified and are contested by the Chinese authorities. Yet there can be no doubt that at least hundreds of thousands Tibetans died by execution, man-made famine, torture, imprisonment and forced labor under lethal conditions, and that the Tibetan people have been exposed for decades to massive and egregious suffering at the hands of the Chinese.

I have maintained elsewhere (Aran, in press) that the Tibetan case cannot be unambiguously classified as genocide because the Chinese policies and actions in Tibet, brutal and murderous as they were, were not motivated by the intention to physically exterminate the Tibetan people (Katz 1994, Ch.4; Charny 1999, pp.5–6). Atrocities inflicted on them were rather a spin-off of a "cultural genocide" (Katz 1994, Ch.4), a coercive strategy intended to obliterate the Tibetan distinctive religious-cultural identity, with the aim to integrate Tibet within the unitary Chinese state. In other words, the massive loss of life and the suffering of the Tibetans at the hands of the Chinese were the result of measures taken to break the Tibetan resistance to have their ancient civilization erased and replaced by new and alien one.[6] However, should a forced annihilation of a nation's identity, without an intention to physically destroy the group, be defined as genocide, then the Tibetan case would qualify for that definition.

II

How do the Tibetans in diaspora deal with the materials of their tragedy? How do they relate to their losses and present them to the world? How do they reconstruct them in their memory, weave them into their historic narrative and use them in reformulating their cultural identity? Which components of the past do they stress, mythologize or forget, and why? And what do they do about commemorating their dead, their lost freedom, the shattered landscape of their spiritual and ritual life?

In order to find at least partial answers to these questions, I have examined books, statements, articles, interviews and public addresses by the Dalai Lama, available in English (the Dalai Lama, 1962; 1982; 1990; 1995; Tenzin Gyatso (the 14th Dalai Lama) 1995; Shiromany, 1996); scholarly and investigative reports and analyses of various aspects of life in the Tibetan Diaspora, including an anthropological study of education in the Tibetan refugee community in India (Stoddard, 1985 and 1994; Nowak, 1984; Strom, 1994 and 1997; Huber, 1997; Kliegler, 1997); a sample of Tibetan refugee community English-language press;[7] a small sample of post-1959 Tibetan literature outside Tibet, and a few informal interviews. In the material examined, I found an overwhelming stress on cultural-religious, rather than human losses; few direct or explicit references to murder, torture and inhuman treatment of innocent people, and an unemotional and subdued tone characterizing these rare references. I found the motif of death and suffering absent from the repertoire of foundational experiences deployed in the reconstruction of the shattered Tibetan identity; and that the self-image of "the new Tibetan," promoted by the Dalai Lama and the educational system in the Tibetan refugee community, is that of a custodian of the Tibetan cultural identity, not a carrier of the memory of its destruction; almost no memorials or monuments to the dead; few commemorative events and only laconic and unemotional references to the dead on the agenda of those events. I found no mention of vengeance, signs of hate or desire to punish the Chinese in any of Dalai Lama's official statements, addresses, interviews and books. Research, translation and publication institutions in the refugee community produce mainly religious texts and books devoted to dissemination of Buddhism in the West, but only few texts documenting the massive loss of life and narrating the human tragedy suffered by the Tibetan people under invasion and occupation; few translations into Tibetan of world literature on science, art or general knowledge (much less than what is produced inside Tibet), and no critical historiography (Stoddard 1994, Huber 1997). I also found little mention of commemorative events, memorial assemblies, and — until 1998 — monuments to the dead.[8] Nowak's study of education in the Tibetan refugee community in India does not mention a single item devoted to the memory of those who perished under occupation in educational programs on any level. The new textbooks (an innovation in the Tibetan educational system) have been carefully designed to promote pan-Tibetan unity, to preserve the memory of the Tibetan landscape, wildlife, astrological animals and various traditional concepts, but do not mention the dead. Extra-curricular activities include religion, culture, history, prayers, sports and celebration of Buddhist holy days, imbued with political awareness, students' newspaper, crafts, compulsory garden, kitchen and cleaning chores, but no memory of the dead. Children's writing shows intense nationalism, faith in Dalai Lama's leadership, in Buddhism and the distinctiveness of the Tibetan culture, as well as preoccupation with the question of identity, but their parents and grandparents who perished a generation earlier have no place in it. This holds also for the small sample of post-1959 Tibetan literature, published outside TAR, that is available for examination.

The Dalai Lama is an appropriate focus because, though not everybody shares his views, his voice is unquestionably the most authoritative among all Tibetan refugees. The Dalai Lama's exalted status among his people rests not on the merits of his performance, which is sometimes severely criticized (though never directly), but on his being the symbol of their identity, especially their special relationship with the compassionate aspect of buddhahood (Chenrezig[9]), which the Dalai Lama not just represents, but of which he is a living manifestation. Even though, during the forty years of exposure to and interaction with the West, he came to formulate his thinking in terms of contemporary Western concerns, which had not been part of the Tibetan discourse in the past, such as independence, nationalism, human rights, ecology and democracy, he still remains not only what anthropologists call the "summarizing symbol" (Ortner 1973) of "tibetanness," but the very embodiment of the Tibetan national and cultural identity in the eyes of most of his compatriots and the rest of the world. Indeed, manifestations of cultural borrowing in Dalai Lama's presentation of Buddhism to the Western world, in his rhetoric as a statesman, his experimentation with education, and the new museum, opened in Dharamsala in

1998 on his initiative, should be seen as an authentic expression of today's Tibetan Diaspora culture, its complexity, its problems, ambiguities and dilemmas. Flanked on one side by what his critics call "reverse orientalism," i.e. excessive accommodation of the Tibetans' own image of their history and their culture to the expectations of their Western sympathizers and supporters, and by unbending traditionalism on the other side, the Dalai Lama's rhetoric, his school system and the new museum, represent the very arena on which the traditional Tibetan and the modern Western cultures meet and negotiate the exchange of their cultural resources in the process of constructing their collective memory and their new identity. The Dalai Lama is undoubtedly the most influential actor on this arena, the leading agent in shaping the Tibetan representations of their past and their deployment in what he sees as the best interests of the Tibetan nation.[10]

Most of the Dalai Lama's books, articles, speeches and interviews deal, above all, with elucidation of various aspects of Buddhism, and with discussion of religious, spiritual and other matters of universal concern, such as ecology, human relations, universal human rights, relations between religions and between religion and science and similar subjects. It seems that, unlike foreign writers on modern Tibet, who tend to underscore the issue of human suffering inflicted on the Tibetan people by the occupying power, the Dalai Lama seems to de-emphasize it,[11] concentrating on an effort to preserve the traditional timeless cultural legacy, through cultivation of such traditional institutions as monasticism. On the international scene, he works toward this end by promoting Buddhism (albeit in its modernized, science-compatible version) as part of the universal cultural discourse, and having the mythologized version of the Tibetan culture accepted as a universal asset and precious gift to the endangered Western spirituality. He complements this effort by projecting current Western concerns, such as environmentalism, human rights and democracy, as constitutive of the Tibetan identity (Lopez 1994, Huber 1997).

In a collection of over forty of Dalai Lama's speeches, interviews and articles (Shiromany 1996), I found four references to the death toll of the Tibetans. In an article in the *New York Times* in 1985, he says:

> It is now over thirty years since Communist China forcefully occupied Tibet. In this period, our religion and culture has been destroyed and the people of Tibet have suffered tremendous physical and economic deprivation. But the greatest loss of all has been the loss of our people's freedom...To date, from information gathered over decades of research, it is estimated that some 6,254 monasteries have been destroyed in Tibet. *In addition* (emphasis L.A.), at least 1.2 million Tibetans have died

as a direct result of the brutal occupation of our country by the Chinese (Shiromany, 1996, p.72) .

This is followed by a long description of the material exploitation of the country and its colonization by Chinese settlers. Another reference to the loss of life under the occupation is in an interview in Switzerland, by *The Guardian Weekly*, 1985. In answer to a question about reported relaxation of Chinese policies in Tibet, the Dalai Lama says:

> In Tibet itself, in the interior of the country, famine no longer exists and this is good news. During the two previous decades a good many people died of starvation or ill-treatment, victims of executions and extremely painful living conditions. Corroborative reports show that 1.2 million of Tibet's 6 million population have disappeared. Compared with that period, things are certainly better today (Shiromany 1996, p.80).

In nine addresses on the occasion of the anniversary of the 1959 Lhasa Uprising, as well as in his statements to the press on the occasion of his birthdays,[12] the Dalai Lama mentions the dead by an almost standard laconic formula, viz.,

> "Finally, I wish to pay homage to the brave men and women of Tibet, who have died for the cause of our freedom. I pray also for our compatriots who are enduring mental and physical suffering in Chinese prisons" (Shiromany 1996, p. 355; H.H.the Dalai Lama 1955, pp. 3, 54, 84, 168, 180, 204, 243).

In yet another press release on the occasion of his 60th birthday, the Dalai Lama refers to the past in the following sentence:

> "In recent times, unspeakable misfortune has overtaken my country, Tibet, because of which more than one hundred thousand Tibetans including myself have had to flee our homeland and live in exile" (Shiromany 1996, p. 365).

In his Nobel Prize acceptance speech the Dalai Lama refers to the past as follows: "The suffering of our people in the past forty years of occupation is well documented" (H.H. the Dalai Lama, 1995, p. 66). In his ten-page long Nobel Prize lecture at Oslo University in December 1989, the Dalai Lama makes the following laconic references to the death toll in Tibet:

> "The suffering of our people in the past forty years of occupation is well documented" (the Dalai Lama 1995, p. 66)

> "More than one sixth of Tibet's population of six million died as a direct result of the Chinese invasion and occupation" (the Dalai Lama 1995, p.77)

In his long Nobel Evening Address, the Dalai Lama speaks of compassion, violence, anger, bees and smiles, but does not mention at all the loss of life under occupation. He announces his decision to divide the Nobel Prize money between the following causes: those facing starvation in various parts of the world; leprosy programs in India; world peace projects; and the establishment of a Tibetan Foundation for Universal Responsibility, devoted to the promotion of the cause of communication between religion and science, human rights, democratic freedoms, non-violence and conservation of "Mother Earth." Conspicuously absent are any commemorative projects, memorials, or research projects on contemporary Tibetan history. There is no sign of a reflexive thought on the meaning of the tragedy, its critical moral evaluation, or a lesson to be learned from it. Even allowing for the festive and in principle non-political nature of the occasion, his reticence with regard to the loss of life and suffering of his people is striking.[13]

The memory of the dead is not a part of the Dalai Lama's presentation of the past. But memory — though part of history — has its own history too. The trajectory of the Tibetan memory of their martyrdom in Dalai Lama's writings shows a rather clear pattern. In his first book, *My Land and My People*, published in 1962,[14] the Dalai Lama makes a much more extensive and expressive reference to the loss of life and the martyrdom of his people than at any time after that. In this book he cites the findings of the International Commission of Jurists (ICJ), who investigated the events by interrogating Tibetan refugees and who, in the Dalai Lama's own words, "brought to light more horrors than even I had heard of." According to the ICJ report,

> Tens of thousands of people have been killed, not only in military actions, but individually and deliberately. They have been killed without trial, on suspicion of opposing communism, of hoarding money, or simply because of their position, or for no reason at all. But mainly and fundamentally, they were killed because they would not renounce their religion. They have not only been shot but beaten to death, crucified, burned alive, drowned, vivisected, starved, strangled, hanged, scalded, buried alive, disemboweled and beheaded. The killings have been done in public. The victims' fellow villagers and friends and neighbors have been made to watch them, and eye witnesses described them to the commission. Men and women have been slowly killed while their own families were forced to watch, and small children have even been forced to shoot their parents. Lamas have been especially prosecuted. The Chinese tried to humiliate them, especially the elderly and most respected, before they tortured them, by harnessing them to ploughs, riding them like horses, whipping and beating them, and other methods too evil to mention. And while they were slowly putting them to death, they taunted them with their religion, calling on them to perform miracles to save themselves from pain and death (International Committee of Jurists 1959 and 1960).

The report goes on describing in detail the brutal killings, torture, imprisonment, deportation and humiliation of monks and peasants and the destruction of monasteries and homes, accusing the Chinese of genocide, i.e. intention to destroy in whole or in part a national, religious, or ethnic group as such, in this case, the Buddhists of Tibet. (International Committee of Jurist Report 1959 and 1960).[15]

This was, to the best of my knowledge, the last (and only) time that the Dalai Lama refers at length, in detail and in a not-entirely-detached tone, to the Chinese atrocities in Tibet. *But note*: he is quoting a report by an international commission. The discrepancy between the terms and the tone of the commission's and the Dalai Lama's own articulation of the Tibetan tragedy is striking and intriguing.

III

It was the great French sociologist, Emile Durkheim, who pointed out that memory, even individual memory, is socially determined. Since the seminal work of Maurice Halbwachs (Halbwachs, 1992), more than half a century ago, it has become a truism that a group's memory of its past is not a replica of past events, but is, at any given time, a product of a social process of reconstruction, affected by the dominant ideas of the time and the group's present needs. Each group member contributes to it, though the weight of different contributions is not equal. Some individuals and social groups have a greater impact than others on the selection of issues to be remembered and those to be put away, and on the construction of meaning of the events selected or those doomed to oblivion, as well as on their role in the present.

Much has been written about manipulation of collective memory by totalitarian and authoritarian regimes, and on the role of the state versus groups in civic societies in this context (Winter and Sivan eds., 1999). But the Tibetan refugee community in India is neither a state nor a civic society, or a group within it. Its regime is neither totalitarian nor truly democratic.[16] It exists as a "deterritorialized" (Appadurai 1981), entity, a guest on the Indian soil, an autonomous, self-governing community,[17] oriented neither toward ultimate absorption in its host society, nor setting itself up as a distinctive minority within it, but devoted entirely to the preservation of its own cultural uniqueness. It is caught in endless internal contradictions and dilemmas. For instance, its mission as a custodian of an ancient civilization under threat of extinction calls for measures which clash with the task of maintaining a viable community and its effectiveness as the spokesman for the occupied Tibet. The image of its leadership as fit to replace the Chinese administration of Tibet demands cultivation of democratic institutions, whereas the effective authority of the present leader rests entirely on his traditional legitimacy as the embodiment of an aspect of the Buddha. Though Tibetans are in some ways unique, many of their problems, created by uprooting, national trauma and the need for reconstruction of a damaged identity, are shared by other refugee and expatriate groups in today's world.

Two questions are posed by these findings, namely, why did the destruction of culture rather than loss of life become the major issue in the Tibetan discourse on their recent tragedy? And what explains the Dalai Lama's reticence to dwell on matters of history in general and memory of the dead in particular?

The most obvious reason to prioritize the issue of the preservation of the cultural legacy, above all religion, is that the Dalai Lama correctly sees the imminent threat to the survival of the Tibetan nation not in physical extermination but in the loss of its national identity, which has always been rooted primarily in its religious and cultural rather than political distinctiveness. He also assumes that religion and culture of Tibet could still be saved by (a) replicating in the Diaspora the traditional cultural infrastructure, above all, monasteries (whose names, architecture and ambiance recreate the sacred geography of Tibet); (b) by achieving a world-wide recognition of Tibetan Buddhist culture as a universal asset.

The Dalai Lama and the Tibetans have always been interested primarily in their religion and culture rather than their political status. I have already noted that after the invasion, there was almost no resistance to the Chinese rule so long as the Tibetans were free to practice their religion and continue their traditional way of life, and the authority of the Dalai Lama was not interfered with. Moreover, the emphasis on culture and religion has been a strategic choice by the Dalai Lama in order to avoid contentious political issues in his interaction with his three main audiences: the Chinese, the West and his own community. It is my contention that underlying the Dalai Lama's choices in reconstructing his people's past and its strategic deployment were both political interests and cultural conditioning.

Reconstruction of the past is invariably replete with dilemmas and the Tibetan case is no exception. "Difficult past" is a term coined by Wagner-Pacifici and Schwartz (1991, p. 376) in the context of the Americans' dilemma of reconciling their loving memory of the killed with their aversion to the memory of the Viet Nam war itself, or the Israelis facing a similar dilemma when remembering the Lebanon war of 1982. The concept is useful also in other cases, such as

Germany, which is under pressure to remember its victims during World War II, but hates to face its Nazi past, or the Japanese remembering their losses and their heroes but embarrassed by the memory of the inhumanity of their invasion of China and elsewhere (Buruma 1994, Olick and Levy 1997, Schwartz 1991, Winter and Sivan 1999). But it is not only perpetrators who have a difficult past. Victims too may have to exercise caution when choosing options in assimilating past events. In his *The Texture of Memory* (1993), James Young shows how different Jewish communities made different choices in remembering the nature of their pre-Holocaust Jewish past. There is much in his own and his country's past the Dalai Lama is likely to consider difficult and would be glad to forget.[18] Like in other cases, in the Tibetan case there is also a "usable past" (Roskies, 1998), which he and other memory weavers would like to make the best of.[19]

Like all his decisions, the choice between different versions of the past requires of the Dalai Lama to keep in mind at least three target audiences, each with its own highly conditioned expectations. The Chinese, on the one hand an enemy, responsible for the terrible suffering of the Tibetan people and their near extinction as a distinct national and cultural group, but on the other hand, a people whom he refuses to hate,[20] and with whom he will ultimately have to negotiate a settlement. After all, compromise and mutual accommodation have been the name of the game of Sino-Tibetan politics for centuries, and the Dalai Lama knows that it is above all the Chinese with whom the Tibetans will have to work out their future. Then, there is the Western world. The Dalai Lama has had no success in changing the position of governments on the question of Tibet's status vis-a-vis China. However, his "presentation of self" to borrow Goffman's famous phrase, has been crucial in mobilizing popular support in the liberal West. His claim to spiritual leadership and moral authority outside the Buddhist world rests, above all, on his commitment to universality, inherent in his being a representative of the Mahayana school of Buddhism, which makes Buddhism relevant to the whole world through its emphasis on compassion *for all* and the aspiration to save *all* human beings. Beyond this, a dose of historic amnesia, and a degree of collusion with his Western admirers and disciples in cultivating the mainly West-created Shangri-La myth and the image of Tibetan wisdom as a panacea for contemporary Western ills, have proven an effective strategy in enlisting popular interest and support. Finally, there is the refugee community itself, divided on many issues, of which events of the recent past are among the most controversial.[21] Survey of publications, including those by circles critical of Dalai Lama's policies, shows that there is a lot of political bickering and factional rivalry there, but the Tibetan catastrophe and the massive loss of life do not seem to have set in motion a significant process of reflexive reevaluation or reinterpretation of the painful events of the recent history. There seems to be little soul-searching, discussion of lessons to be learned or conclusions to be drawn from the recent tragedy. None of such questions seem to be a part of the Tibetan public discourse (Strom 1997).

The Dalai Lama's choice of religion and culture rather than politics and history as the materials for the construction of his people's collective memory serves, among other, as a strategic option, enabling him to deal with these "difficult" and "usable" pasts, as well as the rather difficult present, while avoiding the divisive and stressing the consensual issues.

The manipulative use of the past in structuring their collective memory is especially evident in the Tibetan exiles' choice of events to commemorate. Admittedly, the choice has not been easy. Commemorating defeats is difficult in any case, especially if, unlike the Jews, the victims of the catastrophe prefer not to commemorate it by grieving for their dead.[22] But there is yet another reason that made the choice difficult. I have suggested elsewhere (Aran in press) that one of the reasons for world's indifference to the suffering of the Tibetan people may have been — ironically — its long duration. The murderous events there had been going on for over two decades (1956–1978), with religious persecution and flagrant violation of human rights continuing, with impunity, to this day. Unlike other cases of mass murder, the massive loss of life and almost total destruction of the cultural infrastructure of Tibet has lacked a climax necessary to reduce it to a specific "event" separate from the texture of ordinary life. Its fuzzy temporal and spatial contours defy attempt to contain it "within a frame." It lacks a peak event, a specific date or name of the "killing fields" like Auschwitz, Ponary, the Warsaw ghetto or Babi Yaar, to hang on to as a metonym for what had been happening there for a couple of decades. All this not only decreased the power of the Tibetan tragedy to command attention and mobilize support, but it also posed a problem for the Tibetans' own choice of *the* event to commemorate. They ultimately chose two: the anniversary of the Lhasa uprising in 1959, and the Dalai Lama's birthday (Nowak 1984, p.151). But note: the first is celebrated not by a reenactment of the events of the uprising, the drama of the Dalai Lama's escape from his besieged summer residence, or the tragic aftermath of these. It is celebrated by a reenactment of the two "positive" episodes salvaged from the 1959 catastrophe: (a) the formal proclamation by the Dalai Lama of a provisional Tibetan government on an overnight stop on his flight to India, and

(b) his arrival in India on March 31,1959. In other words: events signifying the beginning of the new era. The narrative has been purged of the events between 1950 and 1959. It may be significant in this context, that in the refugees' parlance, "the tragedy" invariably refers not to the terrible suffering of their own and their fathers' generation, decimated by execution, starvation and torture, but to the fate of the refugees themselves (Nowak 1984, p.11 n.27).

The other occasion celebrated throughout the Tibetan communities, is the Dalai Lama's birthday, not as a biographical detail of a leader's life, but as an illud-tempus, a homage to the holder of sacred power, the repository of ultimate values, and the "summarizing symbol" of "tibetanness" (Nowak 1984, pp. 22–36).

IV

I have discussed several considerations affecting the Dalai Lama's choice of what to remember, what to commemorate and what to forget. They were strategic choices made with a view to avoid burning bridges leading to a possible settlement with China, to maintain the good will and support of the international community,[23] and to promote unity within the Tibetan community. However Dalai Lama's choices are not only, as the constructionists would have it (Mead 1964;) a matter of interests and the strategic needs of the present. The impact of the present on remembering the past is not unlimited (Schwartz 1991). The social construction of a collective memory is part of a political-cultural process, in which past and present interact and, as Olick and Levi (1997) phrased it, "are mutually constitutive." But the past is there not only as a passive bunch of events to be manipulated by "history agents" according to their and the society's present moods and needs. The past imposes itself on the present also through the power of tradition. The Tibetan case illustrates the power of traditional codes to mould attitudes and to affect representations of the past.

The power of cultural codes (or "the mythical"), has been pointed out by Edward Shils already in 1981. It is very much in evidence in the collective memory construction by the Tibetan diaspora leaders, even though the impact of these codes on their motivation may not be necessarily direct.

To understand how cultural tradition interacts with the present in the Tibetan refugee leadership's perception of their people's recent history, we have to make a brief excursus into the cultural legacy which has nurtured their values and attitudes. The first thing it will teach us is that the Dalai Lama prefers teaching compassion and talking about future generations rather than delve into history and remember the dead, above all, simply *because he is a Tibetan and to do so is entirely within the Tibetan cultural tradition.* The Dalai Lama and the Tibetans have always perceived themselves as a civilization rather than a political entity in a modern sense of the term. I have already noted that after the invasion, there was almost no resistance to the Chinese rule so long as the Tibetans were free to practice their religion and continue their traditional way of life, and the authority of the Dalai Lama was not interfered with. Even later, resistance to Chinese occupation had less to do with the question of Tibet's legal or political status than with the threat to the basic codes which have regulated their lives for centuries. These codes were part of a very powerful religious system which provides not only a set of beliefs and practices but also a comprehensive vision of life that orders experience and prescribes conduct, including politics. Moreover, we may be reminded that writing history is not something to be taken for granted. Even the Jews, for whom remembering the past is a religious duty, have abandoned history writing after exile and thus Jewish historiography disappeared for centuries, replaced by the study of the sacred text of the Torah (Yerushalmi 1989). There was practically no Indian historiography until the colonial time. Like the exilic Jews, the Indians were concerned with the eternal — not the passing (Momigliano 1990 and 1994). Tibet inherited the Indian tradition, including Buddhism. Traditional Tibetan history has consisted of hagiography and a record of Buddhist events. It ignored the usual materials of history, such as conquests, defeats, invasions and victories, unless significant in the context of Buddhism. It is only recently, under the occupation, that Tibetans became interested in secular history. Characteristically, one of the pioneers of secular Tibetan historiography, the Amdowan monk-historian, Gendun Choepel, realized the vital necessity of secular history not for its own sake but to boost Tibetan nationalism, destroyed, according to him, by Buddhism (Stoddard 1985).

I propose that the Dalai Lama's training as a Tibetan-Buddhist monk conditions the style of his rhetoric and his presentation of self and his country, and underlies even his instrumental and strategic policy decisions. Thus, for instance, his conciliatory tone in referring to the Chinese and his restraint in referring to their crimes against the Tibetan people expresses not only his political decision to keep the negotiation avenue open, but also reflects his belief in the futility of anger and his life-long training in converting hostility into kindness, as well as a hope born of the Buddhist belief in the human potential for change. Similarly, the Dalai Lama's puzzling omission of Tibetan causes from his humanitarian-causes-agenda to be supported by the Nobel Prize money may be seen not only as a conscious effort to project himself as a universal spiritual leader, but also as a reflection of his genuine conviction that — as the embodiment of *universal* compassion — he must not privilege Tibetan suffering at the expense of others'.[24]

The main cultural variables at the base of the Dalai Lama's decisions on what to include or omit in the presentation of his people's past and in restructuring their identity are the Buddhist conceptions of time, of memory, and of the relative and fleeting nature of the phenomenal life. In the Jewish tradition, remembrance of the past is a deeply ingrained ritualized imperative, time is linear and events are seen as unrepeatable and irreversible (Yerushalmi 1989, pp. 40–42).[25] In contrast, the Indian-Buddhist conception of time is basically cyclical rather than linear, which robs events and lives of their uniqueness and is consequently concerned less with the record of events than with exemplary models and recurrent paradigmatic episodes. In a cosmic perspective, everything repeats itself and the mundane linear time is not a feature of reality but a construction of human mind, in which everything is provisional and relative (Balshev 1993, Pande 1993, Majumdar 1961). This conception of time not only determines the individual's attitude to life, but it also produces a traditional view of its nature and mode of operation. *Above all, it devalues preoccupation with history and works against investing resources in remembrance and commemoration of past events.*

I would not like to be misunderstood. Buddhists mourn and remember their dead just as anybody else does. Relatives, friends and neighbors of the people who perished under occupation in Tibet responded positively to the invitation to come to the new museum in Dharamsala and inscribe their names on a memorial. Hundreds of thousands names have already been inscribed.[26] But it was not their initiative. The Tibetan cultural codes do not require such a project.

In her comparison of the Jewish response to the Holocaust with the Chinese response to their terrible losses in the Cultural Revolution, Sheng-Mei Ma (1987)[27] suggests that whereas the Jews tend to see their Holocaust in metaphysical terms, as an extra-historical event, this attitude seems to the Chinese foreign and inexplicable. For them, the Cultural Revolution is just one of the many violent waves in the ceaseless tides of Chinese civilization and Mao just one of the historical villains who people China's long history. It is not clear to what extent this observation is relevant to the Tibetan attitude to their history, but to the extent that it is, it might shed additional light on the Tibetan Refugee Community tendency toward restraint in their response to their tragedy.

V

The Tibetans often refer to the survival of the Jewish nation after 2000 years of dispersal, due to the Jews' stubborn adherence to their religious-cultural tradition, as a source of encouragement to them. It might be instructive therefore to see the Tibetan case with reference not only to the Jewish response to the Holocaust, but also to their response to yet another of their many catastrophes: the fall of Jerusalem and the destruction of the Second Temple in the first century CE.[28] Following that disaster, the exiled Jews have given up their temple with its priests, its rituals and animal sacrifices, and replaced them with alternative ways to practice and to innovate, appropriate to their new circumstances: the "minyan,"[29] the synagogue, the rabbi, the philosopher, the Talmud,[30] the family. They made their religion "portable," carrying it with them wherever they went. On leaving their ancestral land, the Jews have, so to say, stepped out of history, turning the Jerusalem Temple Mount into a metonym for the lost link with The Place, and longing for it into a symbol of the common Jewish identity.

The Tibetans, on the other hand, saw their best chance for the survival of their identity, threatened with extinction by the Chinese assimilatory policies, in the preservation of their religious tradition *intact*, except for such changes as were necessary for gaining outside support and for the diffusion of Buddhism in the outside world. In contrast to the Jews, they went into exile *with* their high priest, and, under his leadership, have channeled their energy *not* into inventing means to make their religion viable under the new circumstances, but into replicating in the Diaspora their ancient religious infrastructure, rituals and institutions. One may say that the Tibetan refugees settled in India with the Potala[31] on their backs. The few modern institutions, such as secular education or the Tibetan Museum, do not indicate a tendency to modify the cultural tradition, indeed, they are often a necessary concession to the effort precisely to preserve it intact. The Dalai Lama has been successful in "universalizing" Buddhism by presenting it to the West in a Western idiom and by engaging in a dialogue with scientists, intellectuals and religious thinkers, putting Buddhism on the map of the universal intellectual discourse. The influence of all this on the Tibetan Buddhism as practiced by the Tibetans seems to have been so far negligible.

It is ironic that many Jews and Christians turn to Buddhism in search of spirituality unencumbered by the constraints of institutional infrastructure, when, in fact, Tibetan Buddhism within the Tibetan community has remained heavily dependent on the traditional religious infrastructure, the main pillar of which is the monastery.[32]

It is too early to speculate on the future of the Tibetan national and cultural identity. We still have no time perspective. It took the Jews many generations in the Diaspora and more than one calamity[33] to change, while the Tibetan exile is now only just over one generation old. Moreover, traditions and religion in particular tend to emphasize coherence and continuity and only infrequently openly admit change. It takes time to change and even more time to acknowledge it.

NOTES

1. The area of what is at present the Tibetan Autonomous Region (TAR) of the People's Republic of China (PRC) is about 1.3 million square kilometers. The area claimed by the Tibetans as theirs North-East and East of TAR (Amdo and Kham), now incorporated as "autonomous prefectures" and "autonomous districts" of the PRC, covers another 1.2 square kilometers. Thus, the total area claimed by the Tibetans as "Greater Tibet" (Cholka Sum) is about 2.5 million sq.km, which is more than 25 percent of all PRC territory (9.6 million sq.km.) The Tibetan population of TAR is about 2 million; the total Tibetan population is 6 million according to the Tibetan and less than 5 million according to the Chinese sources.

2. The title "Dalai Lama" derives from a Mongolian expression meaning "teacher whose wisdom is great as an ocean." It was conferred on the head of the dominant Tibetan monastic order (Gelugpa) by the Mongol prince Altan Khan in 1578. The fifth Dalai Lama (1617-1682) was the first to consolidate his rule over all Tibet.

3. The Tibetan head lama served as spiritual teacher at the Mongol court in exchange for military protection. This arrangement was continued during the Mongol and later the Manchu rule of China (1244-1368 and 1644-1911 respectively).

4. The selection of the Dalai Lama had been closely watched by the Imperial Colonial Office since 1661, but there had been no direct interference before 1793. Since the Dalai Lama held unquestioned authority for the Tibetan people, manipulation of his selection has remained an important tool of domination of Tibet even by the atheist communist Chinese regime (Crossley 1999, p. 329).

5. As reported in: *Tibet: the Facts*, a report prepared by the Scientific Buddhist Association for the UN Commission on Human Rights, Dharamsala, 1990, p. 279. The figures were obtained by interviewing Tibetan refugees in India. The Chinese called the Tibetan figures preposterous, claiming that Tibet's whole population at the time was only a little over one million. They conceal the fact that this latter figure refers only to Central Tibet, whereas the Tibetan data refer to all Tibetan areas in the PRC, which even by Chinese statistics were over 4 million (*Beijing Review*, 4 April, 1988).

6. This policy has been fully consistent both with China's traditional frontier-country-assimilation ideology and the Marxist-Leninist-Maoist nationalities doctrine. Both

assumed that weaker neighbors should be "assisted" — if necessary, by force — to undergo transformation, which will ultimately make them voluntarily choose to unite with China because of the cultural and economic advantages of doing so. The atrocities in Tibet — like the massive murder of China's own citizens — were, quite unlike the Nazi targeting of the Jews, the unplanned consequences of these policies (Fairbank, 1985, p.11)

7. The *Tibet Journal* and the *Tibetan Bulletin*, published by the Central Tibetan Administration (CTA), sponsored by the Library of Tibetan Works and Archives (LTWA), Dharamsala, and the more independent and politically-oriented *Tibetan Review*, published in New Delhi.

8. This finding is supported by M. McLagan's findings in her study on the "Tibetan Year" events in New York in 1992, including Tibetans' own frustration about the disproportionate emphasis on Buddhism and the exclusively Buddhist definition of Tibetanness (McLagan, 1997 pp. 69-87).

9. Better known under his Sanskrit name as bodhisattva Avalokitesvara.

10. Some critics, Tibetan and foreign, question the wisdom of focusing public attention on the refugee problem, thus "stealing the show" from the situation in Tibet. Others disapprove of what they see as the Dalai Lama's excessive involvement with celebrities and his failure to gain political support.

11. In the opening page of the catalogue of the new Tibet Museum in Dharamsala, devoted to documentation of his people's cultural and religious life prior to its destruction by a brutal force at the cost of hundreds of thousands lives, he refers to the agony of the Tibetan people as "the suffering brought by the changing times" (Catalog of the Tibet Museum, 2000).

12. The two events commemorated in the Tibetan refugee community.

13. In a striking contrast to the Dalai Lama's speech, Eli Wiesel, the Nobel Peace Prize laureate in 1986, devoted most of his lecture to a reflexive reassessment of the Holocaust and the memory of its victims.

14. Republished in 1985.

15. The objectivity of this report has been challenged by several writers, among others Tom Grunfeld (1981 and 1987; Chris Mullin (Greene and Mullin, 1978) and Robert Barnett (Dodin and Rather, 2001, pp.269-316, esp. p.p. 283 and 310. n.41).

16. Despite some formal democratic institutions.

17. The Tibetan community in India counts about 100,000 people; about 30,000 more are dispersed over the world.

18. Among the most embarrassing is the issue of the Tibetan resistance, which the Dalai Lama opposed; his and his government's formal acceptance of Tibet's status as part of China in 1951; and his and the Tibetan elite's collaboration with the Chinese in the nine years prior to the 1959 uprising. It has done irreparable damage to the status of Tibet among nations and in international law.

19. Like, for instance, the memory of poor but serene existence, and a non-material civilization guided by spiritual wisdom, often referred to as the Shangri-la myth.

20. Above all, as a Buddhist; but the Dalai Lama's autobiographical writing also indicates a certain admiration and respect for the Chinese and their achievements.

21. See note 19.

22. Although a memorial to the dead has been set up in the new Tibet Museum in Dharamsala in 1998, it seems to be a concession to a contemporary convention, an

instant of cultural borrowing rather than an expression of a genuine need. The rhetoric surrounding the opening of the museum is not a reliable indication of such a need, considering the heavy involvement of foreign advisers and planners in the project. Jews, on the other hand, whose history has been full of catastrophes, have become experts in commemorating them mainly as metaphors deployed for didactic purposes, occasions for soul-searching and repentance. They have also created a special literary genre of "Lamentations" (Minz, 1984, pp.17-48; Ezrahi, 1978, pp.133-149). The emphasis on remembrance of the dead in all Holocaust commemoration projects is self-evident.

23. The Dalai Lama's success in diffusion of Buddhism in the West has been instrumental in increasing the numbers of supporters of pro-Tibet campaigns and of the refugee community.

24. Personal communication from a friend — a highly educated Tibetan monk.

25. Although Yerushalmi warns us that Jews related to historical time in more than one dimension, sometimes merging verticality with circularity, they were far from the "eternal-return" perception of the Hindus. Historical events of the biblical time — even if experienced cyclically- were seen as unique and irreversible.

26. Personal communication from Ms. Debby Hershman, curatorial adviser to the Tibet Museum, Dharamsala, India.

27. I am grateful to Professor Benny Shanon for suggesting the comparison. The quorum of ten men for prayer. The body of Jewish civil and ceremonial laws created in the Diaspora.

31. The Dalai Lama's official residence in Lhasa and the seat of the Tibetan government since the 17th century.

32. Unlike Christian monasticism, in which monks opt out from the community, leaving it to the clergy to provide it with religious services, there is no professional clergy in Buddhism and monks remain an integral part of the laymen's religious practice. Apart from conducting religious services and supplying ritual expertise, they function as "field of merit" for laymen. First of all, giving is a very important Buddhist virtue, so the monks confer merit on laymen by the mere acceptance of their gifts. Donors also gain merit by enabling the monks to devote themselves to an ideal Buddhist schedule, impossible for the laymen to maintain. No wonder, then, that Tibetan historians perceived the destruction of the economic basis of Tibetan monasticism as the most significant event in their recent history.

33. See Yerushalmi, 1989, for a masterful exposition of changes in Jewish historical memory after their expulsion from Spain in 15th century.

REFERENCES

Appadurai, A. 1981. "The Past as a Scarce Resource." *Man* 16, 201–219.

Aran, Lydia, 2005. *Genocide or Murder of a Civilization: Tibet 1950-2000*. Tel Aviv: Open University (Hebrew), ch.5.

Balshev, A. N. 1993. "Time and the Hindu Experience." In *Religion and Time* edited by Balshev A.N. and J. M. Mohanty. Leiden: Brill.

Bishop, Peter. 1989. *The Myth of Shangri-La: Tibet, Travel Writing and the Creation of Sacred Landscape.* Berkeley: University of California Press.

_____. 1993. *Dreams of Power.* London: Althone Press.

Buruma, Ian. 1994. *Wages of Guilt.* London, Jonathan Cape.

Charny, I.,ed. 1999. *Encyclopedia of Genocide.* Jerusalem: Institute of Holocaust and Genocide Studies.

Crossley, P. K. 1999. *A Translucent Mirror, History and Identity in Qing Imperial Ideology.* Berkeley: University of California Press.

The Dalai Lama, 1962. *My Land and My People.* New York: McGraw Hill.

_____. 1982. *The Collected Statements Interviews and Articles.* Dharamsala, India: Information Office of H.H. the Dalai Lama.

_____. 1990. *Freedom in Exile: The Autobiography of H.H. the Dalai Lama of Tibet.* London: Hodder & Stoughton.

_____. 1995. *Speeches, Statements, Articles,. Interviews 1987-1995.* Dharamsala, India: Department of Information and International Relations (DIIR) of the Central Tibetan Administration (CTA).

DIIR, 1994. *Tibet: Proving Truth from Facts.* Dharamsala, India: Central Tibetan Administration (CTA).

Dodin, Thierry and Rather, Heinz (eds.), 2001. *Imagining Tibet: Perceptions, Projections and Fantasies.* Boston: Wisdom Publications

Ezrachi, Sidra. 1978. "The Holocaust Writer and the Lamentation Tradition: Response to Catastrophe in Jewish Literature." In: *Confronting the Holocaust,* edited by Rosenfeld, A.H. Bloomington, Indiana: Indiana University Press, 133–149.

Fairbank, J.K., 1985. "Dissonance in the Cosmic Harmony." *New York Times Book Review,* 22 December, 11.

Green F. and Mullin C. 1978."The Question of Tibet," *China Now.* London, No.78

Grunfeld, Tom 1981. "Tibetan History: A Somewhat Different Approach." *Tibetan Review,* June 1981.

_____. 1987. *The Making of Modern Tibet.* London: Zed.

Halbwachs, M. 1992. *On Collective Memory,* translation L. A. Coser, Chicago: Chicago University Press.

Huber, Tony 1997. "Green Tibetans: A Brief Social History." In: Tibetan Culture in Diaspora, Proceedings of the 7th Seminar of the International Association of Tibetan Studies, Graz, 1995,

Vol. IV, edited by Korom, F. J., Vienna: The Austrian Academy of Sciences, 103-119.

International Committee of Jurists, 1959-1960. Tibet and the Chinese People's Republic. A Report to the Legal Inquiry Commission. Geneva.

Katz, Steven T. 1994. *The Holocaust in Historical Context.* Vol. I, Ch 4, London: Oxford University Press.

Kliegler, P.C. 1997. "Shangri-La and Hyperreality: a Collision in Tibetan Refugees Expression." In: *Tibetan Culture in Diaspora,* edited by Korom F.J. Vienna: Austrian Academy of Sciences, 59-68.

A Long Look Homeward: Exhibition Catalog, 2000, Dharamsala, India: Tibet Museum.

Lopez, Donald S. 1994. "New Age Orientalism," *Tibetan Review,* May 1994.

_____. 1998. *Prisoners of Shangri-La: Tibetan Buddhism and the West.* Chicago: University of Chicago Press.

Majumdar, R.C. 1961. "Ideas of History in Sanskrit Literature." In: *Historians of India,* edited by Philips, C. H., London: Oxford University Press, 13-28.

McLagan, Meg, 1997. "Mystical Visions in Manhattan: Deploying Culture in the Year of Tibet." In: *Tibetan Culture in the Diaspora,* edited by Korom F.J., Vienna: Austrian Academy of Sciences, 69-90.

Mead, G. H. 1964. "The Nature of the Past" in: *Selected Writings G.H. Mead,* edited by Reck, A. J., Chicago: Chicago University Press, 345-354.

Mintz, Alan, 1984. *Hurban: Responses to Catastrophe in Hebrew Literature,* New York: Columbia University Press, 17-48.

Momigliano, Arnaldo. 1990. *The Classical Foundations of Modern Historiography.* Berkeley, University of California Press.

_____. 1994. "Time in Ancient Historiography." In: *Essays on Ancient and Modern Judaism.* edited by Silvia Berti, Chicago: Chicago University Press.

Nowak, Margaret, 1984. *Tibetan refugees: Youth and the New Generation of Meaning.* New Brunswick, NJ: Rutgers University Press.

Olick, J.K. and D. Levy, 1997. "Collective Memory and Cultural Constraints." *American Sociological Review* 62, 6, 921–936.

Ortner, S. 1973. "On Key Symbols." *American Anthropologist,* 75, 1338–1346

Pande, G. C. 1993. "Time in Buddhism." In: *Religion and Time,* edited by Balshev, A.N. and J.M. Mohanty Leiden: Brill.

Roskies, D.R. 1998. *The Jewish Search for Usable Past.* Bloomington: Indiana University Press.

Schell, Orville, 2000. *Virtual Tibet: Searching for Shangri-La from the Himalaya to Hollywood.* New York: Holt & Co.

Schwartz, Barry, 1991. "Social Change and Collective Memory," *American Sociological Review,* 56 (April), 24–36.

Sheng-Mei Ma, 1987, "Contrasting Two Survival Literatures: On the Jewish Holocaust and the Chinese Cultural Revolution," *Holocaust and Genocide Studies, Vol.2, no.1, 81-93.*

Shils, Edward, 1981. *Tradition.* Chicago: Chicago University Press.

Shiromany, A (ed.) 1996. The Spirit of Tibet: Vision for Human Liberation, Selected Speeches and Writings of H.H. the XIV Dalai Lama. New Delhi: Vikas

Stoddard, Heather, 1985. *Le mendiant de l'Amdo*, Paris:

_____. 1994. "Tibetan Publications and National Identity." In: *Resistance and Reform in Tibet*, edited by Barnett, R. and Akiner, S. London: Hurst and Co., 121-136

Strom, A.K.1994. "Tibetan Refugees in India: Aspects of Socio-Cultural Change." In: *Tibetan Studies*, Vol.2, edited by Per Kvaerne. Oslo: The Institute for Comparative Research in Human Culture, 837–847.

_____. 1997. "Between Tibet and the West: On Traditionality, Modernity and the Development of Monastic Institutions in the Tibetan Diaspora." In: *Tibetan Culture in the Diaspora*, edited by Korom F.J.,Vienna: Austrian Academy of Sciences, 33–50.

Tenzin Gyatso, (the 14th Dalai Lama), 1995. *My Tibet*. Berkeley: University of California Press.

Tibetan Young Buddhist Association,1990, *Tibet, the Facts*, Dharamsala, India: Department of Information and International Relations (DIIR).

Tibet Under the Communist Rule, Compilation of Refugee Statements 1958-1975. 1976. Dharamsala, India: Information and Publicity Office of H.H. the Dalai Lama.

Tibetan Information Network/Human Rights Watch–Asia, 1996, *Cutting off the Serpent's Head*. New York: TIN/HRW-Asia.

Wagner-Pacifici, R. and Barry Schwartz, 1991, "The Viet Nam Veterans' Memorial: Commemoration of a Difficult Past." *American Journal of Sociology*, 97,2, 376–420.

Winter, Jay M. and Emmanuel Sivan (eds.), 1999, *War and Remembrance in the Twentieth Century*. Cambridge: Cambridge University Press, Ch.1.

Yerushalmi, Yoseph Haim, 1989, *Zakhor: Jewish History and Jewish Memory*. New York: Schocken Books.

Young, James, E. 1993, *The Texture of Memory: Holocaust Memorials and Meaning*. New Haven: Yale University Press.

PART IV. COMPARATIVE ANALYSES OF GENOCIDE

Chapter 10. Genocide as a Possible Response to Westernization: Government Treatment of Minorities in Afghanistan and Iran

Raj P. Mohan, Auburn University

> If criminals, according to Hegel, have a right to their punishment and expiation — to restore the cosmic order — the victims are also entitled to know the reasons why suddenly, without their fault, they have been yanked away from their customs, homes, circles of friends and parents — the reasons for their sacrifice. But the Holocaust is not a matter only for the victims and persecutors. It concerns the whole of humanity. No one can be left out. There cannot be neutral observers or bystanders. (Ferrarotti 1994: 91)

The September 11 attacks on New York and Washington, D.C. killed thousands of innocent citizens from many nations, and destroyed property in the billions of dollars. These incidents represent examples of civility gone in reverse (Mennell 1990). How can one explain such inhumane acts of violence? The purpose of this chapter is to explain acts of terror, genocide and other forms of human violence in Afghanistan and Iran with the help of Critical Theory and an examination of specific historical conditions behind intergroup violence.

Although the United Nations definition of genocide has been criticized regarding its scope and applicability, it is important to point out that the treatment of Baha'is in Iran and Hindus and Sikhs in Afghanistan fits the UN definition. This identifies five types of actions, any of which would constitute genocide when there is an intent to destroy a national, racial, religious or ethnic group (Chalk and Jonassohn 1990: 10). As noted in Chapter 4, they are:

1.Killing members of the group.

2.Causing serious bodily or mental harm to the members of the group.

3.Deliberately inflicting on the group conditions of life calculated to bring about its physical destruction in whole or in part.

4.Imposing measures intended to prevent births within the group.

5.Forcibly transferring children of the group to another group.

This definition has been criticized for its lack of distinction between the intended complete destruction of a group and nonlethal attacks on a group, and the exclusion of political groups and social classes in the definition. However, while other definitions may have been developed, this particular one is applicable to the plight of the Baha'is in Iran and Hindus and Sikhs in Afghanistan.

The Relevance of Critical Theory

Given its focus on cultural rather than primarily economic factors (particularly religion), the emergence of destructive cultural fashions, the importance of societal legitimations, the concern with individual reproduction of the larger social system, and psychopathological processes, Critical Theory promises useful and relevant insight into genocidal developments in any society, but particularly countries such as Afghanistan and Iran.

A few years ago, Jurgen Habermas characterized this century as a "catastrophic scene" of worldly destructive campaigns of nations and individuals against themselves. In his analysis, he emphasized the destructive nature that has been taking place in society almost as a "cultural fashion." The adoption of political movements around the world has moved toward the image of "democracy and liberalism" becoming hegemonic without leaving any place for the resistance groups and revolutionary movements which do not show any trait to fight for "liberty."

Habermas (1975: 36-37) also emphasized the importance of "legitimations" as a set of ideas which the political system or any other system generates so that the system will maintain itself and be viable. He says: "In contemporary sociology, the usefulness of the concept of legitimation, which permits a demarcation of types of legitimate authority (in Weber's sense) according to forms and content of legitimation, is undisputed" (Habermas 1975:97). In the case of both the Taliban and Iranian theocracy, such legitimations are created by their own interpretations of the Holy Qu'ran and are supported as official political systems by other political regimes in the neighborhood. Such legitimation as a concept involves the dynamics of the social system as a whole.

According to the Frankfurt School, actors are socially controlled to reproduce socio-political doctrine to maintain the larger social structures they belong to at the time. These ideas echo importantly in the work of Marcuse (1969) who argues that social control pervades the whole cultural world and becomes internalized within the actor's mind. According to him (1969), social structures in decadence, or what Mannell (1990) calls decivilizing process experience, involves a "psychopathological process" which has a negative impact on social actors and results in their revolutionary consciousness. At times this consciousness may not necessarily be constructive.

REACTIONS TO WESTERNIZATION

In general, the impact of Westernization on third world nations, particularly such as those in the Middle East, has included economic exploitation of material resources and labor, ideas such as freedom, progress, nationalism, and individualism which pose a threat to more traditional values, as well as the negative effects of economic development such as increased class differentiation, some of which have resulted in political legitimacy crises, extreme forms of persecution, increased rejection of out-groups, and destructive attempts to return to more traditional types of true values, accompanied by the cultural and physical destruction of minority groups.

Afghanistan, as well as many other Middle Eastern societies whose economies have developed as a result of petroleum exploitation, has experienced major changes in its social structure, morality, religious values and norms because of exposure to modernity and Western ideologies. As Winter (1997:21) notes:

> A crisis of political legitimacy ensued in which secular, authoritarian governments were attacked for corruption, continued subservience to Western powers, and especially for the propagation of supposedly immoral modernists values and institutions. This last point of contention was fuelled by the growth of women's education and employment.

The Taliban in Afghanistan used religion to persecute the diverse cultural and ethnic components of the country as "the ones to blame" for the decay of

Islamic values. The pre-Islamic heritage of Afghanistan included Buddhism; ancient statues of Buddha were destroyed and the National Museum of Afghanistan, which contained many artifacts from the pre-Islamic times, was plundered. They also destroyed the heritage of Hindus and Sikhs, especially relics of their religious and cultural background. Hindus and Sikhs have lived in Afghanistan for centuries and were a very successful minority; they had wealth and power before the Taliban came to power. They represented the forces of modernization and Westernization, as they constantly traveled between India, Afghanistan and other countries. Thus, their situation might be compared to that of Jews in various countries.

The Taliban and, as Marcuse theorizes, the modern world, have reached a stage of supreme domination of individuals where control is so complete that no deliberate actions are required by their leaders. Western ideologies, culture, and capitalism are reaching even the most remote parts of the world, bringing with them promises of progress, freedom, and nationalism, and undermining the values that held various societies together for centuries. The kind of freedom that is promoted threatens fundamentalists around the world, including the Taliban and the Iranian theocracy. The Shah of Iran, for example, was ousted in a reaction against Western-looking movements by the ranks of the Iranian theocracy. The fundamentalist theocrats became the harbingers of movements against modernity and globalization. What the West promotes as liberal democratic ideals are seen as the enemy of the cultural and religious values of "moral societies." These ideas are seen as threatening to destroy the whole society; thus, radical leaders may sense that they must be eliminated at any cost, including a genocidal campaign.

According to Marcuse (1964), domination is sublimated through social institutions such as religion. Religious fanaticism used as a political tool is perhaps one of the most damaging means used in the history of the world to force individuals to exterminate other human beings as a "sacred mission." In this regard, the Taliban have been compared with Nazism and the persecution of many other racial and ethnic groups around the world. They represent a threat to the world in their efforts to emphasize and exacerbate differences between groups of people and to reduce respect for human life generally.

According to Critical Theory, genocide can also be viewed as a product of the economic division of labor and exploitation, creating class gaps which force the system into attempting to conciliate consequent class differences. The Taliban's genocidal behavior not only thrived on the political and ideological (religious) dialectic of social life, but resulted from the direct outcome of some constituent parts of the bourgeoisie and the lower social class.

The economic decline of Afghan society after the so-called liberating civil war in which multinational corporations exploited petroleum and other natural resources resulted in the effect of foreign consumerism within the national commerce. A very skillful Taliban strategy involved taking control of the Afghan economy based upon the persecution of foreign cultures in the name of a "religious war," accompanied by the differentiation of ethnic groups as a new class from which to extract economic benefits. Within this polarized context, genocide ideology could be easily legitimized as a "sacred cause."

Some Neo-Marxists have defined the domination of capitalism as the penetration of the economic considerations into all facets of social existence. In this regard Lukacs sees capitalism as "one form among many regulating the metabolism of human society and the commodity as the universal structuring principle has effect over and above the fact that the commodity relation as an isolated phenomenon exerts a negative influence at best on the structure and organization of society" (Lukacs 1971:85). Genocide triggered by the Taliban, according to Lukacs' notion of Reification, may be viewed as a phenomenon in which the value of commodities, and the mechanization and division of labor, have spread toward the ideological spheres (as religious dogma) to manipulate and force individuals to literally "kill each other." As Lukacs (1971:83-88) points out:

> The essence of commodity-structure has often been pointed out. Its basis is that a relation between people takes on the character of a thing and thus acquires a "phantom objectivity," an autonomy that seems so strictly rational and all-embracing as to conceal every trace of its fundamental nature: the relation between people (83).... [T]his rational mechanization extends right into the worker's soul: even his psychological attributes are separated from his total personality and placed in opposition to it so as to facilitate their integration into the specialized rational systems and their reduction to statistically viable concepts (88).

The magnitude of genocide which has been institutionalized under the Taliban as a religious decree to combat the "community of non-believers" is staggering. In the name of Allah, fundamentalists have found legitimation for their brutal acts of murder and torture and are fighting what they call a "religious war" which has become increasingly intolerant and xenophobic. Under the Taliban, religious and ethnic minorities (i.e. Hindus, Sikhs, Jews and Christians) have been forced to wear distinctive clothing to be publicly recognized and have become target of police and mob violence. As CNN reported on May 24, 2001 from Washington, DC:

The Taliban have demonstrated their capacity to genocidal violence in massacres of civilian members of the Hazara Shi'ite minority in Mazar-e-Sharif in August 1998, Robatak Pass in May 2000, and Yakaolang in January 2001. In Yakaolang, the Taliban rounded up and mass murdered at least 300 civilian men, including staff members of humanitarian organizations.

THE HINDUS, SIKHS AND SHI'ITE MUSLIMS IN AFGHANISTAN

Genocide involves the deliberate and systematic destruction of a group in a number of ways. In this regard, the Taliban ordered that Afghan Hindus and Sikhs wear identity badges on their clothing to differentiate themselves from Muslims, a kind of forced stratification with a distinct identity (CNN.com). Hindus were also ordered to wear yellow cloth markings on their clothes and to post two-meter yellow cloths on their roof tops (genocidewatch.org). They also issued an edict designed to involve a "crackdown" on un-Islamic parts of Afghanistan. In conjunction with this fatwa (religious decree), cultural genocide took place: Buddhist statues were destroyed, sixty-five Hindu and Sikh temples and gurudwaras were razed and the national heritage museum was leveled to intimidate those people whom the Taliban rulers considered "undesirable."

Their approach has evidently worked. For centuries Kandahar was a big commercial center and traders from South Asia, Middle East and Europe walked the trade routes that led to this city which is set in an oasis. In this city Hindu and Sikh merchants and traders once thrived. Afghanistan once had a population of 50,000 Hindus and Sikhs; since the Taliban takeover this has dwindled to a few thousand, after most fled the country (genocidewatch.org). As Andrew Marshall, a reporter for Reuters, wrote in his article, "Afghan Hindus Emerge from the Shadows" (Hindustan Times.Com. Thursday, February 29, 2002):

> Kandahar's last Hindu temple is concealed behind a rotten wooden door at the end of a tiny passage deep in the bazaar. But people who pray there no longer have to hide. The toothless woman who tends to the temple does not know how old she is. She has lived in a small room beside the shrine for decades, while governments came and went and Afghanistan endured anarchic warlord rule and then the harsh grip of the Taliban. She has watched the city's Hindu community dwindle from 500 families to just five. But now, with the city at peace and the Taliban of Mullah Mohammed Omar gone, Hindus say their plight has eased. 'Now we are very happy,' said 43-year-old Roop Chand Batija, head of Kandahar's Hindu and Sikh communities. 'We hope that some of our relatives will come back. It is safe for them now.'

This saga of intimidation, humiliation, torture, persecutions and massacres, furthermore, was not confined to the Hindu and Sikh community: in fact, those who suffered most at the hands of Mullah Omar and his Taliban were fellow Muslims — Kandahar's Shi'ite community, whom the Taliban despised. In northern Afghanistan, during their rule, the Taliban massacred the many members of the Shi'ite community. Those in Kandahar faced a similar fate — persecution, violence and abuse.

In Afghanistan the institutions of religion and politics were synthesized during the Taliban regime: their governmental structure was based on religion — an extreme, fundamentalist interpretation of the Koran. They persecuted all those who did not obey their (or Mullah Omar's) interpretation of the Koran and its numerous laws. Using such an approach they not only took control of the economy but also the cultural matters of the entire society, making it easy for them to curtail the freedom of those they deemed unworthy. Genocide in Afghanistan would have been very limited had the Taliban limited their control to economic factors alone. Their Islamic ideology gave the Taliban power to dominate, discriminate, and eliminate.

Quoting Max Weber, Habermas (1973: 95–96) says: "The basis of legit-imacy reveals 'the ultimate grounds of the "validity" of a domination, in other words ... those grounds upon which there are based the claims of obedience made by the master against the "officials" and of both against the ruled.'" The Taliban utilized legitimation and perpetuated it by creating a shroud of silence and visiting strict and swift discipline on those who deviated from their beliefs. Genocide continued for some time, because of the population's general fear and relative unawareness of what was happening. The Taliban largely controlled the society's means of communication and propagandized the wearing of yellow cloth as a protection for Hindus and Sikhs — not as the discriminatory action it actually was. When a government controls a society's means of communication and knowledge, manipulates them to mystify the masses, and legitimizes them significantly, the probability of emerging genocide increases. It is not surprising, then, that the Taliban manipulated religious, political, and cultural institutions, and not only those institutions that were purely economic, to maximize their power and eliminate possible opposition. This was reinforced, furthermore, by eliminating diversity in the larger society and severely repressing any kind of rebellion. Legitimation was essential to their success; the leaders effectively manipulated the masses by controlling socio-cultural knowledge throughout the society.

In general, then, genocidal reactions to Westernization in Afghanistan under the Taliban have included the physical identification of minorities, group-based murder, and cultural destruction, accompanied by increased elite funda-

mentalism and concerns with legitimation. Clearly, their reaction to this transitional period in their society's history has been overwhelmingly destructive.

THE BAHA'IS AND OTHERS IN IRAN

As Firuz Kazemzadeh (2000) has pointed out, most of the conditions
specified by the UN's definition of genocide have been met in the case of the
Baha'is. More than two hundred of them have been put to death, many of them
community leaders. They also have no civil rights: they cannot hold government
jobs, enforce legal contracts, practice law, collect pensions, attend institutions of
higher learning, and openly practice their faith (Kazemzadeh 2000: 537).

However, the Baha'is are only one group of people singled out in Iran as
unworthy of existence. Ladan and Roya Boroumand have stated that, "since the
beginning of the revolution, thousands of Iranians have been executed for their
'subversive activities,' political opinions, religion, mores, writings, and so on"
(Boroumand 2000: 308). The elimination of people whose views differ from the
ruling theocracy solidified the society's general hegemony.

Furthermore, it is important to emphasize that the elimination of these
people is not effected secretly — there are laws which specifically permit the
killing of people. "In fact, Article 226 of the penal code allows any individual to
kill. All it takes is for the individual to decide on his own that another is an
apostate for the law to authorize him to kill. Even if it means that he has to prove
the crime of apostasy a posteriori" (Kadivar, Payam-e Emrouz, February-March,
1999 p. 19, cited by Boroumand 2000: 320).

As in Afghanistan, the Iranian government has used religion to gain cultural control and thereby dominate the population. As Waters (1994:183) has
put it so well, borrowing from Gramsci, the church "as a critical mobilizer of idea
systems which support the bourgeois control. It can take this role because it
provides an intellectual link between the ruling class and the masses — the
clergy is privileged by the ruling class but revered by the masses." In the cases of
Iran both the ruling class and the clergy are one. Religion provides leadership
and the comfort of being part of the "truth." Once people are protected by the
leadership and comforted by the ruling class and its control over religion, it
becomes easier for the elite to convince the masses that other groups or religions
are a major threat. Conflict among them becomes unavoidable. Through such
violence, a sense of "us" and "them" emerges whereby active consent can be won

among the "us" and the solidarity of "us" is insured through the attack and proposed elimination of "them."

As Trent Schroyer (1973) has made clear, Critical Theory views modern repression as a product of rationality for which it is paramount to use the most efficient means, not economic exploitation alone, to reach an end. In this regard, the rulers of Iran have used technocratic thinking to oppress their victims. Furthermore, denying the Baha'is the right to higher education is a way to oppress and control the intelligence, influence, and power of this minority whom they ultimately wish to destroy.

In the twentieth century, Western ideas flooded Iran. Reza Shah, the king, wanted to make some move toward modernization and this was welcomed by many. However, most of the public was still under the influence of the clergy who rejected both modernization and Westernization, particularly the secularization of the educational system, unveiling of women and implementation of Europeanized legal codes (Kazemzadeh 2000: 539). They saw attempts at Westernization as a subversive threat to Islam. The Iranian clergy associated such reforms with the Baha'is and used their hatred or fear of each to assist in eliminating both.

They began by stating that the Baha'is were running the government and wanted to overthrow Islam. When the Shah was overthrown in 1979 and the clerics took over, they were able to promulgate genocidal acts in order to "save" Islam from Westernization. The Baha'is had been associated with proposed reforms and, therefore, with Westernization; an attack on the Baha'is was an attack on Western ideas, in order to strengthen Islam. The clergy had developed a system of what Habermas calls legitimations. They are designed to "mystify" the political system — to mask what is going on. As Schroyer (1973: 245) says: "legitimation of society is predicated on the promise of survival and mediation of crisis to all those who accept without question the depoliticization of politics and the bureaucratic mystification of the everyday world." The clergy generated negative ideas about Westernization and the Baha'is in order to legitimize their actions and beliefs.

Western ideas such as the free market, despite their relative ineffectiveness, are also anathema to Iranian religious fundamentalists, (cf. Dabashi 2000: 475-476). Western ideas have inadvertently attacked the rules of Islam, thereby threatening the hegemony established by those in power. Consequently, Western ideas are attacked and those in Iran viewed as supporting them, particularly the Baha'is, are defined as worthy of elimination.

The government also used the tactic of dividing people into insiders and outsiders: "These insiders were the defenders of God's rights, their families, and their friends. Any voice of dissent was violently silenced. For the ruling elite, the outsiders were not citizens. They had to passively endure war, violence, and terrorism. In the name of God's rights, a terrorized civil society was kept in the dark, wholly hidden from the outside world" (Boroumand 2000: 303).

This kind of cultural control enabled the elite to divide and control opponents, ruling them more effectively than would have been the case through simple religious dominance. Such behavior may be viewed as highly rational, as were Nazi concentration camps (cf. Ferrarotti 1994).

Critical Theory is also concerned with the consciousness of actors, since control by external forces can preclude their developing a revolutionary consciousness. As Gramsci (1977: 356–357, paraphrased) writes of the proletariat and their consciousness of their own situation:

> It is impossible to imagine the collapse of a centuries-old civilization and the arrival of a new civilization without an apocalyptic upheaval, a tremendous rupture. If a powerful working class-based political force does not emerge from this chaos in the near future; and if this force does not succeed in convincing the majority of the population that an order is immanent in the existing confusion and that this very confusion has its purpose; if this force does not succeed in making the working class appear in the consciousness of the masses and in the political reality of the governmental institutions as a dominant and the leading class — then our country will not be able to overcome the present crisis.

Once this consciousness does occur, it may be revolutionary in nature. President Khatami of Iran advocates the need for a revolutionary consciousness. As Boroumand (2000: 311–312) says,

> Western civilization is not the only challenge to the Islamic revolution. According to Khatami (1997: 160-161), there is another formidable challenge, that of a rigid and reactionary Islamism that rejects any idea of social justice. To survive, therefore, the Islamic regime must wage a war on two fronts: against its own extremists and against the attraction of the humanistic West.

A cultural revolution must take place in Iran in order for its present hegemony to be destroyed. As religion has been an integral part of the cultural domination, it will also be a part of the cultural revolution. "(S)etting up the theologians as political guardians of the people was Khatami's idea (Amir Arjomand 1984: 268 70; Kadivar 1999: 24-5). In the early days of the revolution, the highest ranking ayatollahs argued against this idea with varying degrees of insistence. The grand ayatollahs, Shariat Madari and Qomi were persecuted and arrested for protesting against the direct interaction of the clergy in the affairs of

the state Most of the clergy stayed away from the revolutionary adventure"
(Boroumand 2000: 315). Yet Khatami realizes that in order to have a cultural revolution he must use the tools with which the cultural domination itself is put
into place. Critical theorists highlight the cultural realm of society (rather than
the economic realm as Marx originally did). It is by controlling the cultural
realm (hegemony) that the theocracy in Iran has been able to rule and persecute
as they have. If they only had control of the economic realm then they would not
have the power that they do. Specifically, religion is used to justify and perpetuate their extremist ideas. Once this cultural domination is secure it becomes
easy to control people's beliefs and therefore their actions as well.

Critical theorists recognize that the world is dominated by cultural rather
than economic factors; however cultural control can most certainly lead to economic control. This is especially true when the leaders use legitimations in their
rule. Once cultural control is attained then they can infuse their ideas into minds
of the public convincing them that their ideas, including genocide, are necessary
in order to protect the system in which they live.

The *Economist* (2002, August 3-9: 6) reports that the Revolutionary Court
in Tehran has jailed 33 members of the Iran Freedom Movement Party for up to
ten years on charges they were "trying to overthrow the holy system of the government with new ideas." Their party has also been outlawed.

Bringing the above discussion together, it is evident that post-Western-
ization developments in Iran included the destruction of minorities and removal
of their civil rights in the context of increased cultural and technological control
in the wake of the society's rising economic exploitation and elite domination.

CONCLUSIONS

This chapter has argued for the relevance of Critical Theory to an understanding of genocidal conflict in its emphasis on a society's possible destructive
cultural and ideological intergroup reactions under particular historical conditions. Westernization of Third World countries, with its economic exploitation
of resources and labor, creating major class divisions, and ideas which may be
interpreted as threatening more traditional values, may result in governing elites
feeling particularly vulnerable, thereby attempting to protect and maximize
their dominant power positions by treating minorities in genocidal ways. In the
case of Afghanistan, this involved Taliban identification of particular minorities,

their cultural and physical destruction, and return to traditional ideologies in the form of extreme religious fundamentalism. Given Western economic exploitation of and cultural influences on Iran, genocidal developments there included murder, the destruction of civil rights, cultural control, religious fundamentalism, and rejection of Westernization.

The above factors and case studies highlight the cultural and ideological reactions of particular national elites during transitional periods of Western economic and cultural influence, resulting in genocidal reactions and policies — legal, cultural, and physical. These trends emphasize the need for greater insight into these kinds of situations and processes, with an eye to reducing the potential for genocide in significant ways. Furthermore, in the broader context, genocide may be viewed as tied to culture and civilization. Horkheimer and Adorno in their book, *Dialectic of Enlightenment* (1972: 217) write that:

> The conclusion that terror and civilization are inseparable as drawn by the conservatives, is well founded....Culture has developed with the protection of the executioner... It is impossible to abolish terror and retain civilization. Even a lessening of terror implies a beginning of the process of dissolution.

According to Gramsci (1977: 5):

> Men possess nothing more than a veneer of civilization — one only has to scratch them to lay bare the wolf-skin underneath. Instincts have been tamed, but not destroyed, and still the right of might is the only right that is recognized ... social privileges and differences, being products of society and not of nature, can be overcome. Humanity will need another bloodbath to abolish many of these injustices — and then it will be too late for the rulers to be sorry they left the hordes in that state of ignorance and savagery they enjoy today.

Unfortunately, terror in different forms including genocide is always present under the "mask" of civilization. This is well documented throughout human history. The best a society can hope to do is to keep it under this "mask" and never allow it to reveal the atrocities it is capable of committing.

Genocide may also be examined as part of "civilizing" and "decivilizing" processes: these two represent two sides of the same coin (cf. Elias 1939; 1978; Mennell 1990). The decivilizing process involves the breakdown of the civilizing process just as terror, genocide, etc., are the breakdown of civility. Genocide is the result of the loss of civility and the "mask" which encourages these tendencies to terrorize or engage in genocide under control, as the "mask" breaks apart from time to time cultural and physical destruction result.

Genocide, violence and terror are typical during transitional periods of history. There appear to be certain unsettled periods in societal events when brutality and genocide flourish, as we appear to be seeing, currently. Many states are honeycombed with underground nationalistic, radical, and patriotic move-ments. The result is engagement in activities such as terror, violence or genocide against those who are perceived as the source of major problems. This tends to result from the destruction of the "mask" of civility by a number of possible means (religious, political, cultural, racial or ethnic), leading to the decivilizing process. Again, greater insight into such phenomena is necessary if we are to reduce and hopefully avoid such massive human destruction in the future.

NOTES

* The author is indebted to Mr. James Cassady for his help in the preparation of this paper. He is also grateful to Professor Graham Kinloch for his critical comments on earlier versions of the manuscript and for helping to clarify the author's perspectives.

REFERENCES

Amir Arjomand, S. 1984. *The Shadow of God and Hidden Imam*. Chicago: University of Chicago Press.

Boroumand, Ladan and Roya. 2000. "Illusion and Reality of Civil Society in Iran: An Ideological Debate." *Social Research* 67, 303–344.

Chalk, Frank and Kurt Johanssohn. 1990. *The History and Sociology of Genocide: Analyses and Case Studies*. New Haven: Yale University Press.

Dabashi, Hamid. 2000. "The End of Islamic Ideology." *Social Research* 67, 475–518.

Elias, Norbert. 1939, 1978. *The Civilizing Process. Vol. 1: The History of Manners*. New York: Pantheon Books. (Translated by Edmund Jephcott).

_____. 1982. *The Civilizing Process. Vol. 2: Power and Civility*. New York: Pantheon Books. (Translated by Edmund Jephcott).

Ferrarotti, Franco. 1994. *The Temptation to Forget*. Westport, CT: Greenwood Press.

Gramsci, Antonio. 1977. *Selections from Political Writings (1910–1920)*. London: Lawrence and Wishart.

Habermas, Jürgen. 1975. *Legitimation Crisis*. Boston: Beacon Press.

Jones, G., M. Lowy, G. Therborn, J. Merrington, A. Gorz, R. Aronson, N. Geras, A. Glucksmann and L. Colleti. 1977. *Western Marxism*. London: New Left.

Kadivar, M. 1999. *Anidshe-ye Siasi dar Eslam* (Political Thinking in Islam) Vol. 1, *Nazarieh hay dolt dar Fiche Shih* (Theories of State in Shih Cannon Law). Tehran: Inshore Nay.

Khatami, M. 1997. *Bim-e-Moj* (Fear of Wave). Tehran: Simaye Javan.

Kazemzadeh, Firuz. 2000. "The Baha'is in Iran: Twenty Years of Repression." *Social Research* 67, 537–558.

Lukacs, Georg. 1971. *History and Class Consciousness*. London: Merlin Press.

Marcuse, Herbert. 1964. *One-Dimensional Man*. Boston: Beacon Press.

_____. 1969. *An Essay on Liberation*. Boston: Beacon Press.

Marshall, Andrew. 2002. "Afghan Hindus Emerge from the Shadows." *hindustantimes.Com*

Mennell, Stephen. 1990. "Decivilising Process: Theoretical Significance and Some Lines of Research." *International Sociology* 5, 205–224.

Schroyer, Trent. 1973. *The Critique of Domination*. Boston: Beacon Press.

Tohidi, Nayereh. 1991. "Gender and Islamic Fundamentalism." *www.geocities.com/Islam/capandgen.html*.

Waters, Malcolm. 1994. *Modern Sociological Theory*. London: Sage Publications.

Winter, Bronwyn. 1997. "Fundamental Misunderstandings: Issues in Feminist Approaches to Islamism." *Journal of Women's History* 13: 21.

_____. 2001. Nov. 24. "Taliban Move to Make Afghan Hindus wear ID Badges." *cnn.com*

_____. 2001. May 24. "International Campaign to End Genocide." *www.genocidewatch.org*

_____. YEAR, August 3rd-9th. "The World this Week." *The Economist* 364: 6.

Chapter 11. Conflict Regulation in Chile and Northern Ireland: The Role of Elites

Max Koch, University of Ulster

Introduction

At first sight, mentioning Chile and Northern Ireland in a volume on genocide appears to be misleading, if not misplaced. Indeed, in contrast to the historical cases of genocide discussed in this volume, the scale of violence and the energy of destruction in both countries have been far lower. Chile and Northern Ireland should rather be described as divided societies ridden by conflicts, which have, at times, escalated. Having said this, as Graham C. Kinloch has pointed out, there is "potential for genocide in any society." In understanding genocide as a "continuum," ranging from "ordinary" discrimination to deliberate mass death, the social sciences can contribute to "monitor current and emergent events in the attempt to prevent any movement towards possible minority destruction" (Kinloch 2002, p. 133). Conflicts of any kind might turn into genocidal situations but, fortunately — as in the cases of Chile and Northern Ireland — they normally do not do so.

Both cases can be seen as relatively successful examples of conflict regulation. By highlighting the issues of how a further escalation of conflict was avoided in the two countries, I hope to make a contribution to the general understanding of conflict. As an important factor in this regard, I deal with the role of the elites. During the 1970s and much of the 1980s, the elites of both these countries deemed conflict resolution to be possible only in the context of a military

233

surrender of the opposition groups. At the same time, the opposition did not follow a reformatory and compromise-oriented path of conflict regulation, but rather aimed at a military overthrow of the political and social order. However, neither the government nor the opposition succeeded in defeating their respective opponents and positional warfare claimed several thousand innocent victims on both sides. Towards the end of the 1980s, however, negotiations were taken up and headway was made toward more consensual forms of government, now including many of the previously powerless social groups.

This change in the strategy of governing from constraint to consensus can be seen as crucial in avoiding further escalations of the conflicts in the two societies. To understand the role of the elites in paving the way to peace, I will examine their social composition, the pillars of power as well as the political and economic context in which the mode of the reproduction of their respective forms of capital changed. First, I will examine the cases of Chile and Northern Ireland separately; and then compare both countries. Finally, I will draw some conclusions from the elite-centered approach for the general understanding of conflict in comparative perspective.

CHILE

In the first months after the coup d'état in 1973, the new coalition of power led by a military junta under General Pinochet had no clear idea of how to rule the country. The coup was literally a reactionary action, because the military junta acted against an existing project initiated by the socialist government of the *Unidad Popular* (Koch 2003). Rather than advancing a positive program of its own, this action involved the liberation of the society from Marxism. The subsequent persecutions were supposed to serve this aim and were not only directed against the constitutional government and its allied organizations in particular, but also against those institutions which had allowed the election of a socialist government: political democracy as such. A fundamental reshaping of the society and its key economic and political institutions was deemed necessary.[1] In its first attempts to "modernize" the country, the new elite abolished opposition parties, trade unions, and the democratic institutions. Chile became a dictatorship, and those who had shown even the mildest support for the previous administration were alleged to be in opposition to the new rulers and became the targets of all kinds of exclusion, persecution and state terror.[2]

Who were the societal actors who constituted the pillars of Pinochet's coalition of power? Together with the army and traditional entrepreneurs, whose privileges were under threat from the *Unidad Popular* and who therefore supported all kinds of legal and illegal activities against the government, the new elite consisted of the *Chicago Boys* and new types of joint-stock companies, the *Grupos Economicos* (Koch 1998, pp. 68–70; Koch 1999). The Chicago Boys were a group of young neo-liberal economists who had carried out postgraduate studies in Chicago in the 1950s and early 1960s. Throughout the 1960s, many came back to Chile to hold professorships in universities or top management positions in administration. With Pinochet preventing any interference from the opposition (Osorio and Cabezas 1995), this group was able to transform Chile into a laboratory, based on its ideas of orthodox liberalism. Between 1975 and 1982, the Chicago Boys radically opened the Chilean economy to foreign competition. While many companies whose survival had relied on the internal market and the shelter of the state-sponsored policy of Industrial Import Substitution went bankrupt, those export sectors having comparative cost advantages began to experience success. Those sectors were, above all, those exporting agricultural products.

Another result of the liberalization of the money market was that financial capital advanced rapidly at the expense of productive capital. This led not only to the explosion of the number of small joint-stock companies (*Financieras*) but to the emergence and growth of the large *Grupos Economicos*. From controlling financial capital, they began to purchase companies in the productive sectors of the economy. In the 1970s, the *Grupos* enjoyed spectacular growth rates, which cannot be explained solely by reference to improved efficiency or rational operations on the world market, but also owed a great deal to the "visible hand" of the state represented by neo-liberal economists who were themselves backed by the military junta. It was not that a political-technocratic faction represented the interests of an already established economic elite, but that a technocratic faction of the elite produced the conditions for the advent of a new kind of entrepreneurship.

The transformation from a state-protected growth strategy oriented towards the internal market to an export-oriented capitalism integrated into the world market was completed by approximately 1980. The new "power elite"[3] rested upon three pillars: the military junta with General Pinochet on top, the Chicago Boys and the *Grupos Economicos*. Pinochet virtually monopolized political power, which made the feasibility of the Chicago Boy's neo-liberal ideas a great deal easier. The socio-economic conditions created by the new economic and social policy enabled the *Grupos Economicos* to become dominant. In comparison to this "troika of power," the formerly influential corporative organizations of the traditional entrepreneurs, the *Gremios*, faded into insignificance — a situation which was to reverse partially during the economic crisis of 1982/1983.

During that crisis, the growth model created by the *Chicago Boys* and the *Grupos* collapsed. Faced with an increase in the price of external loans, many companies became heavily indebted. In particular, the *Grupos*, which were especially dependent on international capital, slid into bankruptcy. As the crisis deepened, their activities began to be questioned by the *Gremios* of the small and medium-sized companies. For the first time the government was openly criticized for its one-sided socio-economic policy, which favored almost exclusively the interests of the *Grupos*. In their demand for a more pragmatic line, the *Gremios* were subsequently supported by the biggest employers-organization outside the financial sector, *Confederación de la Producción y de Comercio*, and increasingly by the political opposition. The latter began to recover from its post-coup weakness and organized the resistance against the dictatorship in increasingly effective ways.[4]

Faced with this unexpected challenge from three fronts, the regime was obliged to reshuffle its internal power structures. In order to appease the employers' organizations, many neo-liberal leaders were forced to resign[5] whilst more traditional and corporate politicians were appointed. The state re-activated its role in economic affairs, especially the management of the external debts, and took over the biggest banks and *Grupos*. This resulted in the somewhat paradoxical result of state intervention in the economy being temporarily greater under Pinochet than under Allende (Martinez and Díaz 1995, p. 64).

The state's large debts were subsequently brought under relative control through agreements between the government on the one hand and the World Bank and IMF on the other. Opposition from the employers' organization dwindled as it became clear that banks taken into government control would subsequently be re-transferred to the private sector. Some of the neo-liberal leaders were re-appointed to their influential posts in the economy and administration. With the recovery of the economy, which was to show unprecedented growth rates for the following decade, the street protests of 1983/1984 abated. The crisis in 1982/1983 did not therefore mean the fall of the "troika of power," which had arisen in the 1970s. Their power was interrupted rather than abolished by an episode during which that elite was forced to make concessions to the different opposition strata. Having survived this crisis of hegemony, however, it continued to carry through its market oriented socio-economic reforms.

Although the opposition did not succeed in obliging Pinochet to resign during the protests of the early 1980s, the political space for a long-term strategy for his removal was nonetheless opened. While preparing for the referendum of October 1988, the opposition managed to remain united, and it also succeeded in presenting a common candidate for the subsequent presidential election. The employers' organizations maintained their relative autonomy from the junta by initiating a dialogue with the trade unions as well as with the political opposition. It is true that it supported Pinochet in the referendum as well as Hernan Buechi (Pinochet's chosen candidate) in the subsequent presidential election, but it also stressed its loyalty to the constitution of 1980, which included respect for the newly elected president Patricio Aylwin.

Before the new government took office in 1990, however, the military regime introduced a range of measures to make sure that its main achievements were not reversed by its successors. There was first the law of amnesty, which prevents members of the military government and its allies from prosecution for violations of human rights before 1978. Secondly, the strong position of the armed forces in the constitution was to be maintained according to which they have the majority vote in the National Security Council. By calling a state of emergency, this institution can limit citizenship rights. Another instrument that contributes to the conservation of elements of authoritarian rule is the practice of appointing every fifth member of the Senate instead of electing them. Most of these senators effectively opposed democratic reforms of the society. Pinochet himself remained commander-in-chief of the armed forces until 1998. He subsequently filled one of the non-elected Senator posts.[6] Furthermore he gave senior positions within the armed forces to his comrades-in-arms. Finally, he re-appointed nine out of sixteen judges of the Supreme Court. Since they can remain in office until the age of 75, continuity is also ensured in the judiciary.

The defeat at the referendum might have been problematic for Pinochet and his allies. Their mayor project, however, the transformation of Chilean capitalism, which included the transition from import substitution to a growth strategy based on comparative cost advantages, the strengthening of the private sector and capital at the expense of labor within the industrial relations, was to a large extent achieved. Since continuity was assured in the legal and political field, the armed forces could withdraw from playing a frontline role in politics.

Similarly, the second pillar of power, the *Chicago Boys*, left their government posts and returned to senior positions in the *Grupos Economicos*. Since Chile had been transformed at the socio-economic level and had realized its active integration into the world market, there was no reason for the elite to resist the transition to democracy.

Last but not least, there were international changes. After the fall of the Berlin Wall, the USA, which initially supported the military government as a bulwark against communism in Latin America, became increasingly critical of the ongoing violations of human rights. Terror and state killings, which were initially regarded as necessary in order to carry through socio-economic reforms, were seen more and more as an obstacle to achieving international credibility and as such profitable engagement in the world market. Violations of human rights at first suited the interests of the ruling class, but were now seen to represent a barrier to Chile's full integration in the global economy and society.

NORTHERN IRELAND

Brendan O'Leary and John McCarry (1996) have called the creation of Northern Ireland in 1920 a prime example of a "state and nation building failure." The establishment of Northern Ireland proved not only the bankruptcy of the policy of constructing a British identity throughout Ireland, but was also evidence of the failure of Irish nationalism. The inability of Nationalists to coerce or persuade the Protestants of the benefits of a united Ireland was due to several factors. One factor was their relative military weakness compared to the forces of the British crown, but more importantly Irish Nationalism came to define itself in terms of opposition to the British state, the English language and Protestantism.

Caroline Kennedy-Pipe (2001, p. 25) therefore regards Northern Ireland as "product of varying political power." A 30% minority in the whole island was able to prevent one region from joining the republic, but this region in turn contained a 30% minority in favor of that unification. Until the mid-1960s, Northern Ireland was not fully integrated into either the British or the southern Irish states and little influence was exercised by either Dublin or Westminster on the politics of the province, leaving Stormont, the Northern Irish parliament, to govern. Protestants dominated this and other institutions and made few efforts to win Nationalist support. As Richard Rose (1971) pointed out, Unionist power was dependant upon maintaining the cohesion in the Unionist bloc, and it was Catholic compliance not Catholic consent that was sought. Kennedy-Pipe (2001, p. 26) concludes, that the minority therefore had little stake in maintaining or contributing to this system "and for almost fifty years, Nationalist politicians refused to act as an official opposition, opting out of the business of government."

Protestant rule rested on four pillars. First, there was political domination due to the manipulation of constituency boundaries ("gerrymandering") ensuring that at most electoral levels the Unionist candidates came out on top. Second, there was the monopolization of law and order: until the onset of the policing reforms within the framework of the Good Friday Agreement in 2001, the police force, the Royal Ulster Constabulary (RUC), was over 90% Protestant in composition, and the intelligence services were also predominantly Protestant. Third, there was inequality in the provision and allocation of public housing leading to the creation of ghettos of Catholics in underprivileged areas. And fourth, there was discrimination in employment which led to an overlapping of the class structure with sectarian categories (Aunger 1975).

The opposition movement of the 1960s, of which Catholics were an important but not exclusive part, was aimed not so much at the partition from Britain but rather at the improvement of the economic and social conditions within the existing institutional framework. Heavily influenced by the international civil rights agenda, the opposition started to campaign for equal rights and a reform of rather than an abolition of the assembly in Stormont. This move towards inclusive politics reached its height by 1967 with the foundation of the Northern Ireland Civil Rights Association whose main aim was to abolish the discriminatory practices in the region. The civil rights marchers frequently clashed with Protestant counter-demonstrators leading to an eruption of violence on the streets. Since the RUC soon turned out to be incapable or unwilling to maintain order by de-escalation, Stormont requested additional troops from the Westminster government in 1969.

The deployment of troops, which were initially welcomed by the Catholic community, was not meant to be permanent. It was rather deemed to be a temporary move accompanied by limited action on discrimination (Kennedy-Pipe 2001, p. 28). However, palliative measures satisfied neither Unionists nor Nationalists, because they went too far for the former and not far enough for the latter. On the Unionist side, extremist Loyalists (who regarded the Labour government as too sympathetic to nationalism) gained influence and set up paramilitary organizations, which soon started to terrorize Catholic neighborhoods. On the Nationalist side, the Provisional IRA broke away from the Official IRA and started a violent campaign against the British state. In the meantime, however, a Conservative government was elected in Westminster, which introduced emergency legislation and internment without trial. Special prisons were built and, at least initially, were filled with Catholics.

Rather than containing the conflict, these measures, along with curfews and house raids, accelerated it and led many Catholics to become alienated from the Northern Irish political system. Instead, they increasingly argued that the issues of inequality and discrimination could only be resolved in the context of a united Ireland. Some Catholics showed solidarity with the paramilitaries of the Provisional IRA. Westminster finally announced the end of attempts to reform Stormont by abandoning and introducing Direct Rule (1972). As late as 1994, the prevailing line was that there should be no contact between the governments and paramilitary organizations. The view was held that the Provisionals could be militarily defeated or forced to stop by political change.

But the history of almost thirty years of "Troubles," with its 3600 deaths (from both sides), tells another story. It shows in the first place that neither the IRA nor the British forces were to be "defeated," but that violence on both sides functioned as obstacle for any kind of political initiative. As a consequence, the road back to peace and dialogue was protracted and only began seriously with the Anglo-Irish Agreement (1985), which established collaboration between Westminster and Dublin on Northern Irish affairs. Apart from the changes within the Unionist camp, which will be analyzed in more detail below, further crucial steps for the achievement of peace in Northern Ireland were the beginning of the dialogue between Nationalists and Republicans in the early 1990s[7] and the election of a Labour government in 1997. Taking a different view on Northern Irish issues to its predecessors, who were keen on treating the management of the conflict as a domestic affair, Tony Blair's administration introduced a more pragmatic line. In particular, the mediation of US President Bill Clinton was welcomed. As in the case of Chile, the US had started to show a great deal of interest in bringing about peace in Northern Ireland. This active role became obvious when Gerry Adams was granted a visa to visit the US in 1994, which he had been denied up to this point, and reached its peak when Clinton persuaded both Adams and David Trimble, the leader of the Ulster Unionist Party, to accept the Good Friday Agreement — the current and so far relatively successful attempt at conflict management through devolution.

The Agreement itself, signed on 10 April 1998, is based on the principle of non-violence and mutual respect. It contains four important elements (Bew 2001): first, cross-community executive power sharing; second, proportionality rules applied throughout the relevant governmental and public sectors; third, community self-government and equality in cultural life; and fourth, veto rights for minorities. Further important elements are the release of political prisoners and the setting up of commissions to deal with issues such as equality, policing, human rights and the decommissioning of paramilitary weapons.

The question is why did the majority of Unionists, who had monopolized political and economic power, begin to support power sharing and a peace agreement that questioned some of those privileges? Let us remember that up to this point these privileges were seen as both legitimate and non-negotiable. Protestant supremacy in Stormont was quietly tolerated by the British government until the early 1970s, when Westminster's influence on Northern Irish affairs increased, and resulted eventually in the imposition of Direct Rule in 1972. Subsequently, the British government began to pass laws which facilitated political and socio-economic equality between Catholics and Protestants in the long term. Faced with this unprecedented opposition from a hitherto reliable ally, the previously monolithic block of Unionism began to fragment.

The Ulster Unionist Party (UUP) could no longer mobilize the "Unionist family" and other parties began to emerge. Some made defiant appeals to people who felt a sense of betrayal at the new course of events. Those Unionists opposed to violence and in favor of reconciliation left the UUP and formed the Alliance Party, and those non-violent Protestants against reconciliation formed the Democratic Unionist Party (DUP). In working-class areas especially, dissatisfaction with the political process led to the formation of paramilitary organizations, most notably the Ulster Volunteer Force (UVF) and the Ulster Defence Association (UDA), and their political satellites, the Progressive Unionist Party (close to the UVF) and the Ulster Democratic Party (close to the UDA).[8]

Direct rule and political splits had weakened the Unionist hegemony considerably, and it would take until the mid-1980s until Unionism again spoke with one voice again and was reunited against the Anglo-Irish Agreement. This agreement, since it recognized that the "Troubles" were the business of both Dublin and London, was proof that Unionist influence on British government decisions had dwindled. Protests including large demonstrations and the boycott of public bodies had the support of all the Unionist factions but proved to be ultimately unsuccessful.

After the failed campaign against the Anglo-Irish agreement, Unionist unity disintegrated mainly into two major groups: on the one hand, the traditionalists of the DUP of Ian Paisley and his fundamental opposition to any kind of reconciliation with Catholics, and, on the other hand, the modernizers of the UUP. For the latter, it was becoming clear that abstention would hardly guarantee the restoration of hegemony. In the Ulster Unionists' view, the alleged "sell out" of Northern Ireland by the British would not be reversed and might even be accelerated if Unionists continued to refuse to take part in the negotiations on the future. If the traditional socio-economic privileges could not be defended, perhaps the long term affiliation of Northern Ireland to Britain was achievable. The position of the new leader of the UUP, David Trimble, was that Unionism could no longer afford to remain outside of the political process while others, including the arch-enemy of Unionism, Sinn Fein, negotiated. Instead, he argued that: "It is simply not possible to run Northern Ireland on the basis that excludes the 40% plus who regard themselves as Nationalists. We need to build a stable Northern Ireland. Stability, with the consent principle, guarantees the union" (David Trimble in *The Observer*, November 18, 2001). Walking out of negotiations, by contrast, would leave the union undefended.

Even though some aspects in the Good Friday Agreement are surely problematic for Unionists — among them: the reform of the police service and the equality agenda — two facts seem to justify Trimble's attempt to make the union safer through negotiations. The first fact is that under the new rules Northern Ireland "remains part of the UK and shall not cease to be so without the consent of a majority of the people of Northern Ireland" (Good Friday Agreement, Section 1). A referendum might change this status, but this is generally regarded as "a continuation of the present reality" (Bew 2001, p. 41). So, while the Belfast Agreement (as the Good Friday Agreement is referred to by Unionists) contains a formal and explicit reiteration of British sovereignty, two controversial articles in the Irish Constitution, which claimed Northern Ireland to be a part of the national territory of the Republic of Ireland and claimed jurisdiction over the whole of that territory, were deleted as a result of a referendum in the Republic. Hence, Unionists have the guarantee that Northern Ireland remains part of the UK, and this is no longer contradicted by anything in the Constitution of the Republic of Ireland.

The second issue, which angered Unionists of all camps prior to the Agreement, was cross-border cooperation, which they considered to be an embryonic form of an all-Ireland government. The Anglo-Irish Agreement had clearly called for all-Ireland Institutions to carry out delegated executive, harmonizing and consultative functions. In the Good Friday Agreement, however, words like "executive," "harmonizing" and "dynamic" do not appear. Rather, it was established that cross-border cooperation should be based on practical considerations, and that the institutions were to be accountable to the Northern Assembly, preventing the North-South Council from developing a distinctive life of its own. Since decisions in the Assembly cannot be made without majority support in both camps, Unionists and Nationalists, the former need no longer fear cross-border cooperation: "Unionists will always have a veto" (David Trimble in the *Belfast Newsletter*, April 18, 1998, quoted in Bew 2001, p. 68).

Having successfully avoided the danger of creeping unification through cooperation, the North-South institutions facilitated the economic interests of Northern Ireland's mainly Protestant investors. As in the case of Chile, international economic restructuring was an important factor in bringing about political and social change. As Mike Morrissey (2001, p. 139) points out, Northern Ireland's comparative advantages, which mainly involve cheaper labor compared to the UK, were being "eroded" in the 1990s. Northern Irish factories, the shipyard and textile industry in particular, were especially vulnerable to international restructuring, because "they were small, lacked higher-order activities such as R & D and were making products close to the end to their production cycle." A prime example of the decline of the Northern Irish industry is the Harland & Wolf shipyard in Belfast, which in its heyday employed over 10,000 people, of which less than 1000 survived by the 1990s.

This industrial decline was aggravated by the fact that the readiness of the British government to fund Northern Ireland began to be not as evident as previously. Interestingly, this is a rather recent phenomenon, following from policy suggestions from the New Labour administration. Even though Margaret Thatcher loudly proclaimed an ideology of non-intervention, public sector employment in Northern Ireland steadily increased under her rule. The rise of British subventions from 100 million British Pounds in 1972 to 1.6 billion British pounds in 1988/89 (Morrissey 2001, p. 142) also indicates that the level of intervention from London was a lot higher than during the Labour governments that had preceded Thatcher's administrations. Similar to the teething troubles of Chile's new capitalism, Northern Ireland's economy could not be sustained without massive state intervention.

Last but not least was the economic boom in the Republic of Ireland. Traditionally ridiculed for its alleged "backwardness" by Northern Protestants, the

Republic of Ireland opened its markets almost completely to foreign capital in the early 1990s, and achieved unprecedented growth rates for over a decade. If Chile's development strategy came to be known as a role model for Latin America because of the export of its highly competitive agricultural products, the Republic of Ireland was soon named the "Celtic Tiger" due to its ability to attract international capital, above all in the new technologies. The Southern Irish growth strategy, which is based on a highly skilled work force and capital-oriented labor markets as well as tax regulations, turned out to be extremely attractive to the so-called *New Economy*. Policy makers in Northern Ireland must have feared being left behind. Northern Ireland was less able to take advantage of the boom in the Republic of Ireland because of the ongoing Troubles. US-American companies especially, encouraged by Bill Clinton administration to invest in Northern Ireland, made it crystal clear that they considered peace and the absence of sectarian violence to be a precondition for any kind of economic engagement.

In summary, there were good reasons for the Protestant elites to begin negotiations on the creation of a more peaceful and inclusive environment in Northern Ireland. The old mode of reproduction of their economic and political capital had been based on two pillars and was supported by the British state: an undemocratic political system excluding Catholics from power and a subsidized and sheltered economy. With the change in British policies towards Northern Ireland and restructuring in the international division of labor it became clear that any attempt to defend the old privileges was doomed to failure. Rather, it was in the interest of Unionists to improve the reputation of Northern Ireland, if it was not to be excluded from the benefits of international capital, which had chosen the Republic of Ireland as one of its prime locations. The position taken by David Trimble and the modernizers within Unionism in the negotiations leading to the Good Friday agreement, that is, to accept a greater level of social and political inclusion of Catholics in exchange for the reinforcement of the constitutional affiliation of Northern Ireland to the UK, made sense, because it meant at the same time the reputation of Northern Ireland in international circles would improve.

A COMPARISON OF THE CASE STUDIES

The societies of both Chile and Northern Ireland went into political crisis at the end of the 1960s. In both cases, the privileges of the traditional elites were threatened by social movements which aimed at radical political and economic reforms. It is worthwhile to note that these popular movements did not opt for revolutionary usurpation in this first instance. Instead, they operated within the existing political and social order. In Chile, a socialist party coalition was voted to power in 1970, which nationalized large parts of the country's economy, thereby directly confronting the interests and resources of the traditional elites (the landed gentry and owners of larger private companies). In Northern Ireland, the monopolization of economic and political power by the Protestant elite was questioned by a civil rights movement, which campaigned for reforms of the unjust political system and for socio-economic inclusion (Koch 2004).

In both cases the elites were first unwilling to engage in dialogue and thereby contributed decisively to the escalation of violence. In Northern Ireland, both the British army and the IRA believed they could defeat their opponents using military force. In Chile, throughout the 1970s and much of the 1980s, there was virtually no political dialogue between the military government and the opposition. As a result of this, an increasing number of people supported various kinds of "armed struggle" against the dictatorship in Chile and the presence of the British army in Northern Ireland. Despite international protest, human rights were, on both sides, often ignored. Killings and assassinations, from the state and from the opposition, claimed many innocent victims in both countries.

A third similarity between Chile and Northern Ireland is that their elites had returned to dialogue and negotiations on power sharing with their respective opponents by the end of the 1980s. As has been shown in the case studies, this strategy shift can be linked to the social composition of the elites and the change in the mode of reproduction of their capital. In Chile, the elite consisted of the junta with General Pinochet at the top, creating the conditions for top positions in large corporations and administrative institutions to be taken over by neo-liberal economists. As a result of the political and economic strategy pursued by the Chicago Boys, the final pillar of power, the *Grupos Economicos* emerged. This ruling block carried out a transformation of Chile's capitalism, moving from an economic policy of Import Substitution towards one based on a growth strategy that stressed comparative cost advantages. In contrast to the Chilean case, whose new elite pursued an active project of socio-economic change, the Northern Irish elite remained a conservative social force for decades, and tried to preserve institutions whose days had long passed. The Protestant ruling class did not need to have to be innovative as it enjoyed the advantages of a subsidized economy and a political system that effectively prevented Catholics from challenging the privileges of the ruling class.

In Chile, the decisive factor for the elites in ceding their power through negotiations on power sharing was the after-effects of the debt crisis and the concomitant social consequences. The demonstrations of the early 1980s united the opposition and paved the way for the defeat of Pinochet in the referendum in 1988, which, in turn, assured the re-emergence of democracy. Another important factor was the change in US political pressure towards Chile, which, somewhat surprisingly after supporting the regime for almost two decades, re-discovered the value of human rights and made it clear, that it would not tolerate any kind of attempted coup after a lost referendum.

In Northern Ireland also, the traditional chief ally turned away from the elite. After quietly tolerating Protestant rule in the regional assembly of Stormont, the British government not only introduced direct rule but also passed legislation that enhanced the political rights of Catholics as well as advancing socio-economic equality. Even worse for the old elite was the rapprochement between London and Dublin, leading to the Anglo-Irish agreement (1985), which turned out to be a harbinger for the Good Friday Agreement in 1998. As in the Chilean case, an additional factor was the change in US politics, which was influential in initiating negotiations between the two apparently irreconcilable communities.

A further resemblance, which likewise facilitated the readiness of the elites to engage in negotiations, was the increasing integration of both countries into the international economy. Power sharing with their respective oppositions and the return to democratic and peaceful conditions greatly increased the chance of securing and increasing the assets of the ruling classes in the process of globalization. Far from being brought to account for earlier violations of human rights, the elites in both Chile and Northern Ireland were given a leading role in the emergent political and socio-economic order. In Chile, the continuity of the neo-liberal growth project is ensured through myriad ties with the global economy. Furthermore, the armed forces continue to have an important role in politics. Institutional peculiarities such as the law of amnesty, the appointed senators and the reshuffle of judges of the Supreme Court also inhibit the possibility of drastic change in Chile. In Northern Ireland, the modernizers within

Unionism managed to influence the outcome of negotiations leading to the Good Friday Agreement in such a way that their key interests were not ignored. On the one hand, the constitutional affiliation of Northern Ireland to the United Kingdom had a more secure basis after the agreement than before, on the other hand, the North-South Councils were subject to a Unionist veto. Equally important were the economic interests of the Unionist elite in the "peace dividend," which they hoped would ensue from the increasing attractiveness to international capital in the new more peaceful Northern Ireland.

CONCLUSION

In this chapter, I have analyzed the role of the elites in regulating the conflicts in Chile and Northern Ireland. For this purpose, I examined the social composition of the elites, the structure of their power as well as the political and economic context, which necessitated a change in the mode of reproduction of their capital. For both countries, ties have been found between the specific interests of the elites and the outbreak of violence, on the one hand, and its cessation, on the other hand. The relatively peaceful conflict resolutions, in particular, which characterize recent history in both Chile and Northern Ireland, corresponded well with the elite's need for further integration in increasingly international markets. The return to power sharing and democracy was even easier for the elites because, far from being prosecuted for previous persecutions of human rights, they could be sure of having a leading role in the emergent political and socio-economic order.

What conclusions can be drawn from the two case studies for the general consideration of conflict in comparative perspective? In future cross-country research, we can start from the hypothesis that the likelihood for non-violent conflict resolution increases with the extent of their integration in the international economy and that their elites can hope to secure and transform their capital during the period of political and economic change. Where active integration into global capitalism is possible and appreciated and where the *ancien régime* can hope to play some leading role in the emergent political and social order, the chances for conflict resolution, power sharing and inclusion are better than in cases where countries are excluded from the international distribution of labor and where there is a possibility that former leaders will be prosecuted. In applying this hypothesis, it would be necessary to look at relatively successful examples of conflict management other than Chile and Northern Ireland such as, for example, South Africa and to find out whether there are also connections between their roads to peace and their relative attractiveness to international capital, on the one hand, and the change of the mode of reproduction of the elite's capital, on the other. Cases of unsuccessful conflict resolution, where violence erupted and conflicts escalated, could be examined in relation to the question of whether these countries had any chance of integrating into the world market and the probability of the elite being able to maintain and accumulate capital through negotiations towards power sharing.

NOTES

1. If in the West "September 11" is now associated with terror and mass killing, in Chile this has been the case for over three decades — not least due to the active role played by Western governments in their support of the junta.
2. Measures taken against the internal and external opposition ranged from state killings, the "disappearance" of political suspects, torture, and forced exile, to international state terrorism.
3. Just as Valdés (1989) showed for Chile's *Chicago Boys*, Mills had argued for the US of the 1950s that the high degree of homogeneity of the three factions of the "power elite" — the Major Corporations, the Military, the Federal Government — was down to their common social origins. Members of the power elite were mainly Protestant, native-born Americans, from urban areas in the eastern USA, who shared similar educational backgrounds and socially mixed in the same prestigious clubs.
4. The opposition was fragmented in different sections and there were internal recriminations about the coup. Milestones towards a unification of the movements included the national days of protest, which were carried out once a month beginning on May 11, 1983.
5. The most spectacular resignations were by Sergio De Castro, the leader of the Chicago Boys, and José Piñeras' from their respective posts as secretaries of finance and mining.
6. As a welcome side-affect, the immunity, which corresponds to a Senator post, makes any legal prosecution within Chile very difficult.
7. Most notably the dialogue between the leaders of the Social Democratic and Labour Party, John Hume, and of Sinn Fein, Gerry Adams.
8. Some of these organizations were not new but represented the re-emergence of historically important but currently defunct groups.

REFERENCES

Aunger, Edmund A. 1975. "Religion and Occupational Class in Northern Ireland." *Economic and Social Review* 1, 1–17.

Bew, Paul. 2001. "The Belfast Agreement of 1998: From Ethnic Democracy to a Multicultural, Consociational Settlement?" In *A Farewell to Arms? From 'Long War' to Long Peace in Northern Ireland*, edited by Cox, Michael, Adrian Guelke and Fiona Stephen. Manchester: University Press.

Garretón, Manuel A. 1993. "La crisis de la democracia, el golpe militar y el proyecto contrarrevolucionario," In *FLACSO: Documento de Trabajo, Serie Estudios Políticos*, No. 30. Santiago de Chile.

Kennedy-Pipe, Caroline. 2001. "From War to Peace in Northern Ireland." In *A Farewell to Arms? From 'Long War' to Long Peace in Northern Ireland*, edited by Cox, Michael, Adrian Guelke and Fiona Stephen. Manchester: University Press.

Kinloch, Graham C. 2002. "The Possible Causes and Reduction of Genocide: An Exploration." *International Journal of Contemporary Sociology* 39(2), pp. 131–152.

Koch, Max. 1998. Unternehmen Transformation. Sozialstruktur und gesellschaftlicher Wandel in Chile. Frankfurt / Main: Vervuert.

_____. 1999. "Die kollektiven Akteure im Prozess der Erneuerung des chilenischen Kapitalismus." *Journal für Entwicklungspolitik* 15 (1), pp. 65–80.

_____. 2003. "Die Krise der Demokratie in Chile." *Utopie-kreativ*, No. 155 (September), pp. 789–797.

_____. 2004. "Closure Theory and Citizenship. The Northern Ireland Experience." *Electronic Journal of Sociology* 7 (4), http://www.sociology.org/content/vol7.4/ koch/html

Martínez, Javier and Alvaro Díaz. 1995. Chile: La grán transformación. In *SUR, Documento de Trabajo*, No 148. Santiago de Chile.

Mills, C. Wright. 1956. *The Power Elite*. Oxford: University Press.

Morrissey, Mike. 2001. "Northern Ireland: Developing a Post-Conflict Economy." In *A Farewell to Arms? From 'Long War' to Long Peace in Northern Ireland*, edited by Cox, Michael, Adrian Guelke and Fiona Stephen. Manchester: University Press.

O'Leary, Brendan and John McGarry. 1996. *The Politics of Antagonism. Understanding Northern Ireland*. Second Edition. London & Atlantic Highlands: The Athlone Press.

Osorio, Victor and Iván Cabezas. 1995. *Los hijos de Pinochet*. Santiago de Chile: Planeta.

Rose, Richard. 1971. Governing Without Consensus: An Irish Perspective. London: Faber and Faber.

Valdés, Juan Gabriel. 1989. *La escuela de Chicago: Operación Chile*. Buenos Aires: Grupo Editorial Zeta.

PART V. RESPONSES TO GENOCIDE

CHAPTER 12. WITNESSING THE CATASTROPHE

Kristin Platt

Topical discussions on new conflicts, new violence, new wars, have been accompanied by a new discourse concerning the remembrance of the Holocaust: politicians and intellectuals alike, among them Jacques Derrida, Juergen Habermas and the well-known German sociologist Ulrich Beck (Derrida/Habermas 2003; Beck 2003), have declared a "common memory," a "global memory," to be the basis for European integration and European identity.

This "global memory" promises redemption of "postmodern" crises: particularly with regard to the uncertainties of values, economics or leadership caused by the trans-nationalization of political structures. The declaration of a common experience of violence and the fostering of a common remembrance aims not only to unite people and nations, but also to reconcile them. A closer examination reveals that talking on "global memory" demands the assumption of a common history — which in turn leads to a cancellation of burdens of the past. There is only a small step from promulgation a mutual experience to the argument of equal experience. "Global memory" does not know victims and perpetrators. For this reason the concepts of collective history and global memory needs to be seen in close relation to the setting of a universal phenomenon of modern persecution (especially supported by the terms "ethnic cleansing" and European "expulsions") — and under such conditions, people are freed from the responsibility of considering national intentions to annihilate or to examine specific political motivations.

One could be justified in concluding that the topical German discourse on "global memory" is no mere accident. The discourse on European memory claims to build on the efforts undertaken since the 1990s to reappraise German history in such a way as to reintegrate Germany into world history — but not longer in the role of the historical perpetrator. The topical discourse on global memory, which, it must also be clearly emphasized, assumes a common experience of violence, is a premise that unexpectedly integrates well-known patterns of denial. This is clearly demonstrated, for instance, in statements that most of the German population was also victimized by the National Socialist reign of terror.

But there is no common experience of genocide. There is perhaps a shared history of national homogenization, but contrary to many claims this does not constitute common grounds of historical experience. The experience of genocide separates perpetrators and victims in such an enduring way that this separation is valid for the second or third generation "after." The different experiences caused a clear division between those who are able to write and define history and those who are not really witnesses, not really a juridical proof, not really an accepted voice: the traumatized survivors.

The following chapter aims to emphasize the basic division between the real witness and the survivor, the fundamental differences between history and memory on the one hand and the remembering in the families of survivors on the other. It should be assumed that the reason for these distinctions does not lie in the impossibilities, incomprehensibilities, a specific radicalism, totality or brutality of the recovered violence. The differences follow specific patterns of knowledge, of science and politics — patterns that demonstrate the *social* radicalism of genocidal processes and the *social* validity of their after-effects.

The article focuses on biographical narrations, in particular on autobiographical recollections of survivors of the genocide against the Armenians in the Ottoman Empire (1915/16). The aim of the study, based on semi-structured interviews, was to describe the influence of traumatic experiences on personal development. The project[1] involved a total of 136 interviews lasting between two and 11 hours which were recorded with survivors. These were followed in part by several follow-up interviews and were carried out in countries including Belgium, France, Italy and Cyprus. All interviewees were born between 1890 and 1915. They were requested to describe the course of their own life from their own

---

1. The survey was carried out by Mihran Dabag and Kristin Platt on the Ruhr University of Bochum (1990-1996). The names of the interviewees were not changed for anonymity: it was the explicit wish of the men and women, who are mentioned in this article, to witness their history with their own name.

individual perspective. All biographical accounts integrated self-categorizations into their generations and life views (Platt 1998).

In view of the complexity of the main focuses of academic conceptualizations of narration, recollection and experience, a particular aim of this work is to examine the concept of "survivor trauma."

1. Doubts About the Survivor's Narrative

> I ran away from the massacre, and then someone covered me with sand so I could not be seen, because whoever was seen alive was shot instantly. Underneath the sand I forgot that I was human. You do not believe that you are human anymore, or that you are anyone at all.

(Script interview with Mrs. Aghavni Vartanian, born 1900/01, p. 5, l. 27-32)

At the beginning of the 1990s, a series of publications on contemporary witnesses, survivors, and perpetrators of National Socialism emerged, which linked together historical and sociological perspectives. One of the central stimuli for these works, which were based on large-scale interview projects and surveys of contemporary witnesses, was the *Fortunoff Video Archives for Holocaust Testimonies*, established at Yale University (New Haven, CN) in 1981. The analysis by Lawrence Langer, Shoshana Felman and Dori Laub referred to the records collected in the Fortunoff Archives (Langer 1991, Felman/Laub 1992).

Extensive research projects developed in Germany dealing with survivors, contemporary witnesses of National Socialism or their descendents were inspired by American studies. However, the main focus of the German studies was not on how life stories could be stored and archived as important testimonials of the 20th century. Instead, the main questions concerned what these life stories actually tell and how science can implement them. Accordingly, a methodological approach had to be chosen that allowed the stories told to be dealt with by science. This was found in concepts of sociological research on biography and new hermeneutic methods that had been developed at the end of the 1970s, particularly by Fritz Schütze (Schütze 1983).

The central point of departure of this research perspective was the understanding of individual biography as a reconstructed life story at a point of intersection formed by individual life course and (objective, collective) history. The focus is on typical patterns in the life course, which allow statements to be made about the representativeness of the individual's respective recollection (and the

255

individual development). In biographical research as well as in oral history, individual biographies are treated as a phenomenon that reflects daily life in a specific epoch of history.

At the beginning of the integration of biographical methods into the sciences, a main interest was in the analysis of behavioral motivations, attitudes and habits. On the contrary, in Germany, given the repression of social psychological approaches since the 1930s and the framework of the sociological action paradigm and conception of the action autonomous subject, approaches have emerged which stress the unity of the biography, the *faithfulness* of that which has been narrated to *structure* and *personality*. Sequential analysis or motivational analysis, hermeneutic procedures or approaches of the psychology of personality serve to provide schemata from which patterns of individual biography can be interpreted.

This basic assumption of biography as a *schema characterized storage space for psycho/sociographic information* is founded on the idea of a "natural" production of coherence and continuity in the narration and notion that experiences are internalized in narrative structures. Sociological biography research as well as pedagogical, historically or psychologically oriented analyses are based on the certainty of being able to remove the "text" of the biography from the biographical narrator and standardize it with regard to regularities and conspicuous features. Work with biographical interviews is based on three central tenets:

- The assumption that biography ensues as a "complete narration." Starting points and end points are seen together with beginning and conclusion of individual courses of development. Bridges or jumps are defined as references to processing difficulties, change, or "bridges" in the life course.
- The assumption that the biographical narration presents interpretative schemata at the intersection between individual experience and socio-historical facts, between the self and events, structural contexts and contexts of meaning.
- The assumption that the "socio-graphical" data and sequences of experience presented in the biographical narration are based on a selection which allow conclusions to be drawn about the significance of these sequences for the biographical narrator.

In order to justify this highest unity of structural data and interpretative data, individual and socio-historical development, the individual becomes a "bearer of biography": while he provides evidence "authentically" from his feelings and thoughts, these feelings and thoughts still follow a general structure which enables the researcher to overlook the subjective nature of the biographical construct and to objectify its depictions.

Thus, interviews with survivors initially promised to be of significantly more interest than previous studies of violent youths or unemployed people who had become criminals. However, the flow of such works abated with equal speed since they were declared to be not *typical* and therefore of no interest to social research. The researcher who initiated such studies stood a priori under the suspicion of following non-scientific interests, to be oriented towards normative goals, far removed from all subjectively valid orders of knowledge.

Thus it is notable that today only a mild interest in the stories of the perpetrators remains — these are counted as objectifiable, as typical, and also as a foundation for general statements about social and historical concerns.

The interview with Aghavni Vartanian, from which the passage cited above is taken, was carried out within a project about survivors of the genocide committed against the Armenians in 1915/16 in the Ottoman Empire. Over the course of several years, more than 130 autobiographical interviews were recorded (audio and video) in different European countries. The narrative was initially regarded by the project group as a "bad" interview. Aghavni Vartanian, who was born in 1900/01 in Karahisar near Istanbul, was unable to formulate coherent sequences in her narrative (at the time the interview took place, she was living in an old people's home near Paris and was already clearly alienated from everyday life. Despite this, the interviewer decided to record her narrative after a brief preliminary talk, because he sensed that Aghavni Vartanian did actually understand very well the purpose of a biographical narrative — and in addition, he did not want to disappoint her). Her "failure" to construct a chronologically structured biographical self-presentation has been attributed to a lack of cognitive ability caused both by old age and insufficient education. The "well-meaning" members of the project group argued that it should be considered that a person from a different cultural background might be unable to understand and construct "biography" and that therefore she generally might be unable to "experience" trauma!

In the following excerpt from the beginning of the interview, the interviewer (I.) invites Aghavni Vartanian (V.) to tell her life story in a free autobiographical association — and it is apparent that he is already trying to ease the beginning of the narration with his opening enquiries:

I.: When were you born?

V.: I cannot remember.

I.: How old were you during the genocide?

V.: I was fourteen when we were deported.

I.: That means that you were born in 1900 or 1901?

V.: I don't know how I escaped the massacre.

I.: But by then fourteen years had passed. Can you tell us about these fourteen years? Tell us about your childhood, your father and mother, your family.

V.: First they came and took my parents away ## Did you understand that?

I.: Yes, but please tell me how things were before the genocide. Were you happy? What was your life like?

V.: Yes, very happy. Everything belonged to us, our house, our vineyard, everything was there in abundance. We had everything.

I.: What was your parents' occupation?

V.: They were deported.

(Interview manuscript Vartanian, p 1f.)

(# = indistinct word)

After a continuous breaking away from the attempt to present the memories, which were clearly already becoming overpowering, in a chronological order, the interviewer perseveres and does succeed in leading Ms. Vartanian into a first longer sequence:

I.: No, no. Tell about the time before the deportation. They were farmers, did they have their own land?

V.: Yes. We harvested what we needed for the whole year ourselves. Wheat, everything. We didn't have any worries. We didn't need anything else. Our house was filled to the brim. In winter we had no worries at all. All kinds of fruit, marmalade, because we had a vineyard, an orchard. Everyone had a vineyard in this village...

(Interview manuscript, Vartanian, p. 2)

The design of the interview project, which was started by a group of sociologists and social psychologists at the University of Bochum, was centered around questions relating to how the authenticity, representativeness and truth of the narrations could be ensured (Abels 1991, Abels 1995, Platt 1995): How often would the person to be interviewed have already told their story? Must not a ritualization in the narration of the life story be assumed? Would one then not have to ask whether the interviewee is still reporting the "truth" of the "original" experience and feeling? How can it be established that an individual experience is being described and not perhaps the experiences of another person? How can it be guaranteed that the narration is *typical* for the generation of the survivors? Skepticism was expressed primarily because of the advanced age of the survivors: To what extent would the interviewees be in a position to provide accurate testimony given their age?

In addition, preliminary considerations gave rise to doubts about the "quality" of the interviews due to the fact that even today, the genocide itself is officially denied by Turkish government und scientists. Would the interviews be characterized by ideological statements that would take precedence over patterns of individual identity? To what extent would the narrations be political instead of individual? What role would be given to prejudice against the descendents of the perpetrators? To what extent, in view of expected "political" implications, would it be possible to differentiate between "strategic" and "communicative" statements?

Thus, it was attempted to safeguard the data collection with a special methodological framework. A questionnaire was drawn up with 84(!) individual questions, which included supplementary questions to the biographical narration, integrated in a systematic architecture of "control questions."

The fact that a long-running intensive study resulted from the research design, in which the old age of the interviewees even turned out to be particular advantage, is no thanks to the insight of the project group into the absurdity of the preliminary considerations or the unreasonableness of the questionnaires. It can rather be attributed to the clear reactions and positions of the first interview partners — who critically analyzed the questionnaire and called into question the position of the German researchers (Platt 1995).

Consequently, following a new formation of the project group, a broad, contextually thematic study was carried out along with a general examination of the perspectives of research using interviews with survivors that had become fashionable in the mid 1990s (Platt 1998).

One of the most important points of departure was formed by the attempt to achieve a fundamental critique of the categories of analysis used to attempt to "understand" the narrative of the survivors. It is particularly noticeable that these categories are measured according to standards of the "norm," or to be precise lead to a definition of the norm and deviations from it. The analyses assume from the outset that the object of the examination represents a difference from the general.

Where general biographical patterns are the main focus, when research assumes that the biography represents typical patterns of socially mediated cultural values and that the life course mirrors the order of society (Ochs/Capps 2001), the scientific study of biographical narrations of survivors leads fundamentally to the establishment of "deviations."

It is indisputable that the experiences and narrations of the survivors cannot be studied according to the "normal" categories of experience and event, narration and sorrow.

But the otherness of the memories of the survivors and their constructions of identity is not an abnormality — for, according to the hypothesis that shall be presented in more detail below, it is primarily not a deviation due to characteristics in the personality of the survivor; it is a deviation due to specific historical and social conditions. According to the second main hypothesis, the mechanisms with which the survivor deals with this deviation, with these differences, are methods of action and behavior that cannot solely be described by their symptoms.

The history of the development of the project on Armenian survivors was outlined briefly here since it elucidates the interpretative and analytical concerns of the current analysis. However, it should be stressed from the outset that as yet, research on the survivors ultimately *always* amounts to the establishment of individual "lacks" in personality and individuality. With this, however, the scientific study is itself condemned to marginality, whose results — in contrast to the research on the perpetrators — are not accepted as pure research.

In this project it was the survivors who, referring to the absurdity of the definition of subjective and objective categories, the distinction between the individual and the collective and even the "authentic" and the "constructed," forced the data collection and interpretation concepts to be rethought (indeed, the original group of researchers disintegrated due to their discussions of the data collection and interpretation criteria).

"How should I be able to remember the names of the villages which we forced through 80 years ago?," or in answer to the question whether the person had actually experienced something that he had just related himself: "Of course I experienced this myself. We all experienced this. This is not my experience, it is the experience of an entire generation. It is not important whether I experienced it myself or whether someone else experienced it. We all experienced it." Or a simple initial refusal to tell one's own story since it is absolutely not "worth" anything, and does not amount to anything next to the stories of the deceased; sentences such as these posed initial challenges. For such comments point to obvious "misunderstandings" between narrator and researcher.

It should be emphasized that although studies of coping strategies or patterns of identity examine problems of subjective conditions, they all too often fail to question the conditions of communication and knowledge that determine the narrative construction of biography as well as the fundamental lack of understanding between survivors and researchers.

One of the questions that came up was: What form should the initial condition, the understanding between narrator and listener, interviewer and interviewee, researcher and research subject take, not only with reference to interaction in the interview situation itself, but also with reference to the concepts of recollection and narrative?

It is not only the interview situation that has to be critically assessed — the researcher's interpretation itself has to be analyzed. And this examination goes far beyond the methodological correctness of the data collection.

So it is to find that the interview situation as well as the subsequent interpretative work are determined by an orientation towards omissions: The interviewer pays attention to discontinuities and breaks within the narrative sequences, which he rates as indications of the unconscious, of mechanisms of defense, as a reference to something that can't be told. His attention is focused, first and foremost, more towards omissions than to coherent figures und sequences. The interviewee also focuses on the question of omissions: From the outset he makes conscious decisions about what he does not want to relate, both because he knows he might find it difficult to talk about traumatic events, and because he assumes that the interviewer won't understand. But can it always be assumed that the sequences that the interviewer interprets as unconscious rejection or repression are not actually omitted through a conscious decision on the part of the interviewee?

In spite of all endeavors to justify the evaluations of the interviewer, to allow conclusions of sequences of a narration to sequences of coping with the traumatic traces, the interaction between interviewer and interviewee mostly reflects a totally different understanding of memory and experience. The interviewer expects biographical recollections as a reconstructive order from which he can draw conclusions about coping mechanisms. He works with concepts of traumatic recollection, "deep memory" (Langer 1991), stereotypes and patterns, context and framing, semantic and episodic memory; he might ponder the question of the authenticity of recollection, or of the forming of a myth, or even about the "truth" of the narrative — a question which is particularly problematic, but which frequently arises.

The narratives of the survivors do indeed revolve around the impossibility of narrative. But there is a further aspect besides this "it is impossible to relate, impossible to describe": the evaluation that "I see this in my mind's eye, I see it directly before me and remember it as if it happened yesterday." Are these merely idiomatic phrases? Rhetorical figures on the boundary of that which can be ordered, at the point where the limit of human suffering and endurance was reached?

In order to be able to define the difference in the understanding of recollection, a discussion on experience as the "process," "perception," or even "reaction" on which recollection is based or which it refers to must be taken into account.

In biographical research, it is assumed that occurrence and experience correspond to one another; German discourse features the term *Ereigniserfahrung*, "occurrence-experience" (Schütze 1983). In the relationship between experience and narrative, an incongruent tension exists which is of interest to the researcher, and his concern in this context is with finding or reconstructing objective structures of meaning, assigning meaning, and deciphering intentions; this rests on the assumption that what is subjectively, intentionally expressed is part of a latent structure of meaning.

In particular in the numerous works that have arisen in Germany from doctoral theses, narrations are persistently measured according to a very rigid framework of real events (cf. for example Quindeau 1995). The problem that the narrated sequences do not represent the chronological framework, that the narrator however is still attesting to the truth, is interpreted in terms of the narrator being overpowered by the trauma or attributed to the general unreliability of biographical recollection.

In these works, a type of "evaluation" of recollection, which is apparently oriented towards psychological concepts, is especially noticeable. The interpretations are virtually centered on judgments that a narrative is successful on one point and unsuccessful on another.

To illustrate this with an example — chosen at random and therefore also cited unduly — I would like to refer to a narrative of a Jewish survivor and its interpretation. The researcher writes: "In the interview, Ms. D. is hardly capable of speaking about her recollections of Auschwitz ...," and then goes on to comment on the narrative sequence about the work camp which Ms. D. was transferred to from Auschwitz with the words: "It strikes me that Ms. D. is capable of addressing the topic of her suffering at this point; this is, perhaps, connected with the lesser intensity of the suffering in comparison with previous experiences, which enables her to still put it into words and must not be blocked out to such a great extent" (Quindeau 1995, p. 231).

The difference between occurrence, experience, and recollection could not be clearly shown. Furthermore, it proves itself not to be a difference between an objective and a subjective access to history, but to be the result of a fundamental misunderstanding on the part of the researcher.

How can experiences be described whose violence is carried out in an endless monotony, uniformity, and repetition? How can one describe Auschwitz without a watch, a calendar or diary to structure the experiences? There is no possibility to describe a daily life of uniformity. One can only describe occur-rences: a separation, a specific loss or threat, a specific rescue. Everything else remains unspoken, or has to be linked to frames of place or time. "When the first crocus was out...," "When I was wearing my spring clothes...."

Therefore the impossibility of locating the narrative in a chronologically correct time or place cannot be seen as incompetence on the part of the survivor. Rather, it can be attributed to the exceptional situation of an absolute removal of time and place when experiencing deportation or life in a camp. The dependency of narrative structure and narrated episodes on occurrences calls for a sort of crutch — which is too commonly judged by the researcher as an indication of defense mechanisms.

Thus a phrase like "on that same day I saw my first flower in a long time" need not necessarily serve as the impetus for an analysis of the (symbolic) meaning of the flower for the reawakening of the will to survive — it can, quite simply, be an aid for locating an event in time!

As such the remark "we walked and walked" can also be seen as a "phrase," which allows a concrete location for the survivor. This remark, which was used by many of the Armenian survivors to describe the death marches, cannot be considered to be a metaphor.

Furthermore, in this context the problem of recording sensory recollections also warrants intense consideration. How should a mother be recalled whose image can no longer be brought to mind after 80 years, without a photograph or a single memento? With the majority of scientific analyses the lack of detailed, emotional accounts of the murdered relatives is summed up as a "hardening of the soul" or as "dead feelings" (Gampel 1992, p. 135f). How far are "pragmatic" narrative elements underestimated, to what extent is the idea of unconscious construction preferred over the conscious ordering of the life story?

There are a multitude of other, equally fundamental aspects that need to be taken into consideration in the constitution of the recollective narratives of survivors, which are governed by experience itself. Among them is the diminishment of the capabilities of sensory perception caused by hunger, which will also have effects on the shaping of biographical, retrospective narratives.

In general, it can be established that the analysis of narratives must be linked to an analysis of the conditions and shaping of the *experience* involved — and not to the occurrence. Unfortunately, a focus on the occurrence is attempted, called for, and ensues time and time again when a narrative is to be checked against facts or, as with the work of the *Survivors of the Shoah Visual History Foundation*, is prepared in confrontation with data and facts. However, a detailed analysis of the constructions of recollection is also necessary in order to interpret the narratives of survivors.

Of course from the point of view of functionalist models of recollection a different recollection "concept" between researcher and "research object" is of no relevance. Indeed, works from the areas of biography research, life course research and oral history are supported by the fact that a simple reconstruction relation between experience and recollection is assumed. That recollection, however, results primarily not as a representation of occurrence structures, but rather as a reconstruction on the basis of self-schema and knowledge patterns (cf. Fiske, Taylor 1984; Barclay 1989), that recollection therefore first and foremost says something not about the processing of events but rather about identifiable interpretations, is mostly not taken into account here.

In spite of the explicit references to the studies of Frederic Bartlett and Maurice Halbwachs and the conceptualization of memory as a social or cultural phenomenon, recollection has remained an undefined concept: is it a social or an individual process, a structure, a psychological act, an expression of a relationship to the past?

Although scientific works always make reference to Maurice Halbwachs, his observations have not been discussed in detail or developed much further. According to Halbwachs, recollections are always collective; without a collective background — a group of people, space, or time — they cannot possibly exist; they can only be called forth by events or people, i.e., a person does not "recollect," he "is recollected," or he is "led to recall." Recollections are reflections that are preserved in a context of meaning and triggered by associations. One of Maurice Halbwachs' central prerequisites is that forgetting does not really exist. Forgetting means losing an element that could trigger recollection and occurs through detachment from a group, or by leaving a specific continuity of space and time. Consequently, Halbwachs describes individual memory as "a reference point" (Halbwachs 1985, 31) that overlooks collective memory. It is not possible without the words and images that have shaped an autobiography.

Recollecting cannot be regarded as being detached from frameworks of space and time, or from the historical and autobiographical frame in which it took place. Furthermore, recollection is shaped by the process of "reworking" or "coping" which it underwent in the thought and development of the person remembering, in the course of his life and in the present time. A reawakening of the experience can be brought forth merely through a specific "stimulating" situation which works by association or through questioning.

Taking into account these interrelationships among narrated recollections, social situations, social structures and the individual life course, the biographical recollective narration can no longer be seen as a representation of historical events, but rather as a representation of status passages, social positions, personal norms and values. Of course this is not generally refuted in biographical research — it is clear that, for example, the concept of the status passage (van Gennep 1908, Glazer/Strauss 1971) has spawned a multitude of works on life courses — but such concepts have failed to have a shaping influence on the research on survivor biographies.

Biographical research is interested in a subjective adoption of objective reality, which in turn acquires an objective reality itself in the individual biographical construction, or through the stylizations of the researcher gains a representativeness so that objectivity can be brought about. However, the considerations outlined above already indicate that it is not possible to make a clear distinction between individual and collective experience, between actual experience and a protective narrative, between truth and legend, because the concern here is with analytical distinctions, which not only fail to justify the specifics of the biographical reconstruction, but also fundamentally contradict it. For the unique characteristic of the biography lies in its very résumé both of the personal as well as of the social and the historical. With regard to individual recollection as an adoption of history, this would imply that social aspects, especially the construction of transformation of knowledge, are neglected.

Accordingly, on the basis of the two conditions for recollection already outlined by Maurice Halbwachs, namely sociality and the dependence on reconstruction, and when including new results of psychological and social psychological research, according to references to the importance of the aspect of emotional closeness (cf. Rapaport 1971, Reed 1979), the resistance of survivors against the pathologizing attributions of the researchers is to be supported. Their insistence on formulating both true, i.e., authentic, as well as incomplete, symbolic or metaphoric narrations, becomes even clearer in terms of the discussion of the third aspect in relation to experience, recollection and narration: the aspect of experience.

However, the concept of experience is still rarely examined, even though it is central to the methodological and interpretative circumscription of biographical research and oral history.

Indeed, the different research perspectives in biography can be characterized by their unquestioned habit of standardizing experience: individual and collective, autobiographical or historical, discursive and overwhelming experiences. The main focuses can be categorized as experience as a process of perception and interpretation of history, or discourse on dimensions of experience.

Having an experience, which can be narrated as a biographical experience, means working one's way through a specific occurrence that one characterizes as retrospective. In this context we first recognize an occurrence as such through the fact that it either gives rise to a new experience or reinforces an old one.

When speaking about experience, it is necessary to speak of interconnections or even structures of experience, for each experience is dependent upon a previous one in order to be interpreted as an experience at all. An experience confirms, qualifies, or dismisses previous experiences. Speaking about experience therefore also always means speaking about a complex field of experience, primarily a psychological one.

While we assume an indivisible unity of experience (and not of occurrence), recollection, and narrative, in research studies experience and occurrence differ precisely through an act of synthesis, a function of experience that ascribes meaning, through which an occurrence first "becomes" an experience. Experience is a pattern of re-presentation that is constructed through fragments of the past as well as of the present.

But what does it mean to experience breaches such as the ones that marked the twentieth century? To experience persecution and genocide, annihilation, war, and individual and collective violence? Is such an experience within the realm of possibilities? What forms of reconstruction are accessible apart from the impossibility of reconstruction?

2. LIMITS OF EXPERIENCE

> Each one brought his life along, since what you must take with you, above all, is your life (Delbo 1995, p. 3).

Charlotte Delbo wrote this at the beginning of her *Trilogy*. "They had no idea you could take a train to Hell but since they were there they took their courage in their hands ready to face what's coming / together with their children, their wives and their aged parents / with family mementoes and family papers" (Delbo 1995, p. 4).

In her autobiographical reflections, Delbo constructed with these images a link to a "normality" of the time before: with family (by listing children, women, and elderly parents), with recollection (family mementoes), and with history (papers). The phrase "Each one brought his life along" articulates a clear contradiction of a universalized image of the victim who is already pictured as dead or destined to die, as part of a mass already robbed of its identity and destined to be annihilated. Nevertheless, even the words describing the beginning of the deportation, which Delbo calls "arrival," already remain fragments. How can the beginning of a recollection of violence, loss and survival be constructed? It is notable in the interviews held with Armenian survivors that different attempts and patterns are used to described the various losses and put them in an individual order.

The following examples, which are fairly typical of the narrations, are taken from the biographical narrative of Mr. Aram Güreghian; I cite here from the first ten minutes, starting at the very beginning. Mr. Güreghian had been asked to introduce himself with his name, and his place and date of birth.

> My name is Aram Güreghian, the son of Harutiun and Kohar Güreghian. I was born on March 23, 1904, in Sepastia. Our family had very, very many members. Most of them lived in the country, since Sepastia was an important city, the capital of the governmental district, called Wilajet.
>
> Interviewer: Yes.
>
> The older family members — how many could there have been? — When I think about it, we could have numbered about 200. The old and the young, immediate and distant relatives. Today, at this moment, when I speak about it, that of course from this people, \ — I have to mention first, that I was the only one left in 1918.
>
> (Interview with Mr. Güreghian, p. 1, ln. 8–20.1)

One problem that continually arises in many narratives is the difficulty with recalling losses, such as the loss of one's mother, whose image can no longer be called to mind, but whose loss nonetheless remains present.

> My childhood # my father \ there was a hero named Murat \ was one of the friends of this hero, Murat.
>
> (Interview with Mr. Güreghian, p. 2, ln. 13.3–15)

Aram Güreghian tells about his father, whose face he can no longer recall, by means of his recollection of a hero of literary fame from the 1890s.

The biographical narration shows both motivations placed close together, as can also be seen in the sequence from Charlotte Delbo's *Trilogy* cited above: the attempt to somehow put the losses into words, and the necessity of not addressing the extreme radical nature of the loss in its completeness.

Aram Güreghian's narrative about the dead and the lost is interrupted by chronological breaks into the present as an indicator of a possible future, as well as by the attempt to hold onto past unity, intactness, and a sense of belonging.

> As I already mentioned, my uncle was injured on this day, or on one of those days, and my great-grandfather was killed.... When I came to Paris in 1922 after all of these occurrences ..., someone asked me, "Aha," he said, "you are the son of the Güreghians?" "Yes," I said, "this is what happened"; "But tell me, don't you remember that your grandfather was a very rich man, and possessed an entire village and all of Leghikügh \ and everything belonged to you as far as the eye could see — to your family...
>
> (Interview with Mr. Güreghian, p. 4, ln. 7–36.2)

Although the absoluteness and the totality of the losses are repeatedly emphasized, it is still necessary to reconstruct the pictures and relationships of a family in a narration. In all of the biographical reconstructions of the project, the conjuration of an intact childhood in an active community full of hope and love takes on a central role.

These narrations are not to be read as references to defensive attitudes, as a refusal to accept the "destructive totality" of the genocide or an attempt to not allow oneself to be overcome by this totality. For one thing, the construction of family and with this of origin, enables the creation of one's own history. It becomes possible to draw up patterns for the narration that count as cultural place markers for the development of personality: relationships, closeness and detachment, parents' plans for the future, goals which one achieved independently. In addition to the possibility of creating identity, the concept of family emphasizes the reality of the past. For in order to be able to tell about the violence and the victims, they need to be given back their names, their feelings, their futures.

Thus, although the attempt to tell of the family fails, it is not given up. It is notable that both the failure as well as the attempt at narration itself are explicitly reflected upon by the survivors.

"I make a contribution to the Church and ask that they read a funeral mass. How shall I mourn? For how many, when from five families no one's life was spared...", said Ms. Yüghaper Eftian, born 1901 in Zeytun (Interview with Ms. Eftian, p. 74, ln. 22.2–25.1).

The survivor consciously uses patterns of boundaries as a point of orientation, where mechanisms for coping with "normal" death and constructions of meaning for a (numerically) single death were no longer sufficient. Not because the survivor is overwhelmed, but because no pattern or mechanisms are available (Platt 2001).

Such "limits" of a portrayal have been an established component of analyses since the very beginning of the scientific study of survival in the 1950s — albeit as a reference to *latent* characteristics, to *unconscious* limits of identity formation.

In this way William G. Niederland, in his delimitations of the *Survivor Syndrome*, noted that survivors were marked by an "engram chronicling death," a deep psychological wound stemming from an encounter with death. (Niederland 1980, p. 232; see also Niederland 1968).

Niederland understood trauma as a traumatic *reaction*, with a "repertoire" of available ways of reacting, including: denial, depersonalization, and an automatization of the ego and ego regressions.

Survivor Syndrome, as outlined by Niederland, encompassed a family of symptoms leaving marked impressions through experiences with death, states of fear and agitation, mistrust and tension in dealing with others, a feeling (usually unarticulated) of otherness, a feeling of guilt for surviving; a state of being mentally overwhelmed or deteriorated, a constant presence of the conditions inherent in the survivor's realm of thought, an involvement of the children in this fate of persecution, symptoms resulting from states of fatigue and exhaustion: nervous irritability, uneasiness, tendencies to sudden excitement, moodiness, insomnia, eating disorders, and an incapability of dealing with everyday situations (Niederland 1980, p. 231f).

In their works, Niederland, Henry Krystal, and their colleagues or successors searched for close interconnections between occurrences and traumatic experiences, between traumatization and traumatic reaction.

The most important task expected from work on the concept of trauma consisted, in addition to the description of both physical and mental damage, of proving a relationship between external occurrence and psychological damage as well as between injury and symptoms.

The first historical studies searching for a link between occurrence and psychological injuries described the idea of a *spinal cord concussion*, i.e. a concussion of the neural system (Erichson 1866). The diagnosis of so-called war neurosis after World War I also continued to concentrate on the physical injury that preceded the psychological one; trauma, which was defined as "shell shock," was also to be understood as a syndrome of concussion (Ahrenfeld 1958). Only at the turn of the century did the idea of psychological trauma begin to take shape, to be derived from studies on traumatic neurosis (Clarke/O'Malley 1932).

In Sigmund Freud's analyses, references can be found to aspects of the discussion on "traumatic neurosis" (Oppenheim 1889) as well as the theme of "war neurosis" and "fright neurosis." Two further, complex considerations can be found in Freud's work: the basic thoughts on trauma already outlined in *Studies on hysteria* (1875) and the theme of "war neurosis" and "traumatic neurosis" in *Beyond the pleasure principle*. Freud developed the idea of a "protective barrier" as a central principle of the psychic apparatus, in which defense processes hindered a "flooding of the psychic apparatus with large masses of stimuli" (Freud 1920, p. 648). Types of excitation that penetrated the protective barrier and set off reactions, paralyzing or diminishing psychic capacity (p. 649) should be characterized as traumatic. In his later works, in particular *Inhibitions, Symptoms, and Anxiety*, Freud outlined a conception of trauma that was detached from considerations about neurosis and even from the concept of traumatic neurosis itself. The idea of trauma appears here against the background of discourse on a "danger-situation" which not only displays itself as a situation in which intensive and conflicting instincts are roused in developing fear; but rather, it is also a bio-graphical situation of the ego, which must be viewed as a direct consequence of surviving experiences of existential and mortal fear (Freud 1926, p. 738). Freud ties the conception of such a "danger" to occurrences, such as occurrences of loss (loss of the mother object, loss of love for the superego), and in this framework, he also rejects forms of "primal trauma" to which a "mental content" cannot yet be ascribed. The concern is with a "real danger" or triggering of emotional reactions on the basis of an objective occurrence (p. 738). With the statement that "each situation of danger corresponds to a particular period in life or developmental phase" of the psychic apparatus (p. 743), Freud seeks a reference to history as life history, and of course tries to relate it to the history of the development of instinctive desires and impulses.

The framework, or rather the development, implied in Freud's works is also reflected in the beginnings of later trauma research. Freud traced the effectiveness of trauma back to a disorder of the psychic apparatus. He attributed this in particular to overexertion of the stimuli apparatus. This stimuli apparatus is unable to find an answer to, is unable to process the *internal* stimulus, and ultimately seeks bridging categories to focus on *external* occurrences, which are too different from the character of the experience and which call for psychological reality. In the literature on extreme traumatization of survivors, in contrast, it was necessary to look for reasons for the psychological effect or effectiveness caused by an external occurrence. The question of whether the concern is with subjective experiences or occurrences of an objective character remains as much a component of conceptualizations today as the basic idea of the organism being thrown off balance or the reactive character ascribed to trauma symptoms. Nevertheless, the analysis of emotional disorders and suppressive reactions and, not least, the question of the relationship of the respective adaptation and capacity for adaptation of traumatogenic elements at the moment of experience to later post-situational symptoms also continue to guide central analytic interests.

The Dutch psychiatrist Hans Keilson, in his study on Jewish children (including orphans) who were in hiding during World War II, was the first to attempt to define traumatizing consequences using the definition *traumatic sequences*. He understood a traumatic sequence in this context as a self-contained phase with different traumatogenic elements following a common fundamental pattern. He emphasized that these elements are not necessarily to be identified with the phases of occurrence of traumatization (Keilson 1992).

271

By means of the situation variable, Keilson attempted to take into account the subjective character necessary for understanding extreme traumatization — a character that referred to both experience and occurrence; he sought a consciously broadened perspective with the particular intention of integrating developmental and social psychological aspects. Keilson's broadened outlook is to be understood as a shift in perspective, since he does not explain the conditions that allow an experience to become traumatic through the coping ability and the constitution of the ego before and after persecution. Rather, he seeks to analyze the conditions of the occurrence itself.

In spite of Keilson's work, the study of the effects and consequences of concentration camps remained primarily of interest to the field of diagnosis. However, this was not exclusively due to the necessity of gathering material for claims in the compensation proceedings. Did these studies not also display a reluctance to acknowledge the long-term consequences of persecution, hiding, and camps — because this would also mean that the general reappraisal would not cease? And how unwilling would be the researcher, and particularly the psychotherapist, to accept that this "disorder" of normality, whatever its form, could not be "cured"?

While the first studies on "camp internment and its consequences" still spoke of "later damage," which could turn into "permanent damage," especially with adaptation syndromes in mind (Herberg ed. 1971), the first attempts at coming up with a definition are found in Niederland's concept of *Survivor Syndrome* (1968) and in the conception of *War Sailor Syndrome* (1976/77) and *Rape Trauma Syndrome* (1974). These were followed by a designation for "grave reactions to pressure" in the DSM III (now the DSM IV) and, finally, the contours of PTSD (Posttraumatic Stress Disorder) took shape. Without going into the individual models more specifically here, the importance and the *specific* validity of the concept of PTSD cannot be emphasized enough in this context in order to avoid the simplistic adoption of this conception as a general trauma concept in interdisciplinary discussion: The concept of posttraumatic stress disorder with respect to pressure is a clinical category that infers an accepted link between trauma and occurrence by means of the central idea of stress occurrence and stress reaction. PTSD is a diagnostic category that makes a kind of "snapshot" possible, denying — interestingly enough — a specific course of psychological traumatization and accepting a breadth of variation in symptomatic manifestations. By concentrating on a clear framework of relationships in which a traumatic reaction manifests itself as a stress reaction, the PTSD concept enables a clear categorization of post-situational emotions and symptoms. Certainly, a problem of the PTSD conception must be seen in the idea of the *post*-traumatic itself: Even if the connection between trauma and occurrence laid down in the PTSD concept establishes a marker that was important and long overdue, this relationship already suggests that an occurrence is equated with its consequences.

In the current trauma research two discussions are apparent which take research on the effects of traumatization beyond depth psychology and psychoanalysis (which appears to characterize studies on survivors of the Holocaust as much as ever). These are the discussion surrounding the traumatization of Vietnam veterans and, from the beginning of the 1970s, traumatization caused by sexual abuse. In these discussions, in addition to the latest social and developmental psychology aspects, there are approaches that should be considered highly critically: an example of this is the analysis of endangerment and risk factors, which attempt more to legitimize the reality of the traumatizing situation than to enable conclusions to be drawn about the traumatization.

With regard to the study of extreme traumatizations, in which an analysis of the complex relationship between a traumatic event and a conscious traumatic experience must be pursued with an especially complex, multivariable, and partially ambivalent relation to it, I would like to briefly look at the question of whether it is even possible to assume that a psychological trauma can display the discernible quality of being related to the traumatic occurrence: a quality which can be analyzed in schemes, structures, and sequences. I would like to suggest that we might even have to radically abandon the concept of a situation-reaction context in studying survivor trauma.

For extreme genocidal traumatization, we must assume that traumatization with reference to a historic event can only be spoken of following survival. Only in the traumatic process that follows the physical escape do symptoms and psychopathological syndromes take shape. My concern here is not to argue for a consideration of the intervals between the acute pressure situation and the emergence of symptoms, which aid in diagnosing a "severe disorder with respect to pressure." Rather, I wish to stress that traumatization must be recognized as a specific life-span process for the person persecuted in complex societal processes of violence. I would therefore like to call attention to a very conscious shift of emphasis in the perspective on extreme traumatization.

Biographical long-term interviews illustrate that in general, psychological injuries are coped with, i.e., they find a form of integration into a self-representation which has been brought to a close, no longer changes, and is no longer a challenge, but merely a painful recollection. On the other hand, the processing of complex losses, breaches and humiliations does not occur; it remains fragmented. This cannot be attributed exclusively to psychological coping problems, dissociations, processes of repression or denial. Aspects of regaining, reconstructing, and of maintaining an attachment to what was lost serve to keep the wound (or: the trauma or loss) alive: reconstructions of biography, personality concepts, continuity, and coherence. Maintaining a destroyed continuity, for example, secures the survivor's biographical coherence. The traumatizing process that follows physical survival can be understood as a *reconstruction process*: as a symbolic reconstruction process and as a reconstruction process for attachments and object relationship. The long-term consequences of extreme genocidal traumatizations cannot be explained sufficiently by psychopathology or by analyses of symptom complexes and emotional situations; these consequences predominantly display themselves in problems with forming attachments, and in the constructions of continuity and coherence in the survivor's self-representation.

3. SURVIVING AND TRAUMA

Being a survivor of a catastrophe does not mean having been a participant in a specific historic event; rather, a survivor inevitably becomes the residue left behind by this occurrence. It is the bond with the catastrophe that also governs his life after escaping from immediate physical danger.

Surviving does not mean experiencing a moment or situation of getting away, but rather, it means being a survivor for the rest of a life "afterwards." This fact clearly differentiates survivors from eyewitnesses or those who have been rescued. According to Elie Wiesel, "For the survivors, as for everyone else, the nightmare belongs to the night and its mysterious kingdom. Death no longer lies in wait for them. The enemy no longer has a hold on them. The past? Carried away by the dead ..." (Wiesel 1987, p. 218).

The survivor's present is characterized by the past. Or did he actually in a sense remain there, incapable of regaining a normal daily life, as many articles on survival syndrome maintain?

The question of experiencing persecution and genocide must initially be a question directed to the survivor: which experience does he characterize as the one he survived? This must be an important indication for researchers who take up the search for the "real," unspoken traumatizations by means of the narrative text and who will not accept that losing a beloved domestic animal before deportation could initially be a much stronger traumatic occurrence than that moment in the final time of death when a sister's body was discovered on a pile of corpses in an extermination camp.

There are four primary positions, each formulated as a résumé, which are used to characterize experiences in the narratives of survivors.

One striking metaphor used in autobiographical interviews depicts a wound that cannot and does not heal. Yüghaper Eftian, born in 1901 in Zeytun, stated:

> If you undergo an operation, the scar always remains visible. Or if a glass breaks and you glue it, it still will always be a repaired glass. The wound is very deep... When such a wound exists, seventy-four years can pass and the spot remains, even if it was sutured up. Your heart has been pierced ...
>
> (Interview manuscript Eftian, 79, line 16-28).

The second attitude is the feeling of not being able to return to the realm of the living. Elie Wiesel described this the most graphically, perhaps, in his work *A Plea for the Survivors,* when he spoke of an "invisible ghetto" of survivors: "They do not join in our celebrations, they do not laugh at our jokes. Their frame of reference is not ours. Neither is their vocabulary. Their vocabulary is their code; their memory is their initiation" (Wiesel 1987, p. 222f.).

A third position also closely connected to the two previous ones is the special link to recollection. Charlotte Delbo asks, "Why have I kept my memory? Why this injustice? Why has my memory remained?" (Delbo 1993, 163).

The fourth position, already mentioned above, is the feeling of only being an incomplete fragment, or a very imperfect witness of experience as well as of recollection in the solitude of survival. Yüghaper Eftian says,

> Only I was saved.
>
> (Eftian 42, 34)

and then she makes a transition from this statement to thoughts on the endless loneliness of having survived and the incompleteness of her testimony:

> One cannot understand this from what has been told, one has to know the feeling.
>
> (Eftian 62, 9.2-10).

In order to come close to the specific experience of surviving a genocide, the social conditions of the persecution situation must be considered first of all.

For, living through genocide does not exhibit itself in the breaking of an occurrence into life context, nor in a penetrating annihilation, and nor as a situational, shocking experience of death.

Genocide means the existence of a genocidal situation in which perpetrators and victims develop corresponding ways of acting and behaving. Surviving cannot come to an end with getting through the genocidal situation precisely because of its socializing effects. This is the decisive relationship that differentiates surviving individual catastrophes from surviving a genocidal situation. It is impossible for the victim in question to return to his previous life context, in whatever way it may have been damaged, and he is consequently unable to recover the remains of his previous orientation. For his part, the perpetrator in question is, incidentally, freed from having to confront himself with his deed in the context of his previous life situation, and is consequently freed primarily from one thing: from a confrontation with a counterpart who has not yet become a victim.

Against this background, surviving means having experienced socialization in a time period that cannot be set down chronologically; a period that cannot be interpreted for the survivor either in a past or an historical framework, because the experience is not yet concluded. Furthermore, one special characteristic of the genocide process is that the deportation, the ghetto, the hiding place, and the camp are experienced in a dissolution of temporal structures. The uniformity of the seemingly endless threatening situation reduces the victim's temporal frame of thought to the smallest units, to a life lived from "one moment to the next."

Furthermore, surviving means having experienced socialization in a language that is uncommunicative, i.e. which does not have the task of communicating, but rather of concealing, of being silent, and of formulating metaphors. Language has no vocabulary for a catastrophe. Despite this, language must enable communication within the logic of persecution, it must make the occurrence of persecution expressible in its monstrosity.

Additionally, the socialization of the genocidal situation is not only a socialization of physical and psychological violence, it is also a socialization without fixed places and situations of reference, in particular without families of reference or family members — a socialization without the possibilities of childlike phases of learning and testing, a direct entry.

However, after the escape, after the delivery from terror and persecution, survival is also a confrontation with a new life environment, which initially did not represent everyday life, did not reflect normality, and could not entail finding one's way back to the past. Rather, it meant facing particular challenges: living in DP camps, deciding to make a new home, waiting for official confirmation on those murdered, seeking vocational training without a school education, attempting to return to a job which one has been alienated from for many years. This was initially accompanied by a necessary putting aside of recollections of suffering and of what was lost, but also of many socialization skills. Also, to mention this in passing, actions such as the tendency to improvise or to make rash decisions, which has been observed by survivors of extreme traumatization, cannot only be examined as a regressive, traumatic reaction, but can also be seen as a pattern of action which was learned in terms of socialization. Is there anything that specifically characterizes the recollections of survivors? And what needs to be considered in the process of interpretation?

Biographical narrative in an interview is primarily a narrative of one's recollections about life, a re-constructive ordering in which the years of experiencing segregation, persecution, degradation, loss, death, and survival are involuntarily the center of focus. This specific life narrative very often takes on the character of a "legacy," especially when it is asked about for the first time; a story is "handed over" to the interviewer. Biographical narrative is mainly a matter of testimony, a testimony which only has a marginal obligation to "testifying," however: telling something for which one is the only witness, which no one else can tell, because all the others are dead and everything has been destroyed. This testimony is eyewitness testimony, an attestation, a report from the past. But testimony also restores a loss. Testimony has an important role in the process of grieving.

Is testimony a confirmation of the trauma, a pathological transferal to subsequent generations who remain fettered to the status of the survivor? Or is testimony, repetition, and holding onto fragments of recollection rather also an attempt at forging a link to the breach of annihilation, in order to reconstruct coherence and continuity? A testimony that gains its testimonial character by the very fact that it cannot be experienced?

"True, his survival imposes a duty on him: the duty to testify. Offered to him as a reprieve, his future must find its raison d'être as it relates to his past experience. But how is one to say, how is one to communicate that which by its very nature defies language? How is one to tell without betraying the dead, without betraying oneself? A dialectical trap which leaves no way out. Even if he were to succeed in expressing the unspeakable, his truth would not be whole.

And yet ... In the very beginning, on a continent still in ruins, he forced himself to relent enough to at least lift its veil. Not to free himself of the past; on the contrary, to assert his loyalty. To him, to forget meant a victory for the enemy" (Wiesel 1987, p. 235).

We are therefore dealing with an experience here that can never belong to the past, but that is constantly recreated in narrative and recollection. Relating the catastrophe means retelling and re-experiencing it, again and again. This repetition is not to be viewed primarily as a pathological, compulsive repetition of a traumatic occurrence that has not yet been processed or "worked through." Rather, the concern is with a type of presence that is and must always be re-experienced anew in order to comply with one's own rule of not forgetting, as well as to meet the complexity, extensiveness, and manifold variety which genocide represents. For the initial concern is not with murder or death, but with a long-term breaking in of a situation and the radical change of all areas of life in the past.

For the contemporary witness, violence is a shadow, a dark spot in history; it is disturbance and disappointment. For the survivor, however, violence is an identifiable period of his life which determines everything, actions and recollection, life course and emotions, but which still remains alien to the biography and will never be able to be brought to a close in the biography. The contemporary witness can read the violence as destruction or as a breach of visions of civilization; the narration of the survivors, on the other hand, remains trapped in a subjective closeness, in the after-effects of the injury and the knowledge about vulnerability.

Thus, the external contemporary witness has the possibility of choosing a beginning and an end of the violence in his biography, he has a selection of different perspectives: the uninvolved, the remorseful, the intellectual summarizer, the political critic, the historically interested or the historically disappointed. The survivor, by contrast, is caught in a complex web of recollections and obligations, according to which he constantly has to redefine the beginning of the violence, and is unable to find an ending for the narration of the violence.

The impossibility of finding a coherent pattern of interpretation for the experience, for example in the narration of a horror about the perpetrator who forgets his civilization, and falls back into barbarism and excess, can be related to the impossibility of viewing the experience as a clear, distinguishable — and concluded — experience.

The survivor does not have the possibility of talking about "Auschwitz," "Buchenwald," of the "camp" of the "Nazis" using the fixed connotation with which these terms are associated in history. For the survivor, the meaning of these terms is in no way clear; the senses associated with them are constantly renegotiated. For anyone close to the occurrence, the task of formulating a testimony cannot exist in the search for a direct "authenticity." "There can be no realistic depiction of corpses," as Mark Rothko said in relation to his work and his own integration into tradition and history.

Not because the extent of the corpses was so drastic, but because the extent cannot be described with the picture of the corpses. Not because language is not sufficient to describe the extent of the horror, but because in the process of the genocide the language of the victims was taken away from them.

Certainly the testimony of the survivor is not a coherent, generalizable report. But in his narration there is no failure of language and certainly no silence for failure would mean that the basic rules of language themselves would be removed. Silence would mean presupposing a muting, agreeing to the muting which the National Socialist perpetrators intended.

The spoken testimony of the survivors is not their narration of the experiences and the occurrences; their specific testimony is their present and the present of the subsequent generations who are living in contradiction of the goal of extermination. The testimony of the genocide is marked by the fact that it is always readdressed, i.e. it always has to be proven: not as an authentic attestation of facts of exclusion and murder, but as the attestation of a present, which exterminates, which should be removed from the validities of the future.

CONCLUSION

The considerations outlined above aim, in the context of research on biographical self-depictions of survivors, to critically examine the analytical framework that is currently emerging with regard to the category of trauma. In studying symptoms, emotions, and self-conceptions that allow us to diagnose traumatization, it is certainly possible to detect sequences of stress factors; although we can discern emotions and symptoms that can be traced directly to this process, we cannot define a link between the symptom and the (historic, objective) occurrence. The historic and the traumatic situation seem to give indications of relationship variables — although even these might be lacking. An analysis of the traumatic situation demands a definition of a "situation" which is detached from the factual occurrences of persecution and violence itself, but is also widened by including the experience of violence in its perspective; survival, i.e., the challenges of daily life after the physical escape, must also be considered.

Over and above this, it should also be emphasized that the connections between historical processes cannot be explained by applying the category of trauma to analyses of historical interrelationships, or interrelationships between occurrences. However, inherent in the character of trauma there is no kind of process that might share similarities with characteristics of the thoughts on historical processes and development. The courses that traumatization processes take are not linear, but are determined by variances. They are not evidence of a succession, but of a simultaneousness of different traumatizing elements, first perceived of as traumatizing after survival and first proving to be traumatic elements when faced with a different daily life and a different normality.

Trauma constantly presents itself in a new manner; the representations are sporadic, associative, and oriented to each respective situation. Trauma is first seen clearly in actions, in the formation of identity, in changing life phases, in present-day life decisions. To come close to the traumatic process of the survivors, the only concern can be with the analysis of patterns of relationship (i.e. representations, and also symbolic configurations which are constantly re-emerging or being formulated anew). If the concern is with a relationship trauma, then the relationship to the new life and not to the old one is meant: not a traumatic reaction as an answer to the occurrence of persecution and annihilation, but rather, traumatic representations in relationship to the challenges of a new life, as an answer to a loss which is continuously re-experienced, reconstructed, and re-envisioned in a new and different way in various phases of life.

Translated into English by Sarah Mannion MA (Cantab)

REFERENCES

Abels, Heinz. 1991. "Annäherung an eine Vernichtung." *BIOS* 4(2): 159–190.

_____. 1995. "Zeugnis der Vernichtung. Über strukturelle Erinnerung und Erinnerung als Leitmotiv des Überlebens." In: *Generation und Gedächtnis*, ed. by Mihran Dabag and Kristin Platt. Opladen: Leske+Budrich, pp. 305–337.

Ahrenfeld, Robert H. 1958. *Psychiatry in the British Army in the Second World War*. New York NY/London: Routledge & Kegan.

Barclay, Craig R. 1989. "Schematization of autobiographical memory." In: *Autobiographical memory*, ed. by David C. Rubin. Cambridge/New York NY/Melbourne: Cambridge Univ. Press (first publ. 1986), pp. 82–99.

Beck, Ulrich. 2003. "Ein kosmopolitisches Europa im Zeichen der Erinnerung an den Holocaust." *Die Zeit* (no 29) of 10.07.2003.

Clarke, Edwin and C. D. O'Malley. 1932. *The human brain and spinal cord. A historical study illustrated by writings from antiquity to the twentieth century*. Berkeley CA: Univ. of Calif. Press.

Delbo, Charlotte. 1995. *Auschwitz and after*. New Haven CT/London: Yale Univ. Press 1995 (first publ. Paris 1970).

Derrida, Jacques and Jürgen Habermas. 2003. "Unsere Erneuerung. Nach dem Krieg: Die Wiedergeburt Europas. *Frankfurter Allgemeine Zeitung* of 31.05.2003.

Erichsen, John Eric 1866. *On railway and other injuries of the nervous system*. London/Philadelphia PA: Lea.

Felman, Shoshana and Dori Laub eds. 1992. *Testimony: Crises of witnessing in literature, psychoanalysis, and history*. London/New York NY: Routledge.

Freud, Sigmund 1920. "Beyond the Pleasure Principle." In *The Major Works of Sigmund Freud*. Chicago IL/London/Toronto/Geneva: Encyclopaedia Britannica 1952, pp. 639–663.

Freud, Sigmund. 1926. "Inhibitions, Symptoms, and Anxiety." In *The Major Works of Sigmund Freud*. Chicago IL/London/Toronto/Geneva.: Encyclopaedia Britannica 1952, pp. 718-754.

Gampel, Yolanda. 1992. "Können diese Wunden heilen?" In *Spuren der Verfolgung: Seelische Auswirkungen des Holocaust auf die Opfer und ihre Kinder*, ed. by Gertrud Hardtmann. Gerlingen: Bleicher.

Gennep, Arnold van. 1969. *The Rites of Passages*. Chicago IL: University of Chicago Press (first publ. Paris 1909).

Glazer, Barney and Anselm L. Strauss. 1971. *Statuspassage*. Chicago IL: Aldine.

Halbwachs, Maurice. 1985. *Das kollektive Gedächtnis*. Frankfurt/Main: S. Fischer.

———. 1980. *The collective memory*. New York: Harper & Row.

Herberg, Hans-Joachim ed. 1971. *Spaetschaeden nach Extrembelastung*. Herford: Nicolai.

Interview with Mrs. Yüghaper Eftian, born 1901 in Zeytun, conducted by Mihran Dabag, 14 May 1989 in Paris. Transcript from 10.06.1996.

Interview with Mr. Aram Güreghian, born 1904 in Sepastia, conducted by Mihran Dabag, 17.-19.09.1989 in Alfortville. Transcript from 08.10.1993.

Interview with Mrs. Aghavni Vartanian, born 1900/01 in Karahisar, conducted by Mihran Dabag 01.08.1989, Paris. Transcript from 05.12.1994.

Keilson, Hans. 1992. *Sequential traumatization in children. A clinical and statistical follow-up study on the fate of the Jewish war orphans in the Netherlands.* Jerusalem: Magnes Press (first 1979).

Langer, Lawrence L. 1991. *Holocaust Testimonies. The Ruins of Memory.* New Haven CT: Yale Univ. Press.

Niederland, William G. 1968. "The Problem of the Survivor." In *Massive Psychic Trauma*, ed. by Henry Krystal. New York NY: International Universities Press, pp. 8–22.

_____. 1980. *Folgen der Verfolgung. Das Überlebendensyndrom. Seelenmord.* Frankfurt/Main: Suhrkamp.

Ochs, Elinor and Lisa Capps. 2001. *Living narratives. Creating lives in everyday story-telling.* Cambridge MA: Harvard UP.

Oppenheim, Hermann 1889. *Die traumatischen Neurosen nach den in der Nervenklinik der Charité in den letzten 5 Jahren gesammelten Beobachtungen.* Berlin: Hirschwald 1889.

Platt, Kristin. 1995. "Gedächtniselemente in der Generationenübertragung. Zu biographischen Konstruktionen von Überlebenden des Genozids an den Armeniern." In *Generation und Gedächtnis*, ed. by Kristin Platt and Mihran Dabag. Opladen: Leske+Budrich, pp. 338–376.

_____. 1998. "Gedächtnis, Erinnerung, Verarbeitung. Spuren traumatischer Erfahrung in lebensgeschichtlichen Interviews." *BIOS. Zeitschrift für Biographieforschung und Oral History* vol. 2 (11), 1998, pp. 242–263.

_____. 2000. "Historische und traumatische Situation. Trauma, Erfahrung und Subjekt. Reflexionen über die Motive von Zerstörung und Überleben." In *Gewalt. Strukturen, Formen, Repräsentationen*, ed. by Mihran Dabag, Antje Kapust and Bernhard Waldenfels, München: Fink, pp. 257–275.

_____. 2001. "Trauer und Erzählung an der Grenze der Gewalt." In *Trauer und Geschichte*, ed. by Burkhard Liebsch and Jörn Rüsen. Köln/Weimar/Wien: Böhlau, pp. 161-199.

Quindeau, Ilka. 1995. *Trauma und Geschichte. Interpretationen autobiographischer Erzählungen von Überlebenden des Holocaust.* Frankfurt/Main: Brandes & Apsel.

Schütze, Fritz. 1983. "Biographieforschung und narratives Interview." *Neue Praxis* 13, pp. 283–293.

Wiesel, Elie 1987. "Plädoyer für die Überlebenden." In: *Jude heute. Erzählungen — Essays — Dialoge.* Wien: Hannibal (first publ. Paris 1977), pp. 183–216.

Wiesel, Elie 1979. *A Jew Today.* New York, NY: Vintage Books.

CHAPTER 13. GENOCIDE AND ME

Kurt H. Wolff, Brandeis University

Recently, and I don't know when, where, or why, I was puzzled and shocked when I realized I had never considered the relationship among Nazi genocide, Nazism itself, and my life. I had briefly recovered from my shock when a number of questions arose, particularly how to account for my never having thought of it. I cannot remember ever thinking about what the Nazi genocide had done to me, or more precisely, what Nazism's effect was on me, not just its genocide. One of its first effects involved excluding my studying at Frankfurt University. I had been taking miscellaneous courses, all in the humanities and social sciences, from Gothic to Greek and modern history, until I was suddenly awoken by "that new brilliant professor," Karl Mannheim, who had just arrived from Heidelberg. I was so fascinated by him and everything he had to say, suspecting he was even a poet (Wolff 2002b: 51–54), that I dropped everything else and participated in whatever he offered until many of us, including Mannheim himself, were excluded from university life in Germany.

What could I do in Nazi Germany under these circumstances? I was delighted to accept an invitation from a close friend, a medical student in Florence, for a month in a well-known *pensione*, owned by the Baroness Edith von Munchhausen, a relative of the famous World War I pilot, the "Red Baron." The Baroness generously invited me to stay free of charge if I would help with whatever was needed to be done in the house, including painting and bookkeeping. I soon began to earn money by teaching fellow guests subjects of their choice, particularly Italian, the grammar of which I studied ferociously. During this time a close friend, with whom I kept in touch, urged me to make use of the six semesters I had studied in Germany to complete a doctoral degree in Italy, for which I am profoundly grateful. During the summer of 1934 one of the most important events of my life occurred — I met the woman who was to be my wife until she died in 1990.

At this point I need to emphasize the difference between what I remember clearly and what I refer to as probable. This distinction is vital to an under-standing of this paper's topic, particularly Nazi genocide, since this is not an autobiography but a discussion of Nazi genocide's impact on myself.

I must have decided, no doubt under the influence of my practical friend, to complete my degree and in the summer of fall of 1934 we moved to Florence, a lovely city. At this point in my life the world was indescribably beautiful. I was in love and had little awareness of the world and its major problems. However, in *Vorgang*, a long prose piece I wrote in the summer of 1935, a totally unexpected third part contains an apocalyptic nightmare of the humankind's future (Wolff 2002a: 39–40):

> I dreamed of a big fish, caught by thousands of fishermen, and a few of them had been slain by his movement — now they were stretching and expanding him, the giant ray, boasting so that he darkened the glaring noon, and those who had stood in the sun stood in the fish's shadow... Then we came to a fish shop invited by some-thing in the window that reminded of fish ... and from the triangular fin...they knew it was a shark... "Now, my friends," I told them, "this one is bigger than the fish they caught, and yet he too was caught, but the people have fled in terror before their booty"... As they were snaking from their sites and turned around I heard their high shrill screaming, for I was already snaking myself toward the ray and shark sea to live in it, winding myself, wonder-swelled.

I wrote this in 1935, some years before the Nazis practiced their genocide. Does this represent a prediction of the Apocalypse? Was I anticipating the genocide to come? After so many years, I don't recall whether I thought of the Nazis or the Fascists who surrounded me. At any rate, what I wrote was a fantasy, possibly reflecting some guilt I felt during my happiness, attempting to "make good" by imagining the most horrible punishment that came to mind. Does the end of the quote, involving my leaving my fellow men, reflect a trace of guilt typical of apocalyptic visions? As applied to Nazi genocide, does this mean I feel guilty for escaping the military draft (although for medical reasons) and having little more interest in contemporary history than reading and listening to the news, despite its obvious genocidal events? Was my distancing from the world of everyday reality part of the price I paid for being a poet? What about my interest in sociology? As indicated, this was shaped by Karl Mannheim and certain elements of German culture, including a historical-diagnostic perspective, powerfully exemplified by Weber's *Protestant Ethic and the Spirit of Capitalism*, involving both his ominous feelings regarding Germany, the West, and humankind, along with their immediate dismissal (Weber 1930, p. 182):

> No one knows who will live in this cage [which had derived from the Puritan's "light cloak"] in the future, or whether at the end of this tremendous development entirely new prophets will arise, or there will be a great rebirth of old ideas and ideals, or, if neither, mechanized petrification, embellished with a sort of convulsive self-importance. For the last stage of this cultural development, it might well be truly said: "Specialists without spirit, sensualists without heart; this nullity imagines that it has attained a level of civilization never before achieved." But [Weber at once checks himself] this brings us to the world of judgments of value and of faith, with which this purely historical discussion need not be burdened.

In my conception of sociology, concern with the future is central to its perspective (Wolff 2000). Relevant also is the relationship among its three "worlds" (Shutz 1962), the interaction between everyday life and poetry, and the changing universes in and out of which we move for various lengths of time, from moment to never. The everyday world results from our socialization or acculturation and is culturally relative. It includes the possibility of interruption by other worlds, including poetry and sociology, in which the standards of the interfering rather than everyday life govern us. This is exemplified in Durkheim's attempts to account for the regularity of suicide rates despite individual motives and Weber's discussion of the separation of religion and economy in everyday thought. As for poetry, my example of "apocalyptic" writing might be called a fantasy or vision, something that does not exist in everyday terms nor draws from regular sources of socialization or acculturation. Poetry appeals to feelings which are inseparable from ourselves. Its origins are unclear and such "thoughts" simply appear to "hit" us.

I began my dissertation at Frankfurt University, working on intellectual in Darmstadt, my hometown. When I moved to the University of Florence, I changed my focus to the sociology of knowledge, a specialty unknown in Italy during the 1930s. I was driven out of Italy in 1939 and moved to the United States where I was anxious to become acquainted with sociology in this new setting. My research included papers on Vilfredo Pareto, reflecting my Italian experience, and a field study of the Dallas Jewish community, devoted to my mentor, Walter T. Watson, and his interest in minorities.

These studies were as close as I came sociologically-speaking to Nazism; in reality, I barely touched on the subject. On the other hand, my personal life came much closer: during the late 1930s and early 1940s, I was unaware of the location and fate of my brother and family. During 1944/1945 we learned they had died in Auschwitz. All of this occurred in the everyday world and I had to come to terms with it the best I knew how. A few years later in 1950, however, something happened which made me leave this "everyday" kind of life for other worlds such as poetry or sociology.

I was teaching a course on the study of small communities, my story of "Loma," a small place in New Mexico with which I was enamored and had visited several times in the 1940s. What occurred took place, not in the seminar room, but on a drive with a friend. This resulted in the notions of "surrender and catch," a topic I discussed and published about almost exclusively for the next half century (Wolff 1976). What is particularly important above all in this idea is the suspension of received notion. This may just happen ("surrender") or may be consciously striven for ("surrender to"). The whole experience may be self-consuming or followed by something else such as a decision, essay, personality change, poem, etc., as its "catch." "Surrender" is the most immediate contact with the other, whatever or whoever that may be. I eventually realized that the experience of *Vorgang*, including the Apocalyptic vision quoted above was a case of "surrender," in which everything was different from what it had been, as was myself, with the distinction between subject suspended or un-judged. Originally, I wondered why the word "surrender" did not let me go. Eventually, I realized it was a polemical term, directed against a society dominated by control and manipulation in which such a process meant military defeat. Certainly, Nazism and Totalitarianism were extreme cases of such societies but I made no mention of them except when discussing "total experience," a synonym of "surrender." I argued that this term was polemical also, emphasizing that the "total" experiences of concentration, slave, and death camp inmates were not exclusive examples of this phenomenon.

Clearly, I did not write about Nazism in the society I had left or the fascist situation I moved to, since both of them were outside my realm. My own realm was visionary rather than that of the everyday observer. The closest I came to experiencing Fascism involved an experience one early morning when the police picked up me and my wife and drove us to Genoa to investigate our sending money (legally) for a friend from Germany to a British bank. I implored my wife to tell nothing but the truth to ensure our accounts were consistent. After questioning us for several hours, they let us go with an ominous warning to stop what we had been doing. We were extremely relieved. However, this represented the danger of everyday life, entirely separate from my "real" life. Nazis,

Fascists, Stalinists, Totalitarians and everyday life itself could kill me but this would only end me as someone who sometimes might have a vision.

I will conclude this chapter with two remaining topics: humor and philosophy. While I was not aware of it then, what we experienced in the police station involved a caricature of Italian life, highlighting behavior explicitly forbidden. I remember bank clerks, cigarette between fingers or lips, serving customers directly under "No Smoking" signs. What we experienced there involved a caricature of Germany in which everything is forbidden except what is explicitly permitted. Even the limited and permitted export of money was treated as forbidden, a minute example of what Nazism and totalitarianism imposed on a gigantic scale and to on infinitely more general and tradition laws.

With respect to philosophy, some of you may imagine that what you read is philosophy, perhaps sheer babble, something to think about, a phenomenon such as "surrender-and-catch." I would call it philosophy in the sense that this discussion involves an explication of my approach to the world and my relation to Nazi genocide, an approach that involves us all. I would like to end the chapter by emphasizing that since every living human being has been touched by genocide, Nazi or otherwise, let us embrace and wish each other well!

REFERENCES

Schutz, A. 1962. *Collected Papers: The Problem of Social Reality*. The Hague: Martinus Nijhoff.

Weber, M. 1930. *The Protestant Ethic and the Spirit of Capitalism*, Translated by T. Parsons. New York: Scribner.

Wolff, K. H. 1976. *Surrender and Catch: Experience and Inquiry Today*. Dordrecht and Boston: Heidel.

_____. 2000. "Toward a Conception of Sociology." *International Journal of Contemporary Sociology* 37, 117–127.

_____. 2002a. *A Whole, A Fragment*. Lanham, MD: Lexington Books.

_____. 2002b. *What It Contains*. Lanham, MD: Lexington Books.

GENOCIDE: A BIBLIOGRAPHY

James Jenkins, Auburn University Libraries

REFERENCE

Holocaust and Genocide Studies: an international journal. Washington, DC. United States Holocaust Museum, Oxford-University-Press.

International Journal of Contemporary Sociology. 2002. Special issue on genocide and society. edited by Graham C Kinloch and Raj P. Mohan. 39, no. 2.

Journal of Genocide Research. Oxfordshire, United Kingdom, Carfax-Publishing-Ltd.

Charny, Israel. 1999. *Encyclopedia of genocide.* Santa Barbara, CA: ABC-CLIO.

Charny, Israel W. (Ed.). c1988-c1991. *Genocide : A Critical Bibliographic Review.* New York, NY: Facts on File Publications, 3 volumes.

Dobkowski, Michael and Isidor Wallimann. 1992. *Genocide in Our Time : An Annotated Bibliography with Analytical Introductions.* Ann Arbor, Mich.: Pieran Press.

Drew, Margaret. 1994. *Annotated Bibliography [Holocaust].* Washington, DC: US Holocaust Memorial Museum.

Edelheit, A. and Herschel Edelheit. 1994. *History of the Holocaust : A Handbook and Dictionary.* Boulder, CO: Westview Press.

Fernekes, William R. 2002. *The Oryx Holocaust Sourcebook.* Westport, CT: Oryx Press.

Laqueur, Walter and Judith T. Baumel (Eds.). 2001. *The Holocaust Encyclopedia.* New Haven, CT: Yale University Press.

Rozett, Robert (Ed.). 2000. *Encyclopedia of the Holocaust.* New York, NY: Facts on File.

Rudolph, Joseph R. Jr. 2003. *Encyclopedia of Modern Ethnic Conflicts.* Westport, Conn.: Greenwood Press.

Special Section: Teaching About Genocide. 1991. Genocide_20th century. *Social Education.* 55, no. 2.

UN Genocide Convention. Convention on the Prevention and Punishment of the Crime of Genocide (1948). Bureau of Public Affairs, Dept. of State. 1986.

United States Congress. Genocide Convention Implementation Act: Hearing before the Subcommittee on Immigration, Refugees, and International Law of the Committee on the Judiciary, House of Representatives, One Hundredth Congress, second session, on H.R. 807 ... March 16, 1988.

United States Congress. Investigation into certain past instances of genocide and exploration of policy options for the future: Hearings before the Subcommittee on Future Foreign Policy Research and Development of the Committee on International Relations, House of Representatives, Ninety-fourth Congress, second session, May 11, August 30, 1976.

United States Congress. House Committee on Foreign Affairs. "Expressing the sense of the House of Representatives with respect to ratification of the Convention on the Prevention and Punishment of Genocide : Markup before the Committee on Foreign Affairs and its Subcommittee on Human Rights and International Organizations," House of Representatives, Ninety-ninth Congress, first session, on H. Res. 104; H. Res. 166, April 24 and May 14, 1985.

United States Congress. House Committee on Post Office and Civil Service. "National Day of Remembrance of the Armenian genocide of 1915-23 : Report together with minority and additional views" (to accompany H.J. Res. 132).

United States Congress. Senate Committee on Foreign Relations. "Genocide Convention : Hearing before the Committee on Foreign Relations," United States Senate, Ninety-eighth Congress, second session, on Executive 0, 81st Congress, 1st session, the Convention on the Prevention and Punishment of the Crime of Genocide, September 12, 1984. 266.

United States Congress. Senate Committee on Foreign Relations. "Genocide Convention : Report of the Committee on Foreign Relations," United States Senate, together with additional and supplemental views on The International Convention on the Prevention and Punishment of the Crime of Genocide, Executive O., 81st Congress, 1st session.

United States Congress. Senate Committee on Foreign Relations. "International Convention on the Prevention and Punishment of the Crime of Genocide": Report together with additional views (to accompany Ex. O, 81st Cong., 1st sess.).

United States Congress. Senate Committee on the Judiciary. Subcommittee on the Constitution. "Constitutional issues relating to the proposed Genocide Convention": Hearing before the Subcommittee on the Constitution of the Committee on the Judiciary, United States Senate, Ninety-ninth Congress, first session ... February 26, 1985.

United States Congress. Senate. S. hrg. and 100-1044. "Legislation to implement the Genocide Convention": Hearing before the Committee on the Judiciary, United States Senate, One Hundredth Congress, second session, on S. 1851 ... February 19, 1988.

United States Congress. Senate. S. hrg. and 99-259. "Crime of genocide": hearing before the Committee on Foreign Relations, United States Senate, Ninety-ninth Congress, first session, on the prevention and punishment of the crime of genocide, March 5, 1985.

United States Holocaust Memorial Museum. 1995. *Historical Atlas of the Holocaust*. New York, NY: MacMillan Pub.

Films

Genocide, from Biblical times through the ages. 2002. Princeton, NJ, Films for the Humanities and Sciences. The Genocide Factor.

Genocide in the first half of the 20th century. 2002. Princeton, NJ, Films for the Humanities and Sciences. The Genocide Factor.

Genocide : the horror continues. Robert J. Emery. 2002. Princeton, NJ, Films for the Humanities and Sciences.

Goldman, R. 1994. *The Holocaust : in memory of millions* [videorecording]. Bethesda, Md, Discovery Communications Inc.; Discovery Channel.

Never again? : Genocide since the Holocaust. Robert J. Emery. 2002. Princeton, NJ., Films for the Humanities and Sciences.

Skirball, Sheba F. 1990. Films of the Holocaust : an annotated filmography of collections in Israel. New York, NY: Garland Pub.

White-Stevens, Lillian. 1984. *Holocaust-Genocide Studies : Essential Books and Films, Annotated*. Trenton, NJ: New Jersey State Dept. of Education.

Web Sites

Amnesty International. http://www.amnesty.org/.

Human Rights Watch. Documents by Country. http://www.hrw.org/countries.html.

Prevent Genocide International. 1998. http://www.preventgenocide.org.

United States Holocaust Memorial Museum. Teaching about the Holocaust : a resource book for educators. http://www.ushmm.org/education/foreducators/teachabo/teaching_holcaust.pdf.

University of Michigan-Dearborn. Two Bibliographies on the Armenian Genocide. http://www.umd.umich.edu/dept/armenian/facts/gen_bib.html.

Yale University. Cambodian Genocide Program. http://www.yale.edu/cgp/.

AFRICA

Afflitto, Frank M. 2000. Victimization, survival and the impunity of forced exile: a case study from the Rwandan genocide. *Crime, Law and Social Change* 34, no. 1:77–97.

Aldelman, Howard. 1999. *The Path of a Genocide : The Rwanda Crisis from Uganda to Zaire.* New Brunswick, NJ: Transaction Publishers.

Anderson, Regine. 2000. How multilateral development assistance triggered the conflict in Rwanda. *Third World Quarterly* 21, no. 3:441-456.

Anglin, Douglas G. 2000. Rwanda revisited: Search for the truth (discussing two international reports on the genocide in Rwanda). *International Journal* 56, no. 1:149-169.

Barnett, Michael. 2002. *Eyewitness to a Genocide : The United Nations and Rwanda.* Ithaca : Cornell University Press.

Berger, Ronald J. 2002. *Fathoming the Holocaust : A Social Problems Approach.* New York, NY: Aldine de Gruyter.

Berkeley, Bill. 2001. *The Graves Are Not Yet Full : Race, Tribe and Power in the Heart of Africa.* New York: Basic Books.

Berkeley, Bill. 2001. "Race, Tribe, and Power in the Heart of Africa." *World Policy Journal* 18, no. 1:79–87.

Berry, John and Carol Pott Berry (Eds.). 1999. *Genocide in Rwanda : A Collective Memory.* Washington, DC: Howard University Press.

Bhavnani, Ravi and David Backer. 2000. Localized Ethnic Conflict and Genocide: Accounting for Differences in Rwanda and Burundi. *Journal of Conflict Resolution* 44, no. 3:283–306.

Burton John. 1991. Development and cultural genocide in the Sudan. *The Journal of Modern African Studies*, no. 29:3.

Des Forges, Alison Liebhafsky. 1999. *"Leave None to Tell the Story" : Genocide in Rwanda.* New York: Human Rights Watch.

Destexhe, Alain. 1995. *Rwanda and Genocide in the Twentieth Century.* New York, NY: New York University Press.

Gourevitch, P. 1998. *We Wish to Inform You that Tomorrow We Will Be Killed with Our Families: Stories from Rwanda.* New York: Farrar Straus and Giroux.

Jefremovas, Villia. 2002. *Brickyards to Graveyards : From Production to Genocide in Rwanda.* Albany: State University of New York Press.

Jones, Bruce D. 2001. *Peacemaking in Rwanda : The Dynamics of Failure.* Boulder, CO: Lynne Rienner Publishers.

Klinghoffer, Arthur Jay. 1998. *The International Dimension of Genocide in Rwanda.* New York, NY: New York University Press.

Lemarchand, R. 1995. *Burundi: Ethnic Conflict and Genocide.* Cambridge: Cambridge University Press.

Lemarchand, Rene. 1998. Genocide in the Great Lakes: Which genocide? Whose genocide? (Hutu-Tutsi conflict in Burundi, Rwanda and Congo). *African Studies Review* 41, no. 1:3-16.

Mamdani, Mahmood. 2001. *When Victims Become Killers : Colonialism, Nativism, and the Genocide in Rwanda.* Princeton, NJ: Princeton University Press.

McNulty, Mel. 2000. French arms, war and genocide in Rwanda. *Crime, Law and Social Change* 33, no. 1-2:105-129.

Neuffer, Elizabeth. 2001. *The Key to My Neighbor's House : Seeking Justice in Bosnia and Rwanda.* New York: Picador USA.

Nyankanzi, Edward L. 1998. *Genocide : Rwanda and Burundi.* Rochester, VT: Schenkman Books.

Pottier, Johan. 2002. *Re-imagining Rwanda : Conflict, Survival and Disinformation in the Late Twentieth Century.* Cambridge, UK: Cambridge University Press.

Prunier, Gerard. 1995. *The Rwanda Crisis : History of a Genocide.* New York, NY: Columbia University Press.

Saro-Wiwa, Ken. 1992. *Genocide in Nigeria : The Ogoni Tragedy.* London: Saros International Publishers.

Scharf, Michael P. 1999. Responding to Rwanda: Accountability Mechanisms in the Aftermath of Genocide. *Journal of International Affairs* 52, no. 2: 621-637.

Scherrer, Christian P. 2002. *Genocide and Crisis in Central Africa : Conflict Roots, Mass Violence, and Regional War.* Westport, CT: Praeger.

Semujanga, Josias. 2003. *Origins of Rwandan Genocide.* Amherst, NY: Humanity Books.

Taylor, Christopher C. 1999. *Sacrifice as Terror : The Rwandan Genocide of 1994.* New York, NY: Berg.

Twagilimana, Aimable. 2003. *The Debris of Ham : Ethnicity, Regionalism, and the 1994 Rwandan Genocide.* Lanham, MD: University Press of America.

Uvin, Peter and Charles Mironko. 2003. Western and Local Approaches to Justice in Rwanda. *Global Governance.* 9, no. 2:219-231.

Veale, Angela and Giorgian Dona. 2003. Street children and political violence: a socio-demographic analysis of street children in Rwanda. *Child Abuse and Neglect* 27, no. 3: 253-270.

Verwimp, Philip. 2003. Testing the Double-Genocide Thesis for Central and Southern Rwanda. *Journal of Conflict Resolution. Issue.* 47 , no. 4:423–442.

Weissman, Stephen R. 1998. *Preventing Genocide in Burundi : Lessons from International Diplomacy.* Washington, DC: US Institute of Peace.

Yacoubian, George S. Jr. 2003. Evaluating the efficacy of the international criminal tribunals for Rwanda and the former Yugoslavia: implications for criminology and international criminal law. *World Affairs* 165 (Winter), no. 3:133–142.

Armenia

Adalian, Rouben. 1991. The Armenian genocide: context and legacy. *Social Education.* 55, no. 2:99-104.

Anadolu Basin Birligi. 1986. *The Armenian Murders in Our Century.* Kavaklidere, Ankara.

Anasean, H. S. 1983. *The Armenian Question and Genocide of the Armenians in Turkey : a Brief Bibliography of Russian Materials.* La Verne, CA: American Armenian International College.

Auron, Yair 2000. *The Banality of Indifference : Zionism and the Armenian Genocide.* New Brunswick, NJ: Transaction Publishers.

Auron, Yair. 2003. *The Banality of Denial : Israel and the Armenian Genocide.* New Brunswick, N.J.: Transaction Publishers.

Balakian, Peter. 2003. *The Burning Tigris : The Armenian Genocide and America's Response.* New York, NY: HarperCollins.

Bardakjian, Kevork B. 1985. *Hitler and the Armenian Genocide.* Cambridge, MA: Zoryan Institute.

Boyajian, Dickran H. 1972. *Armenia: The Case for a Forgotten Genocide.* Westwood, NJ: Educational Book Crafters.

Chaliand, Gérard. 1983. *The Armenians, from Genocide to Resistance.* London: Zed Press.

Dadrian, Vahakn N. 1986. *The Naim-Andonian Documents on the World War I Destruction of Ottoman Armenians : The Anatomy of a Genocide.* London : Middle East Studies Association of North America: Cambridge University Press.

Dadrian, Vahakn N. 1997. *The History of the Armenian Genocide : Ethnic Conflict from the Balkans to Anatolia to the Caucasus.* Providence, RI: Berghahn Books, 3rd rev. ed.

Dadrian, Vahakn N. 1999. *Warrant for Genocide : Key Elements of Turko-Armenian Conflict.* New Brunswick, NJ: Transaction Publishers.

Ghazarean, Haykazn G. *Minutes of secret meetings organizing the Turkish genocide of the Armenians: what Turkish sources say on the subject.* Boston, Commemorative Committee on the 50th Anniversary of the Turkish Massacres of the Armenians.: 1965.

Graber, G. S. 1996. *Caravans to Oblivion : The Armenian Genocide, 1915.* New York: J. Wiley.

Guttmann, Josef and Naim Bey. 1965. *The Beginnings of Genocide : An Account of the Armenian Massacres in World War I*. Newton Square, PA. Armenian Historical Research Association.

Hovannisian, Richard G. 1978. *The Armenian Holocaust : A Bibliography Relating to the Deportations, Massacres, and Dispersion of the Armenian People, 1915-1923*. Cambridge, MA. Armenian Heritage Press; National Association for Armenian Studies and Research.

Hovannisian, R. (Ed.). 1991. *The Armenian Genocide in Perspective*. New Brunswick, NJ: Transaction Publishers.

Hovannisian, Richard G. 2003. *Looking Backward, Moving Forward : Confronting the Armenian Genocide*. New Brunswick, NJ: Transaction Publishers.

Hovannisian, Richard G. (Ed.). 1992. *The Armenian Genocide : History, Politics, Ethics*. New York: St. Martin's Press.

Kloian, Richard Diran. 1985. *The Armenian Genocide : News Accounts from the American Press (1915-1922)*. Richmond, CA: Anto Printing. Distributed by ACC Books.

Mazian, Florence. 1990. *Why Genocide? : The Armenian and Jewish Experiences in Perspective*. Ames, IA: Iowa State University Press.

Melson, Robert. 1992. *Revolution and Genocide : The Origins of the Armenian Genocide and the Holocaust*. Chicago: University of Chicago Press.

Nazer, James. 1968. *The First Genocide of the 20th Century; The Story of the Armenian Massacres in Text and Pictures*. New York: T & T Pub.

Parsegian, V. L. 1975. 1975. Human rights and genocide, 1975: The hope, the reality, and still the hope; a status report. New York: Diocese of the Armenian Church of America.

Permanent Peoples' Tribunal. 1985. *A Crime of Silence : The Armenian Genocide*. London: Zed Press.

Sonyel, Salahi Ramsdan. 1987. *The Ottoman Armenians : Victims of Great Power Diplomacy*. London: K. Rustem & Brother.

Stamatov, Vurban. 1987. *Genocide : Against the Bulgarian, Greek, Armenian, Cypriot, and Kurdish People*. Bulgaria. Sofia Press Pub. House.

Ternon, Yves. 1981. *The Armenians : History of a Genocide*. Delmar, NY: Caravan Books.

Toriguian, Shavarsh. 1973. *The Armenian Question and International Law*. Beirut: Hamaskaine Press.

United States. Congress. House. Committee on Post Office and Civil Service. National Day of Remembrance of the Armenian genocide of 1915-23 : report together with minority and additional views (to accompany H.J. Res. 132).

University of Michigan-Dearborn. Two Bibliographies on the Armenian Genocide. http://www.umd.umich.edu/dept/armenian/facts/gen_bib.html.

ASIA INDONESIA AND THE MIDDLE EAST

Barron, John and Anthony Paul. 1977. *Murder of a Gentle Land : The Untold Story of a Communist Genocide in Cambodia.* New York: Reader's Digest Press.

Chandler, D. 1993. *Brother Number One: A Political Biography of Pol Pot.* Sydney: Allen & Unwin.

Chandler, David. 1999. *Voices from S-21 : Terror and History in Pol Pot's Secret Prison.* Berkeley, CA: University of California Press.

Chang, I. 1997. *The Rape of Nanking: The Forgotten Holocaust of World War II.* New York: Basic Books.

De Nike, Howard J. (Ed.). 2000. *Genocide in Cambodia, Documents from the Trial of Pol Pot and Ieng Sary.* Philadelphia: University of Pennsylvania Press.

Fein, Helen. 1993. Revolutionary and Antirevolutionary Genocides: A Comparison of State Murders in Democratic Kampuchea, 1975 to 1979, and in Indonesia, 1965 to 1966. *Comparative Studies in Society and History* 35, no. 4:796–823.

Hinton, Alexander L. 1998. A head for an eye: Revenge in the Cambodian genocide. *American Ethnologist.* 25, no. 3:352-377.

Hinton, Alexander L. 1998. Why did you kill?: The Cambodian genocide and the dark side of face and honor. *Journal of Asian Studies.* 57, no. 1:93–122.

Hogan, M. (Ed.). 1996. *Hiroshima in History and Memory.* Cambridge: Cambridge University Press.

Human Rights Watch/Middle East. 1995. *Iraq's Crime of Genocide : The Anfal Campaign against the Kurds.* New Haven, CT: Yale University Press.

Jackson, Michael G. 2001. Something must be done? Genocidal chaos and world Responses to mass murder in East Timor between 1975 and 1999. *International Journal of Politics and Ethics.*, 1, no. 1:45–71.

Jardine, M. 1995. *East Timor: Genocide in Paradise.* Tucson: Odonian Press.

Kiernan, Ben. 1996. *The Pol Pot Regime : Race, Power, and Genocide in Cambodia under the Khmer Rouge, 1975-79.* New Haven, CT: Yale University Press.

Kiernan, Ben. (Ed.). 1993. *Genocide and Democracy in Cambodia : The Khmer Rouge, the United Nations, and the International Community.* New Haven, CT: Yale University Southeast Asia Studies.

Marks, Stephen P. 1999. Elusive justice for the victims of the Khmer Rouge. *Journal of International Affairs.* 52, no. 2:691–718.

Metzl, J. 1996. *Western Responses to Human Rights Abuses in Cambodia, 1975-1980.* New York: St. Martin's Press.

Phnom Penh : Ministry of Information, Press and Cultural Affairs of the People's Republic of Kampuchea. 1979. People's Revolutionary Tribunal held in Phnom Penh for the trial of the crime of genocide committed by the Pol Pot-Ieng Sary clique : Summary.

Pran, D. 1997. *Children of Cambodia's Killing Fields: Memoirs by Survivors.* New Haven, CT: Yale University Press.

Rummel, R. J. 1991. *China's Bloody Century : Genocide and Mass Murder since 1900.* New Brunswick, NJ: Transaction Publishers.

Saul, Ben. 2001. Was the conflict in East Timor 'genocide' and why does it matter? *Melbourne Journal of International Law.* 2, no. 2:477-523.

Tanaka, Y. 1998. *Hidden Horrors: Japanese War Crimes in World War II.* Boulder, CO: Westview Press.

Um, Khatharya. 1998. Specificities: The broken chain: Genocide in the re-construction and de-struction of Cambodian society. *Social Identities.* 4, no. 1:131-154.

Wang, Cheng-Chih. 2002. *Words Kill : Calling for the Destruction of "Class Enemies" in China, 1949-1953.* New York, NY: Routledge.

Yale University. Cambodian Genocide Program. http://www.yale.edu/cgp/.

BOSNIA HERCEGOVINA YUGOSLAVIA

Amnesty International. 1993. *Genocide: Ethnic Cleansing in Northwestern Bosnia.* Zagreb: Croatian Information Center.

Bell-Fialkoff, Andrew. 1996. *Ethnic Cleansing.* New York, NY: St. Martin's Press.

Bosco, David L. 1998. After genocide: building peace in Bosnia. *The American Prospect.* 39: p. 16-21.

Cigar, Norman L. 1995. *Genocide in Bosnia : The policy of "ethnic cleansing."* College Station: Texas A & M University Press.

Cushman, Thomas and Stjepan G. Mestrovic. (Eds.). 1996. *This Time We Knew : Western Responses to Genocide in Bosnia.* New York: New York University Press.

Ersever, Oya G. 2000. Ethnic groups in Kosovo and the psychological effects of war and genocide. *Peace Research.* 32, no. 3:16–19.

Fraser, John. 1999. Disintegration of Yugoslavia (The politics of Serbia in the 1990s; The war in Bosnia-Herzegovina; Heavenly Serbia: from myth to genocide). *International Journal.* 55, no. 1:146–149.

Hayden, Robert M. 1996. Imagined communities and real victims: self-determination and ethnic cleansing in Yugoslavia. *American Ethnologist.* 23, no. 4:783–801.

Hayden, Robert M. 1996. Schindler's fate: Genocide, ethnic cleansing, and population transfers. *Slavic Review* 55, no. 4:727–748.

Honig, Jan Willem and Norbert Both. 1997. *Srebrenica : Record of a war crime.* New York: Penguin Books.

Naimark, Norman M. 2001. *Fires of hatred : Ethnic Cleansing in Twentieth-Century Europe.* Cambridge, MA: Harvard University Press.

Neuffer, Elizabeth. 2001. *The Key to My Neighbor's House : Seeking Justice in Bosnia and Rwanda.* New York: Picador USA.

Sells, Michael A. 1996. *The Bridge betrayed Religion and Genocide in Bosnia.* Berkeley: University of California Press.

Stiglmayer, A. (Ed.). 1994. *Mass Rape: The War against Women in Bosnia-Herzegovina.* Lincoln: University of Nebraska Press.

Swomley, John M. 1999. Kosovo: Could It Have Been Avoided? *The Humanist.* 59, no. 4:11–14.

Weine, Stevan M. 1999. *When History is a Nightmare : Lives and Memories of Ethnic Cleansing in Bosnia-Herzegovina.* New Brunswick, NJ: Rutgers University Press.

HOLOCAUST

Adler, Jacques. 1987. *The Jews of Paris and the Final Solution : Communal Response and Internal Conflicts, 1940-1944.* New York: Oxford University Press.

Arad, Y. Krakowski S. & Spector S. 1989. *The Einsatzgruppen Reports: Selections from the Dispatches of the Nazi Death Squads' Campaign against the Jews July 1941-January 1943.* New York: Holocaust Library.

Bartov, Omer. 1996. *Murder in Our Midst : The Holocaust, Industrial Killing, and Representation.* New York: Oxford University Press.

Bartov, Omer. 2000. *Holocaust : Origins, Implementation, Aftermath.* New York: Routledge.

Bartov, Omer. 2003. *Germany's War and the Holocaust : Disputed Histories.* Ithaca: Cornell University Press.

Berenbaum, M. and Peck A. (Eds.). 1998. *The Holocaust and History: The Known, the Unknown, the Disputed, and the Reexamined.* Indianapolis: Indiana University Press in association with United States Holocaust Memorial Museum.

Bergen, Doris. 2003. *War & Genocide : A Concise History of the Holocaust.* Lanham, MD: Rowman & Littlefield.

Berger, Ronald J. 2002. *Fathoming the Holocaust : A Social Problems Approach.* New York, NY: Aldine de Gruyter.

Bloxhma, Donald. 2001. *Genocide on Trial : The War Crimes Trials and the Formation of Holocaust History and Memory.* Oxford, England: Oxford University Press.

Braham, Randolph. 2000. *Studies on the Holocaust : Selected Writings.* New York: Rosenthal Institute for Holocaust Studies Graduate Center, City University of New York.

Braham, Randolph. (Ed.). 2000. *The Vatican and the Holocaust : the Catholic Church and the Jews during the Nazi Era.* New York: Rosenthal Institute for Holocaust Studies, Graduate Center/City University of New York.

Breitman, Richard. 1998. *Official Secrets : What the Nazis Planned, What the British and Americans Knew.* New York: Hill & Wang.

Browning, C. R. 1992. *Ordinary Men: Reserve Police Battalion 101 and the Final Solution in Poland.* New York: HarperPerennial.

Burleigh, Michael. 1997. *Ethics, Extermination, and the East : Essays on Nazi Genocide.* New York, NY: Cambridge University Press.

Dulffer, Jost. 1996. *Nazi Germany, 1933-1945 : Faith and Annihilation.* New York, NY: St. Martin's Press.

Eibeshitz, J. & Eibeshitz A. (Eds.). 1993. *Women in the Holocaust - Vols. 1 & 2.* New York: Remember.

Fine, Robert and Charles Turner (Eds.). 2000. *Social Theory after the Holocaust.* Liverpool : Liverpool University Press.

Flescher, Joachim. 1971. *Nazi Holocaust and Mankind's "Final Solution."* New York: D.T.R.B. Editions.

Friedlander, Henry. 1995. *The Origins of Nazi Genocide : From Euthanasia to the Final Solution.* Chapel Hill, NC: University of North Carolina Press.

Friedlander, S. (Ed.). 1992. *Probing the Limits of Representation: Nazism and the "Final Solution."* Cambridge: Harvard University Press.

Gilbert, Martin. 1985. *The Holocaust : The Jewish Tragedy.* London: Collins.

Glass, J. 1997. *"Life Unworthy of Life": Racial Phobia and Mass Murder in Hitler's Germany.* New York: Basic Books.

Goldhagen, Daniel J. 2002. *A Moral Reckoning : The Role of the Catholic Church in the Holocaust and Its Unfulfilled Duty to Repair.* New York, NY: Alfred A. Knopf.

Gordon, Sarah. 1984. *Hitler, Germans, and the "Jewish Question."* Princeton, NJ: Princeton University Press.

Gottlieb, Roger S. 1990. *Thinking the Unthinkable : Meanings of the Holocaust.* New York: Paulist Press.

Gutman, Y. & Berenbaum M. (Eds.). 1994. *Anatomy of the Auschwitz Death Camp.* Bloomington, IN: Indiana University Press.

Hackett, D. A. (Ed.). 1995. *The Buchenwald Report.* Boulder, CO: Westview Press.

Hamburger Institut für Sozialforschung. 1999. *The German Army and Genocide : Crimes against War Prisoners, Jews, and Other Civilians in the East, 1939-1944.* New York: New Press.

Harff, Barbara. 2003. No lessons learned from the Holocaust? Assessing risks of genocide and political mass murder since 1955. *American Political Science Review* 97, no. 1:57–74.

Hass, A. 1995. *The Aftermath: Living with the Holocaust.* Cambridge: Cambridge University Press.

Hilberg, Raul. 1961. *The Destruction of the European Jews.* Chicago: Quadrangle Books.

Hinton, Alexander Laban (Ed.). 2002. *Annihilating difference : The Anthropology of Genocide.* Berkeley: University of California Press.

Hirshfeld, Gerhard. 1986. *The Policies of Genocide : Jews and Soviet Prisoners of War in Nazi Germany.* London: Allen & Unwin.

Holliday, L. (Ed.). 1995. *Children in the Holocaust and World War II: Their Secret Diaries.* New York: Pocket Books.

Jacobson, K. 1994. *Embattled Selves: An Investigation into the Nature of Identity through Oral Histories of Holocaust Survivors.* New York: Atlantic Monthly Press.

Katz, Steven T. 1994. *The Holocaust in Historical Context.* New York: Oxford University Press.

Lang, Beral. 1990. *Act and Idea in the Nazi Genocide.* Chicago, IL: University of Chicago Press.

Levi, N. and Michael Rothberg. (Eds.). 2003. *The Holocaust : Theoretical Readings.* Edinburgh: Edinburgh University Press.

Lifton, R. J. 1986. *The Nazi Doctors: Medical Killing and the Psychology of Genocide.* New York: Basic Books.

Lifton, Robert Jay and Eric Markusen. 1990. *The Genocidal Mentality : Nazi Holocaust and Nuclear Threat.* New York, NY: Basic Books.

Lipstadt, D. 1993. *Denying the Holocaust: The Growing Assault on Truth and Memory.* New York: Plume Books.

Maier, Charles S. 1988. *The Unmasterable Past : History, Holocaust, and German National Identity.* Cambridge, MA: Harvard University Press.

Markusen, David Kopf. 1995. *The Holocaust and Strategic Bombing : Genocide and Total War in the Twentieth Century.* Boulder, CO: Westview Press.

Marrus, Michael Robert. 1988. *The Holocaust in History.* London.: Weidenfeld & Nicolson.

Marrus, Michael (Ed.). 1989. *The Nazi Holocaust : Historical Articles on the Destruction of European Jews* (9 vols.). Westport, CT: Meckler.

Mazian, Florence. 1990. *Why Genocide? : The Armenian and Jewish Experiences in Perspective.* Ames, IA: Iowa State University Press.

Melson, Robert. 1992. *Revolution and Genocide : The Origins of the Armenian Genocide and the Holocaust.* Chicago: University of Chicago Press.

Müller-Hill, Benno. 1987. *Murderous Science : Elimination by Scientific Selection of Jews, Gypsies, and Others, Germany 1933-1945.* New York: Oxford University Press.

Newman, Leonard and Ralph Erber. (Eds.). 2002. *Understanding Genocide : The Social Psychology of the Holocaust.* Oxford: Oxford University Press.

Ofer, D., & Weitzman L. 1998. *Women in the Holocaust.* New Haven: Yale University Press.

Paskuly, S. (Ed.). 1996. *Death Dealer: The Memoirs of the SS Kommandant at Auschwitz Rudolph Hoss.* New York: Da Capo Press.

Phayer, Michael. 2000. *The Catholic Church and the Holocaust, 1930-1965.* Bloomington, IN: Indiana University Press.

Prince, Robert M. 1985. *The Legacy of the Holocaust : Psychohistorical Themes in the Second Generation.* Ann Arbor, MI: UMI Research Press.

Reed-Purvis, Julian. 2003. From "mercy death" to genocide: Julian Reed-Purvis examines the origins and consequences of Nazi euthanasia. (The Unpredictable Past). *History Review* (March): 36-41.

Reitlinger, Gerald. 1987. *The Final Solution : The Attempt to Exterminate the Jews of Europe 1939-45*. London: Jason Aronson.

Rittner, C. & Roth J. K. (Eds.). 1991. *Different voices: Women and the Holocaust*. New York: Paragon House.

Rittner, Carol and John K. Roth (Eds.). 2002. *Pope Pius XII and the Holocaust*. London : Leicester University Press.

Rohrlich, R. 1998. *Resisting the Holocaust*. Oxford: Berg.

Roth, J. K. & Berenbaum M. (Eds.). 1989. *Holocaust: Religious and Philosophical Implications*. New York: Paragon House.

Rubenstein, Richard L. 1987. *Approaches to Auschwitz : The Legacy of the Holocaust*. London: SCM.

Smith, Helmut Walser. Ed. 2002. *The Holocaust and Other Genocides : History, Representation, Ethics*. Nashville TN: Vanderbilt University Press.

Transylvanian World Federation. 1982. Genocide and ethnocide of the Jews and Hungarians in Rumania : Testimony submitted by the Transylvanian World Federation to the International Conference on the Holocaust and Genocide, Tel Aviv, Israel, 1982. Tel Aviv, Israel.

University of the State of New York. 1985. *Teaching about the Holocaust and Genocide*. Albany, N.Y. University of the State of New York, State Education Dept., Bureau of Curriculum Development.

Vidal-Naquet, P. 1992. *Assassins of Memory: Essays on the Denial of the Holocaust*. New York: Columbia University Press.

Weiss, John. 1996. *Ideology of Death: Why the Holocaust Happened in Germany*. Chicago: Ivan R. Dee.

White-Stevens, Lillian. 1984. *Holocaust-Genocide Studies : Essential Books and Films, Annotated*. Trenton, NJ: New Jersey State Dept. of Education.

Wiesel, Elie. 2002. *After the Darkness : Reflections on the Holocaust*. New York, NY.: Schocken Books.

Wiesel, Elie. 1977. *Dimensions of the Holocaust : Lectures at Northwestern University*. Evanston, IL. Northwestern University Press.

Yahil, Leni. 1990. *The Holocaust : The Fate of European Jewry, 1932-1945*. New York, NY: Oxford University Press.

Zygmunt, Bauman. 1989. *Modernity and the Holocaust*. Ithaca, NY: Cornell University Press.

GENERAL

Andreopoulos, George J. 1994. *Genocide : Conceptual and Historical Dimensions*. Philadelphia : University of Pennsylvania Press.

Avarez, Alex. 2001. *Governments, Citizens, and Genocide: A Comparative and Interdisciplinary Approach*. Bloomington: Indiana University Press.

Ball, Howard 1999. *Prosecuting War Crimes and Genocide: The Twentieth-Century Experience*. Lawrence, KS: University Press of Kansas.

Bartov, Omer. 2000. *Mirrors of Destruction: War, Genocide, and Modern Identity*. Oxford: Oxford University Press.

Bartov, Omer and Phyllis Mack. 2001. *In God's Name: Genocide and Religion in the Twentieth Century*. New York, NY: Berghahn Books.

Brantlinger, Patrick. 2003. *Dark Vanishings: Discourse on the Extinction of Primitive Races, 1800-1930*. Ithaca, NY: Cornell University Press.

Campbell, Kenneth J. 2001. *Genocide and the Global Village*. New York, NY: Palgrave.

Chalk, Frank and Kurt Jonassohn. 1990. *The History and Sociology of Genocide: Analyses and Case Studies*. New Haven, CT: Yale University Press.

Churchill, Ward. 1997. *A Little Matter of Genocide: Holocaust and Denial in the Americas, 1492 to the Present*. San Francisco, CA: City Lights Books.

Day, L. and Margaret Vandiver. 2000. Criminology and genocide studies: Notes on what might have been and what could still be. *Crime, Law and Social Change* 34, no. 1:43–59.

Dobkowski, M. & Wallimann I. 1998. *The Coming Age of Scarcity: Preventing Mass Death and Genocide in the Twenty-First Century*. Syracuse: Syracuse University Press.

Gellately, Robert and Ben Kiernan (Eds.). 2003. *The Specter of Genocide: Mass Murder in Historical Perspective*. Cambridge, UK: Cambridge University Press.

Gulden, Timothy. 2002. Spatial and temporal patterns in civil violence: Guatemala, 1977–1986. *Politics and the Life Sciences*. 21, no. 1:26-36.

Heidenrich, John G. 2001. *How to Prevent Genocide: A Guide for Policymakers, Scholars, and the Concerned Citizen*. Westport, CT: Praeger.

Horowitz, Irving Louis. 2002. *Taking Lives: Genocide and State Power*. New Brunswick, NJ: Transaction Publishers.

Jonassohn, Kurt and Karin Solveig Bjornson. 1998. *Genocide and Gross Human Rights Violations in Comparative Perspective*. New Brunswick, NJ: Transaction Publishers.

Kimenyi, Alexandre and Otis L. Scott. (Eds.). 2001. *Anatomy of genocide: State-Sponsored Mass-Killings in the Twentieth Century*. Lewiston, NY: E. Mellen Press.

Kressel, Neil J. 1996. *Mass Hate: The Global Rise of Genocide and Terror*. New York, NY: Plenum Press.

Kuper, L. 1982. *Genocide: Its Political Use in the Twentieth Century*. New Haven: Yale University Press.

LeBlanc, Lawrence J. 1991. *The United States and the genocide convention*. Durham, NC: Duke University Press.

Levene, Mark. 2002. *The Changing Face of Mass Murder: Massacre, Genocide, and Post-Genocide*. *International Social Science Journal*. (December):443-452.

Levene, Mark. 2000. Why is the twentieth century the century of genocide? *Journal of World History*. 11, no. 2:305–336.

Makino, U. 2001. Final solutions, crimes against mankind: On the genesis and criticism of the concept of genocide. *Journal of Genocide Research*. 3, no. 1:49–73.

Markusen, David Kopf. 1995. *The Holocaust and Strategic Bombing: Genocide and Total War in the Twentieth Century*. Boulder, CO: Westview Press.

Mazian, Florence. 1990. *Why Genocide?: The Armenian and Jewish Experiences in Perspective*. Ames, IA: Iowa State University Press.

Mills, Nicolaus and Kira Brunner (Eds.). 2002. *The New Killing Fields: Massacre and the Politics of Intervention*. New York: Basic Books.

Montejo, Victor. 1999. *Voices from Exile: Violence and Survival in Modern Maya History*. Norman, OK: University of Oklahoma Press.

Neuffer, Elizabeth. 2001. *The Key to My Neighbor's House: Seeking Justice in Bosnia and Rwanda*. New York: Picador USA.

Palmer, Alison. 1998. Colonial and modern genocide: Explanations and categories. *Ethnic and Racial Studies* 21, no. 1:89-115.

Power, Samantha. 2002. Stopping genocide and securing "justice": Learning by doing. *Social Research* 69 (Winter), no. 4:1093-1109.

Power, Samantha. 2002. *A Problem from Hell: America and the Age of Genocide*. New York, NY: Basic Books.

Riemer, Neal. 2000. *Protection Against Genocide: Mission Impossible?* Westport, CT: Praeger.

Rittner, Carol, John K. Roth and James M. Smith (Eds.). 2002. *Will Genocide Ever End?* Laxton, UK: Paragon House.

Ronayane, Peter. 2001. *Never Again?: The United States and the Prevention and Punishment of Genocide Since the Holocaust*. Lanham, MD: Rowman & Littlefield Publishers.

Rosenbaum, Alan S. (Ed.). 2001. *Is the Holocaust Unique?: Perspectives on Comparative Genocide*. Boulder, CO: Westview Press. 2nd ed.

Rummel, R. J. 1990. *Lethal Politics: Soviet Genocides and Mass Murders since 1917*. New Brunswick, NJ: Transaction Publishers.

Rummel, R. J. 1994. *Death by Government*. New Brunswick, NJ: Transactions Publishers.

Sanford, Victoria. 2003. *Buried Secrets: Truth and Human Rights in Guatemala*. New York, NY: Palgrave Macmillan.

Schabas, William. 2000. *Genocide in International Law: The crimes of Crimes.* Cambridge, U.K: Cambridge University Press.

Semelin, J. 2001. In consideration of massacres. *Journal of Genocide Research.* 3, no. 3:377–389.

Semelin, Jacques. 2002. From massacre to the genocidal process. *International Social Science Journal* (December): 433–442.

Simpson, Christopher. 1993. *The Splendid Blond Beast: Money, Law, and Genocide in the Twentieth Century.* New York, NY: Grove Press.

Smith, Helmut Walser. (Ed.). 2002. *The Holocaust and Other Genocides: History, Representation, Ethics.* Nashville TN: Vanderbilt University Press.

Stannard, David. 1993. *American Holocaust: The Conquest of the New World.* Oxford: Oxford University Press.

Staub, Ervin. 1989. *The Roots of Evil: The Origins of Genocide and Other Forms of Group Violence.* Cambridge, England: Cambridge University Press.

Strozier, Charles B. and Michael Flynn. (Eds.). 1996. *Genocide, War, and Human Survival, /* edited by B. and Michael Flynn. Lanham, MD: Rowman & Littlefield Publishers.

Sunga, Lyal S. 1992. *Individual Responsibility in International Law for Serious Human Rights Violations.* Norwell, MA.: Kluwer Academic.

Svaldi, David. 1989. *Sand Creek and the Rhetoric of Extermination: A Case Study in Indian-White Relations.* Lanham, MD: University Press of America.

Totten, S. Parsons W. & Charny I. 1997. *Century of Genocide: Eyewitness Accounts and Critical Views.* New York: Garland Publishing.

Totten, Samuel Williams S. Parsons and Israel W. Charny. (Eds.). 1995. *Genocide in the Twentieth Century : Critical Essays and Eyewitness Accounts.* New York, NY: Garland Pub.

Van den Berghe, Peirre L. (Ed.). 1990. *State Violence and Ethnicity.* Niwot, CO: University of Colorado Press.

Waller, James. 2002. *Becoming Evil : How Ordinary People Commit Genocide and Mass Killing.* Oxford, England: Oxford University Press.

Wallimann, Isidor and Dobkowski Michael N. 1987. *Genocide and the Modern Age : Etiology and Case Studies of Mass Death.* New York: Greenwood Press.

Weitz, Eric D. 2003. *A Century of Genocide : Utopias of Race and Nation.* Princeton, NJ: Princeton University Press.

Willis, Brian M and Barry S. Levy. 2000. Recognizing the Public Health Impact of Genocide. *JAMA: Journal of the American Medical Association.* 284, no. 5:612–614.

Yacoubian, George S. Jr. 2003. Evaluating the efficacy of the international criminal tribunals for Rwanda and the former Yugoslavia: Implications for criminology and international criminal law. *World Affairs* 165 (Winter), no. 3:133–142.

NOTES ON CONTRIBUTORS

ERIK ALLARDT is Emeritus Professor of Sociology at the University of Helsinki and former head of the Finnish national science foundation. He has been visiting professor at the University of California (Berkeley), University of Illinois (Urbana), University of Wisconsin (Madison), University of Mannheim (Germany), University of Lund (Sweden), and a fellow of the Wilson Center (Washington, DC). He has published a general textbook in sociology in Finnish and Swedish, and he has written extensively on subjects such as political sociology, social welfare, ethnicity and sociology of science.

LYDIA ARAN, who completed an M.A. degree in the social sciences at the Hebrew University, spent nine years studying Buddhism and Buddhist culture and society in South and South-East Asia. Upon her return to Jerusalem, she became the first teacher of Buddhist subjects in the Department of Indian, Iranian and Armenian Studies at the Hebrew University, where she taught until her retirement in 1997. Her publications include *The Art of Nepal* (1978), *Buddhism: An Introduction To Its Religion and Philosophy* (1993), *Genocide or Murder of a Civilization: Tibet 1950–2000* (2005), along with many articles and book reviews on these and related subjects.

MEDARDUS BREHL studied literature and history. He is research assistant at the Institute for Diaspora and Genocide Studies at the University of Bochum (Germany). His research interest and publications focus on genocide research, discourse theory, the theory of history and literature, the literary construction of social knowledge, colonial discourse and violence, and the history and literature of German colonialism and war poetry. He is co-editor of *Feindschaft* (2003).

MIHRAN DABAG is head of the Institute for Diaspora and Genocide Studies at the University of Bochum (Germany). His recent publications focus on the fields of genocide research, historical philosophy, peace and conflict research, as well as the subjects of remembrance and memory. He is co-editor of *Identitat in der Fremde* (1993); *Generation und Gedachtnis* (1995); *Genozid und Moderne. Strukturen kollektiver Gewalt im 20. Jahrhundert* (1998); and *Gewalt. Strukturen, Formen, Reprasentationen* (2000); and *Kolonialismus. Kolonialdiskurs und Genozid* (2004).

FRANCO FERRAROTTI is Professor Emeritus of Sociology at the University of Rome, "La Sapienza." In 1960 he was awarded the first full sociology chair established in the Italian university system. He founded "Quaderni di Sociologia" in 1951 and presently edits "La Critica Sociologica." He has been a visiting professor at many American universities. In 1978 he was appointed "Directeur d'Etudes" at the "Maison des Sciences de l'homme" in Paris. His many works published in English include *The Myth of Inevitable Progress* (Greenwood), *Time, Memory, and Society* (Greenwood), *Faith Without Dogma* (Transaction Books), *The Temptation to Forget* (Greenwood), and *The Paradox of the Sacred* (Sharpe). His present interest in the analysis of industrial societies focuses on power and rationality within them, particularly in the form of a "civil religion" — a body of values capable of guaranteeing national and international peaceful coexistence. According to Professor Ferrarotti, anti-Semitism, racism, and neo-Nazism represent case studies of the mixed effects of technology on modern society.

JAMES JENKINS is a reference and instruction librarian at the Auburn University libraries. He has completed both a bachelor's degree in sociology and a masters in Library Science at Indiana University. He has published articles on information literacy programs and on health issues pertaining to African Americans. He has been a librarian at Auburn University since 1999.

GRAHAM C. KINLOCH was born in Zimbabwe and has been on the sociology faculty at the Florida State University since 1971. His academic and intellectual interests include sociological theory, the sociology of knowledge, minority and race relations and, more recently, intergroup violence and genocide. He has published a number of books and articles on many of these topics, including *The Dynamics of Race Relations: A Sociological Analysis*, *The Sociology of Minority Group Relations, Ideology and Contemporary Sociological Theory*, and *The Comparative Understanding of Intergroup Relations: A Worldwide Analysis*.

MAX KOCH, Dr. Phil. Habil., teaches at the School of Sociology and Applied Social Studies, University of Ulster. His research interests include sociological theory, the sociology of development, and stratification. He is author of *Vom Strukturwandel einer Flassengesellschaft, Theoretische Diskussion und empirische Analyse, Unternehmen Transformation: Sozialstruktur und gesellschaftlicher Wandel in Chile*, and *Arbeitsmarkte und Sozialstrukturen in Europa: Wege zum Postfordismus in den Niederlanden, Schweden, Spanien, Großbritannien und Deutschland.*

BRIJ MOHAN is author, most recently, of *The Practice of Hope* (2003), *Social Work Revisited* (2002), *Unification of Social Work* (1999) and *Eclipse of Freedom* (1993). As a "post-empiricist" philosopher, Professor Mohan specializes in critical theory of social practice, mental health policy, international social development and philosophy of science. His forthcoming books include *Fallacies of Development*. He is founding Editor-in-Chief of *New Global Development: Journal of International and Comparative Social Welfare* (to be published as *Journal of Comparative Social Welfare* by Taylor and Francis, effective 2006).

RAJ P. MOHAN is Professor of Sociology at Auburn University and editor of *The International Journal of Contemporary Sociology*. He has published a number of books and research articles on a wide range of topics, including the intelligentsia and organizations. He recently co-edited *Ideology and the Social Sciences* with Graham C. Kinloch, published by Greenwood Press in 2000.

TARIQUE NIAZI has a Ph.D. in Environmental Studies from the University of Wisconsin, Madison. He teaches Sociology at the University of Wisconsin, Eau Claire. His teaching areas include Environmental Sociology, Social Problems, and Introduction to Sociology. Dr. Niazi has recently been named as Wisconsin Teaching Scholar for 2002–2003. His research interests include resource-based conflicts, distribution-induced resource scarcities, and sustainable agriculture. He has published his research in national and international research journals, including *International Journal of Contemporary Sociology* (IJCS). He is a member of the Advisory Board of a Pakistan-based Journal of National Development and Security. The US Agency for International Development (USAID) named him Jefferson Scholar for 1990–1992. He is currently working on a book, "Distributional Inequalities, Ecological Deficit, and Social Violence: A Case of Pakistan." He can be reached via email at niazit@uwec.edu.

KRISTIN PLATT has studied sociology, political science and social psychology at the University of Bochum (Germany). Her research focuses on collective violence and genocide, identity patterns in diaspora communities, psychic trauma and biography on both interpersonal and international levels. She is particularly interested in the interrelationships between social structures and general knowledge, specifically political and biographical connections. Since 1992 she has been working on a multistage project concerning psychic trauma and elderly survivors. Currently she serves as Research Director at the

Institute for Diaspora and Genocide Studies. She has authored numerous articles on trauma, biography, Jewish life, and German history. Her major publications include *Nach Afghanistan. Auf dem Weg zu einer neuen Weltordnung?* (2004); *Reden von Gewalt* (ed., 2002); co-editor of: *Identität in der Fremde* (1993), *Generation und Gedächtnis* (1995), *Genozid und Moderne* (1998), and *Feindschaft* (2003).

ARTHUR S. WILKE is an emeritus sociology professor at Auburn University. He is a co-editor of and contributor to the *International Handbook of Contemporary Development in Sociology* (Greenwood Press, 1994). He has written numerous book reviews, articles, and edited sever symposium volumes and chapters. Trained in social theory and the sociology of knowledge, his focus is on social thought and the role of social issues and problems in proscribing political and intellectual activity.

KURT H. WOLFF (deceased) was born in Darmstadt in 1912 and studied in Frankfurt and Florence, focusing on the sociology of knowledge in 1935. He emigrated to the USA. in 1939, where he has taught at Southern Methodist, Ohio State, and Brandeis Universities, as well as Earlham College. Karl Mannheim was his most influential teacher. For a long time his interest involved the development of "surrender and catch," referring to the most immediate kind of contact combined with suspension of one's socialization as far as is bearable. His works in English include *Trying Sociology* (1974), *Surrender and Catch* (1976), *O Loma!* (1989), and *Transformation in the Writing* (1995).

Subject Index

A

Afghanistan, 3, 9, 50, 219–221, 224–226, 229, 308

Africa, 3, 7, 51, 75, 145, 147–148, 150–152, 155–156, 162, 164, 169, 173, 175, 191, 248, 292–293

African Aryans, 170

Aggression, 18–19, 48, 63–64, 66–68, 70, 74

Anglo-Saxon Culture, 84

Annihilation, 3, 16, 44, 46, 48, 51–52, 55, 72, 97, 143–144, 146, 148, 154, 156–158, 198, 267, 276–277, 280, 299

Anti-Semitism, 33, 53, 86

Arusha, 176, 178, 185

Asia, 50, 79, 195, 216, 224, 296, 305

Auschwitz, 59, 61, 96, 102, 110, 206, 263, 279, 281, 286, 299–301

Australia, 25, 35, 75

B

Bahutu Manifesto, 175

Banality, 8, 67, 104, 294

Bangladesh, 24, 34

Banyarwanda, 169

Belgium, 25, 106, 120, 165–166, 169–170, 173–175, 178, 184, 186, 254

Biafra, 24

Biographical Contexts, 9–10

Biographical Research, 256, 262, 265–266

Biographical Self-Depictions, 9–10, 279

Biography, 123–124, 128, 255–257, 260–261, 264, 266, 274, 278, 296, 307

Black Caucasians, 170

Bosnia, 23, 33, 122, 293, 297–298, 303

Brazil, 25, 35, 75

Britain, 74, 148, 239, 242

Buchenwald, 279, 299

Buddhism, 195–196, 198–200, 203, 205, 208–210, 212–213, 215, 222, 305

Burundi, 24, 35, 167, 170, 173, 175–176, 186, 192, 292–294

C

Cambodia, 34, 66, 95, 296–297

Capitalism, 69, 222–223, 235, 237, 243, 245, 247

Case Studies, 7–8, 16, 21, 32, 46, 54–55, 230, 245, 247, 302, 304, 306

Catastrophe, 151, 206, 274, 276, 278

Catholic Church, 173–174, 298–300

Catholics, 239–242, 244, 246

Cattle Chiefs, 173

Chile, 9, 233–235, 238, 240, 243–249, 306

China, 22, 50, 79, 121, 146, 196, 200, 205, 207, 209, 211–212, 214, 297

Civil War, 24–25, 27, 38, 42–43, 47, 176, 178, 223

Coalition for Defense of Rwanda, 168

Co-Existence, 71

Coffee Plantation, 183

Collective Identity, 52, 96, 151

Collective Memory, 96, 100, 200, 203, 206–207, 265, 281, 292

Collective Violence, 38, 42, 45–48, 52–53, 57, 114, 267, 307

Colonial Discourse, 154, 158–159, 305

Colonial War, 156

Colonialism, 3, 8, 10, 19, 24–27, 29, 31–32, 47, 49, 69, 101, 122, 143, 145–146, 148, 150–151, 153–159, 165–167, 169–171, 174–175, 179, 185–186, 188–190, 208, 305

Colonizers, 159, 165, 169–170, 173–174, 176

Coloureds, 169

Commemorate, 53, 206–207

Comparative Sociology, 2

Competition, 8, 17, 20–21, 25–27, 29–32, 235

Conflict, 3–4, 7, 9–11, 15–22, 25–28, 30–32, 41–43, 51, 58, 65, 72, 106, 119, 122, 155, 163, 168, 178, 229, 233–234, 240, 247, 292–294, 297, 305

Conflict Regulation, 233

Conflict Research, 305

Consensus, 113, 130, 134, 234

Critical Theory, 307

Cultural Anthropology, 113, 128

Cultural Co-Tradition, 82

Cultural Dominance, 31

Cultural Evolution, 148–149

Cultural History, 113

Cultural Progress, 149

Cultural Revolution, 228

Cultural Therapy, 95, 97–98, 107

Culture, 2, 16, 22, 28, 41, 43, 50, 65, 67–69, 71, 73–74, 84, 92, 94, 99, 101, 120, 123, 127, 129, 144, 154–155, 158–159, 195–196, 199–200, 204, 206, 222, 230, 284, 305

Culture War, 94

D

Dalai Lama, 9, 195–214, 216

Decisive Generation, 117, 130, 132–133

Democide, 46

Denial, 18, 20, 47, 54, 58, 93, 97, 119, 254, 269, 274, 294, 301–302

Deportation, 43, 45, 197, 202, 258, 263, 267, 275–276

Destruction, 7–8, 15–17, 22–24, 26–27, 29, 31–32, 46, 52, 64–69, 71–74, 81, 100–101, 105, 120, 145, 179, 188, 197–198, 202, 204, 206, 210, 212–213, 220–221, 224–225, 229–231, 233, 278, 294, 297, 299–300, 302

Destructiveness, 65, 67, 72

Deutsch-Südwestafrika, 143, 161

Development, 7–8, 10, 19, 24–25, 28, 30, 32, 47, 49, 51, 63–65, 69–70, 72, 74–75, 80, 104, 130, 148–149, 159, 163, 180, 244, 254, 256, 260, 265, 269, 271, 280, 284, 292, 306–308

Dharamsala, 199, 209, 211–216

Diaspora, 198, 200, 204, 210–211, 213–216, 305, 308

Discourse, 3, 46–48, 52, 54, 56, 58, 69, 102, 118, 128, 131, 134–135, 143–144, 146, 148, 155, 158–159, 199–200, 204, 206, 210, 253, 262, 266, 270, 305

Discrimination, 8–10, 17, 21, 26–27, 32, 77, 82, 93, 167, 233, 239–240

Dublin, 238, 240–241, 246

E

East Timor, 2, 24, 34, 296–297

Ecological Cycle, 17

Ecological Limits, 166, 169, 179

Ecological Overshoot, 166, 169, 179

Ecological Scarcities, 3, 165–166, 179, 183, 185, 189

Economic Development, 25, 221

Element Of Formation, 117, 124, 135

Elimination, 16, 19, 21, 42, 47, 52, 78, 151, 226–227

Elites, 3, 9, 22, 46, 196, 229–230, 233–234, 244–247

Encyclopedia., 289

Enemy, 16, 43, 57, 65, 119, 124, 151, 153, 155–157, 205, 222, 242, 274, 278

Enlightenment, 49, 69, 73, 79, 149, 230

Enmity, 156

Ereigniserfahrung, 262

Ethnic Cleansing, 15, 23, 63, 82, 253, 297–298

Ethnic Identity Cards, 166–167, 176

Ethnic Self-Awareness, 83

Ethnic Violence, 42–43

Ethnicity, 41, 71, 73, 93, 100, 166–167, 170, 176, 304–305

Ethnocentrism, 8, 10, 17–18, 29, 31–32, 98

Ethnocide, 46, 301

Eurocentrism, 77

Evolution, 44, 50, 64–66, 69–70, 94, 157

Exclusion, 3, 8, 10, 41, 43, 45, 57, 122, 143, 145, 158–159, 220, 234, 279

Exclusion Strategies, 143, 159

Exclusivity, 153, 156, 158

Existence, 8, 16, 40, 66, 69, 93, 96, 101, 103, 105, 125, 129, 151, 153, 155, 157, 212, 223, 226, 276

Experience, 20–21, 40, 52, 56, 66, 81, 83, 97, 114–115, 117, 119, 125, 129, 134, 155, 197, 208, 221, 253–257, 259–267, 271–278, 280, 285–286, 302

Extermination, 22, 42–44, 47–49, 52–53, 56–57, 73, 78, 82, 86, 96, 119, 130, 132, 134, 157, 159, 167, 204, 275, 279, 299, 304

External Control, 20–24, 29, 31

External Factors, 19, 29–30

External Threats, 20–22, 30–32

Eyewitness, 56, 277, 304

F

Farmers, 147–148, 154, 164–165, 167, 170, 172, 176, 178, 181–183, 186, 188, 258

Fascism, 39, 53, 55

Films, 9, 95, 291, 301

Fortunoff Video Archives, 255

Framework, 42, 46–47, 54, 65, 93, 98, 115, 117–118, 133, 145, 151, 239, 256, 259, 262, 271–272, 276, 279

Functionalism, 39, 48

Future, 2, 7, 26, 32, 50–52, 57–58, 70, 75, 82, 96, 116–118, 121, 124, 127, 130–133, 135, 157–159, 190, 205, 207, 211, 228, 231, 242, 247, 268–269, 277, 279, 284–285, 289

G

Genç Kalemler (YoungFeathers), 123

General Theory, 28

Generation, 3, 8, 10, 58, 113–119, 123, 125–126, 128–135, 174, 199, 207, 211, 254, 259, 261, 300

Generational Discourse, 114, 125

Generational Knowledge, 114, 125

Generations, 32, 42, 50–52, 57–58, 96, 114–119, 125–126, 128, 130, 132–134, 143, 157, 207, 211, 255, 277, 279

Genocidal consequences, 32

Genocidal continuum, 26–27, 31

Genocidal massacre, 47

Genocidal process, 46, 49, 54–56, 143, 254, 304

Genocidal situation, 7, 18, 233, 276

Genocide Convention, 45, 289–290

Genocide research, 38–42, 44–47, 51, 53–57, 113–114, 133, 135, 143, 159, 305

Genocide studies, 46, 291, 301–302

Genocide survivors, 9–10

Genocide, causes of, 3, 8, 32, 41, 57, 113, 115, 122, 154, 165–167, 179, 184–185, 188–189

German South-West Africa, 8, 143, 145, 149

Germans/Germany, 3, 8, 19, 21–22, 25, 34–35, 37, 45, 47–48, 51–53, 79–80, 84, 95, 106, 114–116, 119–122, 124, 126, 128, 134, 136–138, 143, 145–146, 148–152, 154, 157, 159–162, 165, 169–170, 173–174, 205, 253, 255–256, 259, 262, 283–284, 286–287, 298–301, 305, 308

Global economic development, 10

Global inequality, 71

Global memory, 253

Global sensitivity, 7

Global village, 83–84, 86, 302

Globalization (see also Modernization/ Westernization), 41, 47, 69, 115, 222, 246

H

Habyarimana, 165, 167–168, 176–177, 179, 182, 184–187, 189

Hague Peace Conference, 156

Hamites, 169, 175

Hercegovina, 297

Herero, 3, 51, 60, 143–146, 148, 150–151, 155–159, 161

Herero Rebellion, 145–146

Herero War, 144

Hindus, 213, 219–220, 222–225, 232

Historical process, 49, 150–151, 159, 280

History, 1–3, 8, 10, 15, 19–20, 39–40, 47, 50–56, 64, 68–69, 79–81, 83, 97, 114–117, 119–120, 122–123, 125–126, 130, 132–135, 143–145, 148, 150, 155, 157–159, 168, 171, 199–200, 202, 204, 206–207, 209–210, 213, 222, 226, 230, 240, 247, 253–255, 260, 263–264, 266–267, 269, 271, 278–279, 281, 283–284, 294, 296, 298, 300, 302–303, 305, 308

Hitler, 1, 19, 61, 66, 78–80, 86, 117–118, 124–125, 128, 130, 136, 138, 294, 299

Holocaust, 33, 35, 39, 45, 47, 53–55, 60–61, 67, 77–82, 93–94, 96–97, 101, 105, 108–110, 113, 158, 160, 189, 191, 205, 209–210, 212–216, 219, 253, 255, 273, 281–282, 289–292, 295–296, 298–304

Homogeneity, 23, 122, 248

Homogenization, 41–42, 122, 254

Hope, 33, 65, 67, 69–71, 73–75, 124, 208, 224, 230, 233, 247, 268, 295

Human depravity, 63, 65

Hutu Revolution, 167, 176

Hutus, 81, 163, 165–177, 179, 185–190

I

Identity, 8–10, 47, 50, 52–53, 56–58, 65, 82, 84, 86, 91, 93, 105, 107, 115–116, 119, 128, 134–135, 148, 151, 153–154, 157–160,

167, 176, 190, 197–200, 204, 209–211, 224, 238, 253, 259–261, 267, 269, 280, 300, 302, 307

Ideology, 3, 10, 16–17, 19–24, 26–28, 30–31, 44, 52–53, 71, 73, 84, 104, 133, 211, 221–223, 225, 230, 243

Ignorance, 63, 66–67, 69, 81, 230

Inclusion/exclusion, 3, 8, 10, 41, 43, 45, 57, 122, 143, 145, 158–159, 220, 234, 244–245, 247, 279

India, 25, 72, 76, 195–196, 198, 202–203, 206, 210–216, 222

Indonesia, 60, 161, 296

Inequality, 10, 16, 28–29, 32, 239–240

Injustice, 70–71, 275

Intentionalism, 39, 48

Intentionalist perspective, 113

Interahamwa, 168

Interdisciplinary approach, 8, 10, 38, 302

Internal traits, 20

Invenzi, 176

Iran, 3, 9, 50, 219–220, 222, 226–232

Iraq, 23, 34–35, 66, 82, 296

Israel, 289, 291, 294, 301, 304

Ittihâd Ve Terakki, 120

J

Jews/Jewish community, 2–3, 33, 37, 44, 48, 53, 61, 66, 68, 77–80, 84, 91, 93–94, 108, 121, 123–124, 132, 136–138, 205–206, 208–216, 222–223, 263, 271, 282, 285, 295, 298–301, 303, 308

K

Kayibanda, 165, 167, 175–177, 179, 186

Khmer Rouge, 34, 66, 81, 296

Kigali, 172–173, 176, 184, 188, 192

Kiyarwanda, 169

Knowledge, 15, 41, 48, 57–58, 65, 69, 81, 86, 107, 126–129, 135, 143–145, 150, 157, 160, 199, 203, 225, 254, 257, 261, 264, 266, 278, 285, 305–308

Kurds, 34, 66, 296

L

Land Chiefs, 173
Land Limits, 180
Legitimization, 114, 133, 143, 145, 150, 157
Liberal ethos, 99, 104
Liberalism, 92, 95, 98, 100, 220, 235
Liberalization, 235

M

Mass Media, 81, 95
Massacre, 1, 3, 38–39, 42–43, 47, 54, 57, 65, 68, 119, 163–164, 166–167, 255, 258, 303–304
Memory, 57, 79, 94, 96, 133, 198, 202–204, 209, 212–213, 253–254, 261, 264–265, 275, 281, 291, 296, 298, 300–301, 305
Meta-historical dimension, 82
Middle East, 7, 72, 221, 224, 294, 296
Minorities, 3, 8–10, 16, 19–27, 29–32, 37, 41, 78, 84, 223, 225, 229, 241, 285
Modern societies, Modernity, 41, 57, 69, 135, 221–222
Modernization, Westernization, 3, 9–10, 32, 39, 120, 219, 221–222, 225, 227, 229
Moral life, 8, 103, 107
Moral philosophy, 2
Mourning (see also Remembrance/Forgetting), 3, 198, 201–202, 204, 206–207, 209, 212, 268, 274, 277
Museveni, 177
Mwamis, 172

N

Nama, 145, 147, 150, 161
Namibia, 3, 8, 143, 160–161
Narratives, 262, 264, 268, 275, 282
Nation, 16, 22, 46, 49, 68, 74, 115, 122, 124–125, 127, 130–132, 168, 178, 182–183, 187, 198, 200, 204, 210, 238, 304
Nation state, 49
National character, 127
National consciousness, 117, 128
National discourse, 159

National identity, 83, 117, 124, 130, 195, 204, 300
National Socialism, 37, 48, 53–54, 86, 115–116, 128, 131–133, 135, 255
Nationalism, 17, 22, 41, 127, 129, 199, 208, 221–222, 231, 238–239
Nazi Doctrine, 79
Nazism, 9, 33, 39, 79, 86, 222, 283, 285–287, 299, 306
Neo-Marxism, 223
New Tribalism, 70, 72, 74
Nigeria, 25, 293
Normalization, 18, 45
North America, 33, 80, 83, 294
Northern Ireland, 9, 233–234, 238–240, 242–249

O

Oppression, 70–72, 75
Ottoman Empire, 50, 119, 158, 254, 257

P

Payasannat, 165, 167–168, 176, 180, 182, 186
Perpetrator group, 38, 43, 113, 118
Perpetrator society, 44, 52, 58, 113–114, 134
Persecution, 38, 40, 45, 51–53, 55, 57, 59, 68, 78–79, 86, 113, 206, 221–223, 225, 234, 253, 267, 270, 272, 274–277, 280
philosophy of history, 149
Pol Pot, 34, 95, 296
policy implications, 7–8, 16, 28–29
Political corruption, 74
Political generations, 3, 114
Political violence, 143, 293
Post-Colonial, 9, 20, 25, 165–169, 171, 179, 185, 188–189
Pre-Colonial, 9, 165–166, 169–172, 179, 185–186, 188, 190
Prejudice, 17, 41, 45, 53, 68, 93, 259
Progress, 50, 57, 69, 120, 158, 221–222
Protestants, 238, 241, 243

Psychoanalytic views, 19
PTSD, 94, 272

R

Race, 69, 73, 79, 93–94, 100, 131, 146, 153, 155, 304, 306
racialization, 169–170
Racism, 25–27, 33, 45, 51, 53, 78, 86, 130, 190, 306
Reactions, 9–10, 17–18, 21, 24–25, 27, 31–32, 37, 39, 116, 225, 229–230, 259, 270–272
Religious bigotry, 74
Remembrance/Forgetting, 82, 209, 213, 253, 265, 278, 305
Rwanda, 1, 8, 24, 35, 37, 59, 66, 68, 73, 81, 95, 159, 162–168, 171–177, 179–193, 292–294, 298, 303–304
Rwanda Patriotic Front, 187, 189

S

Science, 1, 3, 39–40, 44, 66, 68–69, 84, 103–104, 129, 134, 199–200, 202, 254–255, 300, 305, 307
Second Generations, 114
Segregation, 26, 59, 277
Self-declaration, 125, 128, 132
Self-definition, 117, 119, 123, 133
Self-perception, 114, 116, 130
September 11, 15, 219, 248
Settlers, 145, 147, 182, 201
Sikhs, 219–220, 222–225
Singularity, 39–40, 47, 53–55, 183
Sinn Fein, 242, 248
Social constructionism, 94
Social Pathology Model, 8, 92–93
Socio-cultural knowledge, 144, 159, 225
Soil limits, 180
Stigmatization, 3, 52, 57, 143
Sudan, 23, 33, 73, 292
Survivors, 4, 56, 96, 133, 190, 197, 254–255, 257, 259–264, 266–267, 269–271, 273–280, 297, 300, 307

T

Taliban, 221–225, 229, 232
Tanzania, 167, 170, 178, 186
Terminology, 56, 82
Testimony, 38, 56, 94, 96, 259, 275, 277, 279
Tibet, 8, 22, 34, 195–198, 200–201, 203–206, 208–209, 211–216, 305
Tibetan Autonomous Region, 211
Totalitarian Control, 72
Totalitarianism, 24, 39, 49, 53–55, 287
Traditional culture, 10, 85
Transformation, 43–44, 51, 64, 75, 143, 212, 235, 237, 245, 266
Transmission, 81, 85, 127, 133, 145
Transnationalization, 115
Trauma, 57, 133, 204, 255, 257, 262, 269–274, 277, 279–280, 307
Tribalism, 10
Turan, 50–51
Turanism, 131
Türk Ocagi (TurkishHearth), 123
Türk Yurdu (TurkishHomeland), 123
Turkey, 22, 51, 58, 120–121, 126, 135, 294
Turkism, 50, 123, 137
Tutsis, 2, 9, 163, 165–179, 185–190
Twas, 165, 169, 171–173, 186, 188
Typology, 40, 69

U

Ulster Democratic Party, 241
Ulster Unionist Party, 240–241
United Nations, 15, 28, 45, 73, 81, 100, 170, 174, 184, 191–192, 219, 292, 296
United States, 15–16, 26–27, 32, 70, 81, 83, 94–95, 97, 100, 106, 192–193, 240, 244, 246, 248, 285, 289–291, 294–295, 298, 303, 307
Unstable diversity, 24, 27
USSR, 21–22, 33, 83

V

Victim Group, 40, 42, 46, 48, 51, 53, 143, 159

Victims, 3–4, 8, 18, 20–23, 29, 31, 39–40, 42–48, 51–53, 56, 58–59, 67, 70, 72, 79, 82, 93–99, 101–102, 107, 113–114, 120, 133, 143, 159, 163, 167–168, 176–177, 201–202, 205–206, 212, 219, 227, 234, 245, 253–254, 267, 269, 276, 279, 293, 296–297

Violence, 7–9, 15, 20, 22–26, 30, 37–38, 40–45, 47–49, 52–59, 66, 73–74, 77, 94, 122, 135, 145, 149, 151, 163–164, 166, 173, 175–176, 185, 188–189, 201, 219, 223–226, 228, 230, 233, 239–241, 244–245, 247–248, 253–254, 263, 267, 269, 273, 276, 278, 280, 293, 302, 304–306

Vision, 43, 50, 70, 74, 115, 174, 197, 208, 285–287

W

War, 15–16, 24, 38–40, 42–44, 52–53, 65, 68, 73, 82, 84, 100, 106, 119, 121, 123, 128, 146–148, 151, 155–156, 158, 164, 168, 171, 178, 187–188, 204, 223, 228, 267, 270, 282, 293, 297–300, 302–305

Westminster, 238–241

Wilderness, 152, 154–155, 158

Witnesses, 56, 59, 254, 275, 277–278

World history, 39, 47, 49, 56, 254

World War I, 19, 60, 68, 80, 93, 96, 104, 106, 115, 120–121, 124, 174, 205, 270–271, 283, 294–297, 300

World War II, 68, 93, 96, 104, 106, 205, 271, 296–297, 300

Y

Young Turks, 44, 50, 119–120, 122–125, 127–128, 133, 135

Yugoslavia, 81, 294, 297, 304

Name Index

A

ABC TV, 68
Abels, Heinz, 259, 280
Adalian, Rouben, 294
Adivar, Hâlide Edib, 131, 136
Adler, Jacques, 298
Adorno, Theodor W., 93–94, 97–98, 107, 230
Afflitto, Frank M., 292
African Rights, 24, 33
Agamben, Giorgio, 158, 160
Agger, Ben, 105, 107–109
Ahrenfeld, Robert H., 270, 281
Aiken, Henry D., 103, 108
Akçura, Yusuf, 126, 136
Aldelman, Howard, 292
Allardt, Erik, 1
Allen, B., 20, 24, 33, 136, 296, 300
Aly, Götz, 44, 59, 61
Amir Arjomand, S., 228, 231
Amnesty International, 190, 291, 297
Anadolu, Basin Birligi, 294
Anderson, Regine, 292
Andre, Catherine, 164, 183–184, 191
Andreopoulos, George J., 302
Angermeier, Heinz, 121, 136
Anglin, Douglas G., 292
Annan, Kofi, 3, 63, 74
Appadurai, A., 203, 213
Arad, Y.K., 298
Aran, Lydia, 2, 4, 9, 195, 197, 206, 213
Arendt, Hannah, 67, 72, 74, 104, 108
Aronson, R., 231, 301
Astourian, Stephan H., 51, 59
Aunger, Edmund A., 239, 249
Auron, Yair, 294
Avarez, Alex, 302

B

Backer, David, 292
Baehr, Peter, 67, 72, 74
Balakian, Peter, 294
Ball, Howard, 302
Balshev, A.N., 209, 213, 215
Banks, W.C., 111
Barclay, Craig R., 264, 281
Bardakjian, Kevork B., 294
Barnett, Michael, 212, 216, 292
Barron, John, 296
Barry Schwartz, 109, 216
Bartlett, Frederic, 264
Bartov, Omer, 116, 136, 298, 302
Bat Ye'or, 119, 136
Bauman, Zygmunt, 3, 96, 108, 154, 160, 301
Baumel, Judith T., 289
Bayer, Maximilian, 155, 160
Beck, Ulrich, 253
Becker, Ernest, 64, 68–69, 74
Bell-Fialkoff, Andrew, 40, 59, 297
Berenbaum, M., 298–299, 301
Berg, Matchew P., 115, 136–137, 293, 301
Bergen, Doris, 298
Berger, Ronald J., 292, 298
Berkeley, Bill, 75, 108, 160, 163, 191, 214–216, 281, 292, 296, 298–299, 305
Berkes, Niyazi, 125, 127, 136
Bernard, Moltmann, 72, 75
Berry, Carol P., 292
Berry, John, 292
Best, Joel, 94, 108, 137
Bew, Paul, 241–243, 249
Bey, Naim, 295
Bhavnani, Ravi, 292
Bishop, Peter, 195, 214
Bjornson, Karin S., 302
Black, E., 22, 33, 35, 84, 170
Bley, Helmut, 145, 160
Blobel, Paul, 132

317

Blumenberg, Hans, 131
Boas, George, 110
Bolz, Norbert, 60, 136, 160–161
Borouman, Ladan, 226, 231
Borouman, Roya, 226
Bosco, David L., 297
Bossuet, J.B., 79, 86
Both, Norbert, 297
Bourdieu, Pierre, 3, 144, 160
Boyajian, Dickran H., 294
Braham, Randolph, 298
Brantlinger, Patrick, 302
Brehl, Medardus, 3, 8, 51, 60, 121, 136, 138, 143, 154, 160–161
Breitman, Richard, 298
Bridgman, Jon M., 145–146, 160
Browning, C.R., 299
Brunner, Kira, 303
Burgess, E.W., 17, 35
Burleigh, Michael, 299
Burton, John, 292
Buruma, Ian, 205, 214
Butcher, M.J., 84, 86

C

Cabezas, Ivan, 235, 249
Campbell, Kenneth J., 302
Capps, Lisa, 260, 282
Cassady, James, 231
Catton, William, 165, 179, 189, 191
Chaliand, Gerard, 294
Chalk, Frank, 16, 34, 40, 46, 60, 219, 231, 302
Chandler, D., 296
Chang, I., 296
Charny, Israel W., 197, 214, 289, 304
Chossudovsky, Michel, 167, 178–179, 183, 187, 191
Churchill, Ward, 27, 33, 66, 68, 106, 302
Cigar, Norman L., 24, 33, 297
Clarke, Edwin, 270, 281
Clarke, Richard A., 270, 281
Clausewitz, Carl von, 156–157, 160
Clay, Daniel C., 164, 180, 183, 191–192
Colleti, L., 231
Conrad, Jospeh, 105, 108
Conroy, J., 18, 33
Crossley, P.K., 211, 214
Cushman, Thomas, 297

D

Dabag, Mihran, 2–3, 8, 37, 50, 55, 60–62, 113, 118–119, 125–126, 136, 143, 149, 157, 159–161, 254, 280–282
Dabashi, H., 227, 231

Dadrian, Vahakn N., 16, 19, 22, 33, 44, 60, 294
Dalai Lama, 9, 195–214, 216
Davis, Bob, 110
Davis, Mike, 105, 108
Davis, Nanette J., 92, 108
Day, L., 290, 295, 302
De Landa, Manual, 106, 108
De Nike, Howard J., 296
de Waal, Alex, 192
Dejaegher, Y.M.J., 182, 192
Dekker, N.K., 33
Delbo, Charlotte, 267–268, 275, 281
Derrida, Jacques, 253, 281
Des Forges, Alison L., 292
Destexhe, Alain, 165, 167–168, 171–178, 191, 292
DIIR, 214, 216
Dilthey, Wilhelm, 79, 86, 114, 119, 136, 149
Diner, Dan, 54, 60
Dionne, E.J., 74
Djemal Pascha, 124
Djordjevic, Djordje, 100, 108
Dobkowski, Michael N., 34, 41, 46, 60, 289, 302, 304
Dodin, Thierry, 195, 212, 214
Domarus, Max, 130, 136, 138
Dona, Giorgian, 293
Dorsey, Learthen, 165–167, 171–173, 175–176, 180–182, 186, 191
Drechsler, Horst, 145, 161
Drew, Margaret, 289
Drost, Pieter N., 41, 60
Dulffer, Jost, 299
Dunlap, R., 189, 191

E

Edelheit, A., 289
Edelheit, Herschel, 289
Eghigian, Greg, 115, 136–137
Ehrenreich, Barbara, 92, 108
Ehrenreich, John, 92, 108
Eibeshitz, A., 299
Eibeshitz, J., 299
Einsatzgruppe, 132
Elias, Norbert, 20, 33, 230–231
Ellingsen, Tanja, 164, 192
Elliott, Michael, 66, 75
Engelman, E., 191
Enver Pascha, 124, 136
Epstein, Jospeh, 95, 108
Erber, Ralph, 300
Erichsen, John E., 281
Ersever, Oya G., 297
Eskin, Blake, 110
Ezrachi, Sidra, 214

F

FAO (Food and Agriculture Organization of the United Nations), 167, 179–181, 191
Fein, Helen, 20, 33, 46, 60, 156, 161, 242, 248, 296
Felman, Shoshana, 255, 281
Fernekes, William R., 289
Ferrarotti, Franco, 2, 8, 20, 33, 77, 86, 219, 228, 231, 306
Fine, Robert, 108, 299
Finkelstein, Norman C., 94–96, 108
Finkielkraut, Alain, 96, 108
Fischer, Adolf, 59, 150, 161, 281
Flescher, Joachim, 299
Flynn, Michael, 304
Fogt, Helmut, 134, 137
Foucault, Michel, 3, 97, 108, 144
François, Curt von, 116, 138, 156, 161
Fraser, John, 297
Frederic, Will, 107, 264
Frenkel-Brunswick, Else, 108
Frenssen, Gustav, 147–151, 154–155, 157, 161
Friedlander, Henry, 22, 33, 299
Fromm, Erich, 64–65, 68
Funck, Marcus, 115, 137

G

Gampel, Yolanda, 264, 281
Gay, Peter, 40, 60
Geiss, Immanuel, 47, 61
Gellately, Robert, 302
Gennep, Arnold van, 265, 281
Geras, Norman, 107, 109, 231
Gerth, Hans, 92, 109
Gewald, Jan-Bart, 145, 161
Ghazarean, Haykazn G., 294
Gilbert, Martin, 22, 34, 299
Glass, J., 299
Glazer, Barney, 265, 281
Glucksmann, A., 231
Goebbels, Joseph, 118, 137
Goertz, Hans J., 54, 61
Goldhagen, Daniel J., 39, 47, 53, 61, 299
Goldman, R., 291
Goltz, Colmar von der, 120, 137
Gordon, Sarah, 299
Gorz, A., 231
Gottfried, Paul E., 92, 109
Gottlieb, Roger S., 299
Gourevitch, P., 292
Graber, G.S., 294
Grabitz, Helge, 132, 137
Graf zu Stolberg-Wernigerode, 137
Gramsci, A., 226, 228, 230–231
Grattet, Ryken, 96, 109

Grebner, Gundula, 115, 139
Green, F., 214
Grosse, Scott, 184, 191
Guinier, Lani, 107, 109
Gulden, Timothy, 302
Gumplowicz, Ludwig, 128, 137–138
Gurr, Ted Robert, 46, 61
Gutman, Y., 299
Guttman, Josef, 295

H

Habermas, J., 220, 225, 227, 231, 253, 281
Hackett, D.A., 299
Hacking, Ian, 94, 109
Halbwachs, Maurice, 91, 109, 203, 214, 264–266, 281
Haney, C., 111
Harff, Barbara, 19, 34, 46, 61, 299
Harnack, Adolf von, 130, 137
Hass, A., 299
Hauge, Wenche, 192
Hayden, Robert M., 297
Hegel, Georg Wilhelm Friedrich, 79, 86, 125, 137, 149, 219
Heim, Susanne, 44, 59, 61
Hentoff, Nat, 73
Herberg, Hans-Joachim, 272, 281
Herbert, Ulrich, 78, 110, 115, 137, 232
Herder, Johann Gottfried, 126, 148
Hilberg, Raul, 43, 61, 113, 137, 299
Hinton, Alexander L., 296, 299
Hitchens, Christopher, 100, 109
Hitler, Adolf, 1, 19, 61, 66, 78–80, 86, 117–118, 124–125, 128, 130, 136, 138, 294, 299
Hobbes, Thomas, 66, 75, 103
Hogan, M., 296
Holliday, L., 300
Homer-Dixon, Thomas, 163–164, 179, 184, 192
Honig, Jan W., 297
Horowitz, Irving Louis, 19–20, 34, 39–40, 61, 302
Hovannisian, Richard G., 59, 295
Huber, Tony, 198, 200, 214
Human Rights Watch, 18–19, 24, 34, 190, 216, 291–292, 296

I

ICE Case Studies, 34
International Committee of Jurists, 202, 214

J

Jackson, Michael G., 296
Jacobson, K., 300
Jaffee, D., 111

Jameson, Fredric, 102, 109
Jarausch, Ferdinand F., 116, 138
Jardine, M., 25, 34, 296
Jefremovas, Villia, 292
Jenkins, James, 9, 289
Jenness, Valerie, 96, 109
Johnson, Nan, 164, 183, 191
Johnstone, Rick, 110
Jones, A., 25, 34
Jones, Bruce D., 293
Jones, Graham, 68, 75, 231

K

Kadivar, M., 226, 228, 231
Kampayana, Theobold, 164, 180, 191
Kant, Immanuel, 129, 148, 161
Katz, Steven T., 45, 61, 197, 215, 300
Kayitsinga, Jean, 164, 180, 191
Kazemzadeh, F., 226–227, 232
Keane, Fergal, 165–169, 171–177, 188, 192
Keilson, Hans, 271–272, 282
Kennedy-Pipe, Caroline, 238–239, 249
Kenrick, D., 22, 34
Khatami, M., 228, 232
Kiernan, Ben, 24, 34, 296, 302
King, Ynestra, 163, 174, 192
Kinloch, Graham C., 1–3, 7–8, 15, 30, 34, 105, 109, 231, 233, 249, 289, 307
Kliegler, P.C., 198, 215
Klinghoffer, Arthur J., 293
Kloian, Richard D., 295
Koch, Max, 3, 9, 233–235, 245, 249
Koestler, A., 18, 34
Kovesi, Julius, 103, 109
Kressel, Neil J., 302
Kristof, Nicholas D., 73
Kroker, A., 85–86
Krystal, Henry, 270, 282
Kuhn, Philalethes, 151, 161
Kuper, Leo, 19–20, 28, 30, 34, 40, 61, 303

L

Landau, Saul, 92, 109
Lang, Beral, 162, 300
Langbehn, A.J., 79, 86
Langer, Lawrence L., 97, 109, 255, 262, 282
Langer, Suzanne, 97, 109, 255, 262, 282
Laqueur, Walter, 289
Larner, Christina, 46, 61
Laub, Dori, 255, 281
Lebed, A., 22, 33
LeBlanc, Lawrence J., 303
Lemarchand, R., 293
Lemert, Charles, 105, 109

Lerner, Richard M., 19–20, 22, 34, 41, 61
LeRoy, P., 181, 191
Leutwein, Theodor, 145
Levene, Mark, 303
Levi, N., 207, 300
Levinson, Daniel J., 108
Levy, Barry S., 304
Levy, D., 205, 215
Levy-Bruhl, Lucien, 126
Lewis, Bernard, 72
Lewis, Laurence A., 180, 182–183, 192
Lichter, S. Robert, 94, 110
Lifton, R.J., 22, 34, 300
Linden, Ian, 173, 192
Lindqvist, Sven, 105, 109
Lipstadt, D., 300
Livingston, Donald W., 109
Loewenberg, P., 19, 34
Loewy, Hanno, 136, 160–161
Lopez, Donald S., 195, 200, 215
Lorenz, K., 18, 35
Lovejoy, Arthur, 110
Lowy, M., 231
Lukacs, G., 223, 232

M

Maechler, Stefan, 110
Maier, Charles S., 300
Makino, U., 303
Mamdani, Mahmood, 163, 168, 174, 192, 293
Mannheim, Karl, 95, 104, 110, 116, 119, 138, 283–284, 305, 308
Mannion, Sarah, 59, 135, 160, 280
Marcuse, Herbert, 99, 104, 110, 221–222, 232
Marks, Stephen P., 296
Markusen, David K., 300, 303
Markusen, Eric, 300
Marrus, Michael R., 300
Marshall, A., 84–85, 224, 232
Martinez, Javier, 236
Mayer, A.J., 78, 86
Mazian, Florence, 295, 300, 303
McDowell, Patrick, 75
McGarry, John, 249
McLagan, Meg, 212, 215
McLemore, S.D., 26, 35
McLuhan, M., 84–86
McNulty, Mel., 293
Mead, G.H., 207, 215
Melson, Robert F., 41, 61, 295, 300
Melvern, Linda, 164, 192
Mennell, St., 33, 219, 230, 232
Mentré, François, 116, 138
Merrington, J., 231
Mestrovic, S.G., 297
Metzl, J., 296

Mills, C. Wright, 84, 92, 95, 98, 110, 248–249, 303
Mills, Nicolaus, 84, 92, 95, 98, 110, 248–249, 303
Mintz, Alan, 215
Mitchell, Tara, 164–165, 167–168, 170, 176–178, 192

Mohan, Brij, 2, 8, 63, 74
Mohan, Raj P., 3, 7, 105, 109, 219, 289
Momigliano, Arnaldo, 208, 215
Montau, Robert, 40, 62
Montejo, Victor, 303
Morrissey, Mike, 243, 249
Morrow, Lance, 73, 75
Moses, A.D., 26, 35
Much, Robert, 203
Mullin, C., 212, 214
Murray, David, 94, 110, 136

N

Naimark, Norman M., 297
Naipaul, V.S., 72, 76
Namik Kemal, 127
Nascimento, A., 20, 26, 35
National Commission on Agriculture, 192
Nazer, James, 295
Neuffer, Elizabeth, 293, 298, 303
Newbury, Catarine, 165, 186, 192
Newman, Leonard, 300
Niazi, Tarique, 3, 8, 163, 307
Niederland, William G., 269–270, 272, 282
Nolte, E., 77–78, 86
Novak, Margaret, 198, 206–207, 215
Nyankanzi, Edward L., 25, 35, 293

O

Ochs, Elinor, 260, 282
Ofer, D., 300
Ohandjanian, Artem, 123, 138
Olick, J.K., 205, 207, 215
Olivetti, A., 83, 86
Olson, Jennifer, 163–164, 192
Omaar, Rakiya, 164, 192
Oppenheim, Hermann, 270, 282
Oppenheimer, Franz, 128, 138
Orne, M.T., 104, 110
Ortega y Gasset, José, 116, 138
Ortner, S., 199, 215
Orwell, G., 82, 87
Osorio, Victor, 235, 249

P

Palmer, Alison, 303
Pande, G.C., 209, 215
Park, R.E., 17, 34–35, 180
Paskuly, S., 300
Paul, Anthony, 109–110, 132, 136–137, 189–190, 192, 249, 296
Peck, A., 298
Percival, Valerie, 163–164, 179, 184, 192
Permanent Peoples' Tribunal, 295
Petersen, Julius, 138
Peukert, Detlev J.K., 115, 138
Phayer, Michael, 300
Piccone, Paul, 92, 110
Pinder, Wilhelm, 116, 138
Plato, 125–126, 138
Platt, Kristin, 4, 9, 49, 56, 60–62, 122, 136, 138, 143, 149, 160–161, 253–255, 259, 269, 280, 282
Platteau, Jean-Philippe, 164, 183–184, 191
Polizzotti, Mark, 110
Porter, J.N., 16–17, 19–20, 35
Pottier, Johan, 293
Power, Samantha, 15, 27, 32–35, 61, 66–67, 70, 75–76, 81, 87, 100–101, 109–110, 160, 174, 191, 214, 231, 246, 249, 292, 303
Pran, D., 297
Prevent Genocide International, 291
Prince, Robert M., 300
Prunier, Gerard, 165, 168, 179, 185, 188, 192, 293
Puxon, G., 22, 34

Q

Quindeau, Ilka, 262–263, 282

R

Rather, Heinz, 122–123, 134, 145, 195, 212, 214, 234, 240, 243–244, 263, 272–273, 277–278
Ratnesar, Ramesh, 76
Raymond, N., 19, 35
Reed-Purvis, Julian, 301
Reitlinger, Gerald, 301
Riemer, Neal, 303
Riesman, David, 115, 139
Rittner, Carol, 301, 303
Roberts, Ulla, 40, 62
Rohrlich, R., 301
Romano, S., 78, 87
Romo, H.D., 26, 35
Ronayane, Peter, 303
Rose, Richard, 238, 249
Rosenbaum, Alan S., 303
Rosenberg, Alfred, 129, 139

Roskies, D.R., 205, 215
Roth, John K., 301, 303
Rothberg, Michael, 300
Rothko, Mark, 279
Rozett, Robert, 289
Rubenstein, Richard L., 19, 35, 301
Rudolph, Jospeh R., 62, 289, 300
Rummel, Rudolph J., 20, 35, 46, 62, 297, 303

S

Salih, K., 24, 35
Saner, Hans, 40, 62
Sanford, Victoria, 303
Saro-Wiwa, Ken, 293
Saul, Ben, 109, 297
Schabas, William, 304
Schell, Orville, 195, 215
Scherrer, Christian P., 293
Schiller, Friedrich, 149
Schmidt, Jeff., 91
Schmitt, Carl, 153, 162
Schroyer, T., 227, 232
Schulz, Andreas, 115, 139
Schutz, A., 287
Schütze, Fritz, 255, 262, 282
Schwabe, Kurd, 62, 155–156, 162
Schwartz, Barry, 205, 207
Schwartz, Joel, 94, 110, 204, 207, 215
Seeckt, Hans von, 120–121, 139
Sells, Michael A., 298
Semelin, J., 304
Semujanga, Josias, 159, 162, 293
Sereny, Gitta, 48, 62
Sheng-Mei, Ma, 209, 215
Sheridan, Alan, 108
Shils, Edward, 207, 215
Shiromany, A., 198, 200–201, 216
Shiva, Dandana, 182, 193
Silliman, Jael, 163, 192
Simpson, Christopher, 20, 35, 304
Sivan, Emmanuel, 203, 205, 216
Skirball, Sheba F., 291
Smith, Adam, 85
Smith, Helmut W., 301, 304
Smith, James M., 303
Smith, Roger W., 62
Sofsky, Wolfgang, 47, 62
Sonyel, Salahi R., 295
Spector, S., 298
Speer, Albert, 118, 139
Spencer, H., 78, 87, 106
Spitzer, Alan B., 116, 139
Stamatov, Vurban, 295
Stannard, David, 304
Staub, Ervin, 19–20, 35, 304
Stiglmayer, A., 298

Stoddard, Heather, 198, 208, 216
Strauss, Anselm L., 115, 265, 281
Strom, A.K., 198, 206, 216
Strozier, Charles B., 304
Sumner, W.G., 17, 35
Sunga, Lyal S., 304
Svaldi, David, 27, 35, 304
Swomley, John M., 298

T

Tanaka, Y., 297
Tansel, Fevziya A., 51, 61–62
Taureck, Bernard H.F., 47, 62
Taylor, Christopher C., 293
Taylor, S., 22, 35
Tenzin Gyatso, 198, 216
Ternon, Yves, 295
Therborn, J., 231
Tibetan Young Buddhist Association, 216
Time Magazine, 77, 87
Titzmann, Michael, 144, 162
Todorov, T., 82, 87
Tohidi, N., 232
Tolnay, S.E., 27, 35
Toriguian, Shavarsh, 295
Torres, Gerald, 107, 109
Totten, S. Parsons, 304
Transylvanian World Federation, 301
Trotha, Lothar von, 40, 62, 146, 156
Trotha, Trutz von, 40, 62, 146, 156
Turner, Charles, 108, 299
Twagilimana, Aimable, 293

U

Um, Khatharya, 136, 297
United Nations, 15, 28, 45, 73, 81, 100, 170, 174, 184, 191–192, 219, 292, 296
United States Congress, 289–290
University of Michigan-Dearborn, 292, 295
University of the State of New York, 301
Urquhart, Brian, 66–67, 76
Uvin, Peter, 164–165, 167–168, 178, 182–183, 185, 187–188, 192, 293

V

Van Biema, David, 65, 76
Van den Berghe, Pierre L., 304
Vandiver, Margaret, 302
Veale, Angela, 293
Verwimp, Philip, 159, 162, 294
Vidal-Naquet, P., 301
Virilio, Paul, 106, 110
Voltaire, F.M.A., 79, 87

W

Wagner-Pacifici, R., 204, 216
Walker, Pat, 108
Waller, David, 165–166, 169–174, 176–178, 182–186, 193, 304
Waller, James, 165–166, 169–174, 176–178, 182–186, 193, 304
Wallimann, Isidor, 34, 41, 46, 60, 289, 302, 304
Wang, Cheng-Chih, 297–298
Waters, M., 226, 232
Watson, Catherine, 167, 170, 175, 186, 193, 285
Weber, Max, 119, 220, 225, 284–285, 287
Weine, Stevan M., 298
Weiss, John, 18–19, 22, 35, 301
Weissman, Stephen R., 294
Weitz, Eric D., 304
Weitzman, L., 300
Welzer, Harald, 40, 62
White-Stevens, Lillian, 291, 301
Wiesel, Elie, 73, 76, 212, 274–275, 278, 282, 301
Wilke, Arthur S., 2, 8, 91, 107, 110

Williamson, Elizabeth, 96, 110
Willis, Brian M., 304
Winter, Bronwyn, 109–110, 203, 205, 216, 221, 232, 294, 303–304
Winter, Jay M., 109–110, 203, 205, 216, 221, 232, 294, 303–304
Wittgenstein, Ludwig, 101, 103, 110
Wohl, Robert, 115–116, 139
Wolff, Kurt H., 2, 9, 105, 110–111, 283–287
World Resources Institute, 182, 193

Y

Yacoubian, George S., 294, 304
Yahil, Ieni, 301
Yerushalmi, Yoseph H., 208–209, 213, 216
Young, James E., 205

Z

Zimbardo, P.G., 104, 107, 111

Printed in the United States
51342LVS00004B/23

9 780875 863795